GIFT

High Technology and Low-Income Communities

High Technology and Low-Income Communities

Prospects for the Positive Use of Advanced Information Technology

Edited by

Donald A. Schön
Bish Sanyal
William J. Mitchell

MIT Press
Cambridge, Massachusetts
London, England

© 1999 Massachusetts Institute of Technology

This book was set in Garamond 3 and Meta by John Macklin using Quark Xpress and was printed and bound in the United States of America.

Library of Congress Cataloging-in-Publication Data

High technology and low-income communities: prospects for the positive
  use of advanced information technology / edited by Donald A. Schön,
  Bish Sanyal, and William J. Mitchell.
      p.   cm.
  Includes bibliographical references and index.
  ISBN 0-262-69199-X (pbk.: alk. paper)
    1. Information technology-Social aspects. 2. Poor.
I. Schön, Donald A. II. Sanyal, Bishwapriya. III. Mitchell, William J.
  (William John), 1944–   .
T58.5.H55   1997
306.4'.6—dc21   97-35754
                                                             CIP

In memory of Don Schön, who passed away on September 13, 1997

Bish Sanyal
William J. Mitchell

Contents

Preface   xi

Introduction   I
Donald A. Schön

Part I: Setting the Context

1. *The Informational City Is a Dual City: Can It Be Reversed?*   25
   Manuel Castells

2. *Changing Geographies: Technology and Income*   43
   Peter Hall

3. *Center Cities as Havens and Traps for Low-Income Communities:*   69
   The Potential Impact of Advanced Information Technology
   Julian Wolpert

4. *The City of Bits Hypothesis*   105
   William J. Mitchell

5. *Information Technology in Historical Perspective*   131
   Leo Marx

Part II: Strategies of Action

The Question of Access

6. *Equitable Access to the Online World*   151
   William J. Mitchell

Governance and Advanced Information Technology

7. *Information Technologies that Change Relationships between*   163
Low-Income Communities and the Public, and Nonprofit Agencies
that Serve Them
Joseph Ferreira, Jr.

8. *Planning Support Systems for Low-Income Communities*   191
Michael J. Shiffer

Entrepreneurial Potential

9. *Software Entrepreneurship among the Urban Poor: Could Bill*   213
Gates Have Succeeded if He Were Black? ... Or Impoverished?
Alice H. Amsden, Jon Collins Clark

The Educational Computer

10. *Action Knowledge and Symbolic Knowledge: The Computer*   235
as Mediator
Jeanne Bamberger

The Community Computer

11. *The Computer Clubhouse: Technological Fluency in the Inner City*   263
Mitchel Resnick, Natalie Rusk, Stina Cooke

12. *Computer as Community Memory: How People in Very Poor*   287
Neighborhoods Made a Computer Their Own
Bruno Tardieu

13. *Social Empowerment through Community Networks*   315
Alan Shaw, Michelle Shaw

14. *Commodity and Community in Personal Computing*   337
Sherry Turkle

15. *Approaches to Community Computing: Bringing Technology*   349
    to Low-Income Groups
    Anne Beamish

Part III: Conclusions

16. *Information Technology and Urban Poverty: The Role of*   371
    Public Policy
    Bish Sanyal, Donald A. Schön

    Index   395

Preface

This book emerged from a colloquium organized by the Department of Urban Studies and Planning (DUSP) at the Massachusetts Institute of Technology in the spring of 1996.

The intellectual initiative for the colloquium, titled *Advanced Information Technology, Low-Income Communities, and the City*, came from two groups of faculty members and students within DUSP. One group comprised the faculty and students who were deeply interested in advanced information technology and its use in urban planning. The other group's primary concern was the plight of America's central cities, particularly the lack of decent housing, employment, and social services in low-income communities. Until the Spring of 1996, the two groups had operated as if their concerns were very different. The first group, known as the Planning Support Systems (PSS), focused on the use of computer technology, with less attention paid to urban poverty. In contrast, the second group, known as the Housing, Community and Economic Development group (HCED), focused its intellectual attention on low-income communities, without much enthusiasm for advanced information technology. This difference in intellectual thrust between the two groups could be traced back to the 1960s when urban riots had erupted amidst startling technological progress which for the first time had put a man on the moon. Since then, advocates for low-income communities had been skeptical of the benefits of technological progress, while the computer enthusiasts, derogatively called "techies," preoccupied themselves with rapid progress in information technology without much concern for its impact on low-income communities.

By the mid 1990s, however, this intellectual division of labor was overwhelmed by two starkly opposite social trends. The positive trend was the wide-spread excitement about the actual achievements and as-yet-unachieved potential of the Internet and the World Wide Web. In the School of Architecture and Planning at MIT, the world wide climate of excitement found strong echoes. Dean William J. Mitchell's book, *City of Bits: Space, Place, and the Infobahn*, had just been published (Mitchell 1995). It heralded a digital revolution in the making, and speculated about the impacts this revolution could have on the functions and meaning of cities.

Mitchell Kapor, founder of the Lotus Corporation, had joined the School as an adjunct professor, bringing with him a profound interest in the policy issues that would determine the future shape of the Internet and the Web. For these individuals, as for many others, the most critical issues of urban planning were those that dealt with the actual and possible future inter-actions of physical space and cyberspace.

In sharp contrast to this widespread excitement about the digital revolution, by the mid-1990s an equally pervasive anxiety about the status of America's central cities marked social, political, and professional dis-courses. By then, the optimism of the 1980s, influenced by President Ronald Reagan's rhetoric of "Morning in America," had vanished in the face of starkly depressing statistics. The evidence showed that income inequality had increased between 1980 and 1990; that the problem of urban poverty had hardened over those years, trapping millions of Ameri-cans in inner-city areas without employment, decent housing and schools, and safe neighborhoods; and more children were going to bed hungry and lacked health care. (Danziger et al. 1994, Wilson 1996).

Who was to be blamed for these reversals in social progress, and what should be done to check it? There was no clear answer at that moment. Some blamed the welfare policies; others pointed to the retrench-ment of social programs in the early 1980s; and still others accused the globalizing forces of the post-industrial economy which, they argued, had exported unskilled jobs out of the United States (Danziger and Gottschalk 1993, Murray 1984). Although these different diagnoses led to different policy prescriptions for improving the quality of life of the urban poor, they concurred on one point: a key factor shaping the policy environment was the rapid progress in advanced information technology (IT).

To be sure, there were sharp differences of opinion about the impact of IT on the urban poor. Within our school, as in policy forums throughout the country, different voices, with different attitudes and assumptions, could be heard. For some individuals, such as Nicholas Negroponte, it was crystal clear that IT was already transforming every aspect of social life, not only in the United States, but also the world at large (Negroponte 1995). It was equally clear that this technology held the key to a radical transformation of social relations, one that would bypass conventional channels for political expression. It was therefore unconscionable that the poor should be left out. Their inclusion in the digital world loomed as a policy issue of paramount importance.

For others, the future looked less rosy. As Mitch Kapor pointed out, it is important to recognize that there are computer haves and computer have-nots. For example: The rural poor rank lowest in terms of computer use; rural blacks have the lowest computer access, followed by central city blacks and central city Hispanics. Senior citizens (55 years and over) in both rural and urban areas rank lowest among all age groups in terms of computer access. There are other differences. With some exceptions (most notably, telephone penetration for the two lowest education categories), the fewer the number of years of education, the lower the telephone, computer, and computer-modem penetration. There are regional variations as well: The lowest telephone and computer penetration is in Northeast central cities (U.S. Department of Commerce 1995).

According to Kapor, these differences in technological endowments are likely to be leveled off in certain ways, but also accentuated in other ways because IT produces effects in opposite directions simultaneously—it acts as a great leveler of opportunity while also being an amplifier of inequity. The implications of Kapor's argument are that without strategic intervention by the government, technologically disadvantaged groups will be left out, stranded on a dirt road adjacent to Vice President Al Gore's "information superhighway." This view was shared by many members of the HCED group, particularly by those in the Community Fellows Program (CFP),[1] which hosts twelve to fifteen community activists from urban, low-income communities each year. In the 1970s, when CFP was started, the community activists generally ignored technological issues, confident that the transformation of the poor required political not technological solutions. But, by 1995, the activists themselves had transformed somewhat: many of them had enrolled in courses focused on IT;[2] several had actively participated in introducing disadvantaged youth to the Internet and the World Wide Web; some were seeking business opportunities to bring IT to low-income areas; while others were interested in utilizing IT for organizing the poor.

There was yet another group of faculty members within the Department, who did not share either Nicholas Negroponte's enthusiasm or Mitch Kapor's concern for IT's distributional impact. These were technology skeptics who dismissed IT's relevance as "hype." They doubted that IT would radically transform the world, pointing out the extravagant claims technology utopians had made in the past, yet some still wanted to learn more about the technology, hoping that they would be proven correct for dismissing IT's importance.

This was the climate of opinion in which, in the fall of 1995, the editors of this book and faculty members from HCED and PSS groups conceived the idea of holding a colloquium on advanced information technology, low-income communities, and the city. We felt that the issues were of critical importance and that the Department had something important to contribute to the national debate—being positioned within MIT, we had a relatively long history of involvement in the application of IT, compared to other leading planning departments. In fact, the PSS group was a product of that involvement. PSS had started the Computer Resource Laboratory which provided up-to-date computer facilities for various planning activities, including spatial analysis and multi-media representation of communities. The HCED group, under which the CFP was housed, had a relatively long history too. Over the last 27 years, CFP, under the leadership of Melvin King, had played a leading role nationally to provide an institutional home to mid-career community activists seeking a year of reflection and retooling, away from the community "battlefields" that exhausted their intellectual stamina.

The CFP alumni, by now nearly 300 in number, are an invaluable resource for the Department to learn, firsthand, the complex reality of American central cities. The colloquium was structured to bring back to the Department the Boston area alumni and join them with the current fellows and other local community activists who are actively engaged in incorporating IT for educating and mobilizing low-income communities. Our goal was to begin a dialogue between these community leaders and the advocates and developers of cyberspace, hoping that such a dialogue would guide IT's use toward livable cities, vital communities, and improved economic prospects for low-income families.

To provide a structure to the dialogue we commissioned and invited a set of papers from distinguished social scientists, planning practitioners and technologists, as well as community organizers and activists.

We requested them to take a pragmatic but critical look at the potential impacts of IT on the form and function of cities, the political and social lives of communities, and the prospects for access to employment and education on the part of low-income populations. We also urged them to critically examine the assumptions underlying proposals for IT's use to enhance access to employment, foster democratic debate and decision-making, and promote dialogue between government agencies providing human services and their clienteles. Our goal was to capture a view of social reality from both "the top" and "the bottom," hoping that such a view would be synergistic and richer than any one view alone; and that such a view would generate effective policies to enhance the quality of life in low-income communities.

The colloquium was open to students and faculty in the Department of Urban Planning, the Department of Architecture, and the Media Laboratory at MIT. The core group of faculty who played an active role in the design and conduct of the colloquium included Professors Alice Amsden, Joseph Ferreira, Mitchell Kapor, Langley Keyes, Melvin King, William Mitchell, Martin Rein, Bish Sanyal, Michael Shiffer, Donald Schön, and Qing Shen. The Community Fellows and other students who participated in the colloquium, and in a parallel course which discussed in greater depth the conceptual issues raised in the colloquium, were Erik Balsley, Reco Bembry, Esperanza Borboa, Cheryl Bursh, Maru Colbert, Tony DeJesus, Elizabeth Espelin, Nils Fonstad, Christina Galli, Amatul Hannan, Alberto Herrera, Matthew Hoffman, Michael Johnson, Christine Kaaihue, Rachel Kimboko, Robinette Livingston, Boramy Ma, Mark Norton, Marla Perez, Lisa Perry, Sumeeta Srinivasan, Marcus Thorne, Lori Treviño, and Akemi Yao.

Much to our delight, there was a significant level of participation by community leaders from the Boston area. Inspired by Melvin King's interest in the colloquium, a large number participated regularly. They included: Jud Dolphin, Kristen Eichleay, Elmer Freeman, Frieda Garcia, Kay Gibbs, Ken Granderson, Roy Guyton, Peter Hardy, Darian Hendricks, Peter Kiang, Ted Landsmark, Nelson Merced, Nestor Rios, Oliver Strimpel, Andrea Swain, and Greg Watson. We owe much to the active participation of these community leaders for raising questions which would not have been raised if the colloquium was restricted to academics only.[3]

A few additional individuals deserve special recognition. Foremost among them is Anne Beamish, a doctoral candidate, who helped structure the colloquium, assisted in running the parallel course, *and* played a key role in the publication of this book. Dean William Mitchell provided both financial and intellectual support and, despite his busy schedule, regularly attended the colloquium. Melvin King, now Director Emeritus of CFP, was the first to conceive the idea of the colloquium. Later, his deep connection with Boston area community activists ensured their active participation in the colloquium. Also, Mel King and Donald Schön co-taught the parallel course mentioned earlier. This course deeply engaged the Community Fellows in deliberating at length on the critical issues raised in the colloquium. Don Schön also chaired the colloquium sessions, gently nudging the participants to express their views. He built the intellectual bridge between the academics and the community leaders.

Last, but not the least important, we received generous financial support from the Kellogg Foundation. This support was crucial for organizing the colloquium and a follow-up meeting to evaluate our effort. The evaluation inspired reflection and generated a range of suggestions about how to move ahead collectively in our effort to harness the immense possibilities of IT for the benefit of low-income communities.

Notes

1. The Community Fellows Program (CFP) is a one year, non-degree program. Started in 1971, it provides an opportunity for mid-career community activists and leaders from communities of color to spend a year at MIT studying, reflecting, and conducting action research. Until 1996, the CFP was led by Melvin H. King, who, prior to joining the Department of Urban Studies and Planning as an adjunct professor and head of CFP, was the director of the New Urban League of Boston. Between 1971 and 1996, the CFP hosted nearly 300 fellows from all parts of the country.

2. In the fall of 1994 Dean William Mitchell and Adjunct Professor Mitch Kapor taught a course titled, "Digital Communities: Urban Planning and Design in Cyberspace." In Spring 1995, Mitch Kapor taught a course titled, "Political Economy of Digital Infrastructure."

3. The colloquium sessions were taped and transcripts of the sessions are available online at: http://sap.mit.edu/projects/colloquium/.

References

Danziger, Sheldon and Peter Gottschalk. 1993. *Uneven Tides: Rising Inequality in America.*
New York: Russell Sage Foundation.

Danziger, Sheldon et al. 1994. *Confronting Poverty: Prescriptions for Change.* Cambridge,
MA: Harvard University Press.

Mitchell, William J. 1995. *City of Bits: Space, Place, and the Infobahn.* Cambridge,
MA: MIT Press.

Murray, Charles. 1984. *Losing Ground: American Social Policy 1950–1980.*
New York: Basic Books.

Negroponte, Nicholas. 1995. *Being Digital.* New York: Knopf.

U.S. Department of Commerce. 1995. *Falling Through the Net: A Survey of the "Have Nots"
in Rural and Urban America.* Washington, DC: The National Telecommunications
and Information Administration (NTIA), U.S. Department of Commerce.

Wilson, W. J. 1996. *When Work Disappears: The World of the New Urban Poor.*
New York: Knopf.

Introduction

Donald A. Schön

In the spring of 1996, the Massachusetts Institute of Technology's School of Architecture and Planning held a colloquium, "Advanced Information Technologies, Low-Income Communities, and the City." The colloquium created a dialogue among parties rarely, if ever, brought together to consider the prospective impacts and potentials of advanced information technologies for low-income populations. The colloquium assembled technologists, planners, educators, and social scientists from MIT and other universities; activists from low-income communities throughout the United States; and representatives of community organizations in the Boston area.

This book brings together the colloquium papers and the discussions to which they gave rise. It reflects the voices of the several types of colloquium participants: "technology enthusiasts" who envisage a bright future in which "being digital" becomes our dominant mode of being; "technology skeptics" who question the positive transformative power of the new technologies, fearing the emergence of new forms of polarization, isolation, and social control; and practical activists, organizers, and planners who give priority to actionable proposals for change.

In this introductory chapter, we present the book's main premise, which is that community leaders and planning professionals who wish to guide the uses of the new technologies toward creating more livable cities, vital communities, and improved economic prospects for low-income populations, need to explore the nature of the changes under way and the policy issues at stake; and that they can be helped in this effort by entering into a dialogue with the advocates and developers of cyberspace. We describe the several senses in which our coauthors use the terms, "low-income community" and "advanced information technologies." We highlight, in advance, the connections between the macro-analyses of Part I, which deal with the wave of sociotechnical change, and the chapters of Part II, which present particular, countercurrent proposals for action in the interests of the poor.

The Main Arguments of Part I

The authors of the five chapters in Part I—Manuel Castells, Peter Hall, Julian Wolpert, William Mitchell, and Leo Marx—present a range of distinct but family-resembling arguments about the rise of advanced information technologies and its significance for low-income urban populations. Each chapter claims that something important—some sweeping sociotechnical change—has been (or is currently) going on. The authors also leave no doubt that low-income people and low-income communities in urban areas are already, or are likely to be affected soon, by the changes in question. Each author believes that these trends and their actual or likely social consequences raise critical policy questions for our society. But beyond these commonalities, subtle, as well as not-so-subtle, differences are evident in what the authors mean by advanced information technology, how they frame the sociotechnical changes under way, whether they view these changes with optimism or foreboding, how they frame the actual or likely impacts of these changes on the urban poor, and what lessons for public policy and action they draw.

Part I presents four principal versions of the underlying argument.

The Argument from the Rise of the "Informational Economy" and Its Impacts on the "Informational City"

In Chapter 1, Manuel Castells depicts a revolution in information technologies that over the last thirty years or so has transformed social life, producing, in interaction with economic, social, cultural, and political changes, "informational cities" that "deepen existing patterns of socio-spatial segregation," creating what Castells dubs the "dual city." According to Castells, this revolution has not *caused* the gap between rich and poor in our society, but has exacerbated it. He frames his argument mainly in terms of the city, seeing it as the subject of sociotechnological changes, taking it as his primary unit of analysis, and treating local urban governments as the most likely agents of change. He sees American cities "evolving toward systemic urban schizophrenia," an image that matches much of what you see as you travel today through American cities. But Castells believes that "The promise of information technology may lead to a different, more humane city, in the framework of a new, more intelligent, and more just society."

In association with this main line of argument, Castells lays out a set of mixed sociospatial trends. Within cities, he sees a trend toward the integration of elite, high-valued people and spaces involved in the informational economy and increasingly polarized from low-valued people and spaces. Within metropolitan regions, he sees a simultaneous concentration of front-office activities and deconcentration of back-office ones. He notes the rise of "milieux of innovation" like Silicon Valley. He describes the "hierarchical diffusion of production, management, and distribution of new products and processes throughout the interconnected nodes of the global system," which "gradually eliminates the distinction between high-tech and low-tech industries." He claims that information technology "reintegrates the functional unity of different economic elements in distant locations," bypassing the devalued spaces of the inner city and making it unnecessary to rehabilitate them. He points out that such "space flows" have the effect of "deepening segregation and accentuating inequality," as central cities lose their economic base except for "islands of prosperity and innovation" that can now bridge directly to their hinterlands.

According to Castells, trends in the job market and labor force parallel these sociospatial trends. There are lots of new jobs, but they demand higher levels of education, which accentuates the mismatch between "embattled urban school systems" and the skill requirements of the expanding sectors of the labor market. The middle class experiences stagnant wages and increasing economic insecurity. The labor force is polarized into a better-educated core and a poorly educated periphery, the latter prone to fall into the growing ranks of the semi-employed. At the same time, the patriarchal family and the welfare state are in crisis. People become trapped in the black holes of the informational city. Castells comes down firmly, as does Julian Wolpert, in support of the view that the inner city is not a "haven" but a "trap."

Peter Hall's perspective is basically consistent with Castells. The informational-digital revolution (which may be read as long and gradual or recent and sudden—and it really doesn't matter) has transformed urban economies. It has divided them into a high end, consisting of information-handling jobs that require "ever-more sophisticated educational qualifications," and a low end made up of dead-end jobs and an unemployed and unemployable segment of the population. Many of these people live in urban housing projects occupied largely by welfare-dependent groups, where young people are trapped in a vicious cycle of undereducation and criminality. This polarization of the urban economy and its labor force plays out in a polarized urban geography: on the one hand, the urban cores that house the activities of the "symbolic analysts," connected by elite corridors to suburban locations; on the other, the islands of poverty and despair in the center city; and in between, the areas that house "ancillary workers."

Hall also makes a subordinate argument about the prospective "death of cities," which he believes will not occur, and about changing intercity patterns: the evolving hierarchy of global, regional, and specialized cities; the "deconcentration" of back-office activities; the differentiation of cities and the coming competition among them; the plight of manufacturing cities like Detroit, "entire islands of multiple deprivation." Hall's subordinate argument is prefigured by earlier remarks about the "death of distance" being exaggerated, the "synergy of electronic and face-to-face communication," and the importance of informal communications that require geographic clustering (as in Silicon Valley). In effect, one argument is about what is happening and what will happen to cities, and the other is about the policy predicament posed by the existence of an urban underclass trapped in center-city islands cut off from the prevailing economy.

Caveats to the Arguments Advanced by Castells and Hall

Is Castells exaggerating the duality of the dual city? How does he distinguish the polarizing effects of the informational economy from the effects of the out-migration of business and the outsourcing of manufacturing? Castell's description of the promise of information technology leading to a different, more humane city is ambiguous. Does he mean that it *will* lead to such an outcome, or that it *might* if we were to act from a vision of the possibilities inherent in advanced information technology? This ambiguity can easily compass the technological utopianism against which Leo Marx inveighs in his chapter.

Additional uncertainties are evident in the main argument

advanced by Castells and Hall. Alice Amsden claims, for example, that the economic success of the Pacific Rim countries is primarily based on *low-* or *middle*-tech industry. In another form, this kind of counterclaim can be based on the examples of networks of flexible/specialized job shops, such as the machine shops and metalworking firms of northern Italy, or the apparel establishments of lower Manhattan, both described by Michael Piore and Charles Sabel in their book, *The Great Industrial Divide.* In a similar vein, Michael Porter has been writing about the "competitive advantages of the inner city," emphasizing the importance of geographic proximities, a workforce skilled in low- or mid-tech crafts, and a sizable center city market for consumer goods and services.

The Argument for "Urban Traps" Rather than "Urban Havens"

In Chapter 3, Julian Wolpert claims that in the large northeastern cities of the United States, the plight of the poor has worsened over the past twenty-five years or so, both in terms of rates of poverty in the center cities and the increasing rate of segregation of poor (and largely black and Hispanic) populations in certain areas of the center city. Wolpert attributes these changes to the flight of businesses from the center city, the loss of blue-collar jobs suitable for low-income people of low educational attainment, and more recently, to the erosion of the safety net provided by social programs sponsored by the federal government. Wolpert argues that the rise of advanced information technology is unlikely, left to itself, to do anything for low-income people, or for the communities of place in which they congregate. The poor lack access to the economic opportunities that advanced information technology might present. This lack of access hinges on issues of transportation, education, work readiness, and computer skills. If anything, Wolpert sees advanced information technology as driving the working poor and layers of middle management out of the mainstream economy, depriving even more people of its benefits.

The Argument of the Technology Enthusiasts — or "Possibilists"

We have no chapter that represents the position of the cyber-utopians, although—in absentia—Nicholas Negroponte's *Being Digital* crops up in a couple of chapters (Marx, Amsden) as an object of attack. Negroponte's digital version of technological utopianism maintains that the new digital world holds the potential for breakthroughs in resolving the social problems of poverty and inequality in American, and for that matter, world, society. According to Negroponte, the digital world holds new forms of community development, independent of communities of place. The isolation of the poor can be ended. Radically new approaches to poverty and social inequality can develop, directly through the cyberworld, without the intermediaries of governmental or traditional political processes. The digital world holds potentials for conferring enormous economic benefits on the society as a whole and its low-income segment in particular. It is for these reasons that Negroponte sees *exclusion* from the digital world as disastrous for those excluded.

In William Mitchell's two chapters, we have a much softer and more reasonable version of Negroponte's utopianism. But the echoes of that utopianism can still be heard.

In Mitchell's view, advanced information technology is in the process of transforming the world in which we live, especially its cities. Everything in the new digital world is—and will be—different: how we work, engage in social relations, consume goods and services, entertain ourselves, study, manage our personal and family economies, take care of our health. We cannot know for sure what the effects of these transformations will be. They are necessarily open-ended. To take the major example that Mitchell has explored in his book, *City of Bits*, which he recapitulates in part in Chapter 4, cities will change radically. New combinations of physical space and cyberspace will appear in every aspect of urban life, although we do not know precisely what forms they will take or how they will develop. Their potentials for good or ill remain wide open. We can *influence* them through the policy choices we make as individuals, institutions, and governments.

All of this applies to the status of low-income individuals and low-income communities. They will surely be radically affected by the digital revolution, which can change their lives for good or for ill. For Mitchell, as for Negroponte, one thing is crystal clear: for the poor to be excluded from the digital world will surely be to their detriment. If they are included in it, they could possibly benefit from it. And the factor on which their inclusion pivots is not education, at least in the first instance, and at least not *formal* education; rather, it is the multilayered issue of *access* to the digital world, which Mitchell discusses in Chapter 6.

Mitchell is careful not to claim that the ongoing digital revolution *will* serve the interests of the disadvantaged. Instead he seeks to open our minds to the view that advanced information *can* offer important benefits to the poor, or can mitigate the otherwise noxious effects of advanced information technology. Mitchell does not argue, as do the other authors in Part I, that to capture the potential benefits of advanced information technology, it is necessary *first* to remedy social inequalities, especially those reflected in our system of public education. Mitchell's view is consistent with advocacy for educational equality, but it is not logically dependent on it. He urges us to keep open the *possibilities* for beneficent social effects, including effects on poverty and inequality, inherent in advanced information technology. He believes that if we imagine such possibilities, and make choices directed to their realization, we may achieve the best of all possible digital worlds, or at least avoid stumbling into the worst of them.

Debunking Digital Utopianism

The case against digital utopianism is made, in its general form, by Leo Marx in Chapter 5. It is made, with respect to the more specific view that advanced information technology may assist low-income people in leap-frogging existing barriers to entrepreneurial success, by Alice Amsden in Chapter 9.

Marx argues that we have no reason to expect the emerging sociotechnical system built around information technology to remedy social inequalities in our society, or to relieve the plight of the poor, any more than other massive sociotechnical changes—for example, those associated with the railroads, electricity, or automotive technology—have had such effects in the recent past. In the short term, the new information-technological system is likely to produce dislocations that affect the weakest first—low-income populations and especially minorities among them. In the long term, widespread adaptations to the new technological system will likely take place, just as broad social adaptations have occurred to other sociotechnological shifts. But these adaptations are unlike to remedy the fundamental, structurally based inequality between the poor and the well-to-do. Structural inequalities can be solved only by attacking them "within the larger historical, cultural, and socioeconomic matrix that generated them."

Alice Amsden asserts in Chapter 9 that advanced information technology offers no realistic opportunity for the poor to leapfrog existing barriers to economic well-being through entrepreneurship. The belief in such opportunities is a myth based on the fact that *one* kind of barrier to entry to the field of software development—physical capital—is relatively low. But another kind of barrier to entry remains high: human and social capital that hinges on educational level, computer-related training, job experience, and economically useful social contacts.

Convergence on Proposals for Change

All of the authors in Part I, with their family-resembling diagnoses of the predicament of low-income urban populations disjunct from the social and economic mainstream, suggest a basic policy prescription: *better and more equal public education.*

There are some interesting variations in the authors' ways of presenting and justifying this proposal. For Castells, "the focus of the corporate-public urban partnerships should be on revamping the quality of the public school system," which he sees as central to the ability of low-income people to take advantage of the emerging opportunities for "entrepreneurialism and teleworking." Moreover, Castells takes very seriously the idea of using information technology in the form of digital communication networks to effect the necessary changes in urban public education. For Hall as well, the "root of the problem" requires "a major reform of our school and preschool systems," a reform that might be hastened through the use of "electronic self-paced education." Wolpert concludes his presentation of the worsening plight of low-income populations in the center cities with a call for renewed commitment to urban revival, which he sees as centering on the need to equip the poor to compete for the "declining number of entry-level positions in the informational economy." He emphasizes the importance for "young people to be computer literate," which calls for "more home computers, more and better equipment in inner city schools, along with trained personnel." Marx sees improved public education as one component of the structural changes necessary to attack deep-seated structural inequalities in our society. Amsden, whose conclusions join the arguments advanced by the authors in Part I, identifies the need to bring "education, training, and job experience up to par" as an essential first step if the urban poor are to set out on "the long road to successful entrepreneurship."

But the policy prescription of better and more equal education is made by these authors in global and rather uncritical terms. There are some significant leaps in the argument, especially the leap in Castells and Hall from the polarized economy to the gap between "information rich and information poor" as indicated by computer access. Information, knowledge, "brain power," education, computer access, all seem to get uneasily joined together here. Information is not knowledge. You can have a lot of information and drown in it; you can have relatively little and yet possess critical bits of know-how that make you a useful economic player. If "education" means formal education, a lot of children and young people seem to learn a great deal (about the uses of computers, for example) out of school, and conversely, a lot of schooling seems to be of dubious economic value. Education, formal or informal, is not equivalent to computer access, and vice versa. If, in Wolpert's view, better public education in the uses of the computer is essential in assisting the poor to compete for a "declining number of entry-level jobs in the informational economy," what about the strides that are likely to be made in educational systems for the nonpoor? On what basis should we expect that improved education for low-income youth will allow them to catch up?

Finally, the broad policy prescription shared by the authors in Part I is made—understandably, given the missions of their chapters—in broad and undifferentiated terms. These authors do not tell us just what "better and more equal education" might mean in practice, nor do they explain in detail just what roles information technology can play in the improvement of public education for low-income people. For these purposes, we must turn to the chapters by Bamberger, Resnick, and Tardieu in Part II.

Part II: The Possible Benefits of Advanced Information Technology for Low-Income Urban Populations

The nine chapters of Part II present a menu of possibilities. They describe ways in which various forms of advanced information technology may be used to enhance the well-being of low-income individuals in urban settings and/or the communities to which they belong. These chapters cluster around different points of entry. Mitchell's Chapter 6 focuses on the variable that he sees as critical to the inclusion of the poor in the advancing digital world: the multileveled problem of access to that world. Mitchell's concern is primarily with digital communications networks, represented by the Internet and the World Wide Web. He argues that the poor tend to be systematically excluded from such access or tend to suffer from a radical inequality of access. Effective access, as he sees it, is a multilayered proposition, consisting of access to the "pipes," the "affordable appliance," the "user-friendly software," and the "will and motivation to exploit all of the above." He claims that each layer of effective access presents its own particular problems, and that the prospects for solution are different in each case. He concludes by making a number of policy recommendations, for example, for "appliance availability" in schools, community centers, and libraries.

Amsden's Chapter 9 is, as we have seen, a mainly skeptical gloss on the possibility that low-income people may be able to exploit the entrepreneurial potentials opened up by the growing field of software development. She and her coauthor Clarke point out that the real barrier to entry is, in this case, not "physical capital" but human capital, which depends on education, training in computer skills, and job experience; and social capital, which consists of the formation of a network of useful business contacts. These are "just the things that poverty denies." Better and more equal education for low-income urban residents, and better access to computer skills, are necessary conditions for entrepreneurial effectiveness in the software field. In their absence, there is no way that persistently poor residents of the center city can leapfrog out of misery.

Chapter 7 by Joseph Ferreira and Chapter 8 by Michael Shiffer are concerned with the uses of information technologies—here conceived as technologies for data collection, storage, and distribution, and for data representation and analysis—to allow low-income people to participate more effectively in urban planning and development. Shiffer's chapter deals first with the uses of information technology to support relevant knowledge for community planning and development, including planning support systems for description, speculation, and recollection, and second with the use of digital communications technology for community networking, collaborative planning, advocacy, and evaluation. Shiffer's examples include the development of an electronic version of the city of St. Louis's strategic plan for the creation of "empowerment zones and enterprise communities." Here, a CD-ROM-based multimedia system "links residential interviews with Geographic Information System (GIS) maps of St. Louis's economic, physical, and demographic characteristics in an interactive presentation that supported the city's bid for federal community development funding." In Boston, a multimedia archive was created to evaluate the effectiveness of an urban revitalization demonstration program for Boston's Mission-Main public housing development. Shiffer claims that video interviews with residents, presented accurately and sensitively in coordination with spatial representations of the physical and demographic characteristics of the development, yield a "dynamic multidimensional case history" that supports effective evaluation and enhances active resident participation. He suggests that the use of these materials on the Internet could support advocacy for the interests of low-income people and provide a more powerful vehicle for communication among area residents, planning professionals, and government officials.

Ferreira's chapter considers how *neighborhood* planners in low-income areas can gain access to and use planning data, first to determine what their interests are and then to give these interests effective voice in public debates over plans and projects. His examples deal with land-use planning, focusing on problems associated with property ownership and arson. He is concerned with developing planning support systems that will encourage a decentralized, grassroots style of neighborhood planning that can feed into and influence urban planning and actions that shape the city in general and low-income neighborhoods in particular. The heart of this chapter is Ferreira's discussion of the *technical* problems that need to be solved to give neighborhood planners access to city data and make "grass-roots" neighborhood planning a reality. First, he argues that apparently trivial problems of ambiguous or indeterminate reference—for example, multiple spellings of the same name, or multiple name-forms for the same property owner (e.g. "Boston," "City of Boston," or "Boston Redevelopment Administration")—turn out to be significant obstacles to the development of a workable planning support system. Second, he recognizes three main strategies for solving such problems: a "top-down" strategy that redesigns the parcel records system to assure consistency and avoid ambiguities, a "bottom-up" strategy in which neighborhood planners work around errors and ambiguities without attempting to change the parcel information system, and a "middle-out" strategy—which he advocates—that uses locally maintained "look-up tables" to cross-reference the official names contained in parcel information systems and their local, neighborhood interpretations.

The chapters by Jeanne Bamberger and Resnick, Rusk, and Cooke explore the computer's potential as a vehicle to educate disadvantaged children and youth. The authors get underneath the vague rubric of "educational uses of the computer" to investigate how computers can enhance an approach to education that emphasizes hands-on design of real objects. The authors draw on experience in settings they have helped create—Bamberger's "Laboratory for Making Things" in the Graham and Parks Alternative Public School in Cambridge, Massachusetts; and Resnick's Computer Clubhouse in Boston, Massachusetts, organized by the Computer Museum and MIT's Media Laboratory. Having noted these significant points of similarity, however, we should also note how very different are the stories told in these two chapters.

Bamberger's Laboratory for Making Things began, as she tells us, with the observation that some children—among them, low-income, minority children, with street smarts—are "virtuosos at building and fixing complicated things (such as bicycles and car motors) in the everyday world around them." Yet these same children tend to have trouble working with common symbolic expressions such as numbers, graphs, and written language; and they are often perceived as failing at school. Bamberger set out to create "an environment where children could easily move back and forth between action and symbolic description, between sensory experience and representations of it, between the virtual world inside 'the box,' and the familiar world of their own powerful know-how in real time/space/motion."

Within this environment, the computer was to play the role of "mediator," helping the children construct the "shared principles that might otherwise have remained hidden in the objects that embodied them." Making objects in the virtual world of the computer requires "describing in symbolic form what you want to happen"; once made and "sent" to the computer, the symbolic description instantly *becomes* the things and actions you have described.

Illustrating an educational use of this unique feature of the computer, Bamberger describes an experience of an African American boy, Lafayette, who talked very little and whose teachers were "often at a loss as to how to reach him." Like many children growing up poor in an unstable world, Lafayette needed to hold things still, quite literally to grasp and hold onto a new idea. His explorations to find out "how numbers could 'teach' the computer to play the synthesizer drums," showed the researchers, in retrospect, "how important it is for him to slow down, to take time to repeat, literally making correspondences between numbers, synthesizer drumming, and his own drumming." In this fully described example, Bamberger shows how the computer can function as mediator between sensory, action know-how, and symbolic representations in a way that allows a child "failing at school" to connect his virtuoso use of objects in space/time with the symbolic world of the school.

Mitchel Resnick's Computer Clubhouse operates outside the world of the school. Like Bamberger's laboratory, Resnick's Clubhouse is based on a distinctive approach to education. It seeks to help its drop-in members, mostly from minority, center city neighborhoods, develop "technological fluency" in the use of "leading-edge software to create their own artwork, animations, simulations, multimedia presentations, virtual worlds, musical creations, Web sites, and robotic constructions." And in the process, the Computer Clubhouse seeks to become "a learning community—where young people and adult mentors work together on projects, using new technologies to explore and experiment in new ways."

Resnick, Rusk and Cooke describe the principles that guide the Clubhouse's approach toward computer-based designing and the software tools it makes available to minority youth. They illustrate how individuals in the learning community of the Clubhouse engage in active, computer-based design in projects of their own creation, and suggest how the

Clubhouse has affected their careers in work and education. Finally, they present their long-term goal of making such experiences available to youth in low-income neighborhoods across the country—"sparking people to rethink their notions of technology, learning, and community."

The four penultimate chapters by Bruno Tardieu, Alan and Michelle Shaw, Sherry Turkle, and Anne Beamish describe different versions of what the members of our colloquium came to call "the community computer"—uses of computers and digital communications systems to contribute to the building and development of communities in low-income areas.

The first of these chapters, by Tardieu, might just as well have been grouped with the two chapters on the educational use of the computer, although its main setting is a poor neighborhood in the South Bronx and it is clearly focused on the strengthening of community bonds in that neighborhood.

The introduction of a computer into a South Bronx neighborhood was a development of the "street libraries" that have long been part of the repertoire of a movement with which Tardieu is associated: the Fourth World Movement, founded in the 1960s in France by Father Joseph Wresinski to fight extreme poverty, initially in France and later throughout the world. Tardieu tells us that for Father Joseph "the central issue of poverty is an exclusion that extends beyond economic resources to being left out of the social, cultural, educational, and political life of the nation." Wresinski believed that the poorest "had to be part of this modern revolution, and not once again left behind."

Tardieu and his colleague, Vincent Fanelli, thought about the possibility of a community computer in the light of a particular view of what a computer was: a system in which words can function either as data or as command, "making things happen," as Bamberger also notes in her treatment of the computer as mediator. They were also struck by the fact that the computer contains an associative memory. Under the influence of these ideas, they introduced an "old-fashioned" computer—an Atari—into the South Bronx street library. Tardieu's chapter describes in detail how members of the community took ownership of the computer, and how he and his colleagues had to learn how to rethink the computer as something that could be "meaningful to all children, that they can master and get involved with." The invention they came up with was a "giant community encyclopedia" to which children in each neighborhood would "contribute what they knew from their lives or from books, entering information in the computer's database, making it possible for them to look up their entries by typing a key word." This project was to "make the computer a *common good*, rather than an exclusive tool."

Tardieu describes the slow, painstaking process through which the children constructed the encyclopedia, learned to get interested in what others had written, and entered into conversations ("Which is the tallest skyscraper? What can you do with a pumpkin? Can bees be bad since they are God's creatures?") within and across communities. In its computer medium, as well as in the form of a huge book, the encyclopedia became a focus of involvement for parents and for the whole community. Eventually, the idea of the computer-based encyclopedia spread, via digital networks, across cities and countries.

The lessons Tardieu draws are not about the community encyclopedia per se, but about the meanings of key terms relevant to the uses of digital technology by the poorest of the poor: not "access" but "reinvention for different aims"; not the "personal computer" but "the community computer"; not "computers to be fed" but "computers to feed"; not "technology to give you answers" but "technology to help you become a researcher and frame your questions."

Like Tardieu and his colleagues, the Shaws sought to develop applications of the computer that would enable poor residents of communities of place to become active producers rather than passive consumers of digital technology. Their chapter describes their development of a networking system that could be used in low-income neighborhoods to support community organization, project development, and—more broadly—the strengthening of social bonds in a neighborhood "village." The software they created—Multi-User Sessions in Community (MUSIC) —employs "Multi-User Dungeons" (MUDs) to "accept network connections from multiple simultaneous users and provide access to a shared database of 'rooms,' 'exits,' and other objects." As neighborhood users browse and manipulate the same database, they encounter other users and their newly created objects, and communicate directly in real time by typing messages that are seen by all other users in the same room.

The Shaws tell how the MUSIC networking system has been used in neighborhoods in Boston and Newark, the latter a functioning resource for a housing development belonging to Newark's New Community Corporation. Users of the system, who live in New Community housing and have a child who attends Newton Street Elementary School, make use of a network of Macintosh computers placed in homes, social service offices, the public library, an area church, and the University of Medicine and Dentistry of New Jersey, to organize projects such as "talent shows, a recycling drive, flea markets, gardening projects, field trips, and fundraisers," as well as for community-wide discussion of issues of community importance, such as the strengthening of security and the prevention of fights in the public school. The Shaws envisage the widespread diffusion of such community networks, which will become economically viable as the computer industry brings networking technology to television sets, cable channels, and phone lines. Driven initially by commercial interests, these technologies can become "tools for local neighborhood development," helping people to "tell their own stories and develop their own programs."

The ways of using the computer highlighted by Bamberger, Tardieu, and the Shaws reveal several crucially important common features. In their applications, the computer is made to respond to a particular situation. It is used to enable particular groups, or individuals, to do the things they want to do. The researcher *learns* what these things are, framing questions and designing adaptations of the computer in response to the discovered interests, needs, and capabilities of particular users. Emphasis is on slowing down, rather than speeding up, and on responsiveness to the users' discovered interests and needs rather than on applications and capabilities that match the designer's prejudgments.

Sherry Turkle's chapter places the community computer, as illustrated by the work of Tardieu and the Shaws, within the context of the recent history of the evolving social meaning of the computer. In the 1970s, she argues, some young people endowed the computer with a political meaning: in contrast to the days when computers were exclusively conceived as "icons of centralized knowledge and power," they could now be put "at the disposal of the grass roots," and thereby "return knowledge to the collectivity." Emphasis was placed on the "transparency" of the machine, and on the "empowerment" of the user. In the 1980s, with the advent of new machines, especially the Apple Macintosh, the earlier dream was "stood on its head," and "the personal computer became a commodity ..." marketed "as an extension of self, a fashionable accessory for isolated, and often elite users." In the early 1990s the expansion of the Internet made the personal machine into a "communications gateway," enabling "international conjunctures" of like-minded people who could discover and share interests and passions, regardless of distance.

In the context of this historical view of the social meaning of the computer, Turkle sees Tardieu and the Shaws as having returned to "what was most robust in the earlier dreams for personal computation." In their hands, the community computer is designed not to bypass but to strengthen communities of place, and to facilitate the discovery of untapped human potential, especially among the disadvantaged.

Anne Beamish's chapter surveys the range of existing approaches to community computing, mapping the larger universe of which Tardieu's community computer and the Shaws' neighborhood networks are outstanding examples, grouping projects by the user populations (for example, individuals, schools, youth, the elderly, community organizations) at which they are aimed and the particular obstacles (of infrastructure, hardware and software, online access, relevant content) to which they are addressed. Illustrating her survey with some thirty community computer projects across the country, Beamish reveals the widespread range and rich variety of such projects, while at the same time she calls attention to the importance of developing a clearer and more specific formulation of the projects' objectives, means, and underlying assumptions, so as to enable us to "imagine, experiment, test, and learn from these experiences."

The Main Terms of the Argument Revisited

The several chapters of Part II that describe possibilities for the beneficial use of advanced information technology by low-income urban populations also reveal important differences in the authors' use of two key terms, "poverty" and "information technology." These distinctions help place the "solutions" proposed in Part II in relation to the different ways of framing the problem proposed in Part I.

Poverty

Amsden distinguishes between "transient" and "persistent" poverty, focusing attention on the potentials for entrepreneurship in software development on the part of the persistently poor. In his discussion of his version
of the community computer, Tardieu concentrates on those who live in
extreme poverty, the poorest of the poor who are of central concern to the
Fourth World Movement. Wolpert, whose statistical approach depends
on the use of the federally defined "poverty line," deals broadly with people
whose household income falls below that line, noting geographic areas of
the city in which concentration of poverty is increasing. He also attends to
the worsening economic plight of the working poor and the increasing rate
at which members of the middle class enter the ranks of the unemployed.

      Several authors make the crucial distinction between low-income
individuals and low-income communities. Amsden, in particular, observes
that when individuals succeed in gaining employment in companies that
develop or use information technology, or when they succeed in entre-
preneuring technology-based businesses, their successes redound to the
benefit of low-income communities of place only when they remain in
their communities of origin.

Information Technology

The pervasive use of such terms as "the computer" or "information technology" masks significant differences in what the various authors actually
mean by these terms. For some authors, such as Resnick and Bamberger,
"the computer" means a type of machine with unique features, coupled
with appropriate software, that lend themselves to an educational function
that can be well adapted to the strengths and weaknesses of low-income,
minority children and youth. For example, an "old-fashioned" computer
(an Apple II) running the LOGO language enables Lafayette to experiment
with the meaning of symbolic descriptions so as to make them actually
"play." The leading-edge software of the Computer Clubhouse enables its
users to design robots or musical instruments. For Tardieu, another "old-
fashioned" computer (an Atari) lends itself, through potentials for "data

as command" and associative memory shared by all computers, to the development of the community encyclopedia.

For Ferreira and Shiffer, "information technology" refers to systems of data collection, storage, analysis, and representation that make up "support systems" for grassroots participation in planning, evaluation, and development. Such forms of digital technology are seen as vehicles for a more decentralized and democratic process of public planning and debate.

But for these authors, as well as others such as Mitchell, the Shaws, and Tardieu (in part), "information technology" also refers to digital communications networks, which are seen as vehicles for dialogue between residents and public officials, or strengthening social bonds in communities of place, or helping create virtual communities among poor people in different places. In some instances, the digital network functions in a given locality to interconnect people who already know one another, enabling them to carry out activities of particular interest to them. In other instances, the digital network takes on a more generic, open-ended meaning. It is seen, for example, as a vehicle which allows low-income people access to a variety of "goods" from which they would otherwise be excluded: information about employment opportunities, opportunities to work at a distance from telecenters, access to educational materials and experiences, access to social or commercial services, entry into broader social networks organized around specialized interests or topics of discussion and debate.

For the authors in Part I, "information technology" has a broader sweep. It refers to a wave of sociotechnical change, comparable to the earlier waves associated with electrification, industrial mass production, the telephone, and the automotive complex. As we have seen, these authors differ in their perceptions of this wave as one that flows from a "control revolution" that began a hundred years ago (Hall), the rise of an "informational economy" over the last thirty years (Castells), or a "digital revolution" that has just begun and is only now in the process of reshaping our cities and our society (Mitchell). What these authors share is the vision of an electronic sociotechnical-economic system of great scope that has transformed, and is likely to further transform, the economies and societies of nations, exacerbating the plight of poor and minority populations in our cities. Through this lens, the authors in Part I (and here we must include Amsden) are broadly concerned with the exclusion of low-income populations from the revolutionary sociotechnical transformations they envisage. They want to find ways of mitigating the dislocating effects of that transformation, or of enabling the excluded to gain entry to "the informational economy," the "electronic business system," or "the digital world," in order to gain access to its possible economic, commercial, or social benefits—or more broadly, in the words of one of our colloquium participants, to avoid being stuck on a dirt road adjacent to the informa-tion superhighway.

Taken together, the chapters of Parts I and II pose a fundamental question: To what extent do the necessarily concrete, particular initiatives set out in Part II represent potential responses to the challenges of the global, problematic transformations described in Part I? What is the longer-term, larger-scale promise of these initiatives? How realistic are they? What impediments must be overcome in order to realize their larger potential? What policies at the federal, state, regional, and urban levels of government are likely to promote the effectiveness of such initiatives? What are their implications for new directions of research? We might also ask: How may these "existence proofs" suggest a reframing of the global problematic situation?

These are questions to which we return in the conclusion.

Part I: Setting the Context

1. The Informational City Is a Dual City: Can It Be Reversed?

Manuel Castells

Introduction

We are living through one of the most fundamental technological and social changes in history. The revolution in information technologies that took shape in the early 1970s, and diffused throughout the economy, society, and culture in the last quarter of the twentieth century, has profoundly transformed the way we live, work, produce, consume, communicate, travel, think, enjoy, make war and peace, give birth, and die. It has also transformed, as have all major technological revolutions, the material foundations of human life, time, and space (Castells 1996). Consequently, the combination of new information technologies and socioeconomic restructuring is reshaping cities and regions, ushering in new urban forms and processes that I identified as the "informational city" (Castells 1989). This multidimensional transformation is not technologically determined. Rather, it is the outcome of an interactive process between technology, economic strategies, social interests, cultural values, and power struggles. Thus, in principle, new social and spatial structures resulting from this multilayered process of change can be modified by social action, private strategies, and public policies. Prevailing trends, however, cloud what could be an exhilarating moment for humankind, opening up extraordinary possibilities for material prosperity and spiritual fulfillment, with the inducement of social exclusion in parallel to social development, deepening existing patterns of sociospatial segregation. These trends are rooted in powerful processes of economic globalization and capitalist restructuring that use to their advantage the potential of new information technologies, conditioning the social trajectory of technological change.

Thus, the emerging, informational city is by and large a dual city. By informational city, I understand an urban system with sociospatial structure and dynamics determined by a reliance of wealth, power, and culture, on knowledge and information processing in global networks, managed and organized through intensive use of information/communication technologies. By dual city, I understand an urban system socially and spatially polarized between high value-making groups and functions on the one hand and devalued social groups and downgraded spaces on the other hand. This polarization induces increasing integration of the social and spatial core of the urban system, at the same time that it fragments devalued spaces and groups, and threatens them with social irrelevance (Mollenkopf and Castells 1991; Castells 1992). I argue that the two processes, informationalization and dualization, are intertwined under the current social, political, and economic conditions in most of the world, certainly including American cities. New information technologies are not the cause of this association between informationalization and sociospatial exclusion. The roots of social exclusion are in the politics of capitalist restructuring that have prevailed in most societies since the 1980s. The power of new information technologies, however, enhances and deepens features present in the social structure and in power relationships. This is why we are at the crossroads of a new urban age. A real possibility exists of evolving toward systemic urban schizophrenia, that is, toward the disso- lution of urban civilization in an undifferentiated exurban sprawl through telecommunicated/freeway-connected, discontinuous spaces, leaving behind "black holes" of poverty, dereliction, and ignorance, abandoned to their fate. Yet it does not have to be that way. The promise of information technology may lead to a different, more humane city, in the framework of a new, more intelligent, and more just society. This chapter examines both possibilities on the basis of available evidence and exploratory thinking.

Information Technology and the Space of Flows

In various quarters of futurology, the diffusion of advanced information and communication technologies has prompted prophetic statements about the end of cities. In fact, a review of empirical evidence on the relationship between telecommunications and urban forms (Graham and Marvin 1996) shows a simultaneous process of concentration and decentralization of activ- ities and population to be the prevailing pattern. Throughout the world, directional centers continue to be concentrated in a few selected nodes of major metropolitan areas precisely because telecommunications and information systems allow directional activities to reach out to the entire country, or to the entire world, from their concentrated locations, be it in the old cores or in the new peripheries of metropolitan areas. Research by Moss (1987), Daniels (1993), and Sassen (1991), among others, shows empirical evidence on the pattern of persistent concentration, and presents arguments for the spatial clustering of corporate centers and their ancillary networks of advanced services: the historical development of a supply base of firms, services, and labor, clustered around corporate centers; the symbolic marking of prestigious space; the face-to-face, secretive interaction required by decision makers at the top; the value of assets invested in prime real estate, precluding a collective flight from business centers that would collapse property values for everybody. Thus, in spite of functional congestion and social problems, most old metropolitan centers continue to thrive, starting with downtown New York, London, and Tokyo; and when new centers are constituted, for example in northern Atlanta or Irvine, they arise in clusters, not along scattered locations on the urban edge.

The geography of innovation, the decisive activity of the informational economy, also shows its spatial clustering in what Peter Hall and I have identified as "milieux of innovation" around the world (Castells and Hall 1994). Innovation may be spurred by synergistic interaction facilitated by territorial complexes of research, design, and production, such as Silicon Valley, Route 128, or Austin in the case of high technology. In Hollywood and San Francisco's South of Market, milieux and innovation arise in the fields of multimedia and computer graphics; on Wall Street in financial products; or in Manhattan or West Los Angeles in fashion design. From these milieux of innovation, telecommunicated information systems ensure the hierarchical diffusion of production, management, and distribution of new products and processes throughout the interconnected nodes of the global system.

The new industrial space reflects this kind of technological/spatial division of labor among centers of innovation, advanced manufacturing, assembly manufacturing, and customized production near the final markets in an asymmetrical set of functional interdependencies. Different locations are selected according to specific characteristics of labor and production inputs, required for each step of the manufacturing process. This changing *spatial* division of labor was first identified in the case of electronics manufacturing and it has been increasingly seen to characterize most industries, as information technology becomes prevalent in all lines of manufacturing, gradually eliminating the old distinction between high-tech and low-tech industries.

Ancillary business activities, such as banking, insurance, and professional services, also follow this "double pattern," concentrating back offices in new suburban centers while diffusing customer-oriented services, some of them automated, throughout the residential sprawl. Social services also concentrate and diffuse simultaneously. For instance, medical services are clustered around major hospitals, while primary care centers are neighborhood based. The higher the specialization, the higher the concentration in a few locations in the metropolitan area and, to the highest level, in the nation (e.g., the Mayo Clinic complex in Rochester, Minnesota). Residential location is increasingly dispersed in suburbs and exurban edges; yet social segregation by income, education, and race still clusters communities, forming a discontinuous space of internally homogeneous social units, both in the city and in the suburbs.

Thus, in all dimensions of the urban/suburban fabric, we observe the emergence of a new form of space: the space of flows, characterized by simultaneous concentration and decentralization of people and activities. Under the new technological conditions the key feature is the linkage of different spatial locations into a new spatial process that reintegrates the functional unity of different elements in distant locations through infor- mation technology. This new spatial logic is present in the location of advanced services centers, in the geography of innovation, in the territorial distribution of services, in the emergence of a new industrial space, and in the variable geometry of residential patterns in the megacities that will characterize third-millennium urbanization (Borja and Castells 1997).

The impact of the space of flows on a highly segregated urban structure deepens segregation and accentuates inequality as a result of several converging processes: (1) traditional manufacturing, based on low-skilled labor, declines in American cities, as it is either automated or relocated to cheaper production sites around the world; (2) large employers of middle- and low-skilled service workers move to the suburbs as back- office complexes escape real estate prices, environmental congestion, and social problems of the central city, following manufacturing's relocation to the suburbs forty years ago; (3) personal and social services also follow the residential sprawl of their users and consumers. Thus most central cities lose their functions and economic base, accelerating the urban decline that took place in the 1960s. But something else is happening. The few nodal functions still located in central cities, around Central Business Districts (CBDs) and high-quality urban spaces, can be bridged to their regional, national, and global hinterlands via telecommunications, fast transportation, and information systems, without needing to renovate their surrounding urban areas. Thus the central city's islands of prosperity and innovation can further isolate themselves from the city, while integrating into the archipelago of the space of flows and delinking themselves from their social and territorial environments. So the space of flows links up *valued* spaces at the same time that it separates and isolates *devalued* spaces in the inner city, and sometimes in the suburbs, where low-income communities, a significant proportion of ethnic minorities, rundown schools, dilapidated housing, the institutions of the urban welfare state, and the shop floors of the criminal economy remain trapped. Given that these spaces, these populations, and these institutions have a decreasing relevance for functions valuable to the central city's islands of prosperity and innovations, from the point of view of the system logic, there is a self-reinforcing process of spatial marginalization, social exclusion, and functional devaluation in these neglected places, which the information highways of the space of flows have bypassed. Under such conditions traditional patterns of urban segregation are deepened. Infor-mationalization induces dualization and reinforces it in the structure and dynamics of space.

The Transformation of Work and Employment

Along with the transformation of space, a major transformation of social structure is also under way, fundamentally rooted in the transformation of work and working arrangements. As in all periods of rapid technological change, the population-at-large has expressed considerable anxiety concerning prospects for employment. Formidable changes are under way, but not in the form of widespread unemployment as a result of the substitution of machines for labor (Carnoy and Castells 1996; Carnoy, Castells, and Benner 1996). Against the prophecies of uninformed doomsayers, America is not experiencing a job shortage. Between 1979 and 1994, 27 million new jobs were created, 60 percent of which were in the technical and professional occupations, thus significantly upgrading the skill profile of the overall occupational structure. From 1992 to 1996, over 10 million new jobs have been created, so that unemployment remains at about 5.5

percent, a low level by historical standards, in spite of the massive incorporation of women into the labor force in the last three decades. Most regular jobs, however, now require some higher level of education, and college education is becoming a requirement for any decently paying job. So, the mismatch between an embattled educational system and the skill requirements of the expanding sectors of the labor market is growing.

People's heightened anxiety concerning new patterns of employment has a different origin, however. On the one hand, it reflects the decline in real wages for full-time male workers, and more recently stagnant wages for women, in spite of the higher skills content of their jobs. On the other hand, it stems from increasing job insecurity and unpredictability, as the traditional model of a stable, full-time job in a large organization with a predictable career pattern fades away. Both aspects are linked: because jobs are no longer secure, and because labor contracts are increasingly individually negotiated, it follows that a downward spiral of wages and working conditions would result in spite of a higher average level of skills and steady job creation. Job instability and lowering of real wages are linked to major structural changes made possible by information technology: globalization of the economy and decentralization of manufacturing and services and transformation of firms' operations through networking and subcontracting. Under such conditions management has a number of options vis-à-vis labor: automate, relocate production, outsource part of the production, downsize, and network. Usually, a combination of all these strategies is pursued: a highly flexible system which is tantamount to the individualization of labor conditions and to the foreseeable end of collective bargaining, except in public services. Our studies on the United States (with Martin Carnoy and Chris Benner) provide evidence of the growing role of different forms of nonstandard, full-time labor: temporary workers, part-time, self-employment, subcontracting, consulting, networking. This desocialization of labor is happening at all levels of skills, not just at the low end. But unskilled workers are the most vulnerable under such new patterns of management/labor relations, and thus they are forced to accept lower wages, job insecurity, and fewer or no benefits. Ethnic minorities and youth are most frequently subject to the devaluation of their labor conditions. The use of information technologies, although not the cause of such labor practices, allows for its diffusion. On the one hand, this is because low- and medium-skilled labor can be automated if it becomes too expensive or too rigid for the requirements imposed by relentless, global competition. On the other hand, it is because the use of information technologies makes it possible to keep the coherence of the production process through a network of interaction among spatially distant units. As a result, a major polarization occurs between a core labor force, with high skills, and a mass of disposable labor that can be used or replaced or employed under different statuses, depending on the needs and requirements of the market. Each discontinuity in the work's trajectory could send into oblivion some workers who, by falling in one of the "black holes" of the new socioeconomic structure, will find it difficult to reinstate themselves in the pool of the fully employable. Thus, even though mass unemployment does not exist, there are growing segments of semi-employed, in and out of the labor market, creating a potential danger for some individuals, particularly among minority youth, to join the ranks of the criminal economy. Decreasing cultural skills forbid entry into the informational labor market that increasingly requires the ability of "symbol processing," in Reich's expression.

To these structural factors of the new labor markets, induced by the combination of informationalization and economic restructuring, we must add the crisis of the patriarchal family, and the weakening of the urban welfare state, currently under the assault of neoconservativism. Thus we observe the formation of a growing segment of urban poor that includes fallen workers, marginal youth, and impoverished families, usually headed by females. These social segments continue to concentrate in the devalued spaces constituted by the process of urban dualism. Given that the school system is spatially segregated, public schools in devalued spaces become mechanisms of reproduction of social devaluation, unable to provide the necessary skills for the informational labor market, and becoming instead training grounds for survival in a world of social irrelevance. Then, the criminal economy takes over these devalued spaces, providing the only alternative for many youths. The justice system (including prisons) links up these devalued spaces, providing the social networks and cultural glue, to develop an alternative form of survival, however precarious. Under such conditions, no telecommunications infrastructure or training programs can save people trapped in these "black holes" of the informational city, as Blakely et al. (1995) have argued in their pioneering study of "the information city and the ghetto" in Los Angeles. Is this self-reproducing process of sociospatial exclusion inevitable and irreversible? Are we creating an Athenian democracy of informational, creative elites while ignoring a derelict mass of slaves and barbarians?

Can the New Urban Informational Dualism Be Reversed? Information Technology with a Human Face

At first sight, the prospect of using the promise of information technology to improve the fate of low-income communities, thus reversing the current trend, appears rather bleak. This is because the informational economy does not have much use for an unskilled, uninformed population, and because the institutional fabric of low-income communities provides scarce opportunity to overcome the vicious cycle of poverty, functional illiteracy, occasional work, social/racial discrimination, and criminalization of misery (Susser 1997). In addition, fashionable neoconservative thinking seems to be ready to give up on inner cities, dooming their dwellers with the dwellings. As George Gilder put it: "The problem with cities today is that they are parasites, and they will have to go off the dole" (1995).

Yet, as Lisa Servon and John Horrigan (1996) argue in their study on urban poverty and information technology in Austin, local governments in several American cities have recorded some successes in enhancing access of low-income communities to information technologies, and putting this access to the benefit of education, job training, and broadening of opportunities to break out of the ghetto, particularly for minority youth. A courageous policy of linking up technological change and social reform is not only possible, albeit difficult, but necessary, not only for moral reasons, but for pragmatic reasons as well. It cannot be seriously argued that a democratic society can live peacefully on the basis of the systemic exclusion of one-quarter to one-third of its people, even confining them spatially in implicit apartheid style. In what follows, I propose some strategic elements of the possible content of a policy using information technology as an additional tool for revitalizing poor communities. These proposals are simply illustrations that should be taken as only hints of what a more detailed, empirically grounded study/design could propose. The basic assumption is that the diffusion of technology is necessary but not at all sufficient to reverse informational inequality. Thus only 10 percent of African American households have personal computers, in contrast to 50 percent of white households. The real issue, however, is how and what to use these computers for.

In terms of strategic goals, in the new sociotechnological structure, the *key* to fighting self-reproducing marginality *is access both to jobs and to income generation*. For this, *education* is a must: general education, not narrow job training. It is increasingly unlikely that investment in the deprived communities will change their fate. Rather, it is the transformation of the residents of these communities, by finding jobs and earning income outside the community, that will change their character. It is important, however, that individual improvement does not translate into immediate residential mobility to the suburbs, leaving trapped behind the less fortunate. Poor communities must find ways to keep their best residents long enough so that the ripple effects of nonmarginal households will enhance the community by their very presence, bringing up the ladder the borderline households. For this, at the roots of *community improvement*, they have to get rid of the criminal economy, which thrives precisely on the deterioration of the community. Innovative urban design (defensible spaces, street life-oriented design, nonpastiche beautification of the neighborhood, etc.) and an active media policy by the community to fight negative images and project the real life of real people to the city at large can also enhance the community. These *efforts, geared toward jobs, education, and community*, require mobilization of social and political resources. At present, *local governments are the key actors in the process*, but they must rely both on citizen participation via community organizations and on the contribution from socially responsible corporate businesses, through *urban partnerships between business, citizens, and local/state governmental agencies*.

All this, however, is not new. It has been tried in many cities over the last three decades, and the positive outcome has been rather meager. Nonetheless, we must try again, this time using experience and knowledge to correct past mistakes (such as excessive reliance on a bureaucratic, urban welfare state), and perhaps marshaling the power of information technology to help innovative programs that, with the support of corporate business, could contribute to breaking the dualizing logic of the informational city.

Six developmental policy initiatives could help cement the proposed interaction between information technology and urban social reform as we approach the twenty-first century.

The first initiative concerns the necessary spurring of *entrepreneurialism and small business* among low-income communities' residents as the most likely way to break through the structural discrimination of the labor market. Indeed, entrepreneurial immigrants are quickly becoming the driving economic force in many poor communities in New York and Los Angeles, thus following the classic, historical pattern of American cities. Online selling, advertising, and contacting over the Net could ease the difficulty of locating these start-up businesses in the invisible, dangerous areas of the city.

The second initiative refers to the expansion of telework not from home but from *community telecenters* set up jointly by governments and corporations, where workers could be employed on a flexible basis without having to commute, thus reducing costs and saving time. Furthermore, these community-based telecenters would keep jobs in the community, while not requiring physical investment by employers in communities that, at least for some time, might constitute hazardous locations.

Naturally, entrepreneurialism and teleworking require a substantial enhancement in the educational potential of residents in low-income communities, which requires reversing the declining quality of public schools and finding additional sources of learning specific to the characteristics of these residents. Thus the third initiative should be a focus of the corporate-public urban partnerships on revamping the quality of the public school system. With the cooperation of Parent-Teacher Associations, schools should be converted in the evening into community centers, open to the society at large, making them less vulnerable to gangs and more in touch with the community's real problems. Experimental programs of tele-education should be geared toward adult education, starting with computer literacy campaigns, followed (not preceded) by rental/donations of computer equipment. Youth could be recruited, and paid, to educate their families in using computers. University extension programs should go online, with subsidized fees for targeted areas, as part of the universities' contribution to the communities. Furthermore, information technology should be called to the rescue of children's education. It is well known that one of the key handicaps for poor children in their education is that their parents do not support them in doing their homework, not because of lack of interest, but because their parents lack education and cultural skills. It is in this way that cultural/social inequality reproduces itself. In some California schools teachers supervise and help their students with their homework online. This practice is often limited to predominantly middle-class schools; its real need, however, is among children of poor families. The building of these programs could start reversing the vicious cycle linking poor families and poor education that would continue in spite of improvement in the schools because of the unsupportive family environment for children's learning.

A fourth initiative can also be used to emphasize the potential of information technology for improving the educational chances of poor populations. It is well known that a significant proportion of poor males, particularly among ethnic minorities, spend considerable amounts of time in prison and in the justice system early in their lives. Indeed, to a large extent, prisons appear to be an extension of the community in many ghetto areas. They are often schools of specific criminal trades. To cut another vicious circle between poverty, racism, discrimination, and jails, *information technology could be used to educate and train the prison population*, to provide opportunities for teleworking and to interact with prospective employers while in prison, so that the link with education and jobs is not lost and, as so often happens, replaced by the link of the criminal economy. This strategy would involve the cooperation of the justice system, the educational system, and corporate sponsorship of experimental programs that could be generalized if successful. We must acknowledge the problem of mass imprisonment of the poor in the United States, and introduce mechanisms to reduce it gradually, starting with the nonreproduction of the criminal system through the institutions of punishment. Telecommunications offer the possibility of keeping the minds linked with, and open to, society, even while the bodies suffer incarceration.

Fifth, if we want to reform, not abandon, cities, community enhancement has to proceed in parallel to educational development and individual job opportunities. Two policy areas could be improved. The first area is *community-based media*, particularly cable television and local radio, that could induce social cohesiveness in the community while projecting its images to broader audiences. The advent of multimedia may help this symbolic interaction, as community-based media could become part of an interactive, electronic hypertext that would broaden the sources of information and images, as well as help citizens to value their own input in the media system. The second area is *urban design in and for poor communities*. The restoration of meaning and culture in communities that have been written off as public spaces for the city implies the search for a new monumentality, for the creation of urban art (e.g., the murals in Latino communities), and for the residents' self-recognition of their public space by being involved in environmental beautification projects. Here information technology is no more than a tool, but an important one, as computer design may considerably help facilitate citizens' participation in the design and redesign of their newly valued space.

None of these policies stands a chance of implementation without the sixth initiative, *revitalizing local governments*. As demonstrated in the 1996 Habitat II United Nations Conference, local governments worldwide are being decisive in improving urban living conditions. Paradoxical as it may seem, in a world dominated by global flows of wealth, information, and power, local governments are as limited in their power as national governments are nowadays, but much more flexible, adaptive, and representative of their constituencies (Castells 1997). When linking up with citizen groups and business partnerships, local governments, under the right political conditions, may become key public entrepreneurs, altering the conditions under which poor communities sink into oblivion. For this, however, they need information and connectivity to compensate for their lower political capacity and financial resources. Information technology provides the tools for local governments to manage in real time the complex interaction between citizens, decentralized public agencies, and business decisions, substituting initiative for bureaucracy through strategic planning and real-time management of multiple initiatives. Furthermore, local governments may network among themselves via shared data banks and online consultations, as is already the case of intermunicipal networks in Europe (Graham 1995). Flexible information systems provide the tools for informed bargaining with corporations and national governments in a resurrection of the vitality of the city-state that characterized the previous period of formation of a world economy in Renaissance Europe. Local governments aim at anchoring spaceless flows in specific places, reversing the structural logic of uncontrolled globalization, and negotiating on behalf of their citizens the conditions under which flows of information and wealth are distributed in local societies. Thus the current powerlessness of localities vis-à-vis the variable geometry of corporations may be reversed, as networks of local communities gradually take up the role of declining national governments in reestablishing social control over the conditions of economic development.

Conclusion: The Politics of Dreams

As in most prospective elaborations aimed at fighting the harsh realities stemming from structural trends, these initiatives may seem like dreams. I would not dispute this characterization, except to emphasize the extremely general, indicative character of my suggestions as I try to propose a style of policymaking rather than present a finished blueprint. I also want to remind the reader that many of these initiatives are being practiced in cities around the world. Yet the fundamental point to be made, following Gilder's cynical statement, is that to accept the current state of affairs is to give up cities. Thus either we accept the ruin of urban civilization, entrapping its last, unfortunate dwellers, and escape into a telecommunicated exurban sprawl, or we take up our courage, invent, calculate, think, fight, and work to turn the extraordinary opportunity of information technology into the promise of a more humane society, based not on social exclusion but on shared creativity. Yet, to do so, dreams have not just to be blueprinted but fought over, because the information age has not changed the reality that the power of technology still depends on the technology of power.

Note

Throughout this chapter, I refer often to my own publications. I do this to avoid repeating data and sources on the whole range of topics presented here that are covered in detail in these publications. Thus each reference to Castells must be considered as a generic reference to the bibliography and evidence provided in each the books cited. Similarly, Graham and Marvin

(1996), Blakely et al. (1995), Servon and Horrigan (1996), and Susser (1997) are useful bibliographic sources to the vast body of information that should be consulted when analyzing in depth the issues explored in this chapter.

References

Blakely, Edward J. et al. 1995. "Information City and the Ghetto—The L.A. Experience." Los Angeles: University of Southern California, Lusk Center Research Institute, Working Paper LCRI-95-10p.

Borja, Jordi and Manuel Castells. 1997. "Global and Local. The Management of Cities in the Information Age." London: Earthscan.

Carnoy, Martin and Manuel Castells. 1996. "Sustainable Flexibility: Work, Family, and Community in the Information Age." Paris: OECD Education Division.

Carnoy, Martin, Manuel Castells, and Chris Benner. 1996. "Flexible Work and Labor Markets in Information Age America." Research report. New York: Russell Sage Foundation.

Castells, Manuel. 1989. *The Informational City: Information Technology, Economic Restructuring, and the Urban-Regional Process*. Oxford: Blackwell.

Castells, Manuel. 1996. *The Information Age: Economy, Society, and Culture. Volume I: The Rise of the Network Society*. Oxford: Blackwell.

Castells, Manuel. 1997. *The Information Age: Economy, Society, and Culture. Volume 2: The Power of Identity*. Oxford: Blackwell.

Castells, Manuel and Peter Hall. 1994. *Technopoles of the World: The Making of 21st Century Industrial Complexes*. London: Routledge.

Daniels, P. W. 1993. *Service Industries in the World Economy*. Oxford: Blackwell.

Gilder, George. 1995. "City vs. Country: Tom Peters and George Gilder Debate the Impact of Technology on Location." *Forbes ASAP*, 27 February, p. 56.

Graham, Stephen. 1995. "From Urban Competition to Urban Collaboration? The Development of Interurban Telematics Networks." *Environment and Planning C* 13: 503–524.

Graham, Stephen and Simon Marvin. 1996. *Telecommunications and the City: Electronic Spaces, Urban Places*. London: Routledge.

Mollenkopf, John and Manuel Castells, eds. 1991. *Dual City: Restructuring New York*. New York: Russell Sage Foundation.

Moss, Mitchell. 1987. "Telecommunications, World Cities, and Urban Policy." *Urban Studies* 24: 534–546.

Sassen, Saskia. 1991. *The Global City*. Princeton: Princeton University Press.

Servon, Lisa and John Horrigan. 1996. "Urban Poverty and Access to Information Technology: A Role for Local Government." Paper delivered at the Annual Meeting of the American Association of Collegiate Schools of Planning. Toronto. 26 July. Unpublished.

Susser, Ida. 1997. "The Construction of Urban Poverty and Homelessness in the New Global Economy." *Annual Reviews of Anthropology*, forthcoming.

2. Changing Geographies: Technology and Income

Peter Hall

Two Parables from London

I begin with two parables from my native London, which I think represent that city—and indeed any major city of the developed world—in the 1990s. The first comes from a recent visit to the National Gallery. In the bookstore there is a glass case containing a display of the Bill Gates Art Gallery of the world: the one he has on display in his house, and is available on a smaller screen version to ordinary mortals like us. A small child about six years old was pushing his fingers against the glass case because he was obviously used to a computer at school that was touch activated; he was trying to change the pictures with his finger. He was getting nowhere because the computer was keyboard operated—at least in principle; in fact it was operating on a fixed time program. I fell to thinking about this typical London child: how soon was he going to learn the keyboard skills and the mouse skills? I figured that if he was in the National Gallery with his parents on a Sunday afternoon, the answer would probably be very soon; indeed, I do not doubt that he is already at work. And soon he may come back to the National Gallery, and before long he may be creating computer art of his own, laying the foundation for a new multimedia business. But will he be doing it in London, or out along the M4 highway west of Heathrow, Britain's high-tech corridor? Or in Silicon Valley, or Southern California, or near Gates in Redmond, Washington?

The second story concerns Harriet Harman, then a member of the Labour Party's shadow cabinet; within a year, since virtually everyone in Britain expected Labour to win the coming general election, she would be secretary of state for health. She decided to send her own eleven-year-old son to a selective grammar school, ten miles away from her home in inner south London, rather than sending him to the neighborhood school. It caused a huge political storm. The reason emerged quickly and clearly: that local school managed last year to get precisely 11 percent of its students through the basic sixteen-year-old hurdle, five grades A through C, which is now the basic passport to entry into the U.K. economy. The school to which she was sending him achieved 99 percent, and it was in the leafy outer London suburbs.

It set off a national debate. And in November 1996, the government again published highly controversial league tables of the performances of pupils at age sixteen in individual schools—controversial because the teacher unions are bitterly opposed to the tables. They showed three things. First, 7.9 percent of all pupils sixteen or older in England failed to achieve even a single GCSE[1] pass at grades A through G, 14.0 percent failed to achieve five passes at this level, and no less than 55.5 percent failed to achieve five passes at grades A through C. Second, all of the twenty worst-performing authorities were big-city ones; and in Kingston upon Hull in Yorkshire, the worst-performing authority, the corresponding figures were 16.3, 26.3, and 77.2 percent respectively; further, of these twenty worst-performing local education authorities, ten were in London. And third, within the London boroughs the spread between the best- and the worst-performing schools was extraordinary: from less than 10 percent passing to more than 90 percent doing so. London, a city that above all depends on successful performance in the informational economy, is massively failing many of its young people. Within the city exists a cycle of privilege, represented by young Joe Harman and the boy in the National Gallery, and a cycle of deprivation, represented by the children in the school that Joe is not going to attend. And for London, substitute Paris, New York, or Boston. Just after these two incidents, the Regional Plan Association published its third regional plan for the Tri-State New York region, entitled *A Region at Risk* (Yaro and Hiss 1996): an entire chapter was devoted to this topic.

These two stories neatly encapsulate two central issues. First, what will the emerging technologies do to the city, and to its economy? Will the new jobs cluster here, or desert the city? Second, and closely related, whatever the answer to the first question, what will be the impact on different groups of the city's—indeed, the world's—population? Will they destroy jobs or create jobs? Almost certainly, both? But what kinds of jobs will these be? What types of skills and aptitudes will they require, and what will be the impacts on different groups of people? Will they narrow or widen income differentials and unemployment differentials? And what will this imply for social cohesion? It is a formidable agenda, and the answers will be far from definite. But some pointers can be given.

The Informationalization of the World

There are two extreme views on what is currently happening to our economies and societies, and between them a host of possible intermediate positions. One is the view of James Beniger: that there has been a century-long "control revolution," a development of increasing sophistication in using information to handle complexity, starting with the classic case of American railroads and the first office technologies of the 1870s and 1880s (1986, 390–391, 401–407, 427–429, 435). And that evolutionary view harks back to Colin Clark, who long ago showed that tertiary-sector employment had been growing steadily throughout the twentieth century, as it has in the six decades since he wrote (Clark 1940, passim). In this view, even the technologies are neither new nor novel: the fax is a nineteenth-century technology, originally used by newspapers to transmit pictures; the compact disk is only a further refinement of the technology of compression that produced the long-playing record of the 1940s; and the VCR represents the domestication of a 1950s videorecording technology.

The opposite view, powerfully argued by Manuel Castells in his chapter, is that on the contrary, something extraordinary is happening: a transition from the industrial to the informational mode of production, associated with total globalization of the organization of production. And this is associated with a very fundamental technological revolution: the digitalization of information, whereby previously separate kinds of information—telephone, radio, television and videorecording, and computing —all become reducible to the same basic information medium, a string of binary digits conveyed along broadband communication channels (Castells 1989, 1997). This, in the view of the advocates, constitutes a basic revolution equal to the invention of writing or printing.

One does not have to accept one position and reject the other: we are seeing some of both. Of course there has been a steady progression toward the information-handling economy during the twentieth century, but equally, the digital revolution is highly significant for us and our cities. In any event, it is clear that already the great majority of the workforce in advanced countries and their cities is in service occupations, and a substantial proportion, approaching 50 percent, are in informational occupations. The old taxonomies of occupations and industries are no longer of much use in economies where only 5 or 10 percent of the workforce are in manufacturing: Robert Reich's distinction between the symbolic analysts and the pure personal service workers is perhaps the most useful one (Reich 1991), although it may need further development and sophistication.

The New Informational Infrastructure

The nature of the digital revolution is clear. It is associated with a bandwidth revolution: for the digital revolution to occur, different pieces of apparatus for the recording, processing, and exchanging of information must be connected by channels of unequaled bandwidth. The previous media, copper wire and airwaves, are no longer adequate for the huge amounts of information that must be conveyed. As Bill Gates writes: "In just the next five years the communications bandwidth available in urban business areas will grow by a factor of 100, as network providers compete to connect concentrations of high-use customers" (Gates 1995, 136). Businesses will be the first users. Hence America, the United Kingdom, and every country in the world must be cabled. Hence also the feverish battle taking place between carriers including TV and telephone companies and the battle over deregulation, culminating in the passage by Congress of the 1996 Telecommunications Act.

According to this view, information rather than physical goods becomes the main emphasis of production and exchange, and a new taxonomy develops, including provision for an infrastructure (the superhighway) and the development of new value-added services carried on that infrastructure. In his book *Being Digital*, Nicholas Negroponte forecasts that "broadcasting" will be replaced by "broadwatching": each individual will pick what she wants from cables full of digital information. There will be no need for "transmission standards": the receiving computer will make sense of anything (Negroponte 1995).

The important point, however, is that we are at a very early stage in this revolution: the parallel is with the automobile in about 1910, when the first Model Ts began to appear. As John Taylor, a British expert, says: "Far from building information motorways, we are just about to begin building some A roads and a few B roads … we are also just beginning to realize that there are indeed some worthwhile or entertaining destinations … the computer industry is at about the stage of the Model-T Ford, when the driver had to be a real enthusiast … anyone who has spent a happy day or two with a stack of floppy disks and manuals bigger than the PC itself will know all about getting out and getting under" (Taylor 1995, 42–44).

Taylor and another British observer, John Goddard, agree in emphasizing that the parallel with the automobile goes further: what was most significant about it was not the manufacture of cars, but the whole set of service industries that grew on top of it (Goddard 1992, 179; Taylor 1995, 42). We can already see the outlines of the new information businesses: they include telemedicine and tele-health care, tele-education, teleshopping and telelearning, online information services, electronic publishing, financial services, trading and brokering, entertainment of all kinds (film, video, theater, music, multimedia pop, animation, virtual reality, games), electronic sports and competitions and virtual reality expressions, security and surveillance, earth resources information, environmental monitoring and control, digital imaging and photography, data mining and processing (GB Office of Science and Technology 1995, 31).

We can also begin to speculate on the ways in which these new services will influence old jobs. Education is a critical example. As Douglas Hague, former chair of Britain's Economic and Social Research Council, has described it, information technology will not destroy the teaching profession—as some fear—but it will change it beyond recognition by allowing teachers to produce high-quality lessons to suit the needs of individual pupils. First-rate remote lectures will replace second- or third-rate direct ones; multimedia presentations will allow students to pace their own learning. Teachers will thus find themselves performing new roles: as "guides" or tutors; as "communicator/interpreters" on TV; as "scholar/interpreters," turning research into teaching material, and as "assemblers," packaging this material into products; all working in teams, on the model set in the 1960s by the United Kingdom's Open University (Hague 1994, 12–13).

The people who design these new applications will be new kinds of people. As *The Economist* put it, the "killer applications" will come from a new breed of high-tech bohemians—call them techno-bohos—who combine computer skills with story-telling and/or artistic flair" (*Economist* 1993). They will have to combine within one person, or at least one team, the "contrary imaginations" of Liam Hudson: the divergent imagination of the artist, and the convergent imagination of the technologist (Hudson 1966). An archetype is DreamWorks SKG, the studio started in October 1994 by film director Steven Spielberg, record titan David Geffen, and former Walt Disney Studios chief Jeffrey Katzenberg, who allied with Silicon Graphics to create an all-digital film production studio in Los Angeles; in a tie-up with Microsoft, they will produce interactive multimedia software, each company investing a minimum of $15 million (Kehoe 1995a; Parkes 1995). Bill Gates made a significant comment: "The potential for combining the incredible stories created by Jeffrey, Steven and David with the innovative technology and amazing interactivity that are possible today and in the future is just awesome to me ... Our partnership with DreamWorks will pave the way for extraordinary new consumer products" (Kehoe 1995b).

The Death of Distance—and the Death of the City?

The first critical issue is the effect of this digital revolution on the city and its people. There is a conventional wisdom: the evolving technology, in the words of an *Economist* supplement, implies "the death of distance" (Cairncross 1995, 39). Once you have paid your monthly subscription to CompuServe or one of its many competitors, the Internet and the World Wide Web are essentially free. This of course is only the culmination of a trend of lowering telephony costs, observable at least since 1950. But it has now reached a stage in which, as Bill Mitchell points out in *City of Bits*, you do not know where you are, or where or who anyone is: "The Net negates geometry ... it is fundamentally and profoundly aspatial. It is nothing like the Piazza Navona or Copley Square ... The Net is ambient—nowhere in particular but everywhere at once" (Mitchell 1995, 8).

But the central question is whether the death of distance implies the death of the city. And no one thinks so, not even Mitchell: "Does development of national and international information infrastructures, and the consequent shift of social and economic activity to cyberspace, mean that existing cities will simply fragment and collapse? Or does Paris have something that telepresence cannot match? Does Rome have an answer to *Neuromancer*? Most of us would bet our bottom bits that the reserves of resilience and adaptability that have allowed great cities to survive (in changed form) the challenges of industrialization and the automobile will similarly enable them to adapt to the bitsphere" (Mitchell 1995, 169).

There are rather good, albeit quite obvious, reasons for this. First, in more than a century of telephony, telecommunications have failed to dissolve the urban glue; on the contrary, their immediate effect has been to increase concentration in the first informational workplace clusters, the skyscraper cities of Chicago and New York of the 1880s and 1890s, and subsequently they have proved to be somewhat neutral in their effects, despite the huge fall in the real cost of long-distance telecommunications over that time. Second, the good reason for this is that much advanced service activity depends on what one can call "access to privileged information": whether in the City of London, or Midtown Manhattan, or Silicon Valley, or Hollywood, higher-level information workers spend a lot of their time picking up informal information, much of it semi-gossip, which is vital to the judgments they make about other more formal information. And the same will undoubtedly be true of the new centers of multimedia production which are now arising in precisely the same kinds of places: Dreamworld Boulevard in Los Angeles, and New York's Silicon Alley are based on just the same principle of networking, which is why new clusters are already beginning to appear.

Third, in these and other similar places we find an extraordinary synergy between telecommunications exchange and face-to-face exchange. That is why, as John Goddard noted in one of his earliest publications, dense telephone traffic for programmed contact is associated with dense taxi traffic for unprogrammed face-to-face contact (Goddard 1975). That is also why the world's first large-scale experiment in telecommunications-based distance learning, the United Kingdom's thirty-year-old Open University, contains such an important summer school program. And it is why, in major metropolitan cities, there is such an important synergy between live artistic performances and broadcast ones: the same actors and producers and designers shuttle constantly between one form and another, even on a daily basis. Out of this, likewise, comes a strong set of linkages between the arts, culture and entertainment industries in cities like London and New York, and the urban tourist industry, which together form a very basic urban economic driver (London Planning Advisory Committee 1991; GB Government Office for London 1996a, 1996b). It is no surprise, then, that over the present century the graphs of long-distance telecommunications traffic have marched in parallel with those for long-distance business travel (Graham and Marvin 1996, 262), or that the two forms of interaction have similar geographies. The one leads to the other.

Some take a more radical view, of course: they argue that we are about to see a revolution, similar to the one wrought by the automobile after World War II, which resulted in the decentralization of cities. Since that process took more than half a century, we might expect some of these impacts to be felt in the first half of the twenty-first century. In particular, telecommuting is being hailed as a transformation of living and working conditions; Mitchell even argues that we are seeing a reversal of the great historic divorce between home and workplace, which Lewis Mumford located in the seventeenth century (Mitchell 1995, 98). Gates reports seven million telecommuters in the United States in 1994, and predicts that millions more will join them at least part-time (Gates 1995, 152).

No one could doubt that telecommuting has a big potential impact: the main problem is to decide just how it is likely to be organized. Reports on the state of California telecommuting experiment, the largest in the world so far, indicate major reductions in commuting, especially at congested peak hours; substantial reductions in overall travel, including nonwork trips; greater reliance on local facilities, meaning less travel; but a minority of telecommuters moving farther from central cities, raising the specter of what Californians are already calling telesprawl (Handy and Mokhtarian 1995, 1996a, 1996b; Jencks and Peterson 1991; cf. Jencks 1992; Mokhtarian 1991; JALA Associates 1990; Mokhtarian 1990, 1991, 1992; Nilles 1991; Pendyala, Goulias, and Kitamura 1991). The question, Patricia Mokhtarian reminds us, is whether such moves might wipe out all the other gains in terms of total vehicle-miles; and these effects might take a very long time to work themselves out. Overall, the study concluded that many state government employees could telecommute, but at least half of them would need to do so not from home but through neighborhood telework centers.

And this perhaps is the most likely scenario: a great deal of part-time teleworking and itinerant work combined with short visits to the home office, or "hot desking." The most dramatic illustration of the part-time work station principle is the growth of remote call centers for airline and hotel reservations, banking or telephone inquiries. They follow the classic Mitchell principle that you do not know where or whom you are calling: Manuel Castells reports that calls for reservations at Best Western motel are handled by inmates at Arizona Women's State Penitentiary; in the United Kingdom, British Airways has decentralized its reservations from Heathrow to provincial cities like Newcastle, Glasgow, New York, and even Bombay, often employing part-time students who have the appropriate telephone manner and are willing to work at unsocial hours (Goddard 1995, 37–38). And, as the Bombay example illustrates, the process can diffuse anywhere worldwide within the obvious linguistic and cultural constraints.

This is a long way from the utopian dream of telecottaging, and it illustrates that the social impact may be far from benign: in the United Kingdom, a study of four hundred teleworkers in the publishing industry, mainly well-educated women, found that most had previously worked in-house, and were now working for their former employers on a casualized[2] basis. Unfortunately, they were socially isolated and financially insecure, with only half making a "living income" from teleworking. Andrew Gillespie and his colleagues at the University of Newcastle upon Tyne, authors of a major study on the subject, comment that "we should be concerned lest teleworking becomes merely another way of disguising poorly-paid casualized work behind a high-tech gloss" (Gillespie, Richardson, and Cornford 1995, 40).

The final verdict on telecommuting, then, must be an open one. Gillespie and his colleagues, who are notably skeptical, conclude that "... ever since teleworking from home became a topic of interest in the mid 1970s, its advocates have always and repeatedly argued that it is on the point of a 'breakthrough' into rapid growth. Rather like the predictions of Armageddon by certain religious sects, however, the breakthrough point has repeatedly been postponed, but only until tomorrow" (Gillespie, Richardson, and Cornford 1995, 141).

To summarize, then: the digital revolution may act to decentralize activities from cities and above all from big cities, but its precise impacts are far from clear. It may simply transfer some activities from some cities to other cities, as is occurring with the call centers in the United Kingdom. It may allow workers to perform some functions at home, or in hotels or other places, while hot desking in shared offices for part of the day or week. It may even—although this is highly speculative—allow some functions to be completely decentralized to home locations, and these may range from routine call center–type functions to more responsible creative jobs such as editing. The critical point, however, is that the functions thus lost from cities, and above all from city centers, may well be replaced by other, still-growing functions that require face-to-face contact: higher-level finance and business services; command and control functions such as headquarters of major corporations, or government; creative and cultural activities, ranging from the live performing arts to the print and electronic media; and tourism, including business tourism. Because these functions are also subject to the constant search for productivity gains, it is possible that big-city employment may decline while big-city value of output continues to grow, as seems to be happening in London and New York. But it would be quite unwise to conclude from this that the death of the city is nigh.

The Information Rich and the Information Poor

The overall prospects for cities, therefore, are likely to be by no means as dire as some commentators suggest. But that does not mean that the prospects for all city people are good; and that brings us to the second theme of this chapter. For the pattern that is emerging is one of huge differences in access to information and in turn to higher levels of education. There is now an accentuating division between the information rich and the information poor: a division applying equally to countries, cities, and individuals within cities.

Conventionally, there are two ways to measure these differences. One is through physical access to the new means of digital information. In January 1995, 3.37 million Internet hosts existed in North America,

1.04 million in Western Europe, 40,000 in Eastern Europe, 150,000 in Asia, 190,000 in the Pacific, and negligible numbers elsewhere in the world; thus, America had twice as many users as the rest of the world put together—in part, no doubt, because the system was developed in America and its main language is English (Anderson 1995, 5). A more recent survey suggests that in Sweden 12 percent of the population are connected at work and 5 percent at home; in Finland, 11 percent and 4 percent; in the United States, 9 percent and 8 percent; and in Great Britain, 6 percent and 3 percent. Thus, even in the most affluent countries, the exposure so far is minimal (Taylor 1996). Elsewhere in the world, even the basic infrastructure is lacking: Africa with 500 million people has fewer telephone lines than Tokyo with 23 million.

The same differences are evident within the advanced economies. Goddard comments that "Far from eliminating differences between places, the use of information and communications technology can permit the exploitation of differences between areas, for example in terms of local labor market conditions, the nature of cultural facilities and of institutional structures" (Goddard 1992, 180). This reflects access to the basic technologies: in the United States in the early 1990s, just under 80 percent of the poorest households in inner cities had a telephone in the home, against almost 99 percent of the richest suburban households; only 4.5 percent of poor rural households had computers available at home, against 66.4 percent of the richest suburban households. In the United Kingdom, telephone penetration ranged from 75 percent of households in the North to 89 percent in the Southeast; in the city of Newcastle upon Tyne, the percentage of households without a telephone varied by ward between 1 and 40 percent, and in one deprived inner city council estate 74 percent lacked phone access (Goddard 1995, 3–4). Goddard concludes that "Far from eliminating the importance of geography, the so-called 'space-transcending' ICTs (Information and Communication Technology), when taken together with other factors, are supporting a more uneven pattern of development within the UK. Information occupations and industries have grown dramatically in London and the Southeast in the past ten years, reflecting the capital's international as well as its national role. This growth has been underpinned by the rapid diffusion of computer networks; these networks are hubbed on London, serving to reinforce its dominant position in the national and international urban system" (Goddard 1992, 199).

The same point is made by Charles Handy: information technology will serve the 20 percent or so of the workforce, Reich's symbolic analysts: their jobs require theoretical abstract intelligence, plus deep and specialized education and knowledge, that remain firmly locked in the cores of the largest western cities (Channel Four 1995, 20). And this is underlined by statistics on educational attainment: within the advanced countries, 30 to 50 percent of the relevant age group now proceed to first-degree level,[3] but, as seen, there is a stubbornly high percentage of students—between 8 and 14 percent of the relevant age group in England, rising to between 16 and 26 percent in the worst-performing city school systems—that leaves without any qualifications at all. Here, surely, is the nub of the problem.

Of course, it can be argued that neither of these criteria is in itself completely relevant or completely definitive. Young people can gain access to computers in places other than home or school; masses of "information" need not be relevant, one can progress on the basis of knowing what is really relevant to the job at hand; schools may do little to advance computer literacy, and better ways may be available to achieve it; formal academic qualifications may not be the only relevant ones for entry to interesting niche jobs in the new economy; and on-the-job training, the kind that gives real understanding of processes, could be much more useful. And maybe, just maybe, we are too locked into the high-tech imagery of the recent past: perhaps, in the future, the relevant skills will be far more the divergent ones of creativity and craziness, which owe much less to formal academic education, and can simply well up out of the native imagination. But maybe not; there is not much evidence of it.

These jobs do not of course represent the sum total of job generation in contemporary cities. For they will generate income multipliers to support a wide range of personal service jobs, involving varied levels of skills, many of which will remain locked into the cities where the informational economy is located. It is common to deride these as entry-level, dead-end, casual jobs, but that may represent too gloomy a view: a whole range of more specialized and more skilled jobs are available: not merely hamburger servers, but top chefs and sommeliers; not merely bellhops, but hotel managers and the architects and engineers who help build new hotels; not merely bartenders, but actors, theatrical designers, art gallery curators. The list is endless; we do not know enough about these jobs and the way they are generated in the contemporary city, and we need a new taxonomy to describe them.

Nonetheless, the widespread fear is that the urban labor force may polarize: as Handy put it, there are the "symbolic analysts" who live in the suburbs and "have a busy life but a nice life," and the rest, "who don't know how to use it, who don't know how to make products out of it. And they live downtown, and they use public transport, and they'll have a tough time. And this is the underclass" (Channel Four 1995, 20). Will Hutton, the British journalist, is even more pessimistic: he writes about the 40:30:30 Society, in which only 40 percent represent the secure and well-paid symbolic analysts; the middle 30 percent consist of a casualized informational proletariat, increasingly in danger of losing its jobs to competitors in other cities and other countries; and the bottom 30 percent constitute an underclass subsisting on welfare payments and casual unskilled labor (Hutton 1995, 105–110).

What seems in no doubt is the proposition that, as economists put it, the rent accruing to brawn is now zero, thanks to what Marxists call the "growing organic composition of capital," while the rent accruing to brainpower, at least at the upper levels, is high and rising—hence the phenomenon, first noticed in the United States and the United Kingdom, but now observable in most advanced countries, of increasingly inegalitarian income distributions. Further, because of this inequality, the historic male advantage over women has disappeared: in certain groups, women have higher employment prospects and lower unemployment rates (as for instance in the United Kingdom), and the most depressed group in the entire labor market consists of undereducated, unskilled, imperfectly socialized young males. The huge loss of jobs in mass-production manufacturing during the 1970s and 1980s, in the older industrial cities of both the United States and the United Kingdom, drastically shrank the job opportunities of undereducated males, although their female equivalents found new niches in unskilled public-service jobs; in the United States, and to some degree in Western Europe, the plight of the males was exacerbated by immigration. All this has a further effect, noted by William Julius

Wilson: that young, undereducated, unskilled males now represent a very poor marriage prospect (Wilson 1987, 1996).

The New Urban Geography

The argument can be summarized in a series of propositions. The informational-digital revolution has transformed urban economies: the brawn jobs that existed in plenty thirty years ago have vanished and will not return; the only jobs that offer any kind of lifetime prospects are in information handling, and they require ever more sophisticated educational qualifications. But substantial numbers of young people, perhaps as many as 40 percent in many western countries, are leaving school without these qualifications and are effectively going onto the streets: youth unemployment is running at over 25 percent in France, over 40 percent in Spain, and among some ethnic-cultural groups the figure is higher: over 60 percent among young African-Caribbean males in London, for instance. These young people are becoming ever more segregated from the mainstream economy because they or their parents live in housing projects largely occupied by welfare-dependent groups; the school systems in these areas go into a downward cycle of achievement. As a result, education and job prospects worsen still further. It is not a pretty prospect, and the evidence suggests that it is not going to get better in a hurry.

Viewed then from a satellite above the Boston-New York corridor or its equivalents in Europe and Japan, a distinctive urban structure is emerging. Still a striking and dominant feature are the skyscrapers representing the traditional central business districts. They are subtly changing form, as they always have: in major cities there is usually more than one core, sometimes two (as in London), sometimes more (as in Tokyo and Los Angeles); some cores may be static, or growing more slowly, while others are expanding; often, there is a new center on reclaimed waterfront land.

These cores employ the symbolic analysts in the activities that now constitute the key urban economic drivers: finance and business services, command and control functions for international companies and agencies, creative and cultural industries, the media, the design professions, international tourism. Some of these workers live locally, in inner-city apartments; many, however, commute from distant suburbs, although significant numbers are concentrated in elite corridors or sectors leading in one or two predominant directions through prosperous inner suburbs to prosperous outer ones. Elsewhere, subways, commuter trains, and expressways hurry people past the inner suburbs at high speed, making them barely noticeable.

These areas are occupied by the casualized middle 30 percent of Hutton's trilevel social structure, or by his bottom 30 percent who are increasingly concentrated in less desirable public housing projects, some of which may be relatively close to the city center, others at the periphery. Wherever located, however, these areas prove to be socially segregated from the rest of the urban economy and society; the irony is that their people often live much closer to the central employment core than do the white-collar commuters, yet effectively they are disconnected from it. (Consider the relation of the South Bronx to Midtown Manhattan, or of Hackney to the City of London or Docklands). Increasingly, the central economy is fed from the elite corridors and the exurbs; the ancillary workers are found in parts of the intervening areas, while other areas become in effect separate islands, no longer functionally connected with the city.

But this is a point-in-time snapshot; in fact, the whole system is in flux. The new technology will probably not lead to the end of the city as we know it, any more than the automobile did. It will in fact have the same impact in the next century as the automobile and the telephone and electrification had in the century now closing: it will allow certain kinds of jobs to move out of city centers, and also down the urban hierarchy—in effect, producing a new urban division of labor. One result is that in the highest-level centers, the labor market will be increasingly polarized between top-level symbolic analysis jobs and bottom-level personal service jobs; less extreme versions of this polarization will appear at the next two or three levels of the new urban hierarchy.

Specifically, a few very high-level cities, the global cities of Saskia Sassen (1991), will perform a range of extremely specialized functions, relating to other similar cities for the exchange of information, but also attracting people worldwide because of the unique cluster of activities they offer. There will be a rather greater number of what one can call "regional cities," embracing the smaller European capitals and the main provincial cities of the larger European nation states as well as about a dozen regional centers in North America, many of which will also occupy special niches for the provision of certain highest-level services (such as financial services, higher education and R & D in Boston, or television news in Atlanta, or television entertainment in Los Angeles). Below them will be a great number of smaller cities, and some of these will cluster around the larger ones in what Lîsch once called "transportation-rich sectors"; some of these, constituting the continuation of elite corridors within the central metropolitan area, will be favored candidates for decentralization of certain activities. Corridors containing major airports are often favored in this regard, as in London, Stockholm, and Washington, D.C. (Hall 1993, 894–896).

Given this pattern, we are likely to find—indeed, are already finding—local deconcentration of back offices along the elite corridors to local subcenters, clustering around these third-level cities at distances up to fifty and even one hundred miles from the global cores. In addition, and more recently, there is deconcentration of pure call centers over much longer distances, to especially favored provincial cities which may be relatively remote, such as Glasgow or Newcastle in the United Kingdom, Omaha in Nebraska, or Salt Lake City in Utah; the common qualities of these cities are not always easy to identify, but the central one is the right kind of labor force. (For instance, American Express traveler's check refund service was relocated to Salt Lake, apparently because ex-Mormon missionaries have a very high level of foreign language competence.) This may cause a very sharp differentiation among cities; it does suggest that educational standards will be a key element in success.

One kind of city is potentially in deep trouble here: it is one that traditionally specialized in a type of manufacturing that has disappeared, because it has migrated out of the region or out of the country altogether. Detroit, Michigan, and Gary, Indiana, are two archetypes of such a city. Here, even the central service functions have disappeared, either because they were producer service offices serving the needs of the manufacturing complex, or because they were consumer services for which effective demand no longer exists. Such cities may come to constitute entire islands of multiple deprivation, gradually reverting back to a pre-urban condition.

And it is notable that they can exist side by side with areas of suburban prosperity only twenty or thirty miles away; here, we see in starkest form the outlines of a new geography of segregation.

Options for Policy

So what is to be done? In *The Truly Disadvantaged*, William J. Wilson believed that we should reflate the economy, because a rising tide lifts all boats. There are several possible responses: no one any longer believes in Keynes, but that does not mean Keynes was wrong, merely that the politicians do not find him a vote getter any more. In any case, the problem is not cyclical but structural. Perhaps, if one believes in Kondratieff waves, one should wait for the next long upswing, which Kondratieff fanciers variously date between now and 2011, and see if that does the trick. Common sense, however, suggests that an unqualified high school dropout will not have very strong prospects in a world where the main economic driver is the processing of information.

Beyond that point, views differ. One is that the United States and the United Kingdom have been wrong in pursuing so wholeheartedly the role of pacesetters of the informational economy: they have notably gone farther along the road of tertiarization than any other advanced countries, even if the others are following behind, and their residual manufacturing sector is heavily skewed toward the highest-technology-content market niches. They would have done better, this argument goes, to have progressed more slowly and more incrementally, improving their technological and marketing competence in sectors for which considerable market demand still exists, such as consumer electronics and automobiles. It is perverse, the argument runs, that America now finds itself uncompetitive in industries like cars and TV sets, where it earlier established a world lead; it should relearn from Japan and the Asian tigers the art of incremental technological improvement in the industries that could reabsorb the discarded urban labor force.

It is a persuasive argument, but the question is whether it now comes too late: Japan is also offshoring its routine production to peripheral regions and to lower-wage countries, and even later developers like Taiwan are now following suit. The logic of globalization is ruthless: cities and countries that pay $32 a day cannot compete with places where equally well-equipped factories employ equally diligent and well-educated labor earning $1 a day. And one might argue that if we have a moral responsibility to the poor, then it should extend to the poorest of the poor in those countries. In any case, even if these industries could recover in the advanced economies, they would be most likely to do so in greenfield areas next to good communications, as has happened with the American automobile industry, not in Detroit.

Unless one is a politically incorrect neoconservative like Richard Herrnstein or Charles Murray, believing that all this is fixed by the bell-shaped curve of intelligence and that nothing much can be done about it (Herrnstein and Murray 1994), the answer to this problem has to be more education and more equal education. Richard Freeman of the London School of Economics has demonstrated a close association between the doubling of the U.S. prison population between 1980 and 1995 and rising unemployment. But he has shown another connection, through education: although 75 percent of the entire population between eighteen and twenty-four failed to finish high school, among the prison population the story was the reverse: nearly 70 percent dropped out. Some 70 percent of all young African American men complete high school; among young black prisoners, only 25 percent do (Balls 1995).

But unfortunately, this is complicated by social geography. As William Julius Wilson has suggested for the African American population, and as other scholars have now proved in detail, the problem is that the more highly educated and qualified members have deserted their traditional residential areas, leading to an increasingly ghettoized underclass in the inner-city public housing projects. In such areas, Wilson says, no one goes to work so there is no tradition of setting the alarm clock. Further, because job prospects are so poor—and may be diminished further by "zip code redlining" among potential employers—the income from crime becomes much more attractive than any possible income from regular work, so drug dealing becomes the chief economic base. As Lawrence M. Friedman puts it: "When the choice is between selling hamburgers at McDonald's for minimum wage and running errands for drug dealers or stealing, the illegal options may seem a lot more attractive. The temptations are great—in this culture" (Friedman 1993, 442).

In other words, there is a rational choice model for undereducated young men: Cokes across the counter versus coke on the curb. And they prove pretty rational. The downside risk is not the fear of arrest and incarceration, which is so low as to be insignificant: Friedman quotes Hans Zeisel's study of New York City in the 1970s: of every 1,000 felonies committed, 540 are reported, resulting in 65 arrests and 36 convictions, in turn resulting in precisely three prison terms of a year or more. Thus, if the system were four times as tough, the figure would be twelve; as Friedman puts it, "Even a tremendous increase in conviction rates, without something more, would hardly make a dent in the problem of crime" (Friedman 1993, 458). In fact, the real downside risk is of murder by rival drug gangs. And this causes a further turn in the vicious downward spiral.

There is almost no doubt that this problem is immeasurably more serious in American cities than in European ones, because of a combination of circumstances: racial prejudice, the arrival of large numbers of unskilled African Americans in northern cities a few years before deindustrialization removed the work they had come north to do, and the fact that they were housed in highly segregated and stigmatized housing projects (Rifkin 1995, 74). The work of Loic Wacquant suggests that the worst European projects would not be regarded as particularly problematic by American standards (Wacquant 1993). But in Britain, Prime Minister Thatcher's right-to-buy policies meant that the superior housing projects became owner occupied, leaving the less attractive residue as a last-resort form of shelter for welfare populations. Certain parts of British cities are acquiring a similar quality of decline, hence the concerns about the school system in London and other large cities. It is no accident that Harriet Harman lives next to one of the largest and most problematic 1960s-style housing projects in London.

The problem lies not in defining the objective, but in discovering how to implement it. First, the evidence is mounting that a segment of the teaching force in the inner-city schools is not up to the job; second, to do anything about it would suggest that teachers would need to be paid more, and that could prove politically unpopular in a world where left-of-center politicians are joining right-of-center ones in cutting welfare-oriented programs. It might just succeed on the basis that it will save on welfare bills in the not-so-long run. In any case, no general improvement is going to work unless it somehow targets the worst-performing schools and pumps extra resources into them: the aim should be deliberately to narrow the spread of performance between school systems and between individual schools. It is significant that these are precisely the policy prescriptions Wilson underlines at the end of *When Work Disappears*: he calls for national standards for high school dropouts, for more even funding of schools (and in particular, for more generous funding for good teachers and for computers in deprived urban schools), and for more preschool education (Wilson 1996; cf. Murnane and Levy 1996).

There are at least two relevant points here. One is that the impact of information technology is not uniform among all sections of the labor force, any more than was the impact of any previous technological revolution. The production of information is one element, and it will involve rather large numbers of the symbolic analysts and the techno-bohos, but almost inevitably it will directly and indirectly involve many other skills too, from bookkeepers through editors and secretaries to canteen cooks and dishwashing personnel. Indeed, many American commentators now argue that there are major deficiencies—for instance, in urban physical infrastructure—that positively need the kinds of low-skill labor that has been discarded by the private sector. Mickey Kaus has suggested a revival of the Works Program Administration (WPA) of the 1930s New Deal, and Wilson endorses him—not least, because it would not specifically target the long-term unemployed, but would naturally reach them.

The other point is that it seems quite possible that the technological revolution could represent an opportunity as much as a threat: electronic self-paced education, with teachers in new roles as mentors, could be the way to achieve convergence, bringing up the standards of inner-city schools while creating all kinds of new jobs in producing the software and in training, or retraining, the teachers for their new roles. Some commentators suggest that the same technologies are already available to the children of the inner city as to the children of the suburbs; the difference is that the latter use it for self-education, the former for computer games, because the machines only show up that way in inner-city corner stores. Society, and the economy, have low expectations of such children, and unsurprisingly they then find themselves justified. These commentators say that we could and should change the rules; others are

more cynical, saying that new technology never did benefit the poor
and never will.

This is probably overly pessimistic: electricity, for instance, did
make an enormous difference to the lives of the poor, releasing them from
drudgery and giving them access to news and entertainment. True, making
the technology work in a positive way, as a driver of education, will be
harder, but not impossible, if we have the will. The question is whether
we have the will. For we need to temper utopian visions with a small dose
of realism: try to imagine that solution in Roxbury or the South Bronx
or the Robert Taylor Homes in Chicago.

It does not seem likely that we can really reach many of these
children unless we disperse them much more thoroughly than we have
proved able to do in the last forty years. Wilson's book is eloquent testi-
mony to the corrosive effect of concentrating low-income poor children
in poorly performing city schools, and it is significant that another part
of his policy proposals deal with ways of achieving greater city-suburb
integration and cooperation. It has happened on a small scale: consider
the Gautreaux program in Wisconsin, operating with success since 1976:
3,900 families dispersed, and helped with jobs to boot. But it poses all
kinds of difficult ethical choices: should we, for instance, keep encouraging
the more educated, the more skilled, the more ambitious to move out as
fast and as far as possible? And what would this mean for the remainder?
Are we condemning them to fester, a lost generation? We may be, but
it may be the least bad solution we can hope to achieve.

Notes

1. The General Certificate of Secondary Education (GCSE) has seven pass grades, A–G,
which are equivalent to A–C in U.S. terminology. GCSE A–C is more like A–B+ in U.S.
terminology, but is basic to entry to higher education.

2. Casual work is not based on a long-term career and often includes short contracts
and no benefits.

3. Equivalent to a bachelor's degree in the United States.

References

Anderson, C. 1995. "The Internet: The Accidental Superhighway." *The Economist*, 1 July.

Balls, E. 1995. "Missing School is Hallmark of Criminal Class." *The Guardian*, 16 October.

Beniger, J. R. 1986. *The Control Revolution: Technological and Economic Origins of the Information Society*. Cambridge, MA: Harvard University Press.

Cairncross, F. 1995. "Telecommunications: The Death of Distance." *The Economist*, 30 September.

Castells, M. 1989. *The Informational City: Information Technology, Economic Restructuring and the Urban-Regional Process*. Oxford: Basil Blackwell.

Channel Four. 1995. *Visions of Heaven and Hell: Will Technology Deliver Us a Bright New Future?* London: Channel Four.

Clark, C. 1940. *The Conditions of Economic Progress*. London: Macmillan.

Economist. 1993. "The Tangled Webs They Weave." *The Economist*, 16 October.

Friedman, L. M. 1993. *Crime and Punishment in American History*. New York: Basic Books.

Gates, W. 1995. *The Road Ahead*. London: Viking.

GB Government Office for London. 1996a. *Four World Cities: A Comparative Analysis of London, Paris, New York and Tokyo*. London: Llewelyn Davies Planning.

GB Government Office for London. 1996b. *London in the UK Economy: A Planning Perspective*. London: Government Office for London/Department of the Environment.

GB Office of Science and Technology. 1995. *Progress through Partnership: Technology Report Foresight Report 8: IT and Electronics*. London: Her Majesty's Stationery Office.

Gillespie, A., R. Richardson, and J. Cornford. 1995. *Review of Telework in Britain: Implications for Public Policy*. Prepared for the Parliamentary Office of Science and Technology. Newcastle upon Tyne: University, Center for Urban and Regional Development Studies.

Goddard, J. B. 1975. *Office Location in Urban and Regional Development*. Oxford: Oxford University Press.

Goddard, J. 1992. "New Technology and the Geography of the UK Information Economy." *Understanding Information Business, Technology and Geography*, edited by K. Robbins, pp. 178–201. London: Belhaven.

Goddard, J. 1995. "Electronic Highways, Cities and Regions: Winners and Losers." Paper presented to Section E (Geography), British Association for the Advancement of Science, Newcastle upon Tyne, September.

Graham, S. and S. Marvin. 1996. *Telecommunications and the City: Electronic Spaces, Urban Places*. London: Routledge.

Hague, D. 1994. "Push Button Professionals." *Demos* 4: 12–15.

Hall, P. 1993. "Forces Shaping Urban Europe." *Urban Studies* 30: 883–898.

Handy, S. L. and P. L. Mokhtarian. 1995. "Planning for Telecommuting: Measurement and Policy Issues." *Journal of the American Planning Association* 61: 99–111.

Handy, S. L. and P. L. Mokhtarian. 1996a. "Forecasting Telecommuting—An Exploration of Methodologies and Research Needs." *Transportation* 23: 163–190.

Handy, S. L. and P. L. Mokhtarian. 1996b. "The Future of Telecommuting."
  Futures 28: 227–240.

Herrnstein, R. J. and C. Murray. 1994. *The Bell Curve: Intelligence and Class Structure in
  American Life*. New York: Simon and Schuster.

Hudson, L. 1966. *Contrary Imaginations: A Psychological Study of the English Schoolboy*.
  London: Methuen.

Hutton, W. 1995. *The State We're In*. London: Jonathan Cape.

JALA Associates. 1990. *The State of California Telecommuting Pilot Project: Final Report*.
  Sacramento: State of California, Department of General Services.

Jencks, C. 1992. *Rethinking Social Policy: Race, Poverty, and the Underclass*. Cambridge, MA:
  Harvard University Press.

Jencks, C. and P. E. Peterson, ed. 1991. *The Urban Underclass*. Washington, DC:
  Brookings Institution.

Kehoe, L. 1995a. "DreamWorks Deal: Say Goodbye to Sillywood." *Financial Times*, 5 June.

Kehoe, L. 1995b. "Microsoft Forms Multimedia Link with DreamWorks." *Financial
  Times*, 23 March.

London Planning Advisory Committee. 1991. *London: World City Moving into the 21st
  Century*. A research project by Richard Kennedy. London: Her Majesty's
  Stationery Office.

Mitchell, W. J. 1995. *City of Bits: Space, Place, and the Infobahn*. Cambridge, MA:
  MIT Press.

Mokhtarian, P. L. 1990. "The State of Telecommuting." *ITS Review* 13(4).

Mokhtarian, P. L. 1991. "Telecommuting and Travel: State of the Practice, State of the
  Art." *Transportation* 18: 319–342.

Mokhtarian, P. L. 1992. "Telecommuting in the United States, Letting Our Fingers Do
  the Commuting." *TR News* 158: 2–7.

Murnane, R. J. and F. Levy. 1996. *Teaching the New Basic Skills: Principles for Educating
  Children to Thrive in a Changing Economy*. New York: Free Press.

Negroponte, N. 1995. *Being Digital*. London: Hodder and Stoughton.

Nilles, J. M. 1991. "Telecommuting and Urban Sprawl: Mitigator or Inciter?"
  Transportation 18: 411–431.

Parkes, C. 1995. "Dream Team for Spielberg's Dream Works." *Financial Times*,
  15 December.

Pendyala, R. M., K. G. Goulias, and R. Kitamura. 1991. "Impact of Telecommuting on
  Spatial and Temporal Patterns of Household Travel." *Transportation* 18: 383–409.

Reich, R. B. 1991. *The Work of Nations: Preparing Ourselves for 21st-Century Capitalism*.
  New York: Random House.

Rifkin, J. 1995. *The End of Work: The Decline of the Global Labor Force and the Dawn of the
  Post-Market Era*. New York: Tarcher/Putnam.

Sassen, S. 1991. *The Global City: London, New York, Tokyo*. Princeton: Princeton
  University Press.

Taylor, J. 1995. "The Networked Home: Domestication of Information." *Journal of the*

Royal Society of Arts 143: 41–53.

Taylor, P. 1996. "Most People in West Aware of the Internet." *Financial Times*, 27 August.

Wacquant, L. J. D. 1993. "Urban Outcasts: Stigma and Division in the Black American Ghetto and the French Urban Periphery." *International Journal of Urban and Regional Research*, 7:366–383.

Wilson, W. J. 1987. *The Truly Disadvantaged: The Inner City, the Underclass, and Public Policy*. Chicago: University of Chicago Press.

Wilson, W. J. 1996. *When Work Disappears: The World of the New Urban Poor*. New York: Knopf.

Yaro, R. D. and A. Hiss. 1996. *A Region at Risk: The Third Regional Plan for the New York-New Jersey-Connecticut Metropolitan Area*. New York: Regional Plan Association.

3. Center Cities as Havens and Traps for Low-Income Communities: The Potential Impact of Advanced Information Technology

Julian Wolpert

Introduction

Has the information revolution been too exclusive or irrelevant for low-income center city communities when more immediate problems dominate people's lives? My analysis concerns how low-income inner-city communities have evolved since the 1960s in northeast cities (where I carried out my previous analyses [Wolpert 1970]), the changing patterns of residence and employment, the evolving roles and positions of low-income people within the center city, their reasons for remaining in the inner city, and finally the impact—if any—the information revolution has been having on their communities. These issues raise some fundamental economic and social concerns that have been analyzed extensively in theoretical and empirical studies such as: the causes and effects of prolonged residence in poor inner-city communities; the causes and impacts of inner-city in- and out-migration; industrial restructuring and job dispersal; the persistence of labor force mismatch (both spatially and in skill requirements); and the effectiveness of social safety nets in helping maintain well-being in center city communities.

Assembling comprehensive evidence on these issues requires addressing a host of empirical questions about changes over the past several decades (some of which go beyond the scope of this chapter) including:

1. How has the relative status of the lowest-income center city communities changed? Have these communities become larger or smaller, less or more income and ethnically segregated, poorer or richer, composed of larger or smaller shares of native-born or immigrant populations; and finally, have they experienced a greater or reduced incidence of social problems? How much population turnover, upward social mobility, and residential relocation have occurred?

2. What is the employment structure of center city low-income communities, and how has it changed? Are fewer or greater numbers employed; are more of the jobs part-time, temporary, and low paying; do more of the jobs require higher-level entry skills; are more male minority teenagers and young adults employed?

3. What are the sources of transfer income in center city low-income communities; how have they changed; and are they likely to change in the near future? Have safety nets and in-kind social and health services

become more or less generous? How will current federal and state legislative proposals affect the well-being and safety nets of low-income people?

4. How have federal, state, and local policy prescriptions and programs for neighborhood development changed? Have schools and employment training programs been preparing center city residents for jobs in the advanced economy? Are center city educational resources for training teenagers and young adults adequate for the knowledge-intensive industries?

5. What are the labor market implications of the information technology revolution in terms of the magnitude of opportunities and requisite entry skills? How are firms that make substantial use of information technology distributed throughout U.S. regional and metropolitan labor markets? What are the current locational trends of these firms? Have programs designed to lure firms in these industries to center city sites been successful? How accessible are these firms to the center city labor force? Have entry-level jobs and training programs in these locationally accessible firms increased? Have reverse commuting opportunities to suburban jobs expanded? Do center city workers have a comparative advantage or disadvantage for these jobs?

How Low-Income Center City Communities Are Evolving

Data and Analysis Sources

Highlights of the data and analyses of national trends and those in some of the largest northeastern center cities and their metropolitan areas are summarized below.[1] The major data gaps are the detailed changes since the 1990 census for specific cities, labor markets, minority groups, and neighborhoods.

Background

Have low-income center city communities and the policy remedies for their revival changed much over the past several decades? Findings from some studies of the economy of center city low-income communities in the 1970s were contrary to then-prevailing paradigms of urban labor markets (see Wolpert 1970). Conventional wisdom stressed the example of upward mobility by earlier immigrant groups and the trickle-down effects of economic expansion. The evidence showed, however, that these communities were both havens and traps for their residents. The haven metaphor suggests a respite of short duration with prospects of something even better; the trap is the snare or penalty for expecting that the haven could be stable. They were havens because mailbox income such as AFDC (Aid to Families with Dependent Children) for households with small children, SSI (Supplemented Security Income) for the handicapped, and Social Security for the elderly provided modest safety nets for a significant share of center city residents in the lowest income communities. These income transfer programs, supplemented by social and health services delivered by locally based nonprofits and access to center city factory and personal service jobs, even if occasional and part-time, were not available in small towns and rural areas. This modest income was even able to sustain some neighborhood retail activity. The community's primary linkage to the advanced economy of the downtown was through occasional low-skill service and assembly jobs.

The study showed that mailbox income could not quite buy a place in neighboring working-class or middle-income communities (Wolpert 1970). Furthermore, available employment opportunities did not enhance residents' job skills at a fast enough pace. Good schools and a culture that stressed upward mobility might help their children escape poverty. Many did, but concentrated neighborhood poverty and deterioration of schools and other public services had the opposite impact over time. The longer children resided in communities with concentrated poverty, the greater the children's downward mobility. Many residents were trapped—they could not stay without harm to themselves and their children, yet they could not leave without inordinate risk to their safety nets and access to local services.

The policy prescriptions were remedial and direct: for example, sustaining human services and the purchasing power of income transfers, and targeting enhancement programs in the public schools, job training, public service jobs, equal opportunity and affirmative action pressures on firms to integrate the city's advanced economy, and housing support programs to foster residential dispersal. These prescriptions presumed

Table 3.1: Center city and suburban population and poverty changes (percentage)

	City Pop. 1980–90	Sub. Pop. 1980–90	City Med. In. 1980–90	Sub. Med. In. 1980–90	Met. Pov. 1989	Met. Pov. 1979–89
Baltimore	−6.5	16.5	18.3	29.6	10.1	−1.8
Boston	2.0	6.2	46.8	34.6	8.3	−1.1
Buffalo	−8.3	−2.7	0.5	2.6	12.2	1.6
Hartford	2.5	7.5	21.2	28.7	7.5	−0.5
New York	3.5	1.7	35.7	33.7	17.5	−0.6
Newark	−16.4	0.4	34.8	31.4	8.9	−2.3
Philadelphia	−6.1	7.9	17.7	24.1	10.4	−1.6
Providence	2.5	6.6	22.0	25.5	10.1	−0.3
Washington, D.C.	−4.9	27.4	19.5	27.1	6.4	−1.7
Total/Average	−3.5	7.9	24.1	26.4	9.1	−0.9

City Pop. = Center city population
Sub. Pop. = Suburban population
City Med. In. = Center city median income
Sub. Med. In. = Suburban median income
Met. Pov. = Metropolitan area level of poverty
City Pov. = Center city level of poverty
City IDR = Center city infant death rate per thousand
Isolation = Isolation of the poor (Source: Abramson and Tobin)
and change in Isolation Index, 1970–90
F. Head = Percentage of households headed by women

Source: Bureau of the Census

generous and progressive public- and private-sector efforts and a growth
economy that would absorb all but a small residual group.

Center City Poverty

What has happened to center city poverty since the 1970s? The severity,
concentration, and persistence of poverty in virtually all American large
cities have been the dominating themes of urban policy analysis during
this period. National demographic and social trends help place current
center city conditions in comparative perspective. These trends include

City Pov. 1989	City Pov. 1979–89	City IDR 1990	Isolation 1990	Isolation 1970–90	F. Head 1980	F. Head 1990
21.9	−0.1	18.0	24.3	1.3	32.5	39.0
18.7	−1.5	13.9	16.2	1.3	29.7	30.4
25.6	4.9	14.6	24.9	9.5	28.0	31.2
27.5	2.3	15.1	25.7	8.8	36.2	35.1
19.3	−0.7	13.2	29.4	7.1	25.8	35.6
26.3	−6.5	19.8	20.7	2.2	40.1	51.0
20.3	−0.3	17.5	25.4	5.9	27.3	32.3
23.0	2.6	12.5	17.1	1.3	25.7	43.6
16.9	−1.7	23.2	14.0	−2.1	35.8	39.0
22.2	−0.2	16.4	22.0	3.9	31.2	37.5

some general observations common to most large cities: continued exodus of whites from center cities, modest suburbanization and interregional relocation of blacks, a substantial influx of Hispanic and Asian immigrants to a few highly targeted cities, and an increase in city-suburban disparities in population growth and economic well-being.

A majority of the nation's lowest-income people now live in cities. Most large cities have or will soon have a "minority majority." In addition, poverty is much more prevalent among blacks and Hispanics than among non-Hispanic whites. One superficial and circular observation attributes center city poverty to large concentrations of minorities and especially

Table 3.2: Persons below the poverty level, 1980–1990 (percentage)

	White 1980	White 1990	Black 1980	Black 1990	Hisp. 1980	Hisp. 1990	Asian 1980	Asian 1990
Baltimore	12.7	12.6	31.0	27.9	30.9	21.5	25.5	24.2
Boston	15.7	13.9	28.6	24.2	41.9	33.9	22.4	29.5
Buffalo	14.1	17.7	36.3	38.3	38.0	52.0	33.5	41.1
Hartford	16.8	16.8	27.5	26.6	49.2	47.4	28.4	22.8
New York	12.9	12.3	30.0	25.3	35.7	33.2	14.9	16.2
Newark	20.2	18.3	37.7	29.0	41.2	30.3	33.5	21.1
Philadelphia	11.7	11.0	32.2	29.0	45.9	45.3	25.2	29.1
Providence	16.9	17.7	36.0	31.1	33.3	36.5	35.7	40.4
Washington, D.C.	9.3	8.2	22.0	20.2	19.3	20.4	16.7	18.2
Average	14.5	14.3	31.3	28.0	37.3	35.6	26.2	27.0

Source: Bureau of the Census

female-headed households who are poor. The evidence provides a more complex set of explanations relating to education and job skills, industrial restructuring, job relocation, and so on. It is instructive, however, to examine the evidence on poverty, first on the national level and then on the level of the center cities.

At the national level overall poverty (i.e., the share of population below the poverty line) was reduced in the 1970s, but has risen steadily since the 1980s. The results, however, are strikingly different among individual cities; among whites, blacks, and Hispanics; and between adults and children. National census tabulation figures show that poverty among whites declined from 9.9 percent in 1970 to 9.0 percent in 1980, but rose to 11.6 percent in 1993. During the same period, poverty among blacks declined from 33.5 percent to 31.0 percent but then increased to 33.3 percent. Poverty among Hispanics increased substantially from 21.8 percent in 1980 to 29.3 percent in 1993. Poverty among white children was 16.0 percent in 1993, while among blacks and Hispanics the figures were

46.8 percent and 38.8 percent, respectively. Among children in female-headed households, the poverty rate in 1993 was 46.2 percent for whites, 69.2 percent for blacks and 68.6 percent for Hispanics.

Center city poverty declined nationally from 18.3 percent in 1960 to 14.3 percent in 1970, then increased to 20.7 percent in 1980 and to 22 percent in 1995. Poverty among center city children dropped from 26.5 percent in 1960 to 14.9 percent in 1970 and then rose to 17.9 percent in 1980 and to 19.9 percent in 1990. In 1995, it stood at more than 20 percent, with levels almost three times greater in female-headed households. White poverty declined by 40 percent and by 50 percent for African American households, from 1960 to 1990. Poverty among Hispanic and female-headed black households, however, is now more pronounced, and the share of these households in center city populations has increased every decade since 1960.

Turning to the major northeastern metropolitan areas, an average of 22 percent of their center city residents fell below the poverty line in 1989, with somewhat higher levels in Buffalo, Hartford, and Newark and somewhat lower levels in Boston, New York, and Washington, D.C. (Table 3.1). These poverty rates are about twice the levels of their respective metropolitan areas. Their rates of center city poverty declined slightly (by 0.2 percent) from 1980 to 1990, but this average masks the substantial increase in poverty in Buffalo and Providence and decline in Newark, Washington, D.C., and Boston. The variation in trends among these northeastern cities suggests some hope that expanding local labor markets can effectively reduce the incidence of poverty.

The more detailed 1980 to 1990 information for the ethnic groups in these northeastern cities shows a steady decline in poverty rates among the groups in most of the cities (Table 3.2). In Boston, for example, poverty rates dropped appreciably for all groups except Asians, but still remain quite high especially among female-headed households. In contrast, poverty rates increased substantially in Buffalo for whites, blacks, Hispanics, and Asians.

Of course, neighborhood turnover has been considerable in the poorest center city neighborhoods. Residents in the 1970s and 1980s were not necessarily the same residents in 1990. All of these northeastern cities

Table 3.3: Changes in ethnic composition, 1980–1990

	White (%) 1980	White (%) 1990	Black (%) 1980	Black (%) 1990	Hisp. (%) 1980	Hisp. (%) 1990
Baltimore	43.6	38.7	54.8	59.2	1.0	1.0
Boston	68.1	58.8	22.5	25.5	6.5	10.4
Buffalo	70.4	63.6	26.7	30.7	2.5	4.7
Hartford	45.2	28.6	33.8	38.9	20.3	31.0
New York	48.7	40.5	25.3	28.8	19.9	23.7
Newark	22.4	15.2	58.3	58.5	18.6	25.1
Philadelphia	57.2	52.1	37.8	39.9	3.8	5.3
Providence	80.7	64.6	11.9	14.6	5.5	14.8
Washington, D.C.	25.9	27.0	70.2	65.9	2.8	5.2
Total/Average	51.4	43.2	37.9	40.2	9.0	13.5

Net H/B/A = Net migration of Hispanics, Blacks and Asians
Immig. 1975–1980 = Residents in 1980 who arrived from abroad 1975–1980
% Pop. 1980 = Share of the 1980 population who arrived from abroad 1975–1980
Immig. 1985–1990 = Residents in 1990 who arrived from abroad 1985–1990
% Pop. 1990 = Share of the 1990 population who arrived from abroad 1985–1990

Source: Bureau of the Census

experienced a good deal of in- and out-migration and a pronounced shift in
their ethnic composition, most notably a substantial increase in Hispanics
and Asians and a further drop in the white share of their population
(Table 3.3).

Income Sorting and Segregation

Abramson and Tobin's 1995 dissimilarity analyses show conclusively
that center city communities have been highly income segregated and are
becoming more so (Table 3.1). Residential patterns in center city communities show increased income sorting and concentration of poverty since
the 1970s. The share of center city poor living in extreme poverty areas
(i.e., poverty rates of 40 percent or more) rose nationally from 16.5 percent

Asian (%) 1980	Asian (%) 1990	Net H/B/A 1970–90	Immig. 1975–80	% Pop. 1980	Immig. 1985–90	% Pop. 1990
0.6	1.1	171,840	5,328	0.7	6,420	0.9
2.9	5.3	353,710	22,543	4.0	36,761	6.7
0.4	1.0	36,620	3,439	1.0	5,357	1.7
0.7	1.5	109,140	9,063	6.6	10,935	8.8
3.5	7.0	2,017,770	342,034	4.8	456,659	6.2
0.7	1.2	272,500	13,532	4.1	14,372	5.6
1.2	2.7	310,420	24,719	1.5	30,204	2.0
1.9	6.0	75,090	6,231	4.0	10,834	7.2
1.1	1.9	651,340	17,077	2.7	24,254	4.3
1.4	3.1	3,998,430	443,966	3.3	595,796	4.8

in 1970 to 22.5 percent in 1980 to 28.2 percent in 1990. Nationwide, more than 20 percent of all black and 16 percent of all Hispanic poor people live in center city neighborhoods of extreme poverty. Nearly two-thirds of the poor in these poorest neighborhoods are black, 10 percent are white, and most of the rest are Hispanic. In Philadelphia, in 1990, for example, 41 percent of non-Hispanic whites lived in poverty zones (i.e., at least 20 percent of the population in poverty), 10 percent in extreme poverty areas, and 5 percent in underclass neighborhoods (i.e., based on the Ricketts and Sawhill measures); this represents an increase from 31 percent, 4 percent, and 2 percent, respectively, in 1970. The corresponding percentages for blacks and Hispanics are up very significantly from 1970. The data for New York City show comparable levels and trends. New York alone accounted for one-fifth of all ghetto poor—

more than 40 percent of blacks in New York live in areas of concentrated poverty. Boston, an exception, had relatively little concentrated poverty in 1990, but a good deal of segregated affluence (Coulter and Pandy 1992).

The segregation of the poor was greatest for African Americans at 41.6 percent in 1990 (Kasarda 1993a). In addition, the number of poor white non-Hispanic areas grew in the 1980s. The degree of current income segregation varies considerably among the metropolitan areas, although levels for both African Americans and Hispanics are highest in the Northeast (Jargowsky 1994). Income segregation is generally most severe in the larger metropolitan areas where population and economic growth has been slowest and poverty has been increasing. Inner-city black communities located in regions experiencing the greatest degree of industrial restructuring had the greatest poverty growth (Galster and Killen 1995).

Extreme poverty zones (i.e., areas with greater than 40 percent living in poverty) expanded spatially during this period, but their populations had a net decline, first through outflows of whites, then through successive filtering of African Americans, Hispanics, and Asians. Some replacement occurred in the zones of extreme poverty largely through in-migration from Southeast Asia, the Caribbean, and Latin America. The poorest groups had the lowest out-mobility rates, especially black households with children. Overall, income segregation rose significantly from 1970 to 1990, while racial and ethnic segregation declined modestly as upwardly mobile black and Hispanic households moved to the suburbs and other metropolitan areas. Some analysts, however, have argued that the growth of minority poverty within segregated communities has contributed more than the outflow of the upwardly mobile to the current degree of concentrated poverty (Massey and Dentan 1993; Coulter and Pandy 1992; Wilson 1987).

Immigration Impacts

The northeastern cities vary considerably in their recent inflows of low-income populations from Asian, Caribbean, and Latin American nations. From 1970 to 1990 the net in-migration to these northeastern metropolitan areas consisted of nearly 4 million Hispanics, blacks, and Asians

(Table 3.3). The New York metropolitan area accounted for almost half of this total, but a substantial net inflow occurred in Washington, D.C., Boston, Philadelphia, and Newark. The immigrants' overwhelming destinations were the center cities. In 1980 nearly 450,000 residents of these cities had arrived from abroad between 1975 and 1980 and almost 600,000 between 1985 and 1990. New York alone accounted for more than 75 percent of these totals; however, it should be noted that New York is the primary point of entry in the northeast region, and many immigrants move on to other destinations. The population impacts of these immigrants were more significant between 1985 and 1990 than between 1975 and 1980. From 1975 to 1980 arrivals to Boston from abroad approximated 4 percent of the city's 1980 population, but the share rose by 1990 to 6.7 percent. The immigration levels and their growth were even higher in Hartford and Providence.

The influx of Hispanic, Haitian, and Asian immigrants replaced upwardly mobile African American residents who had relocated to other city and suburban neighborhoods as well as to southern and western metropolitan areas (Frey and Fielding 1995). Recent data for New York show, however, that median household income for foreign-born black residents (principally from the Caribbean) is more than $28,000, compared with $22,000 for native-born black residents. The data also show that native-born black households moving from gentrifying communities have tended to relocate to poorer neighborhoods.

Urban Social Problems

Concentrated center city poverty has significant side effects. Furthermore, the incidence of social pathology, including personal and property crime, drug dependency, family breakdown, children born to teenagers, infant death rate, low birth weight, child abuse, stress-related diseases, and so on, is highest and growing in neighborhoods where absolute and relative concentrations of the poorest residents are greatest (see Jenks and Mayer 1990; Case and Katz 1991; Kasarda 1993a; Massey and Denton 1993; and Wilson 1987 for comprehensive analyses of the impacts of concentrated poverty).

Shifts in Policy Analysis and Prescriptions

When center cities were more of a haven in the 1960s, especially for low-income, female-headed households, urban pathology was viewed by analysts and policymakers as preventable, curable, and amenable to public-sector intervention. A combination of safety-net support, social services, public service employment, and slum clearance was considered to be adequate for supplementing the trickle-down effects of rapid economic growth and labor market opportunities for advancement. Growing opportunities would presumably lead to successive upward mobility of low-income households into the ranks of the middle class. The population remaining outside the labor force would be small enough to be supported with intensive social and safety net programs to prevent intergenerational poverty.

Policy proposals in the 1960s and 1970s considered center city poverty to be a national problem, and stressed federal involvement to solve the growing problems of urban areas and their residents. Congress and state legislatures forcefully represented the center city agenda. The center city then was still the focus of economic activity, and the appearance of urban decay and poverty were viewed as high-priority national problems that could be surmounted with the right combination of federal money and local initiatives. Now the convergence of analysis and the policy agenda is more local, more reliant on locally based community development activities and private- and nonprofit-sector solutions, and much less ambitious despite the intensification of urban problems (see Buck et al. 1992). The current policy agenda is more inclined to accept failure in solving urban social ills and to cut back on safety nets and social support (see Buck et al. 1992; Katz 1989).

In the 1960s and 1970s a prominent aspect of the policy agenda was the focus on center city redevelopment that would reduce the growing public service disparities and other incentives for residential and job dispersal to the suburbs. Now inequities in access to better jobs and financing of public schools between center cities and the suburbs are even more profound, and the will and commitment to correct the disparities has diminished (see Orfield 1992).

Table 3.4: Employment in metropolitan areas, center cities, and suburbs (percentage)

	City Emp. 1980–1990	Sub. Emp. 1980–1991
Baltimore	2.8	29.6
Boston	12.8	14.9
Buffalo	−0.2	6.9
Hartford	0.0	15.0
New York	11.6	10.2
Newark	−4.1	10.0
Philadelphia	4.3	21.2
Providence	5.2	15.1
Washington, D.C.	2.0	43.5
Total	3.8	18.5

City Emp. = Center city employment
Sub. Emp. = Suburban employment

Source: Bureau of the Census

Employment Patterns In Low-Income Center City Communities

How have employment prospects changed for low-income center city residents over the past few decades? In the comparative center city haven of the 1960s and 1970s there was an abundance of low-end temporary and permanent, part- and full-time factory assembly jobs and service employment in hospitals, building maintenance, and clerical and related occupations in private, public, and nonprofit organizations. Yet low wages in these occupations did not attract much new growth in these jobs in center cities. Other center city costs for these commercial and industrial firms have risen relative to suburban sites, and firms have responded to other locational preferences. Although they were not sufficient to compensate for the lost factory jobs, accessible growth sectors of the 1970s and 1980s for unskilled center city workers were state and local government and

Table 3.5: Metro employment structure, 1970–1990

	Constr. 1970	Constr. 1980	Constr. 1990	Manuf. 1970	Manuf. 1980	Manuf. 1990
Baltimore	52,376	60,835	89,711	197,849	163,017	133,496
Boston	118,411	106,662	147,690	614,969	670,110	533,596
Buffalo	23,093	20,625	29,429	170,191	136,083	101,213
Hartford	26,730	22,818	34,799	157,647	159,573	122,335
New York	153,660	113,991	169,390	869,997	608,315	422,964
Newark	45,152	38,494	48,628	269,404	239,006	168,283
Philadelphia	105,768	100,906	132,602	567,643	458,999	364,403
Providence	17,221	15,906	24,320	119,148	127,503	98,222
Washington, D.C.	91,234	111,145	181,433	66,534	82,704	108,405
Total	633,645	591,382	858,002	3,033,382	2,645,310	2,052,917

Constr. = Construction
Manuf. = Manufacturing
Trans./Util. = Transportation and public utilities
Wh. Trade = Wholesale trade

Source: Bureau of the Census

private and nonprofit service organizations. A positive trend is the current tendency to provide public-sector jobs to AFDC recipients to show that employment training programs are working. Most of the new jobs, however, have been low skilled and low wage, and recent fiscal pressures in public and nonprofit sectors have streamlined their employment roles.

Center city opportunities have traditionally permitted many low-income residents to rise economically and to relocate to working-class and middle-class communities. The upward mobility especially of center city native-born African Americans and Hispanics, however, has been limited by insufficient education and training, recent deindustrialization, cutbacks in public-sector employment, the recent influx of immigrants, and labor market discrimination.

On the whole, the recent immigrants have increased job competition among the shrinking numbers of low-end factory and service jobs.

Trans./Util. 1970	Trans./Util. 1980	Trans./Util. 1990	Wh. Trade 1970	Wh. Trade 1980	Wh. Trade 1990
61,998	62,876	61,186	45,379	57,379	68,658
117,750	124,885	137,499	124,560	152,490	181,906
32,413	28,597	29,048	26,086	29,412	29,881
16,738	21,135	27,513	21,118	31,714	38,136
366,357	308,267	280,825	349,485	313,579	267,405
73,461	71,645	82,954	53,337	65,711	68,754
113,478	108,137	110,215	112,836	128,529	148,577
15,770	13,757	16,413	17,420	20,699	20,466
75,612	84,439	129,369	46,024	65,772	90,534
873,577	823,738	875,022	796,245	865,285	914,317

Findings also show that these immigrants often advance to working- and middle-class status more readily than longer-term residents of the lowest income communities. Immigrants from Asia, Haiti, Jamaica, Russia, and Latin America have introduced a measure of greater entrepreneurship than have native-born residents of low-income communities; but this vibrancy has not yet entered the advanced urban economy.

National trends to keep in mind in reviewing employment changes during the 1980s include: the significant decline in factory jobs; the increase in the number of center city low-wage workers; the dispersal of center city jobs to the suburbs and the greater growth of suburban compared with center city jobs; center city job growth during the 1980s that occurred solely in industries in which most jobs are held by "information processors," while more than half of employed blacks and Hispanics were working in services and in the declining occupations of clerical sup-

Table 3.5 cont.: Metro employment structure, 1970–1990

	Ret. Trade 1970	Ret. Trade 1980	Ret. Trade 1990	Fin./Real 1970	Fin./Real 1980	Fin./Real 1990
Baltimore	152,289	184,982	229,512	63,853	84,913	121,897
Boston	403,356	466,013	565,046	168,394	222,514	289,403
Buffalo	92,833	100,038	122,813	35,117	41,276	42,640
Hartford	74,376	93,789	117,752	57,033	80,743	116,562
New York	584,103	509,020	526,124	599,084	580,236	708,151
Newark	129,356	130,702	146,530	82,269	88,592	119,615
Philadelphia	325,235	358,408	421,581	151,557	183,709	245,479
Providence	59,671	67,737	80,963	21,781	29,428	40,035
Washington, D.C.	227,136	297,663	427,476	120,958	173,543	236,553
Total	2,048,355	2,208,352	2,637,797	1,300,046	1,484,954	1,920,335

Ret. Trade = Retail trade
Fin./Real = Finance, insurance, and real estate
Services = Services
Fed. Gov. = Nonmilitary federal government

Source: Bureau of the Census

port and fabrication or as laborers (Kasarda 1993b). Other trends include: the more than 50 percent decline in poorly educated persons holding jobs between 1980 and 1990 alone (while only 45 percent of black workers and even fewer Hispanic workers in cities had a high school diploma and eight in ten high school dropouts are not even in the labor force); and the lack of a high school diploma among 50–60 percent of the black and Hispanic males living in cities and not working (Kasarda 1993b).

Metropolitan Employment Trends

In the nine northeastern metropolitan areas shown in Table 3.4, total employment in center city jobs grew nearly 4 percent between 1980 and 1990, but the share of center city jobs held by commuters increased and

Services 1970	Services 1980	Services 1990	Fed. Gov. 1970	Fed. Gov. 1980	Fed. Gov. 1990
181,179	258,326	421,574	63,315	77,329	78,274
540,881	769,714	1,151,917	62,610	56,982	60,282
90,661	129,843	183,767	9,661	10,116	10,685
82,330	126,197	195,200	7,017	8,179	9,070
1,142,963	1,311,357	1,733,847	116,323	98,463	89,451
194,000	241,623	346,203	22,568	20,691	21,885
445,084	581,107	859,957	91,332	76,165	82,899
69,479	103,673	148,855	10,880	6,120	6,924
371,876	589,342	1,022,047	346,547	395,351	397,213
3,118,453	4,111,182	6,063,367	730,253	749,396	756,683

suburban jobs grew by 18.5 percent during that period before slowing considerably in the early 1990s. Many of the better jobs in the center cities and some of the employment growth is accounted for by suburban commuters. Furthermore, between 1970 and 1990 more than one million manufacturing jobs were lost, mainly in the center cities of these metropolitan areas (Table 3.5). Almost two-thirds of these losses were in New York and Philadelphia alone. Washington, D.C. was the only metropolitan area in the group to gain manufacturing jobs. Substantial growth over the two decades occurred in construction (35 percent), wholesale trade (15 percent), retail trade (29 percent), finance, real estate, and insurance (48 percent), and services (94 percent). Employment in state and local government expanded by 400,000 in these northeast metropolitan areas during the 1970–1990 period, but the number of federal employees rose by only 4

Table 3.5 cont.: Metro employment structure, 1970–1990

	Military 1970	Military 1980	Military 1990	St./L. Gov. 1970	St./L. Gov. 1980	St./L. Gov. 1990
Baltimore	48,844	30,431	31,191	111,742	144,213	150,400
Boston	68,799	40,993	39,903	233,170	311,870	318,384
Buffalo	6,723	4,065	4,153	75,764	75,668	76,505
Hartford	5,748	4,252	4,369	57,361	70,459	81,309
New York	45,794	28,586	29,809	521,318	482,517	600,483
Newark	10,414	6,940	6,013	89,571	117,966	121,232
Philadelphia	80,808	40,080	41,210	188,465	225,061	226,386
Providence	16,772	5,455	6,401	38,236	48,990	49,714
Washington, D.C.	118,365	81,158	97,546	162,060	211,209	249,658
Total	402,267	241,960	260,595	1,477,687	1,687,953	1,874,071

Military = Military

St./L. Gov. = State and local government

Source: Bureau of the Census

percent, and the military presence declined by 140,000. More recent trends show curtailment in both the civilian and military sectors at federal, state, and local levels.

Employment in some of the Northeast's metropolitan areas grew faster than in others. In the Boston metropolitan area, for example, employment grew nearly 13 percent in the center city and nearly 15 percent in the suburbs between 1980 and 1990; and in New York's center city and suburbs, employment increased 11.6 percent and 10.2 percent respectively, in the same period (Table 3.4). According to Pollard and Storper (1996), the fastest growing metropolitan areas are specialized in innovation-based production (i.e., in industries that employ high proportions of highly skilled, technical labor); however, employment in these industries peaked in the 1980s. Unlike the Sunbelt metropolitan areas, Boston did not have

Total 1970	Total 1980	Total 1990
978,824	1,124,301	1,385,899
2,452,900	2,922,233	3,425,626
562,542	575,723	630,134
506,098	618,859	747,045
4,749,084	4,354,331	4,828,449
969,532	1,021,370	1,130,097
2,182,206	2,261,101	2,633,309
386,378	439,268	492,313
1,626,346	2,092,326	2,940,234
14,413,910	15,409,512	18,213,106

as high a concentration of these industries, but it did have the largest intellectual capital base outside New York of any of the metropolitan areas. Industries in the intellectual capital base maintained higher shares of employment in Boston than in the United States as a whole. New York's concentration of intellectual capital industries is very high, but apparently not sufficient to compensate for losses of production jobs. Data are lacking about the representation of center city and minority workers in these advanced economy jobs, but their numbers are estimated to be very low.

Recent employment trends in parts of the Northeast since 1990 show sluggish job growth in New York, persistent job and population losses with industrial and commercial downsizing in Buffalo and Hartford, and job gains in the health and automobile sectors in Buffalo. As Baltimore continues its transition from manufacturing to services, its metropolitan

Table 3.6: Center city employment structure, 1990 (percentage)

	Constr.	Manuf. Non-Dur.	Manuf. Dur.	Trans.	Com.	Trade Wh.	Trade Ret.	Finan. Ins.
Baltimore	6.3	6.0	6.3	5.3	2.5	3.5	14.1	7.3
Boston	4.0	4.4	5.5	4.4	2.5	2.7	13.9	10.8
Buffalo	3.7	7.3	8.9	4.4	1.9	3.7	17.1	7.1
Hartford	4.7	4.2	11.0	3.8	1.4	2.5	14.0	15.4
New York	4.1	7.2	4.2	6.7	2.7	4.0	13.2	12.3
Newark	6.4	10.0	10.6	8.5	2.9	4.7	12.8	6.7
Philadelphia	4.4	6.9	6.7	5.1	2.4	4.1	15.6	8.2
Providence	4.0	6.5	17.6	2.6	1.7	3.3	15.2	6.1
Washington, D.C.	4.2	3.3	1.0	4.3	2.4	1.5	10.4	7.5
Mean	4.6	6.2	8.0	5.0	2.3	3.3	14.0	9.0

Constr. = Construction
Manuf. Non-dur. = Nondurble manufacturing
Manuf. Dur. = Durable manufacturing
Trans. = Transportation
Com. = Communication
Trade Wh. = Wholesale trade
Trade Ret. = Retail trade
Finan. Ins. = Finance and insurance
Service Bus. = Business services

Service Per. = Personal services
Ent. = Entertainment
Health = Health
Edu. = Education
Other = Other
Public Adm. = Public administration

Source: Bureau of the Census

area has experienced spotty job recovery after the recession in the early
1990s, which was caused by defense cutbacks, banking mergers, and a
decline in construction.

Center City Employment Trends

The employment structure was not very uniform among the nine northeastern cities in 1990 (Table 3.6). Retail trade is the largest sector overall,
but finance, real estate, and insurance are prominent in Hartford, New
York, and Boston; government accounts for 19 percent of employees
in Washington, D.C.; and manufacturing of durables is important in

Service Bus.	Service Per.	Ent.	Health	Edu.	Other	Public Adm.	Total
5.2	3.4	1.1	12.7	8.3	8.1	10.0	100.0
5.8	3.8	1.4	13.3	10.3	11.7	5.6	100.0
4.5	2.9	1.1	13.4	10.1	8.4	5.3	100.0
5.2	2.9	0.9	11.5	8.3	8.5	5.7	100.0
6.5	3.6	1.9	10.7	7.9	10.0	4.9	100.0
6.0	3.1	0.9	9.1	7.4	6.5	4.5	100.0
4.9	2.8	1.2	12.0	9.1	9.0	7.5	100.0
4.3	2.5	1.7	10.0	12.5	7.3	4.7	100.0
6.0	5.0	1.3	7.7	9.4	17.0	19.0	100.0
5.4	3.4	1.3	11.2	9.3	9.6	7.5	100.0

Providence, Hartford, and Newark. The health and education sectors together account for about 20 percent of employment and are especially prominent in Boston, Buffalo, and Providence. Demand for service workers is now bifurcated at the high-skill and low-skill levels with fewer jobs in the middle.

Kasarda's analysis of employment changes shows that jobs in industries classified as "information processors" grew by 30 percent in Philadelphia and 52 percent in New York from 1979 to 1990, while employment in other industries declined 39 percent in Philadelphia and 28 percent in New York (Kasarda 1993b). Jobs held by employees with less than a high school diploma dropped 47 percent in Philadelphia

Table 3.7: Labor force and unemployment, 1980–1990

	Lab. Force Male 1980	Lab. Force Female 1980	Lab. Force Male 1990	Lab. Force Female 1990	Unemp. (%) Male 1980	Unemp. (%) Female 1980
Baltimore	163,194	143,054	157,336	157,352	11.3	10.1
Boston	132,612	123,435	145,862	142,742	7.2	5.0
Buffalo	70,765	60,564	65,984	65,017	14.8	11.1
Hartford	29,267	27,629	29,026	27,844	9.1	6.3
New York	1,593,088	1,325,095	1,710,825	1,546,812	7.7	7.7
Newark	58,651	51,401	55,636	49,917	13.2	13.5
Philadelphia	341,400	283,306	331,875	319,746	11.7	11.1
Providence	35,380	30,406	35,609	33,591	8.8	9.5
Washington, D.C.	144,610	153,497	145,990	158,004	7.5	6.1
Total/Average	2,568,967	2,198,387	2,678,143	2,501,025	10.1	8.9

Lab. Force = Labor force
Unemp. = Unemployment
High Sch. = High school

Source: Bureau of the Census

and 35 percent in New York in the same period, while employees with thirteen or more years of schooling rose 11 percent in Philadelphia and 25 percent in New York. In Kasarda's sample of northeastern cities, 44 percent of black males aged sixteen to sixty-four who were not working in 1988 had less than a high diploma (as opposed to 19 percent in 1970), while 26 percent with a high school diploma, and 15 percent of those with some college or a college diploma were unemployed.

The center city labor market context can be examined through labor force data for the 1980–1990 period that are measured by place of residence, unlike the employment figures gathered at the place of employment. The data show an almost 14 percent growth in the female labor force and 4 percent growth in the male labor force between 1980 and 1990 in the nine northeastern cities (Table 3.7). The changes varied considerably

Unemp. (%) Male 1990	Unemp. (%) Female 1990	High Sch. (%) 1980	High Sch. (%) 1990	College (%) 1980	College (%) 1990
10.0	8.4	51.5	61.6	10.2	14.3
9.8	6.8	72.3	77.6	19.0	28.0
13.0	10.1	58.4	69.5	10.4	15.0
12.6	8.8	55.3	61.5	10.8	12.9
9.3	8.7	61.8	68.8	16.2	21.5
15.0	14.4	47.6	52.9	5.8	7.8
10.6	8.8	57.8	65.9	10.5	14.5
9.8	8.6	59.1	66.2	13.7	18.9
8.3	6.1	68.3	73.7	24.5	30.6
10.9	9.0	59.1	66.4	13.5	18.2

among the cities and declined in Newark for men and women, and in Baltimore, Buffalo, Hartford, and Philadelphia for men. Virtually all the male labor force growth took place in New York and Boston, where the female labor force grew most rapidly as well.

Parallel trends are notable in the unemployment rates, which increased especially for men between 1980 and 1990 (Table 3.7). The unemployment rates for men and women increased significantly in Boston, Hartford, New York, Newark, Providence, and Washington, D.C., and declined in Baltimore, Buffalo, and Philadelphia. Unemployment has been high, even during boom periods and especially for young African American and Hispanic males.

Significant educational gains were made in all nine cities in the shares of both high school and college graduates, but even by 1990 nearly

Table 3.8: Transfer Payments, 1970–1990

	AFDC 1970	AFDC 1980	AFDC 1990	Food Sta. 1970	Food Sta. 1980	Food Sta. 1990	Medic. 1970
Baltimore	52,143	133,901	171,408	12,537	85,129	118,475	103,632
Boston	83,275	122,074	151,283	200	24,039	30,772	159,595
Buffalo	31,765	64,760	121,464	3,463	35,236	69,987	71,802
New York	726,890	1,145,911	1,528,896	31,808	522,896	753,185	1,392,862
Newark	71,134	141,526	132,217	4,905	59,290	93,367	81,650
Philadelphia	145,391	333,209	337,331	9,435	152,504	235,254	202,382
Providence	24,141	52,747	84,577	4,206	23,857	34,181	67,277
Washington, D.C.	32,857	92,003	90,822	11,320	41,049	44,587	61,921
Total	1,167,596	2,086,131	2,617,998	77,874	944,000	1,379,808	2,141,121

Note: All figures are $1,000 current.

AFDC = Aid to Families with Dependent Children
Food Sta. = Food stamps
Medic. = Medicare and medical
SSI = Supplemented Security Income

Source: Bureau of the Census

one-third of residents over age twenty-five on average lacked a high school diploma, and only 18 percent were college graduates (Table 3.7).

The major job gains have been either at the top end in the high-tech sector or in low-end service jobs. During this entire period, income disparities widened between whites and blacks and between those with college degrees and work experience and those without. Recent analyses demonstrate a significant increase in the rate of return from higher education, computer skills, and the use of computers at work (see Krueger 1993). Furthermore, the percentage of people who remain unemployed for more than six months has doubled since 1960. Those who have found work are generally paid less in real wages than they were paid in their previous jobs. National estimates show that millions of center city jobs lost since the 1960s will never exist again.

Medic. 1980	Medic. 1990	SSI 1970	SSI 1980	SSI 1990	Total 1970	Total 1980	Total 1990
485,425	1,158,529	15,770	40,547	87,510	184,082	745,002	1,535,922
442,293	1,301,828	25,120	67,804	94,068	268,190	656,210	1,577,951
285,896	870,688	7,709	33,139	67,619	114,739	419,031	1,129,758
5,053,831	14,411,940	170,003	501,941	996,630	2,321,563	7,224,579	17,690,651
359,404	1,228,216	8,491	31,146	68,422	166,180	591,366	1,522,222
900,770	2,502,310	33,537	95,484	199,188	390,745	1,481,967	3,274,083
251,444	685,291	5,772	19,014	40,626	101,396	347,062	844,675
324,949	876,160	11,533	31,060	54,426	117,631	489,061	1,065,995
8,104,012	23,034,962	277,935	820,135	1,608,489	3,664,526	11,954,278	28,641,257

Employment Trends and Policy Shifts

In the 1960s and 1970s, when center cities were more of a haven, cities were still viewed as the primary centers of labor market opportunities and advancement. Full employment was assumed to be necessary to draw center city low-skilled people into the labor force. The large tax base and civic commitment helped to ensure good educational preparation for the labor force. The strength of labor unions and liberal politics were guarantors of good wages, job protection, and generous benefits during slack periods.

The more recent period since 1980 has witnessed greater polarization of job opportunities and income disparities and shrinkage of entry-level office and factory work. Information technology was assumed to be the salvation for advanced economies and the best way to short-circuit

Table 3.9: State AFDC clients and benefit payments relative to per capita income

	AFDC (%) 1980	AFDC (%) 1987	AFDC (%) 1992	AFDC/PCI 1980	AFDC/PCI 1985	AFDC/PCI 1987	AFDC/PCI 1992
Connecticut	5.2	4.3	6.0	36.7	26.3	23.9	30.9
Delaware	6.6	4.3	5.2	26.3	18.2	16.9	20.9
Washington, D.C.	15.5	11.2	13.3	25.1	12.2	17.8	19.8
Maryland	6.1	5.1	6.0	26.3	20.0	19.2	22.2
Massachusetts	8.3	5.9	7.5	40.4	28.1	29.5	35.0
New Jersey	7.4	5.6	6.1	34.3	20.6	18.0	19.4
New York	8.4	8.0	9.0	43.4	32.2	31.3	33.6
Pennsylvania	6.7	6.1	6.9	37.8	26.7	24.2	27.4
Rhode Island	7.2	6.0	8.0	41.3	31.8	30.2	37.1
Mean	7.9	6.3	7.6	34.6	24.0	23.5	27.4

AFDC (%) = Percentage of state's residents receiving AFDC or SSI benefits
AFDC/PCI = Average family benefits relative to state per capita income

Source: Statistical Abstract of the United States, 1994

educational preparation for the labor force. Yet the downside of the information technology revolution—that is, job displacement—may have overwhelmed its potential upside. The revolution has not been sufficiently accessible to poorly prepared center city populations who lack the requisite entry skills and have been negatively affected by job dispersal.

Assault On the Haven

The relative generosity of income maintenance and safety net services in the Northeast and the Rust Belt has made their center cities both a haven and trap for their low-income populations. Expenditures for virtually all the categories of transfer payments, including AFDC, food stamps, Medicaid, Medicare, and SSI, experienced substantial growth during the 1970s followed by a period of more modest growth in the 1980s, despite the relative constancy in the numbers of the poor during these periods

Table 3.10: Unemployment and social security benefits relative to per capita income

	Unemp. 1980	Unemp. 1987	Unemp. 1989	Unemp. 1992	SS 1980	SS 1987	SS 1989	SS 1992
Connecticut	45.7	40.3	37.8	50.1	33.4	31.7	28.7	39.3
Delaware	54.3	43.0	46.2	56.3	35.9	38.5	35.1	48.8
Washington, D.C.	52.7	45.0	41.7	52.6	25.8	25.9	23.6	29.6
Maryland	46.0	43.3	39.1	49.8	34.3	34.0	30.6	41.7
Massachusetts	49.8	47.3	46.4	61.5	35.8	32.3	29.1	41.1
New Jersey	48.0	42.9	39.4	55.6	35.5	33.0	29.6	40.8
New York	47.1	40.4	36.2	52.7	37.3	36.7	33.6	43.1
Pennsylvania	63.9	54.0	48.9	62.7	39.4	42.0	38.2	48.4
Rhode Island	49.0	46.8	48.1	65.5	38.1	39.5	35.5	47.8
Mean	50.7	44.8	42.7	56.3	35.1	34.8	31.6	42.3

Unemp. = Average unemployment benefits relative to per capita income
SS = Average social security benefits relative to per capita income

Source: Statistical Abstract of the United State, 1994

(Table 3.8). The transfers are dominated by medical payments that are paid not to the poor but to service providers (rising from 60 percent to 80 percent of the transfers while AFDC has shrunk from 32 percent to 9 percent during these two decades).

Historically, transfer payments have been more generous in the Northeast and the Rust Belt than in other parts of the nation and much more generous than in the Caribbean, Latin American, and Asian regions from which recent immigrants have arrived (Table 3.9). The numbers receiving AFDC payments declined from 1980 to 1987, but rose significantly in all these northeastern states from 1987 to 1992.

Yet the assistance programs have not been generous or effective enough—especially since the 1980s—to bring about enough intergenerational progress. Mean AFDC payments to *households* (averaging three persons) in the northeastern states declined from 34.6 percent of per *capita* income in the respective states in 1980 to 24 percent in 1985, and to 23.5

Table 3.11: Private generosity measures for metropolitan areas

	UW/89	Fed./90	NP Supp.	Human	Kidney	AIDS	Con.
Baltimore	33	228	0.29	0.18	0.015	0.35	34
Boston	38	120	1.15	0.08	0.008	0.62	9
Buffalo	38	182	0.29	0.23	0.012	0.36	38
Hartford	71	263	0.44	0.20	0.008	0.57	18
New York	26	73	0.97	0.12	0.020	N/A	10
Newark	38	258	0.12	0.19	0.002	0.10	34
Philadelphia	35	119	0.38	0.15	0.010	0.51	28
Providence	27	269	0.71	0.20	0.011	0.57	25
Washington, D.C.	34	123	1.01	N/A	0.025	1.21	52

UW/89 = United Way contributions per employee in 1989.
Source: United Way of America.
Fed./90 = Contributions per Jewish resident to local Federation.
Source: Council of Jewish Federations.
NP Supp. = Gifts and grants to metro nonprofits per capita, 1989.
Source: Independent sector.
Human = Share of gifts and grants to nonprofits accounted for by human service agencies, 1989.
Source: Independent sector.
Kidney = Donations per capita to the American Kidney Foundation, 1990.
AIDS = Donors per capita to the American Foundation for AIDs Research, 1990.
Con. = American Conservative Union rating of district House members, 1990.

percent in 1987, and then rose to 27.4 percent in 1992 (Table 3.9). This trend is consistent with the changes in real income earned by the lower end of the labor force. Of course, the state-by-state differences even in the Northeast are profound—from a low in 1992 of 19.4 percent in affluent but parsimonious New Jersey to a high of 37.1 percent in generous, but burdened Rhode Island. The contrasts of AFDC with the more generous income transfers to the "more deserving" unemployed and social security recipients are noteworthy (Table 3.10).

A profound threat to low-income neighborhoods as havens is occurring through the assault by Congress and state legislatures on income maintenance and social and health services. The real dollar value of welfare transfers has been declining since the 1970s, and the legislative proposals

Table 3.12: Nonprofit organizations in center cities, 1987–1989

	Human 1989	Change (%) 1987–89	Total 1989	Change (%) 1987–89	Pop./NP 1990
Baltimore	441	13.4	2,690	15.4	286
Boston	872	14.7	5,335	7.5	236
Buffalo	222	15.6	1,167	13.5	281
Harrisburg	125	15.7	518	13.3	185
Harford	200	17.0	1,046	3.3	305
Jersey City	47	34.3	218	18.5	1,202
New Haven	59	−3.3	333	5.0	1,042
New York	2,068	15.0	18,083	11.2	408
Newark	128	7.6	646	9.3	596
Philadelphia	792	13.5	3,687	10.7	462
Providence	168	5.7	984	7.2	282
Rochester	189	9.9	1,195	16.2	194
Syracuse	143	20.2	596	13.3	275
Washington, D.C.	1,302	11.6	4,361	21.5	630

Human = Number of human service organizations.
Total = Total number of nonprofit organizations.
Pop./NP = Population per nonprofit in the center city.

now before Congress will reduce them further. In addition, tens of thousands are likely to be removed from the AFDC and SSI rolls without adequate alternative support, job training, or child-care services (see Hodgkinson et al. 1995; Salamon 1995; Wolpert 1993).

Even though income maintenance and food stamps are not very generous, cutbacks will have a serious multiplier effect on neighborhood retail sales and ability to pay rent. Planned cutbacks in Medicaid services will sharply reduce health care for low-income households, and reductions in housing, heating, and immigrant absorption funding will lead to further deterioration of safety nets.

The legislative proposals will also cut federal funding for nonprofits, such as Catholic charities and the Salvation Army, that provide

a variety of social, educational, and health services in low-income communities and employ large numbers of local residents. The charitable organizations are highly dependent (more than 60 percent) on federal and
state funds for the services they provide to low-income populations (see
Ostrander 1989; Salamon 1995; Smith, Rathgeb, and Lipsky 1993). It
is very unlikely that charitable contributions to nonprofits (especially in
the politically more conservative and less charitable communities) could
offset the deep cuts these organizations have recently sustained (Tables
3.11 and 3.12). United Way contributions per employee averaged only
$35 in Philadelphia in 1989 and only $119 per Jewish resident to the local
branch of the Council of Jewish Federations in 1990. Support for charitable
organizations is generally lowest where needs are greatest and declining
most since 1990, when it had been most generous. The number of nonprofit organizations increased significantly in the late 1980s, especially
in the human service sector, but much of this increase was subsidized by
government contracts that are extremely vulnerable to budget cutting
(Table 3.12). Community residents are already preoccupied with making
ends meet and protecting their children from illness, violence, and other
hazards common in inner-city life. The proposed safety net and service
cutbacks will make the haven even more precarious.

Summary

A preliminary summary of the findings shows that the most fundamental
change for center city low-income residents has been the erosion of the
haven quality relative to the trap for the neediest population groups and
the growing isolation of the center city labor force from jobs—especially in
the advanced urban economy. The analysis of urban change since the 1960s
shows some positive results in reducing poverty through job growth in some
of the Northeast's cities. The findings also demonstrate the costliness of
neglecting to prepare the center city labor force to enter the advanced economy and face the greater difficulties of the current employment challenge.

    The market economy is not rushing into center cities to exploit
the large pool of unskilled workers willing to work for low wages, nor are
entry-level center city jobs with career ladders being created in sufficient
numbers. Center city labor markets have shifted, more low-income house-

holds have arrived, social problems have not yielded to the polity's solutions, and public-sector and charitable generosity have declined. The haven is now quite precarious and likely to get much worse in the short term. The evidence further suggests a comparative disadvantage of the inner-city labor force to benefit from information technology and an accelerating lag that portends poorly for the future. Hopefully, other studies in this series will uncover some beneficial outcomes from the information technology revolution or some prospects of future gains that can be employed to reduce the gaps.

In the 1960s and 1970s our center cities had a form of dual economy that diverged from contemporary theories of urban development. Mailbox income and nonprofit service caretakers provided enough funding and institutional support to maintain safety nets, but not enough, relative to need, to promote upward mobility for more than a fraction of center city residents and their children. We know somewhat more now about effective intervention strategies. The knowledge was available at that time, but political support and funding were not adequate even then to follow the intensive intervention model employed by western European and Pacific Rim nations. This more intrusive model involves more generous safety-net transfers, deliberate assimilation of children into the majority culture, residential dispersal, day care, job training, and adult schools to overcome skill deficiencies.

The center city also provided a minimal haven of safety net support, affordable housing, access to entry-level jobs, supportive ethnic communities and social services, public hospitals, and employment prospects in public- and nonprofit-sector agencies. The downside of the haven was the concentrated poverty, the competition with new arrivals for the shrinking number of low-skill jobs, the difficulties in accumulating savings, and the growing donor and electorate impatience and fatigue with the persistence of need.

This minimal haven is currently under assault by tough love, racist, anti-immigrant, and fiscal conservatives who remind us that American compassion is short-lived and fragmented. Liberal policymakers underestimated the cost of equipping residents to compete in the advanced economy and mistakenly did not try to accomplish more when they had the chance. They failed to recognize how shallow and fleeting the collective commitment was to urban revival. Now, safety nets and support for non-profit services are being reduced drastically while even entry-level jobs are becoming less available.

Without expensive subsidies, information technology firms have little financial incentive to site their facilities in center cities or to make employment opportunities available to low-skill center city residents. The introduction of information technology was clearly not targeted to the special needs of low-income urban people, much like new housing construction which can be occupied by low-income people only after it has been filtered through more affluent groups.

Yet the options are limited—young people need to be computer literate, more home computers are needed, more and better equipment is needed in inner-city schools along with trained personnel. The combination of public schools not adequately equipped to teach needed skills, high drop-out rates, and inadequately financed training programs for adults threaten preparation even for the declining number of entry level positions.

Despite the bleak prospects for information technology to accomplish what the automotive revolution apparently achieved for entry-level wage earners, the center city labor pool must still position itself to take advantage of remaining opportunities and pressure points. This is a tough road into high tech, because the cost of providing jobs is much greater than the combined costs of welfare, food stamps, job training, child care, and Medicaid. At the same time, it is vital to help sustain the existing center city jobs in the lower-skilled service occupations to enable parents to survive and prepare their children for the challenge of securing these better-paying, higher-skilled jobs.

Note

1. Probably the best data collections for analyzing recent changes in low-income communities are the Urban Institute's Underclass Data Base (see Galster; Abramson), University of Michigan's Population Studies Center (Frey) but also the Current Population Survey (CPS), the Survey of Income and Program Participation (SIPP) and the Panel Study of Income Dynamics (PSID) (see Danziger); the data analyses by Massey; Coulton; Kasarda; Hughes; Case; the collection of studies in Lynn and McGeary; and Julius Wilson's book, *When Work Disappears: The World of the New Urban Poor*, which documents center city employment issues very effectively.

References

Abramson, Alan, Mitchell S. Tobin and Matthew R. Vander-Goot. 1995. "The Changing Geography of Metropolitan Opportunity: The Segregation of the Poor in U.S. Metropolitan Areas, 1970 to 1990" *Housing Policy Debate* 6(1): 45–72.

Buck, Nick and Norman Fainstein. 1992. "Dynamics of the Metropolitan Economy." In *Divided Cities,* edited by Susan Fainstein, Ian Gordon and Michael Harloe. Cambridge, MA: Blackwell.

Case, Anne C. and Lawrence F. Katz. 1991. "The Company You Keep: The Effects of Family and Neighborhood on Disadvantaged Youths." Cambridge, MA: National Bureau of Economic Research.

Castells, Manuel. 1985. "High Technology, Economic Restructuring, and the Urban-Regional Process in the United States." *Urban Affairs Annual Review* 28: 11–40.

Coulton, Claudia and Shanta Pandey. 1992. "Geographic Concentration of Poverty and Risk to Children in Urban Neighborhoods." *American Behavioral Scientist* 35: 238–257.

Danziger, S. H. and Gary Sandefur. 1994. *Confronting Poverty*. Cambridge, MA: Harvard University Press.

Frey, William H. 1995. "The New Geography of Population Shifts: Trends Toward Balkanization." In *State of the Union—America in the 1990s*, edited by Reynolds Farley, New York: Russell Sage.

Frey, William H. and Elaine L. Fielding. 1995. "Changing Urban Populations: Regional Restructuring, Racial Polarization, and Poverty Concentration." *Cityscape* 1(2): 1–66.

Galster, George C. and Sean P. Killen. 1995. "The Geography of Metropolitan Opportunity: A Reconnaissance and Conceptual Framework." *Housing Policy Debate* 6(1): 7–44.

Gordon, Ian and Saskia Sassen. 1992. "Restructuring the Urban Labor Markets." In *Divided Cities,* edited by Susan Fainstein, Ian Gordon and Michael Harloe. Cambridge, MA: Blackwell.

Hodgkinson, Virginia A. et al. 1995. *The Impact of Federal Budget Proposals Upon the Activities of Charitable Organizations and the People They Serve*. Washington, DC: Independent Sector.

Hughes, Mark A. 1995. "A Mobility Strategy for Improving Opportunity." *Housing Policy Debate* 6(1): 271–297.

James, Franklin J. 1995. "Urban Economies: Trends, Forces, and Implications for the President's National Urban Policy." *Cityscape* 1(2): 67–124.

Jarkowsky, Paul A. 1994. "Ghetto Poverty among Blacks in the 1990s," *Journal of Policy Analysis and Management* 13: 288–310.

Jenks, Christopher and Susan E. Meyer. 1990. "Residential Segregation, Job Proximity, and Black Job Opportunities." In *Inner-City Poverty in the United States*, edited by Lawrence Lynn and Michael G. H. McGeary. Washington DC: National Academy of Sciences.

Kasarda, John D. 1993a. "Inner-City Concentrated Poverty and Neighborhood Distress: 1970 to 1990." *Housing Policy Debate* 4(3): 253–302.

Kasarda, John D. 1993b. "Inner-City Poverty and Economic Access." In *Rediscovering Urban America,* edited by Jack Sommer and Donald A. Hicks, U.S. Department of Housing and Urban Development, Office of Policy Development and Research.

Katz, Michael. 1989. *The Undeserving Poor: From the War on Poverty to the War on Welfare.* New York: Pantheon Books.

Krueger, Alan B. 1993. "How Computers Have Changed the Wage Structure: Evidence from Microdata, 1984–89." *Quarterly Journal of Economics,* February, pp. 33–60.

Massey, D. S. and N. A. Denton. 1993. *American Apartheid: Segregation and the Making of the Underclass.* Cambridge, MA: Harvard University Press

Orfield, Gary. 1992. "Urban Schooling and the Perpetuation of Job Inequality in Metropolitan Chicago." In *Urban Labor Markets and Job Opportunity,* edited by George E. Peterson and Wayne Vroman. Washington, DC: The Urban Institute Press.

Ostrander, Susan. 1989. "The Problem of Poverty and Why Philanthropy Neglects It." In *The Future of the Nonprofit Sector,* edited by Virginia A. Hodgkinson and Richard W. Lyman. San Francisco: Jossey-Bass.

Peterson, George E. and Wayne Vroman. 1992. *Urban Labor Markets and Job Opportunity.* Washington, DC: The Urban Institute Press.

Pollard, Jane and Michael Storper. 1996. "A Tale of Twelve Cities: Metropolitan Employment Change in Dynamic Industries in the 1980's." *Economic Geography* 72(1): 1–22.

Rosenbaum, James E. 1995. "Changing the Geography of Opportunity by Expanding Residential Choice: Lessons from the Gautreaux Program." *Housing Policy Debate* 6(1): 231–270.

Salamon, Lester M. 1995. *Partners in Public Service: Government—Nonprofit Relations in the Modern Welfare State.* Baltimore: Johns Hopkins University Press.

Smith, Steven Rathgeb and Michael Lipsky. 1993. *Nonprofits for Hire: The Welfare State in the Age of Contracting.* Cambridge, MA: Harvard University Press.

Stenberg, Carl W. and William Colman. 1994. *America's Future Work Force.* Westport, CT: Greenwood Press.

Wilson, Julius. 1987. *The Truly Disadvantaged.* Chicago: University of Chicago Press.

Wilson, Julius. 1996. *When Work Disappears: The World of the New Urban Poor.* Cambridge, MA: Harvard University Press.

Wolpert, Julian. 1970. "Departures from the Usual Environment in Locational Analysis." *Annals: Association of American Geographers* 60(3): 220–229.

Wolpert, Julian. 1993. *Patterns of Generosity in America: Who's Holding the Safety Net?* New York: Twentieth Century Fund.

Wolpert, Julian. 1996. *What Charity Can and Cannot Do.* New York: Twentieth Century Fund.

4. The City of Bits Hypothesis

William J. Mitchell

The Digital Revolution

Historians endlessly contest the question of whether great technological innovations autonomously produce social and cultural transformations, or whether the conditions and desires that yield particular technological innovations are social and cultural constructions—so that we mostly end up with the technologies that we deserve. More accommodating thinkers than the hard-line technological determinists and social constructionists allow that it may be a bit of both; it is hard to imagine technological breakthroughs appearing completely out of nowhere, but it is equally difficult to credit Mother Nature with obligingly coughing up inventions on demand. Perhaps it is most accurate to say that we make our technologies, then our technologies make us, and so on recursively.

In any case, there seems to be little doubt that throughout history new technologies have opened the way to structural and functional transformations of existing towns and cities, and sometimes to the emergence of radically new urban patterns. The wheel and the plough yielded agricultural surpluses that could be transported to central locations, and so allowed large cities to live off their hinterlands. Roman cities depended on infrastructures of roads, aqueducts, and sewers. Mercantile cities needed the capacity to create ports, sailing ships, and navigation instruments. Creation of the Chicago Loop required the railroads, the steel frame, and the elevator. And Phoenix is unimaginable without the automobile and the air conditioner.

Digital electronics is the latest in this long line of enabling and transforming technologies. Its burgeoning power does not derive from just one key invention, but from the growing convergence of several lines of technological development to create a combination of capabilities that is truly unprecedented. Pretty soon—depending on how the business battles and public policy debates of the 1990s work themselves out—we are likely to have a worldwide digital telecommunications infrastructure that combines the pervasiveness and sophisticated switching capability that we associate with the current telephone system with the bandwidth and multimedia capabilities of cable television and the distributed, inexpensive storage and computation capabilities of the personal computer. This will increase the availability of information, create new opportunities for communication, and shrink distances as never before. The rapid growth of the World Wide Web in the late 1990s has been an overture to what is to come. It is entirely appropriate to call this the "digital revolution."

Nobody really knows what the digital revolution will ultimately mean for towns and cities in general, or for low-income communities in particular. Empirical studies have so far been of limited help in understanding it, given that the most important phenomena are just now appearing— and at breakneck speed. Historians may claim that they have seen similar formations in the past, and perhaps can extrapolate from these, but I would not bet on it. Social critics may frame their utopias and dystopias, but that often seems little more than a hasty projection of prefabricated ideology onto the unknown. So, what follows here is mostly frankly hypothetical and in some respects speculative—an effort to set forth some ideas that may serve as postulates for designers and planners who want to explore possible futures, as provocations for critical discussion, and as starting points for framing useful empirical questions.

The New Economy of Presence

To gain a concrete idea of the implications of the digital revolution, let us begin with a simple thought experiment. Imagine that you want to convey some information to a coworker. You can walk to her office and discuss the matter face-to-face; the two of you are physically present in the same place at the same time. If she is not there, you can leave a written note on her desk, and she will find it and read it at some later point; this is using a low-tech form of information storage technology to accomplish a transaction through asynchronous physical presence. A third alternative is to call her telephone extension; if she answers, you accomplish the transaction through synchronous telepresence. Finally, you can exchange e-mail or voicemail; now, you accomplish your goal through asynchronous telepresence—without the need ever to be in the same place or to be available at the same time. It is convenient for our purposes to array these four possibilities in a two-by-two table, as illustrated in Table 4.1.

If we had to rely on our unaided human capabilities, and no technology intervened, all human transactions would fall in the upper left, synchronous presence quadrant of this table. That is how it was in the

Table 4.1: Communication alternatives

	Synchronous	Asynchronous
Presence	Talk face-to-face	Leave note on desk
Telepresence	Talk by telephone	Send e-mail or leave voicemail

past, and still is in some traditional societies. But the development of recording technologies created the possibility of asynchronous communication; writing and associated media for recording and storing text came first, followed by mechanical recording devices such as the camera and the Edison phonograph, and now digital storage of numbers, text, images, sound, and video in RAM and on disks and tape in computer systems. Similarly, the emergence of transmission technologies yielded telepresence; drums, bonfires, and smoke signals, and semaphores were early means of communication at a distance, then came the telegraph, the wireless telegraph, modern radio and television, and now worldwide digital telecommunication networks—such as the Internet—carrying packets of bits.

The combination of recording and transportation technologies produced mail services—a limited capacity, snail's-pace first approximation to asynchronous telepresence. Finally, since the 1960s, digital recording, processing, and telecommunication capabilities have converged to create true asynchronous telepresence—the most familiar forms of which are e-mail, voicemail, World Wide Web (WWW) sites, and video-on-demand servers. So, by the mid-1990s, human transactions were being distributed over all quadrants of the table.

These various modes of communication and conduct of transactions are partially equivalent to each other but not completely interchangeable; they vary considerably in their respective qualities, costs, and most appropriate uses. Face-to-face provides intensity, multimodality, and immediate feedback. It requires putting yourself on the line, sometimes even in physical danger. And when you consider space, transportation, and opportunity costs, it is often very expensive to achieve. Telepresence greatly reduces transportation costs while retaining the possibility of immediate

Table 4.2: Advantages and disadvantages

	Synchronous	Asynchronous
Presence	Intense, multimodal Immediate feedback	Limited by storage and playback capabilities
	High transportation costs	No immediate feedback
	High space costs	No reduction in transportation costs
	Requires coordination of availability	No reduction in space costs
	Requires full attention	No need to coordinate availability
		May allow some division of attention
Telepresence	Limited by bandwidth and interface capabilities	Limited by storage, bandwidth, and interface capabilities
	Retains immediate feedback	No immediate feedback
	Reduces transportation costs	Reduces transportation costs
	Reduces space costs	Reduces space costs
	Requires coordination of availability	No need to coordinate availability
	May allow some division of attention	Allows multiple activities and transactions in parallel

feedback, but the quality of communication is limited by available bandwidth and interface technologies, it still requires coordination of availability, and—as the telephone vividly demonstrates—it can generate unexpected and unwanted interruptions. It also allows some division of attention; you can talk on a cellular telephone while supervising a child's play, for example. Asynchronous communication eliminates the need for coordination of availability, but it also eliminates the possibility of immediate feedback; it does not reduce transportation costs, and it is limited in quality by available recording, storage, and playback capabilities. The most recently emergent possibility—asynchronous telepresence—effectively eliminates transportation costs and the need to coordinate availability, and it allows multiple transactions to take place in parallel through use of software agents and the like, so it is extremely inexpensive and convenient, but it is limited by available storage and bandwidth, and it certainly does not have the intensity and immediacy of a face-to-face encounter. These commonalities and differences are summarized in Table 4.2.

Given this extended range of possible means for conducting our affairs, a number of questions present themselves. What are the best uses of our limited opportunities for face-to-face interaction? When does the value added by the immediacy and high quality of face-to-face interaction justify the high transportation, space, and coordination costs? Conversely, when do the savings on transportation costs outweigh the disadvantages of telepresence? When is immediate feedback essential, and when can we dispense with it? When can we take advantage of the convenience of asynchronous communication without losing something essential? What are the best uses of the low-cost, potentially very high-volume communications capabilities provided by asynchronous telepresence? How can it broaden our opportunities and contacts? How can it free up time and reduce transportation and space demands by eliminating unnecessary face-to-face interactions? More subtly, how can we most effectively use the various available modes in combination—for example, by using many low-cost, convenient e-mail messages to arrange and coordinate much rarer, higher-cost, face-to-face meetings?

Often, the ways that people respond to these sorts of questions are constrained by particular contexts and circumstances. If they are in remote locations that impose particularly high travel costs for face-to-face interaction, for example, then they are likely to rely more heavily than they otherwise would on telepresence. Similarly, if they need to communicate across widely separated time zones, they may prefer asynchronous to synchronous communication because it eliminates the need to coordinate availability. If they have plenty of time on their hands and a narrow range of daily duties they may enjoy doing everything face to face, but if they have numerous responsibilities and are very busy, they may have to rely much more on e-mail and the telephone.

In addition, technological progress influences choices by reducing the costs of the electronically mediated alternatives and increasing their quality—while the cost and quality of face-to-face interactions remain much the same, or even become more expensive as cities become more crowded and jammed with traffic. Processing power, storage capacity, switched connections to remote locations, and high-bandwidth communications channels were all once extremely scarce and expensive commodities but are now becoming very inexpensive; in many practical contexts, we can begin to treat them as almost free resources. Increases in bandwidth have allowed progress from the telegraph's Morse code to high quality voice communication, to increasingly effective teleconferencing, and now (in research contexts at least) to sophisticated shared virtual environments. In the early days of the Internet, remote asynchronous communication was limited to clumsily downloading files from one machine to another and exchanging short, entirely textual e-mail messages; now, the World Wide Web allows smooth navigation of multimedia material at scattered sites simply by pointing and clicking, e-mail is evolving into multimedia mail, and software agents can roam the Net to perform tasks for you while you sleep. The magnitude of these recent changes in cost and quality is so great that the digital world seems qualitatively very different from the world of the early days of electronic recording and telecommunications.

One effect of these increasingly attractive and inexpensive electronic alternatives is to create new kinds of competition for our attention, our business, and our loyalties. You may, for example, have bought this book in the old-fashioned way—by going to an actual bookstore, handing over your cash, and carrying away your purchase—or you may have surfed into an online "virtual" bookstore, browsed through the offerings displayed there, electronically provided your credit card number and address, and had the product delivered from the warehouse directly to your door. In other words, you may have carried out the transaction face to face, during business hours, in a traditional sort of architectural setting, or you may have conducted it remotely and asynchronously through use of electronic infrastructure and appropriate software.

By the mid-1990s growing competition from electronic sites and services was already producing some substitution of connectivity for contiguity, of electronic interaction for travel, and of virtual venues for real estate, and there is likely to be much more of this as high-bandwidth digital telecommunication systems with capabilities far beyond those provided by the Internet and the World Wide Web in the late 1990s become widely accessible. But even more important, we can anticipate that new opportunities for interaction will create new and higher demands, and that both traditional and electronic means will play parts in satisfying these—just as photography did not simply substitute for the sketchbook and the painting but created whole new roles and demands for images, and as the telephone not only substituted for movement, but also created new motivations for travel and an efficient means of arranging and coordinating it.

In sum, we now have a new economy of presence—within which we continually choose among the possibilities of synchronous and asynchronous communication, and presence and telepresence. Given that all the different modes have their respective advantages and disadvantages, we should not (as techno-romantics gleefully anticipate and traditionalists fear) expect wholesale substitution of electronically mediated communication for face-to-face interactions. We are not all going to end up alone in darkened rooms typing e-mail messages to each other. If people are left to themselves, they will make more-or-less informed and rational choices among the available alternatives as appropriate to their particular needs and circumstances. This will result in varying distributions of activity over the quadrants of our table at different historical moments and in different geographic and cultural contexts.

An Illustrative Case: The Fate of the Branch Bank

Different choices of interaction modes create different sorts of space demands, as approximately sketched in Table 4.3.

To sharpen this picture, in a more specific context, let us consider the fate of the neighborhood branch bank. Once, when retail banking transactions were almost entirely conducted face to face, branch bank buildings were found everywhere—in the central city, on main streets of suburban and rural communities, and in drive-up commercial strip locations. You went to the bank to deposit and withdraw cash, to negotiate loans, and so on. The interior of the bank building provided specialized

Table 4.3: Space demands

	Synchronous	Asynchronous
Presence	Meeting spaces	Storage and dispensing or display facilities
Telepresence	Transmission and receiving spaces	Virtual spaces

spaces for these transactions and the people, materials, and equipment
needed to conduct them. The exterior—typically neoclassical, gothic,
or high modern—was designed to express the power and prestige of the
institution in the community. Then, along came automated teller machines
(ATMs) which stored and dispensed cash, did not require their tenders and
customers to be present at the same time, could be located anywhere, and
could operate twenty-four hours a day, seven days a week. Telephone and
even video banking emerged as well; banks now had to create and staff
telephone service centers. Finally, electronic home-banking systems and
electronic cash have begun to shift some banking activities entirely into
cyberspace. Table 4.4 presents the range of possibilities.

Most banks are likely to maintain some mix of these types of
facilities to reach different segments of their markets most effectively, but
we are clearly seeing a massive shift away from face-to-face interactions and
toward various forms of electronic delivery of banking services as costs of
electronic means drop and capabilities improve. Thousands of branch banks
have been shut down—particularly as a consequence of large bank mergers.
Automated teller machines have proliferated, and are no longer just tacked
onto bank building facades to provide extended service hours, but are found
wherever people need cash—in supermarkets, airports, student unions,
casinos, office building lobbies, and busy urban locations generally. And,
for many kinds of transactions, electronic home-banking systems now
completely eliminate the need to go somewhere special.

These developments can have profound consequences for towns
and neighborhoods in general, and for low-income communities in particular. The shutdown of a branch bank can cut off access to banking services

Table 4.4: Banking

	Synchronous	Asynchronous
Presence	Traditional branch banks	Automated teller machines
Telepresence	Phone and video service centers, service delivery kiosks	Electronic home banking and electronic cash systems

if other modes of delivery are not readily available in a community, and it can reduce the presence and commitment of a bank in a community; clearly this can be devastating. Replacement of a centralized location by a decentralized network of ATMs can reduce the traffic in a retail area and contribute to decline in its economic vitality. Since phone and video service centers can be almost anywhere, they can shift jobs from a community to a remote location. On the upside, however, electronic home-banking systems can effectively deliver services to remote and inaccessible locations, and to the aged, the infirm, and the otherwise immobile.

Electronic Delivery of Services in General

Similar analyses can be made of most kinds of services, and of the types and locations of the facilities needed to deliver them. Below I will sketch out some tables of possibilities—which should, at least, be suggestive.

First, let us consider news. Once, it was entirely transmitted through face-to-face meetings at gathering points such as the village well, the coffee shop, or the college dining table, so these sorts of places were essential to maintaining community cohesion. Print brought us newspapers, together with places for buying them (newsstands, newspaper vending machines) and for reading them (armchairs and breakfast tables, reading rooms, waiting rooms, trains, cafés, and so on). Radio and television gave us broadcast news, and the associated architectural demand for transmission spaces (studios, mobile broadcast trucks) and receiving spaces (living rooms organized around television sets). Now—as vividly demonstrated by the huge network traffic on the night of the 1996 presidential

Table 4.5: News

	Synchronous	Asynchronous
Presence	Exchange of gossip at the well or the coffee house, the town crier	Newspaper vending machines, reading rooms
Telepresence	News broadcast studios, television viewing spaces	WWW electronic newspapers and news services, search, filtering, and selection agents

election—remote, asynchronous, electronic news sites are becoming increasingly important, and these create reception locations around network drops and personal computers. Table 4.5 provides a summary.

Similar shifts have developed in entertainment. Traditionally, theaters, clubs, sports venues, and the like have delivered "live" entertainment; you had to be there at the performance time. Recording technology allowed time-shifted reception, and produced some important new architectural types such as recording and movie studios and movie houses. Broadcast media created demands for production and reception spaces; instead of going to a football stadium to watch a game, you might watch a transmission in your living room or a sports bar. And remote audio and video servers are now beginning to deliver recorded entertainment on demand, anywhere you may want it; you do not have to go to a specific location, and you are not bound to any particular performance time. Here, once again, in Table 4.6, is a summary.

These different modes do compete with each other to some extent; on any given evening, you may choose among going to the theater or the movies, watching a sporting event on television, or downloading a video. But they do manage to coexist, and they are sometimes symbiotic—as when record sales create demand for live rock concerts, which in turn boost sales. The same is true of retailing. We can now choose among traditional stores where stock is kept on site and transactions are conducted face to face, vending machines, telemarketing in its various forms, and World Wide Web virtual stores and online malls. The possibilities are shown in Table 4.7.

Table 4.6: Entertainment

	Synchronous	Asynchronous
Presence	Live theaters, clubs, sports venues	Recording and film studios, movie theaters, places for listening to recorded music and videos
Telepresence	Entertainment broadcast studios, living rooms and sports bars	Programmed VCRs, audio and video-on-demand sites, search, filtering, and selection agents

Table 4.7: Retailing

	Synchronous	Asynchronous
Presence	Traditional stores, retail districts, and shopping centers	Vending machines
Telepresence	Telemarketing centers, Home Shopping Network	Mail order, WWW virtual stores and malls, shopping agents

None of these retail modes seems likely to take over completely, to the exclusion of the others. But—as real estate developers are vividly aware—shifts in the distribution of activity among these possibilities have significant implications for the types, amounts, and spatial distributions of retail space. A traditional bookstore requires space on Main Street or in a mall, for example, and it contributes to the commercial vitality of the surrounding area. But a virtual bookstore needs a small electronic operations center (which can be anywhere), a network of strategically located warehouses, and access to an efficient package delivery service. The traditional bookstore usually has very limited stock space and a local clientele, whereas the virtual bookstore can have a much larger stock space and inventory (because it does not have to be located in a high-rent retail area), and can effectively

Table 4.8: Education

	Synchronous	Asynchronous
Presence	Classrooms, lecture halls, schools, university campuses	Libraries, galleries, museums
Telepresence	Educational broadcast studios and viewing spaces, teleconferencing spaces, shared virtual environments, remotely accessed telescopes and other instruments	WWW sites, FTP sites, virtual libraries, newsgroups, listservs, online interactive educational games, software tutors

serve a national or global clientele. In the physical bookstore you browse through the shelves, ask sales staff for assistance, and maybe visit several stores to find what you want; in the virtual bookstore, you use search engines and comparison shopping agents. Going to the physical bookstore may provide a chance to encounter friends and acquaintances, but surfing in to a virtual bookstore does not—at least in the forms that early virtual bookstores have taken.

Books themselves are asynchronous communication devices, and educational institutions have traditionally grown up around places to store and consult them—libraries and reading rooms. To complement these in the educational process, synchronous communication spaces—classrooms, seminar rooms, and lecture halls—were needed. Then the electronic era gave us a series of increasingly sophisticated geographically distributed alternatives—first radio and television broadcasts of presentations, then two-way and multiway teleconferencing, and now shared virtual environments. And the World Wide Web has created an explosion of interest in remote, asynchronous delivery of educational materials, as Table 4.8 demonstrates.

Like delivery of education, delivery of medical services in the past mostly depended on getting the patient and the practitioner together in an appropriately equipped setting—hence, hospital wards, clinics, surgical suites, doctor's offices, and ambulances. But the development of high-bandwidth networks, together with imaging, monitoring, and telerobotic

Table 4.9: Health care

	Synchronous	Asynchronous
Presence	Hospitals, clinics, mobile first-aid facilities	On-site medical records, image collections, and reference libraries. First-aid kits, automated dispensaries
Telepresence	Remote consultation, examination, monitoring, and imaging facilities, remote pathology, telesurgery suites	Networked medical records and reference systems, online image libraries, artificial intelligence medical advice systems

devices that can be operated over these networks, reduces or eliminates the need for patients and practitioners to be physically face to face, and allows consultation, examination, and treatment sites to be distributed rather than tightly clustered. Remote physical examinations and remote pathology become feasible. Suitably equipped homes can become monitoring sites, thus reducing the need for hospital beds. Through a combination of imaging and telerobotics technology, even telesurgery becomes feasible. Less dramatic, but perhaps even more important, medical records and reference material can be delivered asynchronously to wherever they may be needed. Thus the possibilities now look something like those in Table 4.9.

Finally, let us consider safety and security. Police forces, security services, and fire and rescue services have traditionally delivered them by being there, on the spot; guard posts, police stations, and fire stations were placed at strategic locations, and patrols of beat cops and police cruisers extended capabilities of surveillance and response over wider areas. Telecommunication technology opened up the possibility of remote surveillance, and surveillance cameras, in particular, are now ubiquitous. This may be combined with remotely controlled safety and security devices, as when a door lock is operated remotely in response to an intercom or videophone request for entry. Fire alarms, car theft alarms, and even (more violently) defensive booby traps may be put in place at particular locations, to respond to intruders in preprogrammed ways. And increasingly, now, remote and asynchronous capabilities may be combined by connecting

Table 4.10: Safety and security

	Synchronous	Asynchronous
Presence	Police stations, guard posts, fire stations, beat cops, police cruisers	Alarm systems, defensive booby traps
Telepresence	Surveillance cameras, remotely controlled safety and security systems, electronically serviced surveillance and control centers	Alarms and monitoring systems connected to remote sites, firewalls around networks, access controls on files and virtual places

Table 4.11: Office work

	Synchronous	Asynchronous
Presence	Conference rooms, the water cooler	Traditional libraries and file systems
Telepresence	Telephones, videoconferencing, wireless communications, shared virtual environments	WWW, network-accessed file systems and libraries, fax, voicemail, e-mail, multimedia mail, groupware, agents

alarms of various kinds to remote centers of response. So, in summary, we now have the collection of possibilities shown in Table 4.10.

Work and Economic Opportunity

The developments described above clearly change the types, sizes, and locations of some service-sector workplaces. And, if we think of workplaces generally as those particular locations where people, work materials, and tools are brought together to accomplish productive tasks—for a peasant, the field, for an industrial worker, the factory, for a merchant, the store, for a white-collar worker, the office, and so on—we can begin to see that the digital revolution is likely to have very significant effects on workplaces in other sectors as well. From a worker's perspective, this is because it is now possible—and sometimes advantageous—to make effective people-to-people, people-to-materials, and people-to-tools connections remotely and asynchronously. From a management perspective, it follows from the possibility of remote and asynchronous supervision and coordination.

The most obvious potential effects are on office work of all kinds —from routine clerical work to the kind of high-level symbolic analysis that Robert Reich has celebrated. Traditionally, office buildings have been constructed to bring people together for this sort of work; these can be traced back to Giorgio Vasari's Uffizi, in sixteenth-century Florence. The steel frame, the elevator, mechanical HVAC systems, the telephone, and mass-transit systems combined (from the late nineteenth century) to bring large numbers of office workers together in downtown high-rise towers. Later, the automobile and the freeway gave us the suburban office park. Within these various types of office buildings, private cubicles are mostly for processing information, conference rooms (and more informally, the water cooler) for face-to-face synchronous communication, and file systems and libraries for information storage and asynchronous communication. These different kinds of spaces are typically clustered in divisions or departments of an organization to allow efficient circulation and effective supervision, and to promote workgroup cohesion. Now, increasingly, they can fragment. With the telegraph, the telephone, videoconferencing, and now shared virtual environments, more and more effective electronic means have emerged to compete with and complement face-to-face meetings. And digital storage has emerged as an effective, inexpensive alternative to paper. Table 4.11 offers the range of possibilities.

The emergence of powerful and convenient electronic alternatives to traditional means has opened up many new possibilities for the arrangement and distribution of office work space. Through use of portable electronic devices such as cellular telephones, pagers, laptop computers, and personal digital assistants, mobile members of an organization can keep in close touch while in the field or on the road—and may need little or no private office space back at "home base." Consequently, hotel rooms, automobiles, and airplane seats may increasingly be designed and used as workplaces. Within an office building, the capacity to deliver files and communication capabilities anywhere, anytime, may reduce the need for permanent, private offices in fixed locations, and allow much more fluid, flexible space use. Organizations may set up electronically connected satellite offices in suburban locations to tap in to desirable labor markets and reduce rent and commuting costs, or resort offices for concentrated work by project teams. And workplaces may be shifted back into the home to create a telecommuting workforce that does not require much centralized office space, but instead maintains and pays for its own—in widely scattered locations.

In the past, the location of factory work was very tightly constrained by the need for access to raw materials, labor markets, and transportation, and management functions had to be located close to production functions. Suppliers of components and warehouses were often nearby as well. This created intense industrial concentrations at locations where the conditions were just right. However, one very striking effect of telecommunications—intensified by the digital revolution—has been much greater separation of management from production functions. Where managers no longer have to be handy to the factory floor, they frequently move to locations that are closer to customers, closer to other managers, and more pleasant. And, at lower levels in the organizational hierarchy, sensor technology combined with telecommunications may allow remote performance of machine-minding tasks.

Similarly, recording technology allows capture and later use of expertise that was traditionally provided on the spot by skilled craftsmen, designers, and experienced supervisors. This can take the familiar forms of written instructions, step-by-step procedures, shop drawings and specifications, and user manuals for machines. In the digital era such instructions increasingly manifest themselves as CAD/CAM databases, programs for industrial robots, and knowledge-based computer systems for diagnosing problems and providing advice.

Finally, combination of remote and asynchronous capabilities in computer networks allows a steelwork fabricator in Venice to extract CAD/CAM information from a database maintained in Los Angeles, or a programmer in Bangalore to create instructions for an industrial robot in Detroit. Thus we have seen the emergence of computer-integrated global manufacturing enterprises, as strikingly exemplified in the computer

Table 4.12: Factory work

	Synchronous	Asynchronous
Presence	Mill towns, industrial cities	Written instructions and step-by-step procedures, shop drawings and specifications, user manuals, knowledge-based computer systems, industrial robots, CAD/CAM
Telepresence	Separation of management from production, remote machine minding	Computer-integrated global manufacturing enterprises

industry, in today's automobile industry, and in Boeing's celebrated design and production of its 777 aircraft.

To summarize, then, Table 4.12 arrays the possibilities for manufacturing activity and factory work.

All this does not simply add up to decentralization and further suburbanization, as a hasty analysis might suggest. There are multiple—sometimes conflicting—consequences. As has frequently been observed, one such consequence is that places like New York and London, with high concentrations of talent and excellent computer and telecommunications capabilities, have emerged as "global cities" that play worldwide command and control roles. Another result is that high-level, well-rewarded knowledge workers in financial services, the software industry, and the entertainment industry can readily remove themselves to attractive but isolated enclaves like Aspen and Malibu, or even to rural electronic cottages, and operate effectively from there. And a third consequence is that office and manufacturing jobs may shift from traditional central locations to dispersed suburban and rural ones. Or they may shift nationally and internationally to locations where labor markets are particularly attractive, time zones allow work conveniently to be coordinated or handed off, and the flux of global capital causes concentrations of investment in up-to-date, competitive machinery and facilities.

The great danger is that these tides may quickly leave many low-income communities even more isolated in the economic backwaters than they already are, with little to attract investment and few jobs to offer—traps for those without the means or the will to escape. The potential—if there are those with the entrepreneurial skill and vision to grasp it—is that this fluid situation may provide opportunities to break destructive old patterns, and to find new ways to tap and market the talents of community members, and to make productive use of a community's social capital. The successful marketing to wide audiences, through the recording and broadcasting industries, of musical talent nurtured by low-income communities, suggests that this may not be entirely a wishful fantasy; the growing multimedia industry, for example, might create similar opportunities.

Homes and Residential Neighborhoods

Homes have not always contained the mix of activities and spaces that we typically find today. Before the industrial revolution (and still, in some more traditional contexts) homes and workplaces frequently were not separated; we found peasants among their fields and barns, craftsmen and merchants living above their shops, and so on. And often, in the past, homes did not fit into the one-bedroom, two-bedroom, and three-bedroom formats of today, but were built to accommodate extended families. Now, the digital revolution is producing another change in the mix by shifting many activities back into the home. Telework may bring the workplace back to the home (although in some very different forms), and electronic delivery of services is likely to shift many retailing, banking, entertainment, educational, health care, and other activities from central commercial and institutional locations to collections of decentralized, private, domestic ones.

This has quite dramatic implications for residential design and for residential real estate markets. To function effectively in the digital world, homes will need reliable, inexpensive, high-bandwidth network connections; these will soon seem as essential as connections to electric, water, gas, sewer, and telephone utilities. And because many of the newly domesticated or redomesticated activities are incompatible with each other (teleworking does not easily coexist in the living room with watching a video, for example), and because these incompatibilities cannot always be handled by scheduling them at different times, there will probably be demand for larger amounts of space in residential units, and for greater division and differentiation of space. Housing stock that can accommodate these changes will tend to gain in desirability and value, while stock that cannot will lose.

If significant numbers of jobs do eventually shift from central office, commercial, and industrial locations to residential neighborhoods, this will reduce the daytime populations of the old centers and increase the daytime populations of bedroom suburbs and other predominantly residential areas. This should, in turn, increase the demand in those residential areas for on-the-spot services—health clubs, lunchtime restaurants, day care, copy shops, package drop-off and delivery points, and the like. So there may be very interesting opportunities to create cohesive, small-scale, pedestrian-oriented or bicycle-oriented neighborhoods that combine lively local social interaction focused on neighborhood service centers with electronic access to a much wider world of jobs and services.

The obvious danger is that many such neighborhoods could become walled, gated enclaves of privilege. The challenge, for those who believe that social and cultural diversity and a balanced mix of income levels are crucial components of healthy communities, will be to find ways to achieve diversity and balance that are compatible with the new residential patterns that are likely to emerge from the digital revolution.

Maintaining Community Cohesion

Urban theorists from Plato and Aristotle onward have argued that successful towns and cities require an appropriate balance of residential space, work areas, and essential services (the elements that have so far been considered here) tied together into a coherent unit by circulation and utility networks and containing generally accessible places for public life and political and religious activities. From this, they have derived ideal populations and dimensions for settlements. Aristotle's *Politics*, for example, recommends a city that is small enough to be held together by pedestrian circulation, for the citizens to know each other, and for public life to take place in the central agora. Today's New Urbanists propose

Figure 4.1: Physical and virtual structures and their interrelationships

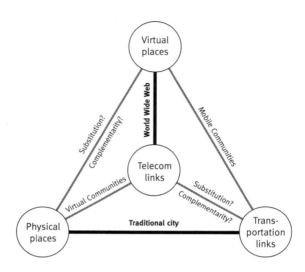

neighborhoods along very similar lines. And planners of modern cities, generally, have been concerned with creating and maintaining the right balance of land use and transportation—with making the best use of available land, keeping travel times to work and services within acceptable bounds, and with minimizing transportation congestion. Now, however, we need to consider virtual places as well as physical ones, telecommunication links in addition to transportation connections, and the interrelationships among all of these, as illustrated in Figure 4.1.

A traditional city — as it appears on a map — is a structure of physical places and transportation links. Analogously, the World Wide Web is a structure of sites (virtual places) tied together electronically by hyperlinks. But the physical world and the electronic virtual world are not separate, as much current discussion might lead one to believe; in fact, as the light-colored links in Figure 4.1 suggest, they are intricately intertwined. Consider, for example, the connection of physical places by telecommunication links; this creates the potential for telecommuting, and for the establishment of geographically distributed virtual communities. Conversely, the combination of virtual places with transportation supports such practices as taking your office on the road — for example, by carrying a laptop with appropriate software and dialing in to a server to gain access to e-mail, files, and other resources. Furthermore, we can imagine that telecommunication and transportation links may either substitute for one another or complement each other. And the same goes for virtual and physical places.

The burden of sustaining a community interaction and cohesion may now be carried by any or all of these means. We should not expect uniformity. In different contexts, very different patterns and mixes may make sense; architects, urban designers, and planners will need to consider the tradeoffs among the many emerging possibilities. Services may be delivered in traditional sorts of physical settings, by electronic means, or through some mix of the two. Community members may travel to work to conduct transactions and to socialize, or they may accomplish many of the necessary connections electronically. Efficient transfer of people and goods may be accomplished by locating origins and destinations as near to each other as possible, or by building high-speed transportation linkages between them. Thus the old yardsticks of accessibility and overall cohesion —walking distance and travel time—no longer apply in straightforward ways.

Within these hybrid structures of real estate and virtual places, held together by both transportation and telecommunication linkages, public space may appear in a variety of guises—some ancient and some very new. There may be traditional, physical venues for face-to-face encounters —agoras, forums, squares, piazzas, streets, public parks and gardens, and so on. Public monuments, museums, galleries, and libraries may be important repositories of community memory, and allow asynchronous communication across generations. Radio and television talk shows, online chat rooms, and MUDs, MOOs, and other kinds of shared virtual environments may employ telecommunications capabilities to create placeless, electronic

Table 4.13: Public space

	Synchronous	Asynchronous
Presence	Agoras, forums, squares, piazzas, streets, public parks and gardens	Public monuments, museums, galleries, and libraries
Telepresence	Radio and television talk shows, online chat rooms, MUDs and MOOs, shared virtual environments	Online newsgroups, bulletin boards, communal Web sites

agoras. And online newsgroups, bulletin boards, and Web sites function as remotely accessed, asynchronously visited public places. Table 4.13 provides a summary of the possibilities.

With these observations in mind, we can now develop a new kind of urban typology. At one end of the spectrum are completely traditional, place-based communities—composed entirely of physical spaces, organized around traditional types of public spaces, and held together by physical circulation through streets and transportation networks. At the other end of the spectrum are fully virtual communities. These consist of widely and randomly scattered physical places, together with many virtual places—including virtual public places—held together primarily by electronic connection rather than physical transportation. In between are numerous possible hybrids, in which both physical and virtual places play significant roles, and in which linkages are formed both by transportation and electronic connections. These hybrids include established cities and university campuses on which community networks have been overlaid, scattered rural communities tied together by networks, small communities that extend themselves virtually, and so on.

Communities like these are not necessarily discrete and clearly bounded, as more traditional ones typically have been. They may overlap and intersect in complex ways. And, given that electronic connections are much more easily changed than physical adjacencies and transportation linkages, they may be a lot less stable in their sizes and configurations. The

Deleuzian terminology is useful here; we might say that the global urban system is becoming less hierarchical and more rhyzomic in character.

Conclusions

The digital revolution, like the agricultural and industrial revolutions before it, opens up new possibilities for urban form and organization and creates powerful pressure for change. Under the emerging new conditions, established concepts and methods of urban analysis and design may no longer suffice, and familiar nostrums for urban problems may no longer work. We need to consider the roles of virtual places as well as physical ones, of electronic connections as well as transportation linkages, and of asynchronous encounters and transactions in addition to synchronous ones. If we want to understand the plight of low-income communities in the twenty-first century, and find policies and design strategies to alleviate it, we will have to set the problem firmly in the context of the unfolding digital revolution and its urban consequences.

5. Information Technology in Historical Perspective

Leo Marx

My aim here is to consider what we can learn from history about the promise that information technology holds for low-income urban communities. Are we justified in assuming, as many apparently do, that this new technology can play a decisive role in resolving the problems of the poor minority populations of our inner cities? I am skeptical, but not about the capacity or the need of inner-city youngsters to master the new technologies of communication. Today computer literacy is a prerequisite for most desirable jobs, and access to the new technology is every child's democratic right. On its face, however, the idea that computer technology will be the crucial factor in transforming the lives of urban minorities strikes me as counterintuitive.

Why? Because computation is a technology to which access is limited by peculiarly exacting qualifications in the degree of literacy, general education, self-confidence, and—especially—the verbal facility needed for its use. To adult neophytes the computer often seems a forbiddingly esoteric instrument: its arcane operations are hidden from view, and the standard instructions for its use often are couched in an esoteric idiom. Yet we are asked to believe that the most disadvantaged fraction of the population, through mastery of this intimidating technology, can expect to compete successfully for the available jobs and escape from poverty. This prospect seems even less plausible when we recall that our leading economists regard a 6 percent or 8 percent rate of unemployment as the norm for our market economy. If the nation's policy is to tolerate this level of unemployment, can there be much doubt about which groups are the most likely candidates for joblessness? It hard to reconcile these facts with the laudable outcome we seek for the inner-city population.

But Americans have always been optimistic—to put it mildly— about the benefits of technological innovation. It would in fact be more accurate to say that they invariably have had unrealistic expectations about these benefits. Consider, for example, a respected historian's summary of the dominant American reaction, as expressed by Thomas Edison, to the coming of electricity:[1]

> [Edison] ... expressed utopian ideas about it that were characteristic of the popular press. He predicted that electrification of the home would eliminate the distinction between night and day

and speed up women's mental development, making them the intellectual equals of men. Constant light might lead to the elimination of sleep. In later years he even hinted that he was experimenting with electrical ways to communicate with the dead.

As such predictions suggest, electrification became inextricably bound up with ideas of social progress in the transformation of human nature. (Nye 1990, p. 147)

Here are some of the felicities that electricity was expected to bestow on the nation.

In the beginning, Americans believed that electricity would free them from toil, as prophesied in the popular press, utopian works, feminist proposals, and back-to-the-land movements. Extravagant predictions about the electrified future were an integral part of the new technology's social meaning. Americans learned that they might use electricity to abolish sleep, cure disease, lose weight, quicken intelligence, eliminate pollution, banish housework and much more.

What really happened, at least in the short term, was very different.

But the actual development of electrical technologies seldom lived up to expectations. Electric trolleys did provide economical mass transport, but they did not lead to urban deconcentration into a pastoral utopia, and in any case they were abandoned in favor of automobiles. Productivity rose in the electrified factory, permitting shorter hours, higher pay and more consumer goods. Yet pressures on the job also increased as managers achieved greater technical control over work, and in contrast to the dream of automated factories that eliminated human toil, came either a stepped-up piecework system or the assembly line. ... Electricity improved working conditions on the farm, but instead of revitalizing agrarianism as some had predicted, soaring productivity made most farmers superfluous, and urban centers became even more dominant. (Nye 1990, p. 386)

Comparably extravagant expectations have been evoked by other—earlier and later—new technologies: the railroad and the telegraph, for example, and more recently, nuclear power. After Hiroshima, ironically, it was widely believed that limitless, free energy would soon be available. But few inventions have been as stimulating to the technocratic imagination as the computer. In his recent book, *Being Digital*, Nicholas Negroponte (1995), director of the celebrated MIT Media Laboratory, foresees the triumph of individualistic consumerism in a future that will be dominated by information technology. The computer's capacity for customizing the preferences of individual consumers will transform our daily lives, our very beings. We will become—we will literally *be*—digitalized: "In being digital I am *me*, not a statistical subset. *Me* includes information and events that have no demographic or statistical meaning. Where my mother-in-law lives, whom I had dinner with last night, and what time my flight departs for Richmond this afternoon have absolutely no correlation or statistical basis from which to derive suitable narrow-cast services." (Negroponte 1995, p. 164)

This transformation of humanity will be accomplished, in part, by replacing the old "broadcast" services, applicable to everyone on a statistical basis, with the new "narrowcast" services specially designed for each person.

> That unique information about me determines news [sic]
> services I might want to receive about a small obscure town, a
> not so famous person, and (for today) the anticipated weather
> conditions in Virginia. Classic demographics do not scale down
> to the digital individual. Thinking of the post-information age
> as infinitesimal demographics or ultrafocused narrowcasting is
> about as personalized as Burger King's "Have It Your Way."
>
> True personalization is now upon us. It's not just a
> matter of selecting relish over mustard once. The post-informa-
> tion age is about acquaintance over time: machines understand-
> ing individuals with the same degree of subtlety (or more than)
> we can expect from other human beings, including idiosyncrasies
> (like always wearing a blue striped shirt) and totally random
> events, good and bad, in the unfolding narrative of our lives.

> For example, having heard from the liquor store's agent, a machine could call to your attention a sale on a particular Chardonnay or beer that it knows the guests you have coming to dinner tomorrow night liked the last time. It could remind you to drop the car off at a garage near where you are going because the car told it that it needs new tires. It could clip a review of a new restaurant because you are going to that city in ten days. (Negroponte 1995, pp. 164–165)

In imagining this digitalized future, Negroponte may not have had the residents of the inner city expressly in mind, but he reassuringly predicts that the new technology will allow us to dispense—or very largely dispense —with old-fashioned political means of resolving social problems. In "the digital world," he predicts, new global means of communication will transcend old social boundaries, and "previously impossible solutions become viable."

> Today when 20 percent of the world consumes 80 percent of its resources, when a quarter of us have an acceptable standard of living and three quarters don't, how can this divide possibly come together? While the politicians struggle with the baggage of history a new generation is emerging from the digital landscape free of many of the old prejudices. These kids are released from the limitation of geographic proximity as the sole basis of friend- ship, collaboration, play and neighborhood. Digital technology can be a natural force drawing people into greater world harmony. (Negroponte 1995, p. 230)

These predictions exemplify the utopian thinking provoked by the advent of the new information technologies. An especially popular vision—it had been evoked by the coming of the railroad, the telegraph, the telephone, the radio—is of unprecedented harmony that will replace social stratifica- tion. The new means of communication will bring strangers together. Such futuristic visions also reveal the character of prevailing assumptions about "technology" itself—the sort of entity it is. It often is depicted as if it were a palpable *thing*—a complicated kind of tool devised by a few geniuses, members of a technically gifted elite—and an embodiment of virtual autonomy and agency. "Technology" is tacitly accorded autonomous power in that its efficacy is perceived as largely unconstrained by the circumstances of its origin or dissemination, and it often is implicitly endowed with agency, as if it is inherently capable of making things happen—of determining the tenor of human behavior and, indeed, the course of human events.[2] As Negroponte contends, and all of us can plainly see, the new information technology is in fact having a profound effect on the way we live; in short, it looks like a primary causal agent of social change. But whether it will free humanity from the need to make painful political decisions, as hopeful futurists often suggest, seems unlikely.[3]

How, when, where, do these utopian expectations originate? Much of their origin is traceable, I believe, to certain historical developments in nineteenth-century America, and here I propose to examine two of the more important among them: one ideological, and the other material or, as it were, artifactual. Both changed the character and status of the mechanic arts, a change that helps to explain the emergence and, eventually, the popular currency of the very concept—the word—"technology." Although it may not be news to many people, it is important, if we are to develop a critical understanding of the way we think about technological innovation, to recognize that "technology" is a concept of relatively recent origin. The English word, in its current sense, did not exist at the time of the late eighteenth- and early nineteenth-century industrial revolution, when the material foundation of urban industrial capitalism—as exemplified by mechanized motive power (the steam engine), iron construction, the factory system, the railroad—was laid. At that time the word "technology" referred to a kind of book, or treatise, in the mechanic arts. Only in the first decades of this century did the word "technology"—in today's wider sense, referring to the mechanic arts themselves (collectively)—gain currency.

Cultural historians, it should be said, regard the emergence of a word (and concept) that acquires a pivotal role in public discourse (as "technology" has done) as a significant historical landmark. It is likely to mark an important, subtle, complex change in the society and culture. To assess the significance of such a new word, the historian compares it with its precursors: words that formerly had been its nearest equivalents. By examining the specific contexts in which the word first appeared, its emergence can be linked with other specific changes in the society and culture. Historians thus can account for the semantic void the word serves to fill; or, to be more specific, they can identify the ideas and feelings— the hitherto inexpressible views—to which the new word now provides expression. As the cultural critic Raymond Williams (1983) famously observed, there is a curious, complex reflexivity, or circularity, in this process. He noted that certain key words in his analysis of changes occurring in that era—words like *culture, class, democracy, industry*—had been called into existence by (or acquired wholly new meanings as a result of) the very historical developments he was analyzing. The same may be said, here, about the emergence of the concept, *technology*. This makes such analyses particularly challenging, for to explain why the concept was needed calls for an understanding of an absence, or "semantic void"—the inadequately developed state of the collective consciousness, or vocabulary, *before* the new word and concept's emergence.

In the case of "technology," the traditional terms that preceded its appearance included *mechanism* (as a mode of thought), *invention, mechanism* (a device), *machine*, and above all, the *mechanic* (or *useful* or *practical* or *industrial*) *arts*. But in English, "technology" (in our sense) did not come into general use until roughly the time of World War I.[4] Why was a new concept needed? What purposes did it serve that its precursors did not? Of course a new concept is not conceived in isolation: it arises within a specific cultural matrix, as an aspect of a collective mentality. Most of the precursors of "technology" just mentioned had prominent places in the vocabulary of "the Enlightenment Project," the name given recently to the movement of intellectuals committed to the superiority of scientific (or instrumental) rationality in the era, roughly, between 1750 and 1825. This project marked the great watershed between the feudal era and the emergence of democracy, the market economy, or, in a word, modernity.

A major ideological contribution of the Enlightenment Project was the idea of progress. But to call the new sense of progress an "idea," as if it were merely another among myriad ideas, is to trivialize it. Originally, to be sure, progress, in the obvious, unproblematic, common sense of the word—an advance toward a specific goal—was applied to many innovations of the great sixteenth- and seventeenth-century scientific revolution.

Progress was exemplified by radical innovations within such clearly bounded fields of research as those leading to the invention of, say, the microscope or telescope. By the time of the late eighteenth-century political revolutions (in America and France), however, progress was being made on so many fronts that it was extended to the entire course of human events. Now "progress" expressed the belief that history itself is a record of the steady, continuous, cumulative expansion of human knowledge of— and power over—nature, exemplified above all by advances in science and the mechanic arts, and that it will result in a general improvement in the human condition. Most of those who formulated the progressive ideology were radical republican revolutionaries (like Condorcet and Turgot, Paine and Priestley, Franklin and Jefferson); to them advances in science and the mechanic arts were merely the *means* of arriving at vital political *ends*: liberation from monarchical, aristocratic, and ecclesiastical domination, and the establishment of a more just, peaceful society.[5]

This hugely expanded, metaphysical idea of boundless Progress became the fulcrum of the dominant nineteenth-century secular world view. Over the last two hundred years, when exponents of Progress required an illustrative example, they almost always chose an innovation in the mechanic arts. For one thing, as John Stuart Mill (1865, p. 148) noted, the mere sight of a steam locomotive or other striking mechanical invention— wordlessly disseminates the belief that the present is (and hence the future also is likely to be) an improvement on the past. The universality of the nineteenth-century belief in Progress is indicated by the fact that it was embraced by both the most ardent apologists for industrial capitalism, and by its most cogent critics, the Marxists. The idea that history is inherently progressive plays a role in the culture of modernity comparable, in its centrality, to that of religious myths of origin in traditional, premodern cultures. All of which helps explain why technological innovations became the chief icons of the modern faith in Progress.

The belief in progress was pivotal in the official culture of the West in the nineteenth century, but the scope of that belief nonetheless was limited. Although it was ardently affirmed by spokespersons for the dominant groups in society—privileged, educated, articulate, property-owning white males north of the Mason-Dixon line—these groups did not include a large part, perhaps most, of the population. It is difficult, therefore, to establish the precise reach of such a belief system.[6] Still, we know there were groups whose experience was not comport with the prevailing faith in Progress.

A well-documented example of some relevance to our subject—the benefits that technological innovations offer to entry-level workers—is the celebrated case of the female labor force in the Lowell textile mills. In 1813 the Boston Associates, a group of wealthy merchant capitalists, built textile factories in Lowell, Massachusetts. To cope with a serious labor shortage, they set about recruiting young women from New England farms—their average age was nineteen or twenty—to work in their mills. Eager to avoid being associated with the British textile industry and its dismal reputation for exploiting and maltreating workers, especially women and children, the Lowell mill owners adopted a highly paternalistic set of practices. By today's standards, to be sure, work at the new mechanized looms was intolerably protracted, nerve-racking, and exhausting; the noise in the large, crowded workrooms was deafening, and during the first two decades or so the women worked six twelve-hour days a week. (This was not generally considered excessive at the time.) In many ways, indeed, the working conditions in the Lowell mills were considered ideal. The owners provided the women with newly built, clean dormitories staffed by matronly chaperons who were in effect the girls' moral guardians. On the whole, the owners succeeded in creating what was widely seen as a showcase of enlightened industrial capitalism. Famous visitors from all over the world—Charles Dickens among them—came to see, and in many cases to write about the exemplary Lowell factories and their lovely, rosy-cheeked, contented workers.

The Lowell mill girls were in fact an exceptional workforce. The owners carefully recruited the young women from New England farms for their health, their upright character, and their industriousness. Many of the women in turn assumed that they would work in the mills only long enough to accumulate a decent dowry; hence, they eagerly submitted to the rigorous discipline of factory life. (The only alternative for most was the prospect of lifelong spinsterhood on an isolated family farm.) Besides, they found it exciting to live in close quarters with their peers in town; at first they created a somewhat satisfying feminine workers' culture with a certain amount of social activity, including their own newspaper. In the early Lowell years, accordingly, they shared in the optimism associated with innovative technologies.

Before long, however, the Lowell mill girls' situation deteriorated. An economic recession in 1836 led the owners to demand more, faster work for less pay, and eventually the disenchanted women went on strike. Although they struck twice, they failed in their attempt to organize a durable labor union. Then, in the 1840s a wave of desperately poor Irish immigrants of both sexes, escapees from the Great Hunger, came to Lowell and competed for the women's jobs. The owners faced an increasingly competitive market; the American women soon lost most of their power to keep wages up; and ultimately much of the hope aroused by the Lowell venture was dashed. This sequence of events prefigured the disenchanting experience over the next century of many entry-level workers, especially women, in industries with new, innovative technologies. From a long-term perspective, it is true, the Lowell experiment may be seen as part of a process leading toward greater equality for women workers. It also should be noted that, unlike the factory system, which required the services of many largely unskilled workers, our new information technologies seem to be eradicating the need for precisely that kind of labor force. But perhaps the more important lesson, in the present context, is that new, innovative technologies seldom if ever have altered the fundamental economic structure, with its inherently stratified—and in recent decades increasingly stratified—distribution of wealth, power, and status.[7]

During the same years, popular spokesmen for the dominant culture like Daniel Webster were busy disseminating the ideology of progress, including the visionary idea, legacy of the Enlightenment, that innovations in science and the mechanic arts issue in universal social progress. That this remained the primary—the most widely expressed and almost certainly the most popular—response to new machines seems incontrovertible. The rhetoric habitually used to describe it expresses the unquestioning assurance of its exponents. Thus Webster, speaking at the opening ceremony for a new railroad at Lebanon, New Hampshire, in 1847, proclaimed:

It is an extraordinary era in which we live. It is altogether new. The world has seen nothing like it before. I will not pretend. No one can pretend to discern the end. But everybody knows that the age is remarkable for scientific research into the heavens, the earth and what is beneath the earth. And perhaps more remarkable still for the application of the scientific research to the pursuits of life. The ancients saw nothing like it. The moderns have seen nothing like it until the present generation. We see the ocean navigated and the solid land traversed by steam power and intelligence communicated by electricity. Truly this is a miraculous era. What is before us no one can say. What is upon us no one can hardly realize. The progress of the age has outstripped human belief. The future is known only to Omniscience. (Webster 1905)[8]

If Webster saw the railroad as a miracle that outstripped human belief, what might he have said about our electronic technologies! Indeed, it is precisely their power to evoke awe and wonder that often leads us to depict them in cloudy, undiscriminating language. Notice, in any case, that Webster did not use—possibly did not even know—the word technology. Nevertheless, his speech illustrates two kinds of change that help to explain the advent of this new concept. The first is his evident belief that mechanical innovations, in themselves, confirm the reality of—indeed constitute—historical progress. This marked a subtle, highly significant change in the doctrine of progress that initially had been formulated by the radical republican thinkers of the revolutionary generation of the late eighteenth century. They valued scientific and mechanical innovations chiefly as a means of reaching a political goal: a less hierarchical, more peaceful, just polity—a republican government based on the consent of the governed. By Webster's time, however, that political criterion of progress had lost much of its force. Many Americans complacently assumed that the political aims of the revolution had been achieved, and others—especially the wealthy captains of the new manufacturing industries—now regarded economic growth as the primary criterion of progress. Thus Webster assumes that the stunning innovations of science and the mechanic arts, and their "application … to the pursuits of life," provide a sufficient confirmation of the progressive faith. Compared with precursor terms like "mechanic arts," the term "technology," by virtue of its inclusive, nonarti-factual, nonspecific character, accords with the generalizing, reified, well-nigh metaphysical tenor of the faith in universal Progress.

Webster's own career illustrates the elevation of material pros-perity to supremacy over the fulfillment of political principles as the chief criterion of progress. Originally, he had been a senator from New Hampshire, but he later changed his residence to Massachusetts largely to represent the new manufacturing interests. For him the identification of technological innovation and its benefits with the political agenda of the economically privileged was obvious, unproblematic, or, in a word, natural. He accepted a regular secret retainer from Nicholas Biddle, head of the national bank. And three years after the Lebanon speech, Webster lost many of his best-known New England followers, notably Emerson and the Concord intellectuals, when he endorsed the Compromise of 1850, which included the infamous Fugitive Slave Law requiring every citizen to assist in the capture of escaped slaves—or face being charged with a felony. Issues of social justice clearly had become less important to Webster than the economic well-being of his constituents, the textile manufacturers who relied on slave-produced cotton as their chief raw material. This attitude comported with his fervent praise of the scientific and technological innovations which were a primary basis for their growing wealth.

The second precondition for the emergence of the new concept of technology marked by Webster's speech is an implicit change in the material, or artifactual, character of the mechanic arts. This change also is exemplified by the new steam locomotives or, rather, by the new railroad systems. Previously, the chief icons of innovation in the mechanic arts had been single pieces of equipment—free-standing devices like the spinning machine, the stocking frame, the power loom, or the steam engine. (That phase of the industrial revolution was widely referred to as the "Age of the Machine.") In the railroad era, however, particular mechanical artifacts, like the steam locomotive, were incorporated into increasingly elaborate systems with many more nonartifactual components. In tracing the origins of professional management, Alfred Chandler (1977) demonstrated how a large system like the railroad made it imperative to replace the traditional family firm, characteristically run by a father and his sons, with the newly invented large, impersonal, professionally managed corporation. In addition to the locomotive, therefore, a railroad consists of thousands of miles of track, many cars and other pieces of equipment, including telegraph lines—all operated by a specially trained workforce: engineers, switchmen, conductors, telegraphers, and skilled managers, on duty night and day, in every kind of weather, operating many trains traveling over all kinds of terrain every season of the year. The railroad, like other burgeoning new technological systems, required all sorts of basic changes in social behavior, such as the new mode of timekeeping by fixed geographical zones made necessary by the exact timing and safety requirements of railroad schedules. A railroad, far from being a single tool-like device, or machine, is a complex system of which the mechanical parts—the "technology" in the literal sense—are only one component.

In the late nineteenth century, innovations in the mechanic arts increasingly took on the character of such large complex systems: the electric power-generating-and-delivery system, the telephone system, the mass production (assembly-line) system of the automobile manufacture-and-use industry, the airline system, or—coming down to yesterday—the worldwide information superhighway. In addition to their material components (or "hardware"), these systems invariably require special bodies of technical knowledge and skill: knowledge that increasingly consisted of—or drew upon—advances in physics, chemistry, biology, and the other sciences[9]; professional education or training in those skills; a cohort of specialized workers and managers; the production or manufacture of raw materials and components; access to ancillary materials, and so on. These complex systems were so extensive, and they entailed such a wide range of practices, that they far outreached the conventional denotations of terms like "the mechanic [or practical, or industrial] arts," or "the machine." This increasing disparity between the language and its presumed referents —the entities to which it was supposed to refer—created the semantic void that "technology" gradually filled.

What makes the emergence of the concept of "technology" significant, especially when used as a singular noun, is the heavy load of ideological assumptions that it carries—particularly when used in the singular. To see this, one need only compare the connotations of its precursors, "the mechanic [or 'useful' or 'practical'] arts," with those of "technology." The mechanic arts conjure up the image of a craftsman at a workbench; he has a special artisanal skill (carpentry, machine-tool making, plumbing, welding): he is a manual worker in soiled overalls. It is noteworthy that "mechanic arts" is a plural term—it distinguishes them from the expressive (or 'fine' or 'high' arts)—whereas "technology" is routinely used in the singular.[10] It is in fact a bloodless abstraction that represents no particular person or thing, no specific skill, vocation, or other institution; so far as it conjures up a vocational type, it is a crisply dressed technician peering at an instrument panel, console, or computer screen. "Technology" carries a distinctive aura of disinterested, precise, scientific measurement quite unlike the rule-of-thumb mode of the mechanic arts.

Particularly relevant here is the tendency, beginning when the concept first gained currency, to see "technology" as a substitute for political means of resolving problems. In the writings of Veblen, who began publishing at the turn of the century, and who taught at the New School for social research after World War I; in Frederick Winslow Taylor's application of "scientific" principles to the discipline of the workplace; and in the avowedly political "technocracy" movement led by Howard Scott in the 1930s, technology was presented as a more efficient, rational, and effective mode of resolving difficult social problems than the usual mode of political debate and conflict. This vein of utopian thinking, which was implicit in Webster's rhetoric, is often made explicit. Take, for example, Nicholas Negroponte's 1994 proposal for meeting the problem of homelessness by giving each homeless person a laptop computer, or the tendency to see the new information technology as a panacea for the problems of the inner-city population.

Indeed, it is precisely the abstract, bloodless, indeterminate quality—the ambiguity—of the concept of "technology" that accounts for its marked affinity with the new era, and for its susceptibility to mystification or metaphysicalization. As the line between the literal mechanical (artifactual) and other (human, socioeconomic, or ideological) components of the large new systems became blurred, it also became difficult to locate the boundaries separating these systems from the rest of society and culture. What, in fact, are the defining attributes of such a technology? Where do we draw the boundary between it and the rest of culture? Take, for example, the automobile. Apart from the internal combustion engine—or the vehicle itself—which aspect do we include in the rubric of automotive technology? The production industry—say, the Ford (or other) Motor Company—with its assembly lines, engineers, workers, dealers, delivery systems? What about the "feeder" industries: steel, glass, rubber, aluminum, plastic, petroleum? (Petroleum, with its oil fields, ships, refineries, delivery systems, and service stations, is a vast worldwide system in itself.) Or the road-building and road maintenance industries? Trucking? The automobile regulatory agencies? The automotive engineering profession? The list could be extended. In all its aspects, indeed, automotive technology has been said to encompass about 25 percent of the American workforce and a large part of the nation's material armature. It is impossible, finally, to make any sensible distinction between American "society" today and this or other major (technological) systems of production, transportation, and communication. To speak, as we habitually do, about the "impact" of the automobile "on" society is misleading: it is like speaking of the "impact" of the bone structure or the nervous system on the human body. By now these systems are inextricably embedded in—they are constitutive of—the whole society and culture. If all our automobiles or electric power stations stopped functioning, the society would be paralyzed.

In American public speech nowadays we incessantly hear "technology" invoked as if it were an entity that possesses autonomy and agency —an independent capacity to change things. And yet, paradoxically, if you ask Americans what a "technology" is, my impression is that most people still think of it as a kind of *thing*—a tool-like machine or device, in which case it is a magical thing, an all-powerful agent of change, bearer of the historical legacy I have tried to describe. Inherent in it is a capacity to generate Progress and to determine the direction of social change. It is not surprising, under the circumstances, that many of us invest hope in the new information technologies as a cure-all for deprived inner-city populations.

The primary significance of information technologies today, however, is their pivotal role in the new, postmodern global economy. They make possible the instantaneous global transmission of financial and other economic data, as well as the mass-produced products of popular culture or "infotainment." They are a vital part of the technical armature of the transnational corporate economy, and of an emerging worldwide popular culture. They surely herald sweeping, unpredictable global change. But it is important to take account of the effect the new order is having on corporate employment, especially the process of "downsizing" that entails the dismissal of thousands of highly qualified, experienced, well-educated, white employees. Is it realistic, under the circumstances, to expect the advent of the new information technologies to resolve the specific problems of the inner-city population? If the historical record is any indication, these innovations by themselves are most unlikely to ameliorate the deprivations that afflict residents of the inner city. Only by attacking their problems within the larger historical, cultural, and socioeconomic matrix that generated them, are they likely to devise effective ways to use the new technologies. But that is another subject. Meanwhile, the chief lesson to be drawn from the history of technological innovation and its social consequences in the United States is largely cautionary. Although the new information technologies surely will help to effect many radical changes in our society, it would be foolish to rely on them as a "fix" for the afflictions of racial and economic injustice.

Notes

1. For a helpful general survey, see Segal (1985).

2. On the autonomous character of technology, see Langdon Winner, *Autonomous Technology: Techniques-Out-of-Control as a Theme in Political Thought* (Cambridge: MIT Press, 1977); on technology as the primary agent of social change, see David F. Noble, *America By Design: Science, Technology, and the Rise of Corporate Capitalism* (New York: Knopf, 1977), and Leo Marx, "American Literary Culture and the Fatalistic View of Technology," in *The Pilot and the Passenger: Essays on Literature, Technology, and Culture in the United States* (New York: Oxford University Press, 1988), pp. 179–207.

3. For a critical assessment of this view, see Merritt Roe Smith and Leo Marx, eds., *Does Technology Drive History? The Dilemma of Technological Determinism* (Cambridge: MIT Press, 1995).

4. Jacob Bigelow, a physician and Harvard professor, was a pioneer in attaching the new meaning to the word in a series of lectures, published as *Elements of Technology* (Boston: Boston Press, 1829). No comprehensive history of the concept technology presently exists.

5. For a recent collection of critical essays assessing the new implications of the progressive world view, see Leo Marx and Bruce Mazlish, eds., *Progress: Fact or Illusion?* (Ann Arbor: University of Michigan Press, 1996).

6. Since the largely written sources on which historians rely tend to reflect the views of the most privileged groups, the extent to which the contrary-minded, less privileged, less articulate members of society—the poor and propertyless and illiterate; the women,

children, servants, and slaves—actually embraced the dominant belief system is never easy to establish. But there is every reason to assume that a sizable fraction of the under-privileged was less enthusiastic, if not downright skeptical, about the doctrine of universal progress.

7. For an illuminating survey of the Lowell experiment, see Thomas Dublin, *Women at Work* (New York: 1979).

8. Opening of the Northern Railroad, remarks made at Lebanon, New Hampshire, in *The Writings and Speeches of Daniel Webster* (Boston: 1905), IV, 105–117. For a more detailed analysis of Webster's ambivalent feelings about the new technology, see Leo Marx, *The Machine in the Garden: Technology and the Pastoral Ideal in America* (New York: Oxford University Press, 1964), pp. 209–215.

9. The extensive convergence, in the nineteenth century, of science and technology—especially in the emergence of the science-based electrical and chemical industries—probably deserves (if space allows) treatment as a separate factor contributing to the transition from the single technical device to the large complex system and, consequently, to the advent of the concept of technology.

10. The importance of this distinction, for my argument, cannot be exaggerated. References to "technology" used in the singular, without any specifying adjective (e.g., computer technology), as the name of an entire class of things and practices, are hospitable to many kinds of mystification to which references, explicit or implied, to particular "technologies" are not.

References

Chandler, Jr., Alfred D. 1977. *The Visible Hand: The Managerial Revolution in American Business*. Cambridge MA: Harvard University Press.

Mill, John Stuart. 1865. "M. de Tocqueville on Democracy in America." *Edinburgh Review*, October, 1840, rpt. *Dissertations and Discussions: Political, Philosophical, and Historical*. Boston. 2:148.

Negroponte, Nicholas. 1994. Op-Ed page essay, *The New York Times*, December 16.

Negroponte, Nicholas. 1995. *Being Digital*. Cambridge, MA: MIT Press.

Nye, David. 1990. *Electrifying America: Social Meanings of a New Technology*. Cambridge, MA: MIT Press.

Webster, Daniel. 1905. "Opening of the Northern Railroad." In *The Writings and Speeches of Daniel Webster*. Boston. 4:105–117.

Williams, Raymond. 1983. *Culture & Society: 1780–1950*. New York: Columbia University Press. Originally published in 1958.

Part II: Strategies of Action

6. Equitable Access to the Online World

William J. Mitchell

When access to jobs and services is delivered electronically, those who have good network connections will have an advantage, whereas those with poor service or no service will be disadvantaged and marginalized. So common justice clearly demands that we should strive for equitable access—and, in particular, to ensure that members of low-income communities are not further disadvantaged by exclusion from the digital world. But this goal—although simply stated—probably cannot be achieved in any simple way. The problem turns out to be complex and multilayered, requiring a combination of measures for its solution.

Getting Connected

Becoming connected to a new kind of utility is the most obvious problem. As with water, sewer, gas, and electric service, members of low-income communities need to get the "pipes"—in this case, pipes for digital information—connected to their homes, workplaces, schools, libraries, community centers, and other potentially important delivery points. The connections must be reliable and provide enough bandwidth for effective use; a system that is overloaded, slow, and goes down all the time provides little real benefit.

Connections should also be two-way, and—I would argue—symmetrical. One-way connections, like those established by broadcast media, create a rigid division between producers and consumers of information. Asymmetrical two-way connections, like those established by cable television systems, allow large quantities of information to flow in one direction but only allow a trickle to flow back. Two-way symmetrical connections, as in a telephone conversation, allow exchanges of information on an equal footing; this is an important dimension of equity in the digital world.

Alternative Means

Many competing ways are available to provide the necessary connections to the Internet and other digital networks, and these have different costs and qualities. The existing telephone network offers the most straightforward, short-term solution in most contexts. You can buy a modem, subscribe to an Internet access provider or a bulletin board system, and make dial-in connections. If the provider is reasonably close by, the cost of an online session is typically that of a local telephone call plus a fee charged by the provider. The fundamental limitation is that dial-in connections operate at limited speed—at the time of writing, the speed of a 14.4 or 28.8 kbps modem; this is good for electronic mail, marginally adequate for access to graphic World Wide Web pages, and unacceptable for videoconferencing.

Higher speed access, at higher cost, can be provided via ISDN connection. With a single line you can surf the Web more effectively than with a standard telephone connection, and with multiple lines you can get the speed needed for reasonably good videoconferencing. The technology is not new, but by the mid-1990s telecommunications providers had deployed it very unevenly, both within the United States and internationally; in some areas it was readily and inexpensively available, and in others it was not.

A third alternative is to employ cable modems and existing cable television networks. This has some attractions, because it employs existing, widely available infrastructure, and it can provide high-speed connections. But cable networks do not have the sophisticated switching capabilities of telephone networks, and considerable doubt exists about whether they could actually provide high-quality interactive access to large numbers of users; certainly this had not been convincingly demonstrated, on any significant scale, at the time of writing.

If you have the capacity to make a major investment, you can buy or lease a dedicated high-speed line that connects you directly to the high-speed backbone of the Internet or some private network. This solves the technical problem, but it is unlikely to be a feasible option in most low-income community contexts.

Finally, you might get access wirelessly, using cellular telephone or pager systems, satellites, and the like. This eliminates the need to run wires or cables, so it is particularly appropriate for mobile connections in developing countries, where there is suddenly a great need for service but little wired infrastructure in place, and in isolated rural settings. But it differs fundamentally from wired connection in that there is only a limited amount of communication capacity in the electromagnetic spectrum, while we can always create more wired capacity by laying more cables. This means that wireless connections are often expensive, and that—although they will continue to have their uses—they are unlikely to provide the long-term solution to the problem of providing good, high-speed connections to large numbers of users.

Who Pays and Who Plays?

To make connections to end users, infrastructure investments are typically necessary at several levels. These investments need to be paid for somehow. And levels of accessibility to particular groups and locations are often determined, in practice, by who pays and how.

At the largest scale, long-distance telecommunications providers lay high-speed cables on land and under the sea, deploy satellites, and seek returns on these large investments. Local telecommunications providers wire cities and want to take their cut. Corporations, universities, and other organizations arrange and pay for their own on-site infrastructures. Ultimately, someone has to run wires through buildings to points of use, and lack of this last link in the chain can often be a significant barrier to delivery of services to inhabitants of old and poorly maintained structures —such as inner-city schools. Increasingly, these various types of infrastructures are integrated into one complex, multilayered, international system involving many different providers and employing many different media —twisted pair, coaxial cable, optical fiber, and wireless transmission.

Service providers can potentially use a variety of methods to account and recover costs. They can charge monthly or yearly fees for connection and unlimited use; this is simple, but it penalizes light users and favors heavy ones. They can meter connect time and charge for it; this is more complex, and it discourages experimental, exploratory uses. They can charge by the transaction, or by numbers of messages sent or received —which can be onerous; for example, e-mail users in some developing countries are charged high rates for each message *received*, which makes junk e-mail very unwelcome. They can provide "free" services supported by advertising; these services may become the last resort of those who cannot pay to avoid them. And—as in the so-called Free-Nets and in volunteer bulletin board services—they can use various combinations of tax dollars, charitable contributions, and volunteer efforts to provide generally available services for the public good.

The implications are obvious. Unless somebody is willing and able to make the infrastructure investments necessary to provide connectivity in a low-income community, that community will remain without service. Even if connectivity is physically available, there will be little actual use if prices are too high or if pricing strategies and structures create disincentives for significant numbers of users. And generally, the quality and sophistication of service will depend on the income stream that supports it; premium commercial services are usually a lot better than shoe-string, volunteer Free-Nets or bulletin board services.

Markets and Regulators

Similar problems were faced in the past, as the telephone system grew. In many parts of the world these problems were solved, with some effectiveness, by adopting universal access policies. Essentially, regulators offered monopolies or near monopolies to telephone service providers in return for commitments to provide services at uniform prices not only where it was profitable to do so, but also where it was not. This usually meant that lucrative service to businesses, and to the more affluent urban residential areas, cross-subsidized service to much less profitable rural and low-income residential areas. It became a means of redistribution and spatial equalization.

From an equity perspective, universal access policies seem an attractive way of assuring that the potential benefits of digital telecommunications extend to low-income communities. Providers and free-market advocates typically counter that this is simply not realistic—at least in the short term. They point out that the adventurous early adopters of new telecommunications technology are too few in number to allow providers to benefit from economies of scale, so providers will only have sufficient incentive to roll out new services if they can do so first in the markets that are willing and able to pay premium prices.

The standard arguments on both sides are well known. Battles over who gets service, when, and at what price will continue to be fought among large and powerful players both in business and in the public policy arena. Where market forces have the upper hand, it is not easy to be optimistic that low-income communities will be well served. But it is also probably true that overly restrictive regulation will simply mean that *nobody* gets advanced service for a very long time.

Low-Cost Access Appliances

Unfortunately, having the digital "pipes" is not enough; you do not have useful access unless you have an appropriate electronic appliance to connect to them. Typically, such appliances have been expensive—creating another access barrier for low-income communities. But this is likely to change as the demand for access grows, as the market for inexpensive access devices correspondingly expands, and as industrial capacity to serve that market develops.

As the Internet and commercial online services were growing explosively in the mid-1990s, the standard appliance at the user end was a personal computer. Despite great advantages in computer technology and the development of a huge market, the prices of personal computers were high compared with other household items (considerably more than a television set or a refrigerator but less than an automobile), and had remained quite stable for many years—essentially because manufacturers had chosen to increase performance at a given price point as the technology improved, rather than to keep performance at roughly the same level and drop the price. The market, apparently, would bear it. By 1997, however, some manufacturers were finding it attractive to seek the lower end of the market by introducing very low-cost models at about the price of a good color television set, and others were radically rethinking the basic idea of a personal computer—leading them to experiment with greatly simplified machines that could not operate independently, but could be very effective when drawing on the resources of a network.

At about the same time, we saw the introduction of inexpensive set-top boxes that converted ordinary television sets into World Wide Web access devices. And, as the French Minitel system had been demonstrating for years, it was also possible to think of providing network access through a more sophisticated version of the humble telephone.

In general, the possibility of widespread connectivity in low-income communities depends not only on sufficiently inexpensive network access, but also on the capacity of the computer and consumer electronics industries to produce effective, inexpensive access appliances. The evidence of progress in this direction is growing. In the meantime, as long as access devices remain relatively expensive, it will be crucially important, at least, to provide as many of them as possible at strategic central locations, such as schools and libraries, in low-income communities.

Appropriate Software

If we could somehow put a powerful UNIX workstation, connected by high-speed link to the Internet, into every home in the country, we would still not have provided wide accessibility. The technical capability would certainly be there, but most people would find these machines far too complex and difficult to operate. Well-educated younger people probably would not have much trouble, but the poorly educated, the elderly, those who did not speak English, many of the disabled, and those who found the look and feel of these machines intimidating, would encounter a barrier. There is, then, a further need—for interface software that is easy and attractive to use.

An important step in this direction was taken in the mid-1990s, when graphic browsers for the World Wide Web first appeared—first NCSA Mosaic, then Netscape and others. These proved to be very simple to use, and opened the way for the Web to grow explosively. Soon after, classification and search services such as Yahoo made the Web surfer's life even easier. These pieces of software and related online services were aimed at mass markets, so they were made available free of charge or at very low cost.

It might seem that the software problem had largely been solved at this point, but it is worth observing that most Web content and tools of this era were squarely directed at well-educated, middle-class, English speakers. You were out of luck if you were illiterate, or if you spoke another language, or if the presentation of material seemed alien and forbidding. Despite the Web's growing popularity, many subgroups of society—particularly those already marginalized—were not effectively served by it.

The Consequences of Commercialization

The Internet and the World Wide Web initially developed as mechanisms for the unrestricted interchange of information within the academic world. To most users they presented themselves as free resources; individual users generally were not charged for connect time, for access to Web sites, or for transmission of e-mail messages. In the mid-1990s, however, the Internet and the Web experienced rapid commercialization; a much wider range of online products and services developed, and creators of many of these products and services—naturally enough—were interested in making money from them. Pundits, venture capitalists, and Wall Street analysts began to recognize that providing online content (that is, adding value to bits) could be a much better business than merely providing the channels and servers to pump the bits around. Consequently, the culture of the Internet and the Web began to change rapidly.

One way to make money from a Web site is to sell advertising on it, so Web advertising quickly proliferated. Another way is to impose access controls, then charge for entry to the site. The charge might be a subscription on the magazine model. It might be on an event-by-event or download-by-download model, as with movie theaters and pay-per-view television. Or it might be by connect time—a common strategy for access to premium database services.

A consequence of this growing commercialization is that general access to the Internet and the Web is no longer enough. To get access to some of the most valuable services, you now must have a way of paying for them—which can be another problem for low-income communities. So, for example, an online encyclopedia provides no benefit to a school in a low-income community if the school does not have the funds to pay the access fees. A real danger exists that, in a commercialized online world, the most valuable products and services will be available only to the affluent.

One bright spot in this picture, however, is that online intellectual property does not behave like more traditional kinds of intellectual property. If a provider gives away a copy of a print encyclopedia or some seats at a showing of a movie, there is usually an appreciable loss of sales income—which obviously limits the capacity of even the most socially conscious and generous providers to extend these services to those who cannot pay. But providing a poor school with a free subscription to an online encyclopedia costs very little, and probably has a negligible effect on sales income; the only downside for the provider is a little more server traffic. So, one very positive consequence of the growing commercialization of the Internet and the Web, and of the online publication of increasing quantities of valuable educational and other material, is that this material —once available online—can potentially reach segments of society that would otherwise be denied it. There is scope here both for public policy initiatives and for private charitable efforts.

Servers Too

Another bright spot is that the Internet and the Web inherently can provide much wider access to the means of publication and distribution than print, radio, or television. Anyone with a relatively powerful personal computer, some inexpensive software, and a reasonably good Internet connection can set up a Web site and publish material to the whole world. Costs are low and distribution is very effective. So, if mainstream media do not find it worthwhile to serve low-income communities, or simply choose to ignore marginalized groups, an effective, low-cost alternative is now widely available. A few hours surfing the Web will quickly demonstrate that many such groups are already making effective use of it.

One model for providing server access in low-income communities is to make servers available as public resources at schools, libraries, community centers, and storefront computer access centers. (As long as you can log in remotely, a server does not actually have to be there, on the spot—but you do need an account, some disk space, and a machine from which to operate.) This provides teachers, librarians, ministers, local merchants, and community activists with a way to publish material of value and interest within the community, to create "community memories" such as local history sites, and to make the community's resources and potential visible to the outside world. Another model is to treat servers as engines of economic advancement, and to find ways of encouraging entrepreneurial efforts to supply online products and services from within low-income communities. In any case, the important point is that accessibility should not be defined just in terms of consuming online products and services, but also in terms of producing them.

Skills and Motivation

Even if all the technological and economic barriers described here can be overcome, and the members of a low-income community do have effective electronic access to services and economic opportunities, they still may not make much use of that access. If important usage is to develop, community members must be motivated—in other words, they must feel that it is worth their time and effort—and they must have the necessary skills. And we should not assume that the motivating factors at work in more-affluent and better-educated communities will have the same effect in low-income communities, where so far little direct experience of the benefits of the digital revolution has been realized, and where the buzz generated by *Wired* and the business pages of the *Wall Street Journal* is less likely to resonate.

Schools have a vital part to play here. They are natural sites for establishing access points, they can benefit immediately from use of online material, and children usually have less difficulty than their elders in engaging computer technology. Wiring schools, training teachers, and educating students for the digital world is probably the most effective strategy for using the very scarce human and economic resources that are likely to be available to assure that low-income communities will not be left hopelessly behind. Volunteer, foundation-funded, and government-funded computer clubhouses and storefront drop-in centers can play important complementary roles.

It is sometimes objected that such efforts divert resources from even more basic and desperate needs. This is clearly a danger to consider carefully. But it will be less and less of an issue as computer networks grow in importance as deliverers of important services and economic opportunities.

Conclusions

Throughout history, the affluent and the privileged have been in a far better position to benefit immediately from new technologies than the poor and the marginalized. Other things being equal, the same will be true of digital technology and computer networks; low-income communities will probably find it more difficult than affluent ones to get wired and connected, they will be less able to pay for the necessary electronic appliances, they will not be such attractive markets for software and online content, and they have fewer resources to educate their members to meet the new challenges and opportunities of the digital age. In the longer term, however, digital technology should have a powerful equalizing effect by delivering services and opportunities to those who would otherwise be excluded by location or lack of mobility, and by creating products and services that can be shared widely at very low cost. The great challenge before us is to find ways of mitigating the short-term problems while moving as rapidly as possible to achieve the long-term benefits.

7. Information Technologies that Change Relationships between Low-Income Communities and the Public, and Nonprofit Agencies that Serve Them

Joseph Ferreira, Jr.

What are the prospective benefits for service providers and service recipients of decentralized access to information about populations and their needs, service systems, and operations? Will growing access to such information be, on the whole, enfranchising for community members, or will it subject them to increased centralized control? This chapter examines particular ways in which information technologies (IT) can make land-use planning (and other aspects of metropolitan evolution) more transparent and understandable to individuals and communities. The point is not that such a use of IT is possible; rather, it is to better understand how it might empower or disenfranchise low-income communities, promote efficiency through improved self-governance, or further centralize authority in the hands of government and other large-scale data providers.

I begin by focusing on a simple, seemingly straightforward example of the use of IT: to computerize inquiries about land use and ownership of land and property in the city. This "simple" example of decentralized data access becomes complicated, however, as soon as the issues of maintenance and updating are addressed. Moreover, various IT strategies for addressing these issues have significantly different impacts on whether or not data access promotes effective decentralization and citizen empowerment. A careful examination of some of the issues and options involved in this simple example improves our ability to draw inferences about how access to information can and should foster improved metropolitan governance and broader public participation in urban and regional planning. The real potential for capitalizing on IT to improve governance is not simply a matter of automating government services, nor is it a question of whether or not to introduce IT. Shaping planning processes to capitalize on IT are crucial in improving local governance through reduced bureaucracy and devolution of authority. My reasoning is consistent with recent observations in the management literature by Shoshana Zuboff, Tom Peters, and others about IT-driven restructuring of work in U.S. corporations (Peters 1992; Zuboff 1988).

Supporting Urban Revitalization with Data and Information Systems

The role and relevance of information in urban planning is a broad, complex, and much-debated issue (Harris 1989; Innes 1995, Schön 1983).

Here I focus on a few practices (of data gathering and analysis) that are common in urban revitalization, concentrating on how the design and implementation of a metropolitan area's information infrastructure can affect the usefulness of such practices to constituencies typically involved in urban revitalization.

Urban planning can be about the public investment, authorization, and support for improved infrastructure (roads, transit, water and sewer, etc.), and for other public works and services (parks, buildings, public housing, garbage collection, job training, public safety, health care, etc.). It can also be about the regulatory processes that set, monitor, and enforce land-use and zoning regulations, environmental controls, economic development incentives, design guidelines, and the like. Land-use functions—the focus of this chapter—are typically undertaken by institutions that exist in different sectors (public, private, and nonprofit) and at different levels of government (federal, state, metropolitan, city, and neighborhood). In Boston, for example, the Boston Redevelopment Authority (BRA) plays a key role in land-use planning. It is usually responsible for planning studies of major real estate investment projects such as Government Center, the Prudential Center complex, and more recently, the controversial "megaplex" proposals to develop a convention center and related commercial and sports facilities in South Boston. But the Boston Housing Authority (BHA), which owns and manages housing for more than 10 percent of the city's residents, is the lead agency for two Housing and Urban Development (HUD)-financed urban revitalization demonstration programs costing more than $80 million over a five-year period. Neither authority is completely under the mayor's control, nor are they the only citywide agencies with significant authority in land-use planning. Boston's Public Facilities Department (PFD) is responsible for land and facilities owned by the city (including, for example, abandoned property); it is also heavily involved in Boston's "Empowerment Zone" planning.[1]

Other federal-, state-, and metropolitan-level agencies and authorities are also significant players in urban redevelopment. HUD and the Massachusetts Housing Finance Agency (MHFA) are major underwriters of subsidized housing in the region; the Massachusetts Water Resource Authority (MWRA) is in the midst of multi-billion dollar projects to upgrade the region's water and sewer system; and the Central Artery

Project is managing the $7 billion decade-long transportation improvement project to sink Boston's Central Artery and build a third harbor tunnel. Also, the Massachusetts Bay Transit Authority (MBTA) and related transit and transportation planning agencies have a considerable impact (through their control of transit routes and transportation investment) on the accessibility of inner-city residents to jobs and services; and federal and state environmental protection agencies regulate the reuse of the many "brownfields"[2] in inner-city areas that have questionable land-use history.

Private agencies are also important in land-use planning. The Metropolitan Boston Housing Partnership (MBHP), a regional nonprofit organization, manages the pass-through of state and federal housing subsidies for more than five thousand households. Along with large landlords, community development corporations, neighborhood and church associations, private developers, and the like, such groups represent significant interests and planning/management capabilities that are vocal, more or less organized to represent their interests, and likely to grow in size and/or number as federal efforts continue to decentralize control of programs for housing, economic development, and social services.

To develop new land-use plans and proposals (or to form opinions as new opportunities and proposals surface), all of these agencies typically spend considerable energy researching and analyzing land use and ownership in the neighborhoods surrounding the sites that are targeted in the plans. This work (along with other related studies) is then used to develop tables, charts, and maps that summarize patterns of land-use and ownership and that estimate the size and nature of changes in both the physical and socioeconomic environment that are likely to result from one or another of the proposed changes in land use.[3] For large proposals with relatively formal review and approval processes, the results of this work are typically included in an environmental impact assessment (EIA) report and/or in various related planning reports and documents that critique, amend, or expand upon the EIA. In the case of large and controversial projects, the public review process can be long and complex; and public (or mandated private) funds are often used for separate studies and technical reports, so different interest groups can be more evenly balanced as they debate relevant issues and expectations.

The land-use and ownership studies are only one part of a complex land-use planning process, and their effects on urban revitalization are indirect. Nevertheless, they help us explore the planning uses of emerging computing technologies, because they show how unexpected difficulties can arise in a seemingly simple data-processing setting. And, these difficulties highlight a generic issue. Much urban planning focuses on understanding places and spatial relationships. Computing technologies have only recently had the horsepower and computer graphics tools to track, digest, and visualize complex urban settings. But to understand the plans and build consensus on action, we need to integrate and reinterpret many data sources now dispersed among agencies and groups that are administratively isolated and focused on different issues and goals. Moreover, they often use different accounting systems to name, measure, and value urban activity.

Although I am optimistic about our learning to deal with these difficulties, the devil is in the details. In forecasting the impacts of computing technologies, it is often easy to take for granted elementary operations that bog down when they assume the scale and complexity needed to address real-world settings. This is especially true if, as I believe, the important benefits of data-processing systems for urban planning are not so much in gaining *access* to detailed urban data, but in having *decentralized* access in a way that allows *meaningful dialogue* as part of an ongoing planning process of design, discussion, and consensus building across many diverse and relatively autonomous groups. With this in mind, I examine how Boston's parcel database is used to identify and categorize land-use and ownership patterns. I then discuss how emerging information technologies might assist us in the development of improved planning for urban revitalization.

Researching Land-Use and Ownership Patterns

As suggested earlier, many neighborhood planning activities—from economic development studies and urban revitalization projects to community organizing, community development corporations (CDC) development, and site planning—begin with a study of patterns of land use and ownership. In the old days this meant spending considerable time in the Assessor's Office and at the Registry of Deeds. Today, most parcel owner-

Table 7.1: Sample parcel data for residential housing in East Boston

PARCEL_ID	OWNER	NO	STREET	USE	LANDVAL (dollars)	BUILDVA (dollars)	LOTSIZE (sq. ft.)
0100001000	PASCUCCI CARLO	105A	PUTNAM ST	R3	39400	55500	1,150
0100002000	MASTRORILLO ANGELO P	197	LEXINGTON ST	R3	39400	59600	1,150
0100003000	HASELTON PETER	199	LEXINGTON ST	R3	39400	48400	1,150
0100004000	DILLON KELLEY A	201	LEXINGTON ST	R3	39400	73400	1,150
0100005000	DIGIROLAMO JOHN F	203	LEXINGTON ST	R2	40900	73700	2,010
0100006000	BOTTE FRANK A	205	LEXINGTON ST	R3	41600	65100	2,500
0100007000	PORCELLA RACHELA	209	LEXINGTON ST	R3	41600	79700	2,500
0100021000	CIOTO ROBERT	245H	LEXINGTON ST	R1	39200	37900	1,238
0100022000	CAHILL STEPHEN F	245	LEXINGTON ST	R3	41200	72300	2,250
0100023000	MIANO MARIA ETAL	247	LEXINGTON ST	R3	39800	54300	1,838
0100024000	SHEA RAFFAELA	249	LEXINGTON ST	R3	40100	67800	1,835
0100026000	CARUSO SYLVIA HELEN	31	PRESCOTT ST	R1	39300	42700	1,263
0100027000	PATTI RALPH ETAL	33	PRESCOTT ST	R1	39700	70000	1,650
0100028000	MELE ANTHONY	35	PRESCOTT ST	R2	39700	68400	1,650
0100029000	STEWART ROBERT	37	PRESCOTT ST	R3	39600	87900	1,700
0100030000	SLOWEY JAMES J	252	PRINCETON ST	R3	41600	95300	2,500
0100031000	BOSSI MICHAEL ETAL	250	PRINCETON ST	R3	41600	99200	2,500
0100032000	TONTODONATO SANDRA M	248	PRINCETON ST	R1	41600	61900	2,500
0100033000	MARSIGLIA MARILYN G	246	PRINCETON ST	R1	41600	43100	2,500
0100034000	CAPO JOHN A & MARY B	244	PRINCETON ST	R2	41600	61200	2,500

Source: Boston Assessing Office data from February 1, 1996,
Parcel Records for Boston, Massachusetts.

ship and land-use records are computerized, so that information can be obtained by searching digital databases for a parcel's address, owner name, and the like. A sample of such parcel data for one- to three-family residential housing in East Boston is shown in Table 7.1.[4] The addresses and owner names are shown for several dozen residential parcels, along with their lot sizes and the February 1, 1996, assessed values for the land and buildings. In many U.S. cities and counties electronic access to such parcel data is provided from terminals in a limited number of government offices through the use of database applications. These allow the user to select from a limited set of text-based inquiry "screens" in order to find and display information about a single parcel. Providing citizens with direct access to these terminals in government offices became relatively common during the 1980s. More recently, some cities and counties in the United

States have begun to provide more flexible and widespread access to parcel data through use of the Internet or CD-ROM distribution and, in recent months, through map-based interfaces that make it easy to identify relevant properties and compare the characteristics of neighboring properties.[5]

Compared with poring over printed records of parcel information, electronic access speeds up research into land use and ownership. This is especially true now that Internet or CD-ROM access can run queries from a desktop computer (rather than a customized dial-up terminal) so that the results can be "cut-and-pasted" into the neighborhood planner's spreadsheet or report. The latest database technologies and mapping software enable users to construct spatial and textual queries; find, map, and aggregate significant amounts of digested parcel data; and download these data to the desktop in user-determined formats that become local tables, maps, and spreadsheets.

Using IT to accelerate the process of researching land use and ownership is a typical example of enhanced efficiency through IT *automation*. But, this "speed-up" effect is only the most obvious of the possible impacts we might imagine; and, as it turns out, it may not make much of a dent in the considerable amount of time that our prototypical neighborhood planner must spend studying land use and ownership.[6] We shall see why in the following two sections. In subsequent sections, I shall suggest how computerizing parcel records might result in a deeper restructuring of neighborhood planning activities.

Exploring Land Ownership Patterns

A typical land-use and ownership study might examine in detail the records for a few hundred to perhaps a thousand parcels. Boston has approximately 138,000 parcels distributed among 16 primary neighborhoods, 22 political wards, 64 sub-neighborhoods, and about 4,500 city blocks.[7] Hence, a typical land-use and ownership study might focus on an area smaller than a BRA sub-neighborhood, one that ranges from a few dozen to a hundred blocks. To explore the characteristics of computerized parcel records, however, we need not limit ourselves to a sub-neighborhood. Since we have access to a "snapshot" of 1996 Boston parcel records stored on a fast network server with relational database management tools, we can

Table 7.2: Residential holdings of the largest Boston property owners using "official" owner names as of February 1, 1996

OWNER	PARCELS	TOTVAL_K ($ x 1000)	ACRES
CITY OF BOSTON	1,589	506	271.9
CITY OF BOSTON BY FCL	944	168	81.2
	102	7,664	8.3
BOSTON REDEVELOPMENTAUTH	83	0	11.9
CITY OF BOSTON FCL	71	0	4.5
WEST ROX CRUSHED STONE CO	46	883	8.6
BOSTON HOUSING AUTHORITY	37	0	4.5
CITY OF BOSTON MUNICIPAL CP	35	0	3.3
UNITED STATES OF AMERICA	35	95	12.1
SAMIA LEONARD J	34	7,135	3.3
MERCURI ANTHONY C	30	547	5.3
ABBEY ST GERMAIN LP	28	9,554	0.8
W ROX CRUSHED STONE CO	27	1,500	41.7
OBRIEN PATRICK	24	4,012	4.1
HYDE SQUARE CO OP	22	1,929	1.6
RAND MORRIS TRST	22	91	0.5
FEDERAL HOME LOAN MGT CP	21	2,398	2.2
JONES JOHN C	21	1,189	1.7
SECRETARY OF HOUSING	21	1,651	2.5
TODESCA CHARLES ETAL	21	456	2.5

explore land ownership patterns by sorting, aggregating, and summarizing the parcel data for all of Boston.[8] By doing so, it will be easier to spot data ambiguities and problems that might have an impact on the accuracy and generality of a small area study.

For example, Table 7.2 lists the owners of the largest amounts of residential property throughout Boston. The listing is the output of a query written in Structured Query Language (SQL), which has become the *lingua franca* of database interoperability.[9] For each unique owner name in the official records, the query counts the number of parcels owned and sums the total lot size and the total assessed value.[10] Since we have been discussing *neighborhood* planning, we focus only on those 80,842 parcels zoned for residential use (that is, those with a land-use classification code beginning with "R").[11] Of these 80,842 residential parcels, 3,213 were owned by the top-20 owners shown in Table 7.2.

A look at the owners' names in Table 7.2 suggests that a problem must be solved in order to make good use of this computerized listing of the official parcel records. It is not surprising to find that the city of Boston owns most of the parcels. But the city is also second, fourth, fifth, seventh, and eighth in this top-20 listing. The BY FCL in CITY OF BOSTON BY FCL stands for "by foreclosure" and represents foreclosures for nonpayment of taxes. Seven hundred forty-four such parcels are listed, but another 71 parcels list "CITY OF BOSTON BY FCL" as the owner and are presumably more of the same. The BRA, the BHA, and the CITY OF BOSTON MUNICIPAL CP are also among the top-20 residential landowners and should probably be treated as municipal ownership in any land ownership study. Note also that 102 residential parcels have the owner name missing and that the UNITED STATES OF AMERICA, the FEDERAL HOME LOAN MGT CP, and the SECRETARY OF HOUSING make the top-20 owner list. Almost all of the U.S.-owned parcels are on the Stony Brook Reservation in Hyde Park, whereas the Federal Home Loan and Secretary of Housing parcels are spread around town and probably represent foreclosed residential property owned (as of February 1996) by the Federal Home Loan Mortgage Corporation and HUD. In all likelihood, these properties should also be treated as "municipal ownership" in a land ownership study aimed, say, at understanding property ownership for the purpose of designing a program of urban revitalization.

Difficulties in Categorizing Owner Names

If the parcel data recorded ownership in a way that matched the needs of such a study, then access to the computerized records through powerful data query tools such as SQL would be especially useful. But variations in spelling and the need to group official names into broader categories of ownership complicate our efforts to capitalize on the speed and cross-referencing capabilities of tools for processing digital parcel records. Of course, spelling errors could be corrected, and we could take steps to categorize ownership. But there are several ways of making such corrections and categories, and the choice can make more difference for planning and policy analysis purposes than we might at first think.

If the only issue were an occasional spelling error in owner names,

Table 7.3: Residential holdings of Boston property owners with "CITY" included in the official owner name as of February 1, 1996

OWNER	PARCELS	TOTVAL_K	ACRES
CITY OF BOSTON	1,589	506	271.9
CITY OF BOSTON BY FCL	944	168	81.2
CITY OF BOSTON FCL	71	0	4.5
CITY OF BOSTON MUNICIPAL CP	35	0	3.3
BOSTON CITYWIDE LAND TR INC	7	4,330	0.3
CITY OF BOSTON FCL.	7	0	0.3
CITY OF BOSTON PWD	6	0	0.9
CITY OF BOSTON BY F CL	3	0	0.1
CITY OF BOSTON BY FCL	2	0	0.1
CITY SUITES BOSTON INC	2	873	0.0
BOSTON CITYWIDE LAND	1	186	0.0
CITY OF BOSTON PUBLIC FACLTS	1	0	0.1
CITY OF BOSTON-MUNICIPAL CP	1	0	0.1
CITY OF BSOTON BY FCL	1	0	0.1
CITY OF BOSTON BY FCL.	1	0	0.1
CITY OF BOSTON MUNICIPAL	1	0	3.3

then almost any solution would be effective. Occasional errors would not have a big impact on our totals and summary statistics, and we could still save a lot of the legwork involved in chasing down owner names for the bulk of the parcels recorded correctly in the database. But a closer look at the 1996 parcel database reveals more than an occasional spelling error or omitted name. The West Roxbury Crushed Stone Company shows up twice in the top-20 list with a total of seventy-three parcels of (mostly unusable) residential land. The owner name, WEST ROX CRUSHED STONE CO, is associated with forty-six of the parcels, and the other twenty-seven parcels are recorded under the owner name W ROX CRUSHED STONE CO. The two spellings might result from different choices about how to abbreviate the long name in order to fit it within the thirty characters allowed in the parcel database. The database comes from official "owner of record" information generated when the deed of ownership is recorded. Hence, standardizing the owner names used to record land ownership would not be an easy task—especially since the "owner" might include multiple individuals, corporations, trusts, and the like.

Examining a few more ways of trying to account for parcels owned by the city of Boston will help clarify the nature and extent of the difficulties involved in interpreting the "official" names of the parcel owners. Table 7.3 lists all owners of record for residential parcels containing the word "city" in the owner name. Thirteen of the sixteen names do appear to indicate city ownership, and the vast majority of city-owned parcels are associated with the first two spellings. But the other three listings— BOSTON CITYWIDE LAND TR INC, CITY SUITES BOSTON INC, and BOSTON CITYWIDE LAND—appear to be nongovernmental entities. Note also that the BOSTON CITYWIDE LAND name might seem to indicate city ownership except that BOSTON CITYWIDE LAND TR INC also appears on this list, which suggests that the entity is a private trust and not the city.[12]

Furthermore, this list does not include many other public entities that are directly or indirectly controlled by the city. Both the BRA and the BHA own hundreds of Boston parcels and should probably be counted as city-controlled agencies even though the word "city" does not appear in their name. Table 7.4 indicates that at least seventeen different spellings of the Boston Redevelopment Authority are involved in accounting for some 605 parcels that they own. Additional parcels with other abbreviations or misspellings might also be owned by the BRA.[13] Note that no one way of spelling BRA accounts for even 40 percent of these parcels, and a considerable amount of investigation might be needed to find all the parcels that the BRA owns. Likewise, the Public Facilities Department is directly under the mayor's control and owns a number of residential and nonresidentially zoned parcels under an owner name that contains neither "city" nor "Boston".[14] Sorting through various spellings of corporate, nonprofit, and individual ownership cases can be even more problematic; for example, we found twenty-seven different spellings indicating Boston University ownership.

Strategies for Standardizing Owner Names

The point of these examples is to illustrate why it is unrealistic to expect that computerizing parcel records will, by itself, turn land-use and ownership studies into trivial, push-button tasks. The land-use planning studies

Table 7.4: Boston Redevelopment Authority parcels listed under
seventeen different owner name spellings (February 1, 1996)

OWNER	PARCELS	TOTVAL_K	ACRES
BOSTON REDEVELOMENT AUTH	1	327	0.2
BOSTON REDEVELOPMENT	5	157	0.5
BOSTON REDEVELOPMENT AUTH	231	106,863	123.9
BOSTON REDEVELOPMENT AUTHRTY	3	61	0.1
BOSTON REDEVELOPMENTAUTH	83	0	11.9
BOSTON REDEVELOPMENTAUTHRTY	1	0	0.1
BOSTON REDEVELOPMNT AUTH	82	32,975	23.3
BOSTON REDEVELPMENT AUTH	41	1,418	3.0
BOSTON REDEVELPMNT AUTH	22	5,073	2.4
BOSTON REDEVELPOMENT AUTH	1	33	0.2
BOSTON REDEVLPMNT AUTH	28	7,488	3.2
BOSTON REDEVLPMNT AUTHOR	29	2,955	3.3
BOSTON REDEVLPMNT AV	1	0	0.0
BOSTON REDVLPMNT AUTH	60	2,472	7.8
BOSTON REDVLPMNT AUTHOR	15	3,416	1.8
BOSTON REDVLPMNT AUTHORITY	1	1,095	0.5
BOSTON REDVLPMNT CORP	1	662	0.1

try to identify and interpret various spatial patterns of common land use,
ownership, and control; but the parcel records merely indicate the "owners
of record" as each property changes hands. Variations in spelling, and other
ambiguities in interpreting the official owner names, hamper the planner's
ability to digest the detailed parcel data quickly. One can imagine several
ways of addressing the problem of the lack of standardized owner names.
I focus on three strategies—bottom-up, top-down, and middle-out—which
have very different implications for both the efficiency and the degree of
decentralization of the kinds of prototypical neighborhood planning studies we have been contemplating.

Bottom-Up Strategy

In this case, one accepts spelling variations and simply tries to find a work-
around without changing the parcel information system. One might say,
for example, "I'm studying only 250 parcels. Just give me a copy of the
parcel records. I'll correct the spelling errors as I find them and get on with
the task at hand." Computerizing the parcel records automates the copying

process and allows the planner to enter the copied records into a desktop database or spreadsheet that can be readily updated as spelling errors are found and corrected. But the process is still time consuming because, as I have shown, there are many spelling variations for key owners, as well as many cases in which it is not obvious how to determine who has controlling interest in the property from the name of the owner-of-record, even if that name is correctly spelled.

If a study of parcel data focuses on a relatively small neighborhood, this strategy may work; but the time and effort required to research land use and ownership in one such case is not easily transferable to others. All the effort goes into correcting the planner's *copy* of the parcel records; the original data lie beyond the planner's control. Moreover, the parcel records are constantly changing. When next year's parcel data arrives, the planner will have to spend additional time transferring all the corrections and adjustments already made in the old parcel records so they are not overwritten by the new year's parcel data; hence, our planner's corrected parcel records will not be very easily maintained. Indeed, most such land-use and ownership studies are one-shot efforts that provide no lasting body of knowledge that can either accelerate or improve the quality of subsequent land-use and ownership studies.

Top-Down Strategy

This traditional approach, especially familiar in data-processing circles within management information system departments, involves standardizing the spelling of owner names and redesigning the parcel records system to ensure consistency and avoid spelling errors and other ambiguities. Modern relational database management systems provide a rich array of data-entry tools and multiuser, distributed access capabilities. Parcel record updates can be made using "forms" packages that run as "clients" on local desktop machines and can run edit checks of owner names against shared master files located and maintained on a central machine. Standardizing names through the use of such technology would eliminate the seventeen different spellings of the Boston Redevelopment Authority and the twenty-seven different variations of Boston University. As part of the redesign, one could also add a few additional fields for use in categorizing ownership—for example, a category that distinguished among levels of public, private, corporate, and individual ownership.

Such a redesign would go a long way toward eliminating the difficulties of researching land ownership; but this strategy also has its drawbacks. As with many top-down central planning efforts, such a system takes months or years to design and implement, is hard to implement incrementally, and tends to be rigid and not easily adapted to changing circumstances and needs. Handling the multiple spellings of Boston Redevelopment Authority and Boston University is one thing, but standardizing the names of not-yet-formed corporations, partnerships, joint owners, and the like is more difficult. Do we want a data-entry clerk to have the authority to alter the names of the owners of record as recorded on the deed in order to conform to standardized spellings? Can we go far enough in standardizing names like "John A. and Jane B. Smith et al."? Moreover, the official owner name is unlikely to be the desired grouping in any case. Perhaps John A. Smith owns many properties with different partners, or through various corporations. Matching the official owner name would not be sufficient to track the common thread of ownership. Likewise, the categorizations of ownership—for example, public/private, state/local, corporate/individual—are useful but limited in that no one set of categories suits all purposes; in addition, the categorization is likely to involve enough subtleties and ambiguities that self-reported categories would have to be double-checked by professionals.

Middle-Out Strategy

This strategy tries to combine the best of both worlds so that the end-user flexibility of the bottom-up approach is not lost in the effort to ensure consistent recording of owner names. The basic idea is to leave the official parcel data untouched and build local "lookup" tables that accumulate owner name corrections and interpretations. These tables can then be cross-referenced as needed with official parcel data so as to aggregate and map patterns of land use and ownership. While the idea is simple, its implementation in decentralized settings challenges modern database technology and requires more understanding of end-users' data management than the typical "turnkey" database application. But it can also lead to a very different view of how to share data in ways that allow one to decentralize *interpretations* of data. Such an approach could support a form of "grassroots" self-help planning while maintaining an acceptable level of coordination and standardization. Through shared data and data analysis tools, it could reduce the inefficiency, fragmentation, and delay that tends to plague decentralized, inclusive approaches to planning. In the following sections, I consider a specific example of the middle-out strategy.

Using Lookup Tables to Correct Spelling Errors

Instead of correcting spelling errors in our copy of the official parcel data, we can create a new lookup table that lists each of our corrections next to its original name. Relational database management tools make this easy. First, we use SQL to pull all unique owner names that appear in the original parcel records and store them in a new table called "own_lookup". We also add two new columns to this table—one for storing our spelling corrections and the other to hold categories of ownership (e.g., public, private, local, institutional, etc.) that we might want to assign to various owners later on. Table 7.5 shows a portion of this table for some of the entries that contain "Boston" in the official owner name.[15] Since we have not yet corrected spellings or categorized ownership, the second and third columns retain the "xxx" and "yyy" code we have used to indicate missing values.

Next, we write a series of SQL statements to update the own_ lookup table as we identify various spelling corrections and assign ownership categories. If the lookup table had fewer rows, we could update by hand; however, it is useful to take the time to write update statements that make the changes, so as to avoid hard-to-find typographical errors that result from handwritten corrections, and to archive precise update statements that can be reused as needed. Table 7.6 lists a selection of such update statements. The first one simply sets all names in the "fixowner" column to be the same as the original "oldowner" names; we use this as our starting point. The next two update statements standardize several of the variations of "City of Boston" found in Table 7.5. The last update illustrates a more complicated statement that does what the previous two updates did and then some. It corrects owner names and categorizes the "owngrp"

```
CREATE  TABLE own_lookup AS
SELECT  DISTINCT owner oldowner,
        'xxxxxxxxxxxxxxxxxxxxxxxxxxxxxx' fixowner,
        'yyyyyyyyyy' owngrp
  FROM  parcel96;

SELECT  oldowner, fixowner, owngrp
  FROM  own_lookup
 WHERE  oldowner LIKE '%BOSTON%' AND oldowner LIKE '%CITY%';
```

OLDOWNER	FIXOWNER	OWNGRP
BOSTON CITY LIGHTS FOUNDATON	xxxxxxxxxxxxxxxxxxxxxxxxxxxxxx	yyyyyyyyyy
BOSTON CITYWIDE LAND	xxxxxxxxxxxxxxxxxxxxxxxxxxxxxx	yyyyyyyyyy
BOSTON CITYWIDE LAND TR INC	xxxxxxxxxxxxxxxxxxxxxxxxxxxxxx	yyyyyyyyyy
BOSTON CITYWIDE LAND TRUST	xxxxxxxxxxxxxxxxxxxxxxxxxxxxxx	yyyyyyyyyy
BOSTON CITYWIDE LAND TRUST I	xxxxxxxxxxxxxxxxxxxxxxxxxxxxxx	yyyyyyyyyy
CITY OF BOSTON	xxxxxxxxxxxxxxxxxxxxxxxxxxxxxx	yyyyyyyyyy
CITY OF BOSTON	xxxxxxxxxxxxxxxxxxxxxxxxxxxxxx	yyyyyyyyyy
CITY OF BOSTON MUNICIPAL	xxxxxxxxxxxxxxxxxxxxxxxxxxxxxx	yyyyyyyyyy
CITY OF BOSTON BY FCL	xxxxxxxxxxxxxxxxxxxxxxxxxxxxxx	yyyyyyyyyy
CITY OF BOSTON BY F CL	xxxxxxxxxxxxxxxxxxxxxxxxxxxxxx	yyyyyyyyyy
CITY OF BOSTON BY FCL	xxxxxxxxxxxxxxxxxxxxxxxxxxxxxx	yyyyyyyyyy
CITY OF BOSTON BY FCL.	xxxxxxxxxxxxxxxxxxxxxxxxxxxxxx	yyyyyyyyyy
CITY OF BOSTON BY FL	xxxxxxxxxxxxxxxxxxxxxxxxxxxxxx	yyyyyyyyyy
...		

as PUBLIC for those parcels that have both CITY and BOSTON (or BSOTON) in their owner name—as long as the name does not also have CITYWIDE or SUITES in it.[16] As a planner digs into the official land use and ownership data, she will discover a number of such spelling corrections and name interpretations that can be accumulated and stored in such update statements. Table 7.7 shows the results of applying the Table 7.6 updates to the same rows of the "own_lookup" table that were shown above in Table 7.5.

After making our spelling corrections and owner groupings in this manner, we can use the lookup table to interpret the official parcel table along the lines suggested earlier in Tables 7.2 and 7.3. Suppose we want to look again at the residential holdings of the largest Boston property owners. We can run the same query we ran earlier for Table 7.2, but now,

Table 7.6: Updating the lookup table to correct spelling errors

```
UPDATE own_lookup SET fixowner = oldowner;

UPDATE own_lookup
   SET fixowner = 'CITY OF BOSTON'
 WHERE oldowner = 'CITY  OF BOSTON';

UPDATE own_lookup
   SET fixowner = 'CITY OF BOSTON'
 WHERE oldowner = 'CITY OF BOSTON BY   FCL';

UPDATE own_lookup
   SET fixowner = 'CITY OF BOSTON', owngrp = 'PUBLIC'
 WHERE oldowner LIKE '%CITY %' AND ((oldowner LIKE '%BOSTON%' and
       oldowner NOT LIKE '%CITYWIDE%' AND
       oldowner NOT LIKE '%SUITES%')
    OR (oldowner LIKE '%BSOTON%' ));
```

instead of grouping owners by their *official* owner name, we link the parcel table to the own_lookup table (using the official owner name) and then use the "fixowner" column in the lookup table to lump together parcels that have the same *fixed* owner name. Table 7.8 illustrates how the relational algebra of SQL links rows in the parcel table with rows in the lookup table.[17] Several parcels in the parcel table may have the same spelling for their owner name, in which case they will match up to the same entry in the lookup table. In addition, the lookup table will match many different original spellings of, say, CITY OF BOSTON BY FCL with the same "fixowner" spelling (viz. CITY OF BOSTON). Once the tables are linked in this fashion, the SQL query language enables us to count parcels, sum acres, and the like by grouping parcels according to the values of any field in *either* of the linked tables. We can link the tables using the original owner names, but then count parcels, value, and acreage by lumping together all parcels with the same "fixowner" name. Table 7.9 uses this technique to recompute the residential holdings of Boston's largest property owners (cf., Table 7.2) after making only those owner name corrections listed in Table 7.7.[18]

We see in Table 7.9 that Boston's land ownership now includes 2,662 residential parcels. This includes the 2,639 parcels for the four

Table 7.7: Viewing the updated lookup table

```
SELECT  oldowner, fixowner, owngrp
  from  own_lookup
 where  owner like "%BOSTON%";
```

OLDOWNER	FIXOWNER	OWNGRP
BOSTON CITYWIDE LAND TRUST I	BOSTON CITYWIDE LAND TRUST I	xxxxxxxxxxxxxxxxxx
CITY OF BOSTON	CITY OF BOSTON	PUBLIC
CITY OF BOSTON	CITY OF BOSTON	PUBLIC
CITY OF BOSTON MUNICIPAL	CITY OF BOSTON	PUBLIC
CITY OF BOSTON BY FCL	CITY OF BOSTON BY FCL	PUBLIC
CITY OF BOSTON BY F CL	CITY OF BOSTON BY FCL	PUBLIC
BOSTON HOSPITAL FOR WOMEN	BOSTON HOSPITAL FOR WOMEN	xxxxxxxxxxxxxxxxxx
BOSTON HOTEL LP	BOSTON HOTEL LP	xxxxxxxxxxxxxxxxxx
BOSTON HOUSING AUTH	BOSTON HOUSING AUTHORITY	PUBLIC
BOSTON HOUSING AUTHORITY	BOSTON HOUSING AUTHORITY	PUBLIC
BOSTON HOUSING AUTHOURTY	BOSTON HOUSING AUTHORITY	PUBLIC

entries in Table 7.2 that have both "city" and "Boston" in the (old) owner name plus another 23 residential parcels that did not show up on the Table 7.2 list of landowners with 20-plus parcels but were identified as having city of Boston ownership in our Table 7.7 updates. Evidently, there were nine different spellings of Boston for these cases since the total number of spellings collapsed into the CITY OF BOSTON row is 13. Note that, thus far, we have only standardized those names containing both "city" and "Boston."[19] The results in Table 7.9 do not lump together any other spellings indicating Boston ownership, such as the two Boston Housing Authority and Boston Redevelopment Authority entries, which remain as they were in Table 7.2.

We could easily construct another set of updates to handle the various spellings of BHA and BRA. In fact, we can accumulate any number of corrections and categorizations of owner names in our lookup table. Then, whenever we want to probe a question of multiple parcel ownership or perform some other land ownership analysis, we can use the *same* query used earlier to produce Table 7.9, in order to generate a revised table or map that reflects the impact of the latest corrections and categorizations in our lookup table.

Table 7.8: Using the lookup table

Official Parcel Data

PARCEL_ID	OWNER	STCLASS
0306490000	BOSTON REDVLPMNT AUTH	132
0306535000	CITY OF BOSTON	131
0400945010	SOUTH BOSTON-II LP	102
0401479008	NEW BOSTON INVESTMENTS IN	102
0401479018	NEW BOSTON INVESTMENTS IN	102
0402209000	SHAWMUT BANK OF BOSTON NA	132
0600624000	CITY OF BOSTON BY FCL	132
0600648000	CITY OF BOSTON BY FCL	104
0600654000	CITY OF BOSTON	132
0600655000	CITY OF BOSTON BY F CL	132
0600656000	CITY OF BOSTON	132

Lookup Table for Categorizing Owners

OLDOWNER	OWNGRP
AUTO CITY INC	xxxxxxxxxxxxxxxxxxxx
CITY OF BOSTON	BOSTON
CITY DEVELOPMENT CORP TRST	xxxxxxxxxxxxxxxxxxxx
CITY DEVELOPMENT CORP	xxxxxxxxxxxxxxxxxxxx
CITY HEIGHTS CONDOMINIUM TR	xxxxxxxxxxxxxxxxxxxx
CITY OF BOSTON	BOSTON
CITY OF BOSTON MUNICIPAL	BOSTON
CITY OF BOSTON BY FCL	BOSTON FORECLOSURE
CITY OF BOSTON BY F CL	BOSTON FORECLOSURE
CITY OF BOSTON BY FCL	BOSTON FORECLOSURE
CITY OF BOSTON BY FCL.	BOSTON FORECLOSURE

Table 7.9: Residential holdings of the largest Boston property owners
(reworked Table 7.2 results after standardizing "city of Boston")

FIXOWNER	SPELLINGS	PARCELS	TOTVAL_K	ACRES
CITY OF BOSTON	13	2,662	673	366.0
BOSTON REDEVELOPMENTAUTH	1	83	0	11.9
WEST ROX CRUSHED STONE CO	1	46	883	8.6
BOSTON HOUSING AUTHORITY	1	37	0	4.5
UNITED STATES OF AMERICA	1	35	95	12.1
SAMIA LEONARD J	1	34	7,135	3.3
MERCURI ANTHONY C	1	30	547	5.3
ABBEY ST GERMAIN LP	1	28	9,554	0.8
W ROX CRUSHED STONE CO	1	27	1,500	41.7
OBRIEN PATRICK	1	24	4,012	4.1
HYDE SQUARE CO OP	1	22	1,929	1.6
RAND MORRIS TRST	1	22	91	0.5
FEDERAL HOME LOAN MGT CP	1	21	2,398	2.2
JONES JOHN C	1	21	1,189	1.7
SECRETARY OF HOUSING	1	21	1,651	2.5
TODESCA CHARLES ETAL	1	21	456	2.5

Accumulating Knowledge about Land Ownership

This last point suggests how a middle-out approach that makes use of
SQL and relational tools could support distributed, decentralized planning
more effectively than top-down or bottom-up approaches. Rather than
seeing the middle-out approach as an elaborate way of handling spelling
errors, we can see it as a robust strategy for decentralizing city data in
ways that empower end-users to analyze data through the lens of their own
interpretations and accumulated knowledge. Conventional "citizen inquiry
systems"[20] restrict users to a limited set of narrow, predefined questions;
they do not help users to adjust or aggregate data to suit their own concep-
tions of reality. Conventional systems may suffice for predictable day-to-
day queries, such as "What's my assessed value?" or "Did you get my tax
payment?" But they do not support the creation of an inclusive, decentralized planning process that would enable individuals at the neighborhood
level to query city data efficiently in the light of questions they invent
in the service of their own interests.

Interpretations of official owner names can take time to research and compile, and findings may vary from organization to organization, or change from time to time. It is better to isolate such volatile local information from a central list of official owner names and records that serves a variety of purposes for different agencies and may be needed, unchanged, as a basis for cross reference to other official records. In addition, I should note that official parcel records are reasonably well maintained in a central city department such as "Assessing" or "Management Information Systems"; but lookup tables can be generated and maintained by any number of independent planners and researchers, and spread among departments and neighborhood groups throughout the city, so long as local planners have the network access, data-processing tools, and the know-how to tap into the city's databases.

Distributed, networked databases coupled with end-users who are skilled at cross-referencing data may look like exotic technology today. Nevertheless, the core elements of this technology are progressing rapidly. They include the Internet, multitasking desktop machines, inexpensive large-volume storage devices, and powerful user interfaces that support mapping and visualization. Standards for encoding and processing digital spatial data are also improving rapidly. It is already possible, through open database connection (ODBC) tools and object linking and embedding (OLE) tools, to construct lookup tables locally. The tables can be contained in a spreadsheet or desktop database package and cross-referenced, with the click of a few buttons, with remotely stored databases such as the parcel database. These databases exist on database servers accessible through the Internet, and employ a variety of software packages for database management. In classes for planning students at MIT—not necessarily computing majors—we are doing this already. Moreover, we are able to link the work of data analysis with map and image servers that provide visual assistance in locating and interpreting data, without bogging down in the complex manipulation of sophisticated geographic information systems.

Individual citizens may not need such technology. But a growing number of local organizations involved in bottom-up planning for urban revitalization already have some capacity to access and use computing technologies, and could make good use of the technologies described above.

Conclusion

The middle-out approach to data access and analysis has many applications beyond land ownership accounting. For example, neighborhood groups, concerned about conditions that provide economic incentives for arson, sometimes form arson-prevention teams. Such teams try to keep track of landlords who are delinquent in their tax payments, often appear in housing court over disputes with tenants, disinvest in their property, or even amass land with run-down or abandoned buildings in the hope of clearing it for other uses via arson. It takes considerable time and energy to investigate such landlords, since they tend to use "shells" to hide their identity. The middle-out approach enables local agents to accumulate knowledge in a lookup table (noting, for example, that "John Smith controls the XYZ Corporation"). The lookup table can be used from time to time to reinterpret official data about land ownership contained in central parcel databases that lie outside the control of local actors. When such results are linked to parcel maps of a neighborhood, they allow for quick, visual inspection of ownership patterns. Indeed, as software evolves and "intelligent agents" become more practical, one can imagine programming an "agent" to help plan such detective work. "Take a look at this block," the agent might suggest. "I've looked around, and I suspect that if you examine what's happening with its twenty 'uncategorized-ownership' parcels, you'll find cause for concern!"

There are many other questions of interest to neighborhood planners that lend themselves to a middle-out approach. Which housing near a BHA site should be first targeted for acquisition? What is a good location for a new day-care or job-training center? Which landlords are overdue on taxes and likely to abandon their property, or milk it dry, before converting to high-rise buildings or condos? Who else is heavily involved in housing in the neighborhood? Does the neighborhood have the local buying power to sustain a bigger grocery store?

The middle-out approach to data processing is important because both top-down and bottom-up approaches prevent neighborhood groups, or neighborhood departments of city agencies, from interactively engaging and keeping pace with the city planning process. Access to official databases, spelling errors and all, will not suffice to enable neighborhood groups, or smaller agencies and nonprofit organizations, to digest the relevant data in time to engage urgent planning issues and decisions—not so long as they have to construct their own data analyses for themselves, from scratch, for each new project. Moreover, neighborhood groups and organizations have local knowledge that the city lacks—for example, knowledge about the actual uses of land and space—but no efficient way to share that knowledge with the city, or with other organizations. If we could count on the availability of data in the flexible and decentralized manner supported by the middle-out approach to data processing, then the stage would be set for a truly interactive, timely planning dialogue between neighborhood planners and city agencies—as well as for a mode of interagency coordination that might allow agencies to keep pace with one another.

Notes

Partial support for the data management and analyses in this paper was provided by the MIT Architecture and Planning School's Bemis Fund. The author wishes to thank the Boston's Assessing Office and Public Facility Department for providing the parcel-level database for Boston and the research and technical staff of MIT's Computer Resource Lab and Planning Support Systems group for assistance in data management. The author also wishes to thank Don Schön for many helpful suggestions and comments in my effort to make the technical content of the paper more clear and relevant to a broader audience.

1. In 1993, the U.S. Federal Government began an "Empowerment Zones/Enterprise Communities Program" aimed at revitalizing inner-city neighborhoods through tax incentives and other federally funded assistance intended to stimulate economic development within impoverished urban communities.

2. "Brownfields" refer to parcels of land whose land use history makes them suspect as the location of hazardous waste such as contaminated soil or undocumented and leaky underground oil tanks. The uncertainty regarding their history and the (limited) prospect of collecting on their prior owners' liability clouds efforts to promote their reuse and adds financial risk and delay to land-use planning efforts in their vicinity.

3. For example, such studies might employ the land-use and ownership data to develop a series of (before and after) parcel- or block-level maps of the neighborhood showing land-use (residential, retail, commercial, etc.) demographics, population, density, job locations, transit stops, rent levels, vacancy rates and the like. These maps are then used to characterize the proposed plans as having small (or large) impacts, being similar to (or different from) current patterns, and so on. Neighborhood and community groups familiar with the neighborhood still spend considerable time amassing such data to provide systematic and credible justification for their proposals and opinions and to reduce to common terms their anecdotal impressions and recollections of land use and ownership.

4. Of course, the "official" records are more complex than the single-table "flat file" extract shown in Table 7.1. Not only are there many more variances associated with each parcel (e.g., building characteristics, square footage, owner's mailing address, etc.), but there are "one-to-many" relationships (e.g., multiple owners of a parcel, multiple buildings on a parcel, condominium ownership, etc.), and complex changes in the data as various transactions occur (e.g., the sale of buildings and parcels, subdivisions of land, construction and renovation, etc.). Nevertheless, most of today's land records can distill from the more complex databases a "snapshot" of current information such as shown in Table 7.1.

5. For example, the Oakland, California, Community and Economic Development Agency has recently begun providing an online "map room" on the Internet that allows the public to zoom in on a neighborhood or parcel and obtain parcel-specific ownership and land-use information. See the "Map Room" and "Permit Counter" on the City of Oakland Virtual Permit Center and web page at http://ceda.ci.oakland.ca.us.

6. Note that computerizing parcel ownership and tax records has a significant impact on the day-to-day operations of the Assessor's Office and Registry of Deeds in that it enables many individual inquiries about property characteristics and ownership to be handled much more quickly and reliably and from decentralized locations. But our focus is whether and how IT innovations influence land-use planning and policymaking activities rather than on the use of automation to improve the efficiency of specific operations involved in delivering urban services.

7. These 64 sub-neighborhoods were defined by the Boston Redevelopment Authority and Boston's Public Facility Department as neighborhood statistical areas for the purpose of aggregating 1980 U.S. Census data.

8. The parcel data are stored (along with other Boston data, maps, and GIS tools) in an Oracle relational database on a SPARCServer 1000E with half its 128 megabytes of RAM dedicated to relational data processing.

9. The SQL used by Oracle Release 7.1 conforms to the SQL-2 standard. In this case, the query is:

```
SELECT  owner, count(*) parcels, sum (totalval) /1000 totalval_k,
        sum (lot size) /43560 acres
  FROM  parcel 96
 WHERE  land-use LIKE 'R%'
```

```
GROUP BY  owner HAVING count (*) > 20
ORDER BY  count (*) DESC;
```

10. The total assessed value of zero shown is not a coding error. For most tax-exempt property, the assessor's office does not try to determine and record the market value of the land and buildings.

11. A three-digit land-use code is also available for each parcel and provides a more precise definition of property use. For this example, however, we used a simpler (albeit less precise measure)—whether city land-use code begins with "R." This convenient approximation is sufficient for the purposes of discussing encoding and interpretation issues that are of interest in this chapter.

12. If we had not restricted the research to residential parcels, the presence of the word "CITY" in the owner name would have been more ambiguous as an indicator of municipal ownership. Among all parcels, 4,356 were owned by 41 different owner names containing the word "city," and these owner names included BOSTON CITYWIDE LAND, CITY OF BOSTON MUNICIPAL CP, CITY OF BOSTON TRST, and CITY DEVELOPMENT CORP TRST.

13. The query in Table 7.4 was not restricted to residential parcels:

```
SELECT  owner, count (*) parcels, sum(totalval) /1000 totalval_k
        sum (lotsize)/43560 acres
  FROM  parcel96
 WHERE  owner LIKE '%BOSTON%' AND
        (owner LIKE '%REDEV%' or owner LIKE '%REDEV%'
GROUP BY  owner;
```

There are 154 residential parcels among the 605 BRA parcels summarized in Table 7.4 and these 154 residential parcels utilized 11 different spellings of the Boston Redevelopment Authority.

14. The CITY OF BOSTON PUBLIC FACLTS name in Table 7.3 probably refers to the Public Facilities Department. But in other cases, the owner is listed as PUBLIC FACILITIES.

15. There are 103,281 unique owner names in Boston's parcel database.

16. Examination of owner names using other SQL statements indicated that the only *nonpublic* owner names having both "Boston" and "city" in them were names containing "citywide" or "suites."

17. Table 7.8 is not wide enough to fit all columns of the lookup table. The "fixowner" column is omitted and the "oldowner" column is displayed along with the "owngrp" column, in which updates not discussed in the chapter have been used to group city-owned properties into various Boston-xxx categories.

18. The SQL query used to produce Table 7.9 is:

```
SELECT  fixowner, count(distinct oldowner) spellings, count(p.parcel_id) parcels
        sum(totalval)/1000 totalval_k, sum(p.lotsize)/43560 acres
  FROM  own_lookup g,parcel96 p
 WHERE  p.owner=g.oldowner and land-use like 'R%'
```

```
GROUP BY  fixowner HAVING count(p.parcel_id) > 20
ORDER BY  count(p.parcel_id) DESC;
```

19. Note also that the 102 parcels from Table 7.2 with a missing owner name drop out of Table 7.9 since they do not match up with any name on the lookup table.

20. For example, most assessor's offices allow citizens to have access to their records by coming to the office and thumbing through voluminous printouts of owner names, addresses, and assessed values that are sorted alphabetically by owner name and street address. Within the past two decades, many such offices have switched from printouts to terminal screens — i.e., computer monitors that are 'dumb' terminals directly wired to minicomputers and mainframes. However, these terminals do not provide the open-ended inquiry and cross-referencing discussed in this paper. Rather, they automate the answering of a few specific questions such as, "Who owns the property at 45 Main St." The result is a screenful of information for the one property that is found and, while the citizen might be able to obtain a printout of the screen, they cannot take away an electronic record of the information that can be readily merged and cross-referenced with other information.

References

Harris, Britton. 1989. "Beyond Geographic Information Systems: Computers and the Planning Professional," *American Planning Association Journal* (Winter): 85–90.

Innes, Judith E. 1995. "Planning Theory's Emerging Paradigm : Communicative Action and Interactive Practice," *Journal of Planning Education and Research* 14: 183–189.

Peters, Tom. 1992. *Liberation Management: Necessary Disorganization for the Nonosecond Nineties*. New York: Alfred A. Knopf.

Schön, Donald A. 1983. *The Reflective Practitioner : How Professionals Think in Action*. New York, Basic Books.

Zuboff, Shoshana. 1988. *In the Age of the Smart Machine: The Future of Work and Power*. New York: Basic Books.

8. Planning Support Systems for Low-Income Communities

Michael J. Shiffer

Introduction: The Planning and Community Development Context

This chapter's primary area of investigation is to determine how emerging information technologies (IT), such as the Internet and multimedia representational aids, can be used to better inform (or misinform) discourse in planning and community-related settings. More specifically, in the context of providing community-related information, the question becomes: How do we enhance the capability of citizens to function intelligently and creatively?

It is often said that information is power; however, it can be argued that information is only powerful when it is effectively comprehended by those who would use it. It could therefore be argued that *knowledge* is power. IT can help people comprehend information (thereby delivering knowledge). Therefore, IT has the capacity to endow citizens with greater political power when it is effectively delivered (Sawicki and Craig 1996).

This chapter is primarily concerned with illustrating how IT can deliver relevant knowledge in a community development and planning context that involves deliberation and decision making in both public and private arenas. The actors in these contexts are typically associated with "grassroots" community groups, city planning agencies, community development corporations, state and federal agencies, and other governmental and nongovernmental bodies.

In this case "relevant knowledge" is defined as a recognition of problems and issues faced by a community, an understanding of the range of alternative scenarios that can begin to address these problems and issues, an acknowledgment of the actors and institutional mechanisms available to support action, and some appreciation of the implications of action based on an understanding of present conditions and past trends. This knowledge is typically shared through varying degrees of recollection, description, and speculation. While recollecting the past history of a given site or planning issue, human conversations may revolve around what was said, what was done, or what a place was like, among other things. Descriptions of present conditions are generally used to familiarize participants in a collaborative situation with an area being discussed so that everyone can work from a common base of knowledge (frequently augmented with maps and/or imagery). Finally, speculation about the future of an area generally involves experienced individuals extrapolating measurable phenomena from past experience and applying it to the future using informal mental models, hand calculations, and computer-based analysis tools.

This chapter identifies three categories of IT that can support such discourse and then discusses several examples of implementations. Finally, it closes with a discussion of some early lessons learned from these implementations.

IT Roles for Community Development and Planning

While one can imagine a broad variety of roles for IT in addressing the needs of distressed urban communities, here I focus on the following categories: community networking, collaborative planning, and representation. These categories can support various stages of a planning process. For example, a community group or planning organization may need to solicit community perspectives when setting forth the goals and objectives of a strategic plan. (This may be facilitated to a certain degree with *community networks*.) They also may need access to relevant data sets, advanced analysis tools and the expertise of staff and related professionals when preparing the plan. (This can be aided through *collaborative planning systems*.) Finally, they need to effectively communicate that plan to key stakeholders and agencies possessing the resources to effectively evaluate it and bring it to realization. (This involves using IT as a *representational application*.) In this context, community networking tends to primarily support a process of information gathering. Collaborative planning supports information processing, deliberation, rhetorical conversations, and sometimes confrontation. Finally, representational applications support advocacy, information dissemination, and to a certain degree evaluation.

Community Networks

IT seems to hold a significant promise for distressed urban communities in its ability to function as an effective communications medium (Barndt and Craig 1994). Community-based network sites are numerous and growing. They are delivered by *grassroots organizations, governments,* and *entrepreneurs—*

Figure 8.1: A text-based menu in Milwaukee Omnifest

```
Community Center

1) About the Community Center
2) Ethnic and Religious Areas
3) Health and Safety
4) Non-Profit Community Calendar
5) Political Focus
6) Senior Center
7) Support Services
8) Youth Serving Organizations
———————————————————————
h = help q = quit system
p = previous menu t = top (main) menu

Enter selection ==> 3
```

each with their own strengths and weaknesses as described by Beamish (1995). Nevertheless, community networks are rapidly proving to be a significant channel of communication among like-minded people. They can offer an effective medium through which success stories of community revitalization can be shared.

For example, Milwaukee's Omnifest is a text-based community information system that users can connect to with fairly low-end modems and PCs. Accessing this community information system provides one with a menu that includes "ethnic and religious" areas, "health and safety," a nonprofit "community calendar," some degree of political focus, a "senior center," support services, and so forth (see Figure 8.1).

Through the menu structure, the user can jump into various sections of the system, such as the section on "health and safety" issues. In this section one is faced with a number of different issues, for example, "street gang problems." On this subject, the user can jump to an online public discussion or an anonymous questions board. Even though Omnifest is

Figure 8.2: A WWW-based menu for Buffalo

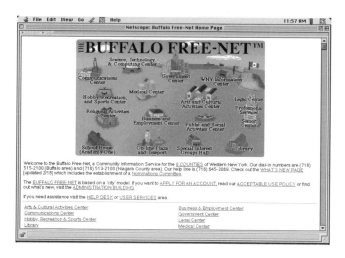

an example of an older text-based approach to community information systems, it is nonetheless an effective one.

Buffalo Free-Net provides an example of a community information network that makes use of the World Wide Web (WWW). This offers a greater degree of interactivity by virtue of the WWW's graphical interface. In many ways the information contained within this system is similar to that of Milwaukee, except that it is supplemented with graphics and hypertext that allows the user to navigate by selecting highlighted words with a pointing device (see Figure 8.2).

Using this interface, the user can jump into a communications center and have access to Usenet News Groups. This offers access to nationally and internationally posted bulletin boards that can facilitate discussion perhaps more richly than a small local bulletin board. But it also has the capacity to give people access to a variety of local topics such as the "senior

Figure 8.3: A WWW-based menu for St. Louis

center" where one can read about "coordinated care services" for the elderly. One can also jump to a subject such as "home health care" and read about related resources. The Milwaukee and Buffalo systems provide examples of community networking at the grassroots level.

The city of St. Louis, and its Community Development Agency, provides an example of a community information system that is provided by a local government (Posey 1996). Here one finds a relatively "rich" base of information. The system offers information on a variety of topics, including "economic development," "St. Louis's Enterprise Community," "arts and entertainment," "the government," "neighborhoods," "community resources," and "education." If, for example, one would like to read more about "economic development," by pointing and clicking one can learn about the range of development organizations existing in the community (see Figure 8.3). One can then contact those organizations, find out what

Figure 8.4: A WWW-based mechanism for citizen access to city government in St. Louis

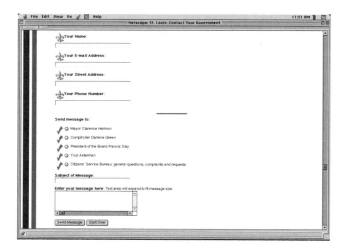

they can do, what kind of assistance they can provide, and so on. Information about housing development programs, various home buyers' support services, and home owners' assistance and other housing programs in St. Louis can also be found. It thus provides a valuable resource for accessing information that might be used to deal with some of the sustainability problems that a community might be facing.

Another interesting part of the St. Louis system is the section that describes the various aspects of the city's neighborhoods. Residents can display neighborhood-related information either from an online city map or from a list of neighborhood names. One can read about a neighborhood's institutions and see where the neighborhood is located in relation to the rest of the city. A list of the selected neighborhood's resources is also available, along with facts and figures about the people who live there. This can be quite useful if one is evaluating revitalization projects or trying to get a sense of the demographic characteristics of a particular community. Another particularly useful element of this system is its capacity to provide contact with a local government representative (in this case an alderman) via e-mail (see Figure 8.4). Other members of the government responsible for the neighborhood may also receive e-mail messages. Thus this system offers the ability to effectively connect with the government in ways that may have been previously difficult because of incompatible personal schedules.

Finally, a growing number of community information systems are being provided as entrepreneurial efforts, such as "Inner City Access," which is located in Boston. Their approach is typically to garner community support through a marketing perspective so that their existence can be financed through corporate and small business sponsorship. Users can often find out about what's going on in their community or learn about local businesses through these sites.

Collaborative Planning Support

A second potential role for IT in community development and planning involves the use of collaborative planning systems (Shiffer 1992). Planning support has traditionally been provided using analytical tools such as geographic information systems (GIS) and various types of forecasting models (Klosterman 1992; Harris and Batty 1993). Nevertheless, augmentation of discourse using these analytic tools has traditionally been handicapped by a lack of immediate response and abstract output that tends to exclude from such conversations those who are not technologically sophisticated (Shiffer 1995a). For example, it has often been difficult to interact with an analytic tool, such as a GIS, in the context of a meeting room and expect the immediate response necessary to support a conversation. Furthermore, technical output, such as a predicted automobile traffic level of thirteen thousand cars a day, can have little meaning for nontransportation specialists. The issues of speed and responsiveness can be addressed to a limited extent with advances in processing speed as well as through the employment of direct manipulation computer interfaces that allow users to push buttons and slide levers to elicit an immediate response from the computer (Hutchins, Hollan, and Norman 1986). The issue of relatively abstract output can be addressed using multimedia representational aids such as images and sound that can portray the output of analytic tools more descriptively (Rasmussen 1986). For example, an expert's quantitative representation of automobile traffic scenarios can be augmented using visual imagery and sound linked to forecasting models with simple-to-use, manipulable, graphic displays.

In one case, a collaborative planning system (CPS) was designed to support an exploration of reuse alternatives for a former air force base as described in Shiffer (1995a). In this situation, one would follow the agenda of the meeting and use the system to access information about the various locations within the air force base for display to the group using a portable computer and projector. Such information would include descriptive text and 360-degree panoramic views of the base from key locations identified on a digital map. One could also listen to the environmental noise implications of proposed aircraft operations at selected locations around the former air force base.

In this case, the area in question had not experienced aircraft operations for about twenty-five years prior to this study. Thus most of the people in the community had poor recollections of the aircraft noise intensity (frequently described as "pretty loud," "loud," or "really loud"). Yet one of the issues discussed was whether to allow a commercial aircraft repair facility to operate at the site. A number of different variables can go into the calculation of noise impacts—(topography of the region, prevailing winds, and so forth). If one constrains most of these variables and leaves manipulable the one that is likely to be a point of negotiation (such as the number of aircraft operations allowed in a 24-hour period), it becomes possible to limit the number of alternatives that are considered—while still broadening the range of alternatives that would not have been considered using conventional methods of environmental analysis.

The user can identify the frequency of operation and the preferred runway to see noise contours drawn on a projected map. One can learn more about the noise contours by selecting them with a pointing device which yields the contour's value represented as "Ldn" (decibel level over time with nighttime noise events weighted more heavily than daytime noises). Questions about the meaning of Ldn would still remain, however. These would be addressed by a representational aid that would use descriptive

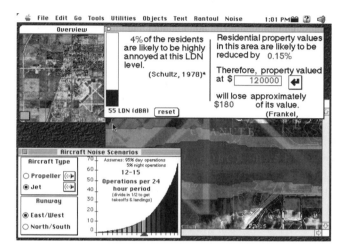

text to illustrate the percentage of residents likely to be highly annoyed (see Figure 8.5).

To understand how a value such as "public annoyance" is derived, the user can click on the citation and see the formula that it is based on and a reference to the journal article that the formula was published in (Schultz 1978). Even though this type of reference can provide a level of accountability for this information, it is not necessarily a precise representation, but it does give the user some idea of "likely" scenarios. One can also interpolate between contours by sliding a graphical bar up and down to play "what if" games. Although this simply involves manipulating spreadsheet calculations using graphics, it affords a greater degree of interactivity that leads to a clearer understanding of the issues at hand.

It is also possible to convey an idea of what it is like to hear aircraft operations in the field. This is made possible using noise samples from a comparable airport that have been geocoded to match this location. By selecting a location on the projected map, one can hear what the aircraft might sound like taking off at the decibel level experienced in the field, provided that the noise level in the meeting room is calibrated using an amplification system such as that pioneered by Dubbink (1989).

Representational Applications

The third potential role for IT in community development involves using the technology as a representational application. In this case we explore how the persuasive aspects of multimedia can be used to advocate specific projects that may improve the quality of life in distressed urban communities. We also explore how the technology might be used to assist in the evaluation of community revitalization efforts through the juxtaposition of the physical and demographic characteristics of an area with individual perspectives related through video interviews.

The first example of a representational application involves looking at the city of St. Louis once again. In this case, a CD-ROM-based multimedia system linked residential interviews with GIS maps of St. Louis's economic, physical, and demographic characteristics in an interactive presentation that supported that city's bid for community development federal funding.

In 1994 the Clinton administration accepted applications for funding "empowerment zones and enterprise communities" as a means to address the issue of distressed urban areas in the United States. Central to each application was the development of a strategic plan for the community in question. The strategic plan was to act as a blueprint for community empowerment. As such, community involvement typically played a role in the development of the plan.

After defining an area that qualified for the funding program, the city of St. Louis developed such a strategic plan (Posey 1996). This involved the identification of goals, objectives, and actions that formed the plan's critical base. The planning process also involved community input through meetings and interviews with residents. The result was a fairly sizable paper document that described an associative relationship of goals, objectives, and action plans for the area.

Concerned about the communicative limitations of a paper document, the city worked with MIT's Department of Urban Studies and Planning to create an electronic version of the plan using interactive multimedia technology. The intent of the electronic version was to use it as a point of reference (projected on a wall) during discussions and meetings that centered on various aspects of the plan. The electronic version of the strategic plan linked its text with descriptive maps of the affected areas. Relevant elements of the plan were also linked to interactive video interviews with community members, business leaders, and other parties with an interest in the affected areas. The technology carried community concerns (voiced by the stakeholders themselves) to local planning meetings and offices. It also was used to carry these concerns to places where they may not have been heard previously (such as within large federal agencies). In these environments, the technology can be used as an evaluative mechanism for those concerned with improving the quality of life in a distressed community.

Such evaluative measures were also a goal of a multimedia archive that was designed to describe various characteristics of an urban revitalization demonstration program for Boston's Mission-Main public housing development. This system also juxtaposed physical and demographic characteristics with individual perspectives in a manner similar to the St. Louis system (see Figure 8.6). In the Boston case, however, the video interviews with residents were more extensive and structured. When represented accurately and sensitively, these videos would provide a sense of ownership for the stakeholders in the community. A key to this success was the long-term involvement of the "filmmaker" with the community. In this case the filmmaker was an MIT student who worked in this community for several months. Only after gaining a significant degree of trust could she expect residents to be open and forthcoming in sharing their views about their community's issues (Guiterrez 1996). When the interactive video documentary was combined with spatial representations of the physical and demographic characteristics of the development, the result was a dynamic multidimensional case history.

Both the St. Louis and the Mission-Main projects resulted in a rich and compelling "snapshot" of an urban community and its associated issues. Such snapshots can be combined over time to tell a story about the

Figure 8.6: A multimedia representation describing Boston's Mission-Main public housing development

relative successes or failures of an urban intervention, thus providing an effective evaluative mechanism. Because of the large amounts of digital video and graphics, these tools were initially delivered on CD-ROM. As video compression technologies mature, this can be more effectively implemented in a networked environment such as the Internet. Thus the use of multimedia for representation of distressed communities has the capacity to provide a foundation for an enhanced "community voice" through a broadened degree of communication among area residents, planning professionals, and government officials.

Early Lessons

To summarize, IT can play a role in addressing the needs of distressed urban communities through *community networking, collaborative planning support,* and *multimedia representational mechanisms.* Much of the evidence about IT's impact on communities that has been developed to date is somewhat loose and anecdotal. This is primarily because much of what has been implemented had been available for less than five years as of this writing. Nevertheless, initial observations lead one to reconsider the functions that such systems play by reflecting (at least initially) on three questions: Do community networks lead to community networking? How do collaborative planning systems support rhetoric? Can representational applications play a role as strategic weapons for advocacy?

Do Community Networks Lead to Community Networking?

Community networks can eliminate time and place constraints so that people with incompatible schedules can discuss issues of common interest more effectively. They also provide a rather crude "filtering" mechanism so that people of like minds can find a virtual place to share their ideas. Finally, they offer rapid progress reports and updates for projects that are under way in a particular community. In this manner, they furnish an effective mechanism for community "networking." Therefore, one can surmise that community information systems have the capacity to give a broad reach to entirely new constituencies. For example, residents may have difficulty participating in neighborhood activities, primarily if they are still at work when neighborhood meetings are held. A community information system could allow residents to be informed of proposed changes to their community, post messages to a bulletin board, and voice their opinions to elected officials where they might not have been able to participate in the past.

In spite of this, there are still some drawbacks and concerns related to community information systems. Beyond the obvious issues of access to the technology, one challenge involves gaining a critical mass of users to sustain such a system (Markus 1987). Many community information systems, especially highly localized ones, contain minimal amounts of information. One might speculate that the reason for this is that few people participate in highly localized information systems. This results in a lack of message activity at a particular site. Conversely, a lack of message activity at a particular site may lead to a lack of participants. This can lead to a vicious circle that ultimately results in the failure of an online information system. While one might speculate that the community information systems explored here have indeed attained the critical mass necessary to be sustainable over time, the question remains as to exactly what is needed to achieve a critical level of activity.

Other concerns relating to the characteristics of interaction on the Internet may be beyond the capacity of the local community information provider to address. For example, the specialization of subject matter online may result in a sympathetic yet narrow audience of similarly situated groups. In other words, if one tries to bring attention to pedestrian issues in their community, other people who are also concerned with these issues will probably read these messages and continue to post messages related to that issue. But the sympathy or the attention of people who can address these issues will not necessarily be gained. Related to this issue is the concern that the effectiveness of the WWW as a medium for increasing general public awareness about specific issues is likely to drop as the number of individuals and groups using the medium as a platform for discussion continues to grow. In other words, when there are fifty voices out there speaking, it is easy to pay attention to those fifty voices. But when there are five thousand voices, one may become much more selective and tend to gravitate much more to issues that one is particularly concerned with. Thus an important issue to be reckoned with is the apparent parochialization of discussions on the Internet.

How Do Collaborative Planning Systems Support Rhetoric?

The simple linking of maps and images in collaborative planning systems provide a significant conversational (or rhetorical) aid, particularly when individual frames of reference—which may be based on physical landmarks, noise, and other environmental characteristics—need to be reconciled with geographic or spatial abstractions (usually represented as maps).

Thus conversations would frequently turn from an extended attempt to resolve questions of "where we are" or "what is there" toward more meaningful questions centering on "how it is likely to change." In this manner, the technology has the capacity to speed up the process of "recollection and description" to allow more time for "informed speculation." This was observed informally in several instances where groups considering physical interventions to specific areas spent less time talking about the physical characteristics of the area and more time exploring the (in this case visual) implications of change. This is not to say that the importance of recollection and description was minimized; on the contrary, by virtue of the fact that recollection and description could be aided with multimedia representational aids, such discourse could take place more efficiently.

Collaborative planning systems also afford a visualization of otherwise abstract environmental impacts. They also allow for the consideration of a broader range of alternative scenarios that can be discussed. And they offer an integration of analytic tools, relevant media, and cognitive information, especially if they are implemented in a place where people can interact with one another along with these information systems.

Cost and sustainability of such systems are of particular concern. Depending on the scale of implementation and the richness of the data contained in them, these systems can vary widely in terms of both development and maintenance costs (Thompson 1989). Another issue is accessibility. Where is one going to be able to use this? How is one going to get everybody into the room at the right time?

With respect to computer-user interface issues, the initial intention of these information systems was to provide a laser pointer that could be passed among the participants of a meeting. Yet it was found that many of the people in meetings were reluctant to pick up a laser pointer and interact with the system. In an implementation of a collaborative planning system in Washington, D.C. (Shiffer 1995b), it was discovered that a very effective approach was to implement an interface approach called "Leo." "Leo" is not an acronym: it was actually a person named Leo who sat in the back of the room! Leo would follow the conversation and had some sense of what was inside the information system. So he could then predict what was going to be presented next and display relevant information on the screen. Or somebody could ask, "Leo, would you show us this, or Leo, would you show us that?" and he would do so, acting as the intermediary between the information system and the meeting participants. In this respect, Leo's presence was tremendously helpful.

Another very important concern about collaborative planning tools is that the information they contain is not value neutral. Just as these tools can be used to create compelling representations of urban futures, they can create compelling misrepresentations (Monmonier 1991). Also, it is easy to imagine how collaborative planning uses of this technology might lead to paralysis of the planning process resulting from a never-ending analysis and generation of alternatives. Thus it is important to consider where the use of these tools may be appropriate or inappropriate.

Finally, community groups have the capacity to become more technologically autonomous as advanced IT tools (such as authoring, serving, and client software for the WWW) become more accessible. Nevertheless, these groups will likely need expert help to get started. Furthermore, spatial analysis and other activities that rely on sophisticated tools and information infrastructure will continue to require specialized skills or expert help.

Can Representational Applications Play a Role as Strategic Weapons for Advocacy?

The positive aspects of persuasion can be put to a significant test when IT is used to represent competing views of the future. After demonstrating the capabilities of one particular prototype, a planning commission member enthusiastically commented: "This is really great! We've been 'out-gunned' for years. Now we have a chance to give them a taste of their own medicine!" In this case "them" referred to well-funded special interests and project proponents who prepare highly polished presentations to support a specific view of the future. This form of persuasion has been manifest in traditional media as position papers, proposals, feature articles, television news stories, and documentary pieces that describe a plight (or put forward a proposal) from a specific point of view. While traditional media has served to amplify special interests in many of these contexts, it has also given "voice to the voiceless." Of course, one could argue that this has not occurred in many instances, given the high costs and significant social barriers that may make access to even the most receptive media outlets and advocates difficult. While the capacity of IT (such as the WWW) to allow for a greater degree of self-publication may significantly lower such barriers, it remains to be seen whether this will truly broaden access to a receptive and relevant audience or simply lead to one's voice becoming lost in the "din" of the Internet.

The process of dueling views has recently been observed in one instance in which competing views were represented using videotape. The discussion began when the developer of a large chain store submitted a standardized videotape (that had been used in several similar areas) to put forth a persuasive argument about why the proposed store would be good for the community. Such tapes may lead to an overwhelming degree of persuasion when presenting one specific side of an argument; in this case, however, a well-organized opposition to this particular chain submitted their own version of the effects of such developments. The media was non-interactive in this case. It still created a (perhaps false) sense of legitimacy for both sides, however. While one's initial fear would be that the decision makers and the public would be confused by such a juxtaposition, people in this case had a tremendous capacity to act as their own filter, and it could be argued that the medium actually allowed a much broader degree of information to be conveyed in a relatively short period of time.

If one were to extrapolate the admittedly limited lessons from these experiences and apply them to future implementations of (more interactive) multimedia, one might see less of a propensity to "spew" a large amount of information and greater attention paid to selective filtering. With the capacity of multimedia representational aids to shift the focus of a conversation toward a more meaningful look at specific issues, the technology has the capacity to effectively target a selected audience. As noted earlier, just as this technology has the capacity to create a rich and compelling representation, it has the capacity to create a rich and compelling misrepresentation (intentionally or unintentionally). The careful planner will want to be concerned with how people are represented in these systems as well as how information is represented. Finally, there is the issue of sustainability. If this is going to be used as an archival mechanism, one needs to determine who is responsible for the maintenance and integrity of information contained within this. Challenges will continue to center on the legitimacy of arguments, the validity of data, and the various assumptions and premises that went into the formulation of a position. These challenges, however, are not unique to interactive multimedia, and one could argue that the characteristics of the IT actually brings these out into the open more readily.

Not all community groups and planning agencies need to strive to possess this technology. But they should possess an understanding of its power and limitations so that they can view it from a critical perspective. Without the ability to effectively experiment with IT, it can be difficult to fully understand the implications of its use through mere speculation.

References

Barndt, M. G. and W. J. Craig. 1994. "Data Providers Empower Community GIS Efforts." *GIS World* 7(7): 49–51.

Beamish, A. 1995. "Communities On-Line: Community-Based Computer Networks." Master's thesis, Massachusetts Institute of Technology.

Dubbink, D. T. 1989. "Use of Acoustic Examples in Airport Noise Planning and Decision Making." In *Airport Landside Planning Techniques: Transportation Research Record* 1199. 64–70. Washington, D.C.: National Research Council.

Guiterrez, E. 1996. "Representing a Community Interactively: A Multimedia Study of the Mission-Main HOPE VI Project." Master's thesis, Massachusetts Institute of Technology.

Harris, B. and M. Batty. 1993. "Locational Models, Geographic Information and Planning Support Systems." *Journal of Planning Education and Research* 12: 184–198.

Hutchins, E. L., J. D. Hollan, and D. A. Norman. 1986. "Direct Manipulation Interfaces." In *User Centered System Design: New Perspectives on Human Computer Interaction,* edited by D. A. Norman and S. W. Draper, 87–124, Hillsdale, NJ: Lawrence Erlbaum.

Klosterman, R. E. 1992. "Evolving Views of Computer-Aided Planning." *Journal of Planning Literature* 6(3): 249–260.

Markus, M. L. 1987. "Toward A 'Critical Mass' Theory of Interactive Media: Universal Access." *Communication Research* 14(5): 491–511.

Monmonier, M. 1991. *How to Lie with Maps.* Chicago: University of Chicago Press.

Posey, J. 1996. "The St. Louis Community Information Network: A Case Study." In *Urban and Regional Information Systems Association 1996 Annual Conference Proceedings,* edited by M. Salling, 29–43. Cleveland: URISA.

Rasmussen, J. 1986. *Information Processing and Human Machine Interaction: An Approach to Cognitive Engineering.* New York: North Holland.

Sawicki, D. S. and W. J. Craig. 1996. "The Democratization of Data: Bridging the Gap for Community Groups." *Journal of the American Planning Association* 62(4): 512–523.

Schultz, T. J. 1978. "Synthesis of Social Surveys on Noise Annoyance." *Journal of the Acoustical Society of America* 64: 377–405.

Shiffer, M. J. 1992. "Towards a Collaborative Planning System." *Environment and Planning B: Planning and Design* 19: 709–722.

Shiffer, M. J. 1995a. "Environmental Review with Hypermedia Systems." *Environment and Planning B: Planning and Design* 22: 359–372.

Shiffer, M. J. 1995b. "Interactive Multimedia Planning Support: Moving from Stand-Alone Systems to the World Wide Web." *Environment and Planning B: Planning and Design* 22: 649–664.

Thompson, B. 1989. "The Dazzling Benefits (and Hidden Costs) of Computerized Mapping." *Governing* 3(3): 40–46.

9. Software Entrepreneurship among the Urban Poor: Could Bill Gates Have Succeeded if He Were Black? … Or Impoverished?

Alice H. Amsden
Jon Collins Clark

Introduction: The Gumption Factor

The computer software industry is a bastion of entrepreneurship in the late twentieth century. Drug dealing aside, it is one of the few industries associated with the "third industrial revolution" in which the individual entrepreneur can become a multimillionaire overnight.[1] The best example is Bill Gates, whose entrepreneurship and ten-digit financial fortune have been the subject of admiration and awe in at least three popular books in print in the 1990s.

The software industry has been identified as a fertile field for aspiring modern-day Horatio Algers because of its perceived low start-up requirements and barriers to entry. Take, for instance, the following citation from a contemporary conference on the subject of entrepreneurship: "The microcomputer software industry is both a throwback to the classic cottage industry of entrepreneurship and at the same time a leading edge of the new wave of technological entrepreneurship. Like the cottage industry of old, the barriers to entry are modest in the extreme. An investment of a few hundred dollars in hardware; a corner in a room; combined with commitment and hard work can, in most cases, produce a product, and in a few cases, a business" (Teach, Tarpley and Schwartz 1985, p. 546).

This supposed ease of entry for entrepreneurs into software production presumes that even society's most disadvantaged can reap potential gains in this industry. Because barriers to entry are supposedly so low, individuals from the ranks of the urban poor can make it as computer software entrepreneurs alongside individuals from the ranks of the wealthy and privileged. All that is needed is imagination, perseverance, and painstaking effort—"gumption" for short.

We have sought to examine the validity of this proposition. It is intriguing because entrepreneurship is an enchanted and extraordinary talent that seems to emerge from unexpected soils—impoverished youth, as in the case of Andrew Carnegie and Henry Ford, and especially the cultures of persecuted minority groups, as in the Jews, French Huguenots, Indians in East Africa, Chinese in Southeast Asia, and so forth. If entrepreneurship can blossom in these inhospitable climes, then why not in the software industry among the urban poor in American cities, which are typically rife with persecuted minorities?

By entrepreneurship we mean a process whereby an individual or group of individuals perceive a new profit-making opportunity, coordinate and mobilize the resources necessary to implement the original idea, and then monitor the implementation procedures necessary to ensure the efficient execution of plans. This is more or less the definition of entrepreneurship provided by Joseph Schumpeter, an innovative economist in his own right (Schumpeter 1938).

In the 1950s Schumpeter's conception of entrepreneurship inspired a large body of literature on whether different developing countries were likely to spawn an entrepreneurial elite (see, for example, Harbison 1956, Glade 1967, and Marris 1968). This research, however, tended to go nowhere analytically and empirically because entrepreneurship was conceived of simply as genius, a magical quality, or a *je ne sais quoi*, all of which defied systematic investigation.

Certainly entrepreneurship is rare and inspired, and more of an art than a science. Nevertheless, from data on who has innovated in the American software industry, it appears that entrepreneurship is not nearly as quirky as once believed. As we hope to show:

1. American software entrepreneurs tend to have standard characteristics: a very large portion of them are white, male, and extremely well educated. They may all have gumption, but the gumption factor *alone* works in only a very small number of cases (the details of which are in any event unclear).

2. Entry barriers into the software industry may be low in terms of physical capital but are high in terms of human capital, which is generally a key difference between the second and third industrial revolutions. "Human capital" refers to education and work experience. Also important for success is "social capital," or the contacts and networks that facilitate business interactions (Putnam 1993).

3. The category of "entrepreneur" in the United States—which we proxy statistically with certain subcategories of "self-employed"—includes a large number of African Americans. Being black and being an entrepreneur (even in software) are not mutually exclusive, although blacks tend to have a lower incidence of entrepreneurship than whites for reasons that are discussed later in this chapter.

4. We infer from this that what restrains entrepreneurship in industries like software in American inner cities is not race but rather *poverty*, with characteristics of low education and an absence of influential business contacts that are antagonistic to those required for entry into the new high-tech information sectors.

5. Quick fixes—like the dumping of computers into inner-city schools—may encourage the necessary tinkering with hardware that seems to flow in the veins of software engineers. But such gestures are far from sufficient to ensure even a small, steady stream of inner-city entrepreneurial talent. Even before that flow can start to trickle, imbalances must first be addressed in the state of education in general, computer education in particular, job training and job availability, and other factors that currently serve to make real levels of human capital so disparate among different economic classes in the United States.

Entrepreneurship and the Software Industry

Who Are Entrepreneurs?

To understand software entrepreneurship, it is instructive to have some background information on the demographics of entrepreneurs in general. Most research concentrates on the category of the "self-employed" rather than of the "entrepreneur" because no data are available directly on the latter. These two populations overlap considerably, but they are by no means identical (see Reynolds 1995 and Becker 1984). Some self-employed are not entrepreneurs and some entrepreneurs are not self-employed.[2]

The ranks of the self-employed contain many independent professionals who by most definitions, including ours, would not be considered entrepreneurs. "More than half of all dentists, veterinarians, optometrists, podiatrists, and other health diagnosing technicians, authors, painters and sculptors, auctioneers, street and door-to-door sales workers, barbers, child-care workers, and farm operators and managers were self employed in 1983" (Becker 1984, p. 17). Given the heterogeneity of this classification, inferences about entrepreneurs drawn from this population must be taken gingerly.

Research shows that the self-employed are disproportionately represented by native-born white males. Put another way, the self-employment rates among both women and minorities are significantly lower than those among white men. Among minorities, rates of self-employment are lowest among African Americans, somewhat higher among Hispanics, and in the case of Asian Americans, almost equal to that of native-born whites (Aronson 1991; Reynolds 1995; Butler 1991). Just why this has been the case has been the cause for much debate and will be discussed in further detail later in this chapter.

The self-employed are generally older and have some work experience. "The probability of being self-employed increases with labor market experience" (Evans and Leighton 1989, p. 532). In other words, most self-employed are not high school dropouts, college dropouts, or even recent high school or college graduates; they are former employees with real job experience. There is also some evidence of convexity in this trend; one study found that the largest number of entrepreneurs fell within the category of 25–34-year-olds (Reynolds 1995).

On average, the self-employed are better educated than the population at large. This holds true even when controlling for the "professional" contingent among the self-employed—that is, independent lawyers, doctors, and so on—(see Evans and Leighton 1989 and Light 1995). This suggests a quality about entrepreneurs that tends to make them better educated, all else being equal.

The self-employed are generally wealthier than the labor force at large. The significance of the level of monetary assets in explaining either self-employment or a business start-up, however, is somewhat dubious and leaves considerable room for debate. Capital requirements for aspiring entrepreneurs continue to be surprisingly lower than one would expect (Evans and Leighton 1989; Evans and Jovanovic 1989).

The Software Industry

As can be seen in Table 9.1, today's aspiring software entrepreneurs will find that the computer software and services market is still large and growing rapidly, with forecasts predicting more of the same in the coming years. Estimates of the size of the software industry alone put revenues

Table 9.1: Size and growth of U.S. markets for computer software

	Software/Services Total ($ billions)	Software/Services Growth (%)	U.S. Services Total ($ billions)	U.S. Services Growth (%)
1970	2.5		284.0	
1971	3.0	20.0	310.7	9.4
1972	3.4	13.3	341.3	9.8
1973	4.3	26.5	373.0	9.3
1974	5.5	27.9	411.9	10.4
1975	6.5	18.2	461.2	12.0
1976	7.0	7.7	515.9	11.9
1977	8.0	14.3	582.3	12.9
1978	10.0	25.0	656.1	12.7
1979	13.5	35.0	734.6	12.0
1980	18.0	33.3	831.9	13.2
1981	21.0	16.7	934.7	12.4
1982	23.5	11.9	1027.0	9.9
1983	28.2	20.0	1128.7	9.9
1984	35.3	25.2	1227.6	8.8
1985	40.7	15.3	1345.6	9.6
1986	45.0	10.6	1449.5	7.7
1987	53.9	19.8	1584.7	9.3
1988	68.1	26.3	1720.7	8.6
1989	79.9	17.3	1845.5	7.3
1990	94.1	17.8	1983.3	7.5
1991	107.2	13.9	2124.6	7.1
(1992)	(122.0)	(13.8)	(2275.4)	(7.1)
(1993)	(138.9)	(13.9)	(2435.9)	(7.1)
(1994)	(157.2)	(13.2)	(2612.5)	(7.2)
(1995)	(177.5)	(12.9)	(2801.9)	(7.2)
(1996)	(200.6)	(13.0)	(3007.8)	(7.3)
(2002)	(401.2)		(4685.7)	
Compound growth rates (%)				
1971–1981	21.5		11.6	
1981–1991	17.7		8.6	
1991–2002	(12.7)		(7.5)	

Parentheses indicate projected values.
Source: CBEMA (Computer and Business Equipment Manufacturers Association), 1992,
The Information Technology Industry Data Book 1960–2002, Washington, D.C.,
as adapted from (Juliussen 1993).

at about $42 billion in 1991 and projected at over $100 billion by 1995. Approximately 70 percent of those sales were in prepackaged software, the remaining 30 percent being in customized software services (Merges 1996).

Nonetheless, devotees of small-scale entrepreneurship are concerned that the software industry is quickly becoming dominated by industry giants. The concern, as expressed by one analyst, is that "... as entry barriers in the industry increase, the financial resources, technical capabilities, and marketing skills required for a new software organization may constrain the entrepreneurial process" (Haug 1991, p. 878).

As far back as 1986, *Business Week* warned that the increasing importance of corporations as buyers of software was leading to rising concentration on the supply side: "This is leaving the bulk of the market to a few winners. Last year the top 15 companies in personal-computer software accounted for 72 percent of sales of all general application programs, up from only 37 percent in 1981. The products of the three biggest companies —Lotus, Ashton-Tate, and Microsoft—accounted for 35 percent of these revenues" (Field and Harris 1986, p. 129). From this point of view, the best hope for small, independent, software entrepreneurs will be to "dovetail their products much more closely with the majors" (Field and Harris 1986, p. 129), that is, to provide products in market niches that complement (rather than substitute for) the products of the software industry's dominant players.

Despite the increasing market share of industry giants, however, the continued existence of a large number of small firms suggests that there is still ample room in the market for small-scale entrepreneurs. Of the software firms already in existence, most tend to be relatively small operations (in terms of employment), lending support to the notion that there is still room for small players in the market. One recent U.S. survey of software companies found that 18 percent of respondents had 5 employees or less, 38 percent had fifteen or fewer, and roughly 50 percent had thirty or fewer (Merges 1996). The Haug study of the software industry in the state of Washington found that 63 percent of the firms surveyed had fewer than nine employees. The average number of employees among software companies was approximately twenty-two. In another survey, software firms in the United States were found to have, on average, twenty-eight employees as compared to the services sector's overall average of more than forty (cited in Haug 1991).

If industry analysts are correct, this proliferation of small firms in the software industry may very well be curtailed in the near future, although new technologies, such as the Internet, make future projections hazardous. Suffice it to say that prohibitive entry barriers do not appear to exist for budding entrepreneurial talent in industries related to information technology.

Software Entrepreneurship

Fortunately, some specific research has been conducted on the demographic profile of software entrepreneurs themselves (Teach, Tarpley, and Schwartz 1986). Perhaps the most important insight gained is that most software entrepreneurs *are extremely well educated*. A whopping 86 percent of the software entrepreneurs analyzed in one sample (approximately two hundred software firms) had at least a college degree, and 47 percent held advanced degrees (Teach, Tarpley, and Schwartz 1985). Another study in 1987 found similar results among a sample of over two hundred high-tech firms (Goslin 1987). This entry qualification of high educational credentials appears to have accelerated over time. A follow-up study to the 1987 study provided evidence of "... the virtual disappearance of the 'computer jock' without a college degree" (Teach et al. 1987, p. 465).

Software entrepreneurs also usually have some work experience prior to opening their own businesses. The Haug (1991) study of the software industry in Washington state found that only 3 percent of software company founders launched their companies directly out of high school or college. Approximately 86 percent had previously held some position in industry working for another firm, and a majority (approximately 57 percent) had been employed by a software company. In the Teach, Tarpley, and Schwartz (1985) study, less than 2 percent reported that their current position was their first position. Over 40 percent had worked as employees in the software industry.

Research confirms the notion that *physical* capital requirements for software entrepreneurs are relatively low. Initial capitalization levels of the firms in the Teach, Tarpley, and Schwartz (1985) study were relatively

Table 9.2: Composition of the urban poor

	Persistently Poor (8 or more years, 1974–1983)	Poor in 1979	Total U.S. urban population
Ethnicity (%)			
Black	66	51	21
White	34	49	79
Education Among Heads of Household (%)			
K–8 grades	49	29	12
9–11 grades	29	27	17
12 grades	18	32	33
13 or more	4	11	38

Source: Survey Research Center, 1984, User Guide to the Panel Study of Income Dynamics, University of Michigan, Ann Arbor, as adapted from (Adams, et al. 1988)

small. Roughly 50 percent reported initial capitalization levels of $10,000 or less. A follow-up investigation in 1986 found that over 75 percent of firms were initially capitalized exclusively with the personal funds of the principals (Teach, Tarpley, and Schwartz 1986).

The Haug (1991) study found that approximately 83 percent of software companies were initially capitalized through the personal funds of the principals and/or their families and friends. In the Goslin (1987) study, 71 percent of firms were capitalized exclusively with the personal funds of the principals. These findings are consistent with those of Light (1995) and others who have found that physical capital requirements for *all* entrepreneurs, regardless of industry, tend to be relatively lower than one might expect (see also Reynolds 1995).

Finally, software entrepreneurs appear to be predominantly male. Only 15 percent of those in the Teach, Tarpley, and Schwartz (1985) sample were women. This proportion is significantly lower than that of women found among the self-employed as a whole, most estimates of which range between 30 and 40 percent (Becker 1984 and Reynolds 1995).

The Urban Poor: Software Entrepreneurs-in-Waiting?

Urban Poor

The urban poor have become of greater interest to policymakers and social scientists alike because they represent an increasing proportion of the total poor in the United States (Sandefur 1988). The steady increase in the "spatial concentration" of poverty in American inner cities has led us to consider ways of addressing poverty particularly in these geographical centers (see Adams et al. 1988; Danziger 1987; Goldsmith and Blakely 1992; Wilson 1987).

Poverty in U.S. urban centers often has a dual nature. Two kinds of poor are present in the inner city at any given time: first there are the transient poor (poor at a given moment but not likely to be so in the near future), and second are the "persistent poor" (those who have been and are likely to remain in a state of poverty) (Adams et al. 1988). We are mostly concerned with the persistent poor—not with those who are transiently poor on the basis of their reported income in a given year.[3]

As can be seen in Table 9.2, the urban poor are mostly black. Notice that 66 percent of the *persistent* poor were black, whereas the corresponding number of blacks in the urban population as a whole was only 21 percent. Perhaps most significantly for the purposes of this study, the urban poor as described in Table 9.2 are poorly educated. Among the persistently poor, 78 percent of the heads of the household did not graduate from high school. Only 4 percent had even one year of schooling beyond high school.

As a final note, it is important to recognize that the urban poor are often unemployed or out of the labor force altogether. The correlation between poverty and unemployment is widely acknowledged and is possibly becoming stronger (Wilson 1996). For instance, a 1986 study found that "a reduction in the unemployment rate from 6 to 5.5 percent would reduce the number of poor people by about 2.5 million" (Lynn and McGreary 1990, p. 261). For our purposes, it is important to be aware that those living in poverty, because they are often unemployed, are likely to have no recent job experience in any industry whatsoever (see also Lichter 1988).

Urban Poor and Software Entrepreneurs: How Do They Match Up?

Now that we have two basic demographic portraits, of software entrepreneurs and of the urban poor, the question is how they match up. We know that software entrepreneurs are, on average, white, male, college-educated professionals with some job experience, often in the field of computers. Among the urban poor, we know that they are, on average, black, have not graduated from high school, and are often currently unemployed or out of the workforce altogether. Many are also female heads of households.[4] Clearly, these two groups do not seem to overlap very much.

Urban Entrepreneurs

Nevertheless, the set of general demographic characteristics among the urban poor that we have provided here does not altogether preclude the existence of entrepreneurship in urban areas. There are, in fact, urban entrepreneurs. Rates of entrepreneurship in the inner city, however, fall significantly below those in the country as a whole. "Entrepreneurship is patently suboptimal in the dilapidated inner cities of the United States" (Light 1995, p. 224).

Among the urban poor, those who are entrepreneurs are likely to be "value entrepreneurs": those choosing the low returns of self-employment over the low returns from a low-wage job. "Franchises and home-enterprises" are likely endeavors for the urban poor—undertakings requiring low levels of education and learned job skills (Balkin 1989, pp. 44–45).

Race and Entrepreneurship

Thus far the evidence does not suggest that skin color is a prerequisite for success in entrepreneurial endeavors, whatever their nature. It is true that rates of self-employment among blacks and Hispanics have lagged behind those of nonminorities, as noted earlier, and there has been considerable debate as to the cause of this disparity. Much of the variation in rates of self-employment is *not* explained by independent variables such as education, age, and income (Butler 1991 and Light 1995).

Instead, some have argued that cultural differences among ethnic groups have been the greatest source of differing rates of self-employment (Light 1995). But other factors must also be considered. For instance, it may be that racial discrimination on the demand side may influence the decision of minorities to become self-employed. The more (perceived) discrimination, the greater the risk of failure and, therefore, the higher the opportunity costs of investing in entrepreneurship. A related hypothesis is that affirmative action in the labor market may have made the opportunity costs associated with self-employment significantly higher for minorities than for other ethnic groups (Butler 1991). Others have suggested that a lack of past experience in business and a consequent underdevelopment of social and business networks for some ethnic groups is a crucial contributing factor (Fratoe 1988).

But despite variations in the proportions of those who are self-employed among different ethnic groups, there is still a substantial number of self-employed who are from minority groups. Moreover, concrete evidence suggests that their characteristics and experiences are remarkably similar to those of the nonminority self-employed. Based on 1980 census data, Bate's 1987 study of the self-employed found that among those whose self-employment income was *below* average, the characteristics and earnings of minorities and nonminorities were almost identical. The results of this study are provided in Table 9.3.

As can be seen in the table, the same commonalties cannot be said to be true among those with *above* average earnings. In the high-earner category, nonminorities appear to have earned approximately 20 percent more than their minority counterparts. Most of this disparity in earnings, however, can be accounted for by differences in three independent variables: age, education, and sex (Bates 1987).

Although in smaller proportions to those in nonminority groups, it is still worth noting that minorities are becoming entrepreneurs in all types of fields—increasingly so in high-skilled and high-earning fields (Bates 1987). These fields include the computer and software industries: 4 percent of the entrepreneurs in one sample had initiated ventures in computer services (Hisrich and Brush 1986).

Research also shows that the qualities that make high-earning entrepreneurs among minorities are the same qualities that make high-

Table 9.3: Mean traits of above average versus below average earners of self-employment income

| | Low Earners | | High Earners | |
	Minorities	Non-Minorities	Minorities	Non-Minorities
Age	43.5	44.5	43.1	44.7
Education	10.9	12.3	12.1	13.4
Proportion Female	0.322	0.337	0.133	0.091
1979 Self-Employment Income ($)	4,446	4,447	22,689	27,199
1979 Income From All Sources ($)	7,028	8,878	25,792	31,676
1979 Household Income ($)	17,710	20,211	34,297	38,263
No. of Observations	13,845	3,414	7,119	1,805

High earners are those earning self-employment income above the sample mean of $10,640.
Low earners fall below the mean. Data exclude doctors and lawyers; nonfarm agricultural industries
are included. Self-employment earnings include nonfarm earnings only.

Source: 1980 Census of Population Public Use Samples as cited in (Bates 1987).

earning entrepreneurs among nonminorities; namely, among both demographic groups, those with higher levels of education and with some working experience earn more than those with less education and experience (all
else being equal) (Bates 1987; Fratoe 1988; Hisrich and Brush 1986).

Thus, as a step toward answering the question we posed in the
title of this chapter—Could Bill Gates have succeeded were he black (or a
member of another minority)?—our answer is yes, he could have succeeded,
all else being equal. Nevertheless, all else is typically not equal. The incidence of poverty is significantly higher among most minorities than in the
population at large. As we show in the following section, it is the pathology
of poverty, including low levels of human and social capital, that is most
inimical to entrepreneurship.

What Does It Take?

Human and Social Capital

Even though race may not be a determining factor in the success of prospective entrepreneurs, evidence strongly suggests that both human and

social capital are critical ingredients of success. As mentioned in the previous section, successful minority entrepreneurs have the same characteristics as nonminority entrepreneurs: they are well educated and usually have relevant job experience. In other words, they have higher levels of human capital. They also have higher levels of social capital, in part as a result of their better education and richer job experience.

Research concerning the importance of formal education in the success of entrepreneurs has been extensive and conclusive. Study after study indicates that successful entrepreneurs have above-average levels of education (see Aronson 1991, Bates 1987, Hisrich and Brush 1986, and Light 1995). We have every reason to believe, then, that formal schooling is becoming increasingly important as a determinant of high self-employed earnings, just as it is in the labor force at large (Danziger 1987).

More specifically, advanced business degrees and entrepreneurial-specific training seem to serve as important assets to entrepreneurs in general, including those in software. One study of software venture teams found that those that contained at least one member with an advanced business degree were more successful than those that did not (Teach, Tarpley, and Schwartz 1985). Specific courses that targeted potential entrepreneurs and taught them the practical know-how needed to start their own businesses have also been shown to be effective (Balkin 1989; Price 1991; Rush et al. 1987).

Not only an advanced degree but a college degree in any discipline seems to contribute to entrepreneurial success. The nature of that degree, if not in business, would most likely depend on the nature of the entrepreneur's intended industry. For instance, the Teach, Tarpley, and Schwartz (1985) study of software entrepreneurs found that a majority of the respondents had undergraduate degrees in a technical field (engineering, math, science, or computer science). Another quarter of the respondents, however, had degrees in liberal arts or humanities. This suggests that beyond the specific nature of the degree, there are other benefits that a college degree can provide to the potential entrepreneur.

One such potential benefit is the opportunity it can provide for the degree holder to gain relevant job experience and make social contacts. This is especially true when one considers what we already know about the importance to entrepreneurs of having previous job experience.

Another potential benefit of a college degree is the membership it can provide graduates in instrumental peer networks. A great deal of research has been done on the importance of social connections for entrepreneurial success. Researchers have found that higher levels of social capital contribute to an increased probability of entrepreneurial success (Fratoe 1988); for instance, peer networks have been shown to contribute to the development of marketing and subcontracting among new firms (Holt 1987 and Rush et al. 1987). It is this development of social capital no less than human capital that has contributed to entrepreneurial success among those with undergraduate and graduate degrees.

Computer Education and Software Entrepreneurship

Given the abundant evidence that successful entrepreneurship, whether in software or other endeavors, is strongly associated with high levels of education, the hypothesis of low entry barriers into the software industry requires serious revision. Barriers in the form of physical capital may be relatively low, but those in the form of human and social capital appear substantial. Thus, even though the eccentric individual with megadoses of gumption may succeed as an entrepreneur whatever his or her background, population groups with low levels of human and social capital are unlikely *on average* to pioneer new, legitimate business ventures, small or large.

Nevertheless, the cherished American ideal that anyone with gumption can make it as an entrepreneur lives on with respect to information technology. Consequently, there has been a vigorous attempt on the part of government and business to blanket the inner cities with computers and computer-related crash courses, the hardware and software supposedly needed for anyone with a dream to become a software entrepreneur. The increased proliferation of computers throughout American public schools has thus rekindled the old American dream of equal opportunity. Nevertheless, a closer look at the nature of computer education in poor urban schools shows why this dream is seriously out of focus.

It is true that in recent years much has been done to increase the number of computers in poor urban schools. Initiatives have been launched by large private corporations such as AT&T, Microsoft, and Xerox to place computers and develop computer networks in public schools (U.S. Department of Education 1996). Local private companies have complemented these initiatives by donating their outdated computers. Meanwhile, the federal government has begun to pay more attention to the importance of computer education, a visible example being President Clinton's recent campaign promise to "put a computer in every classroom" and to link these computers on the Internet. Nevertheless, the impact these developments have had on the overall quality of computer education among the poor remains suspect for the following reasons.

First, although the absolute number of computers in poorer schools has increased, it still appears to fall short of the number in more wealthy classrooms. Picciano's 1991 study comparing computer education in schools in Westchester County, New York, with those in New York City found that the ratio of computers to students was more than twice as high in Westchester. Another study found similar degrees of imbalance in the computer-to-student ratio between suburban and urban districts (Quality Education Data 1991). Thus, although it may be true that some effort has been made to address the discrepancy in access to computers in poor and rich schools, serious imbalances persist.

Perhaps even more important, researchers have found that there are significant differences in how computers are used in school districts with different income levels. According to Owens (1995, p. 84), "urban schools with predominantly minority students have been found typically to use computers for tutorial and rote drill-and-practice programs, while suburban schools with students from higher-income families have generally been found to use computers for problem solving and programming." In eighth-grade mathematics classes, "urban teachers reported that they were more likely than suburban and rural teachers to use computers for remedial purposes" (Owens 1995, p. 90). Thus, there is reason to believe that the overall quality of computer education in inner-city schools suffers compared with that of suburban schools; the nature of "literacy" is different.

Alongside the inequities in computer education that exist in the nation's schools, one must further consider the inequities that characterize young people's access to computers at home. Intuition, rather than systematic research, suggests that access to computers at home as well as at school is an important condition for the nurturing of software entrepreneurship. A 1994 national survey found that the degree of technology used in the home was largely dependent on income: "college graduates and families with high incomes were more likely to own several types of electronic technology" (Black Child Advocate 1995, p. 3).

Young people who have exposure to creative uses for computers, and continued access to and experience with computers in their own homes, are far more likely to tinker in creating software than those who do not. These and other inequities in asset endowments put the poor at a distinct disadvantage in fulfilling any entrepreneurial dreams with respect to information technology.

Conclusion

The urban poor are not likely on average to become software entrepreneurs for many of the same reasons they are not likely to become brain surgeons, investment bankers, or CEOs of Fortune 500 companies—they simply do not have the requisite educational and social capital. We have focused on the paucity of their human and social skills, although this is not the only factor inhibiting the development of high-earning entrepreneurs in the inner city. To our minds, however, it is the primary one in light of the technological requirements of the third industrial revolution through which the United States and other advanced economies are now passing. Were education, training, and job experience brought up to par, then policymakers could begin to address other entry barriers to small-firm entrepreneurship, such as access to finance capital.[5] But these other barriers will remain moot as long as the urban poor remain insufficiently skilled to take the first step on the long road to successful entrepreneurship—the mere conception of a novel product or process that sufficient numbers of people with high enough levels of income are willing and able to buy.

Thus, even though Bill Gates may be the *un*characteristic software entrepreneur for having dropped out of college (Harvard no less), he is typical insofar as he enjoyed membership in a privileged American economic and social elite. The odds that he would have succeeded had his social world been that of the urban ghetto may be predicted to be infinitesimally small.

All this puts an enormous burden on education to bootstrap the poor. We would suggest, however, that although better education in poor neighborhoods may increase the number of successful entrepreneurs, it is insufficient for a technomodernization of the American inner city itself. This may be illustrated briefly by drawing an analogy between poor people in rich countries and poor countries in the world economy. After World War II a large number of extremely poor underdeveloped countries attempted to industrialize. Most failed because they started from a capital base (physical, human, and social) that was too low to allow them to compete in world markets. But a few enjoyed spectacular success, in particular South Korea and Taiwan, which were very poor initially but which had exceptionally equal income distributions (a result of land reform) and unusually high levels of education (in part as a consequence of the geopolitics underlying American foreign aid allocation). What is noteworthy about South Korea and Taiwan, however, is that initially their high investments in education resulted not in rapid domestic economic growth but in a "brain drain"—the educated migrated abroad to high-wage countries and only returned home once endogenous growth had begun—by a variety of complex and controversial means, although none of these means involved the exploitation of high technology. The industries in which South Korea and Taiwan (and Japan before it) prospered involved first low- and then mid-technology, such as steel, industrial chemicals, and later automobiles (Hikino and Amsden 1994).

So, too, we would suggest, better education of the poor will initially result in their migration out of the inner city, and not necessarily in an immediate improvement in living standards of the inner city proper. What remains unclear—and controversial—is how the inner city itself is to be modernized, and what role high technology, specifically information technology, will play in that process.

Notes

We wish to thank Robert Bauer, David Friend, Takashi Hikino, Stanley Kugel, Sarah Kuhn, and John Seely Brown for helpful insights.

1. The "third industrial revolution" is associated with innovations in electronics, communications, chemicals, and pharmaceuticals, including biotechnology, which is

also friendly toward the small entrepreneur (Chandler Jr. and Hikino 1997).

2. "Downsizing" in large American corporations appears to have swelled the ranks of the "self-employed" in the form of a burgeoning number of underemployed "consultants."

3. We are concerned with the persistent poor in order to understand the entrepreneur-ship among the most disadvantaged. The transient poor may well have a higher incidence of entrepreneurship than the persistent poor; more research is required.

4. Roughly 70 percent of a sample of poor urban households were found to be headed by females (Adams et al. 1988).

5. Teach, Tarpley and Schwartz (1985) found that a large percentage of software entrepreneurs borrowed large sums of money from friends and family. How many among the urban poor could do so?

References

Adams, T., G. Duncan, and W. Rogers. 1988. "The Persistence of Urban Poverty." In *Quiet Riots*, edited by F. Harris and R. Wilkins, pp. 78–99. New York: Pantheon Books.

Aronson, R. L. 1991. *Self-Employment: A Labor Market Perspective.* Ithaca, NY: ILR Press.

Balkin, S. 1989. *Self Employment for Low-Income People.* New York: Praeger.

Bates, T. 1987. "Self-Employed Minorities: Traits and Trends." *Social Science Quarterly* 68: 539–551.

Becker, E. 1984. "Self-Employed Workers: An Update to 1983." *Monthly Labor Review* 107(7): 14–18.

Butler, J. S. C. H. 1991. "Ethnicity and Entrepreneurship in America: Toward an Explanation of Racial and Ethnic Group Variations in Self-Employment." *Sociological Perspectives* 34(1): 79–94.

Chandler Jr., A. D. and T. Hikino. 1997. "The Large Industrial Enterprise and the Dynamics of Modern Economic Growth." In *Big Business and the Wealth of Nations*, edited by A.D. Chandler Jr., F. Amatori, and T. Hikino. Cambridge: Cambridge University Press.

Danziger, S. P. G. 1987. "Continuing Black Poverty: Earnings Inequality, the Spatial Concentration of Poverty, and the Underclass." *American Economic Review* 77(2): 211–215.

Evans, D. and B. Jovanovic. 1989. "An Estimated Model of Entrepreneurial Choice Under Liquidity Constraints." *Journal of Political Economy* 97(4): 808–827.

Evans, D. and L. Leighton. 1989. "Some Empirical Aspects of Entrepreneurship." *American Economic Review* 79(3): 519–535.

Field, A. and C. Harris. 1986. "Software: The Growing Gets Rough." *Business Week*: (March 24): 128–134.

Fratoe, F. 1988. "Social Capital of Black Business Owners." *Development of Black Political Economy* 16(4): 33–50.

Glade, W. P. 1967. "Approaches to a Theory of Entrepreneurship Formation." *Explorations in Entrepreneurial History* 5(3).

Goldsmith, W. and E. Blakely. 1992. *Separate Societies: Poverty and Inequality in U.S. Cities.* Philadelphia: Temple University Press.

Goslin, L. N. 1987. "Characteristics of Successful High-Tech Start-Up Firms." In *Frontiers of Entrepreneurship Research*, edited by N. Churchill, B. Kirchhoff, W. Krasner, and K. Vesper. Wellesley, MA: Babson College.

Harbison, F. H. 1956. "Entrepreneurial Organization as a Factor in Economic Development." *Quarterly Journal of Economics* 70(3).

Haug, P. 1991. "Regional Formation of High-Technology Service Industries: The Software Industry in Washington State." *Environment and Planning A* 23: 869–884.

Hikino, T. and A. H. Amsden. 1994. "Staying Behind, Stumbling Back, Sneaking Up, Soaring Ahead: Late Industrialization in Historical Perspective." In *Convergence of Productivity: Cross-National Studies and Historical Evidence*, edited by W. J. Baumol, R. R. Nelson, and E. N. Wolff, pp. 285–315. New York: Oxford University Press.

Hisrich, R., and C. Brush. 1986. "Characteristics of the Minority Entrepreneur." *Journal of Small Business Management* 24(4): 1–8.

Holt, D. 1987. "Network Support Systems: How Communities Can Encourage Entrepreneurship." In *Frontiers of Entrepreneurship Research*, edited by N. Churchill, R. Kirchoff, W. Krasner, and K. Vespero. Wellesley, MA: Babson College.

Juliussen, K. and E. Juliussen. 1993. *The 1993 Computer Industry Almanac*. Austin, The Reference Press Inc.

Lichter, D. 1988. "Racial Differences in Underemployment in American Cities." *American Journal of Sociology* 93(4): 771–792.

Light, I. C. R. 1995. *Race, Ethnicity, and Entrepreneurship in Urban America*. New York: Aldine De Gruyter.

Lynn, L. E, and M. H. H. McGreary, eds. 1990. *Inner-City Poverty in the United States.* Washington, DC: National Academy Press.

Marris, P. 1968. "The Social Barriers to African Entrepreneurship." *Journal of Development Studies* 5(1).

Merges, R. P. 1996. "A Comparative Look at Intellectual Property Rights and the Software Industry." In *The International Computer Software Industry*, edited by D. Mowery, pp. 272–303. New York: Oxford University Press.

Owens, E. H. W. 1995. "Differences Among Urban, Suburban, and Rural Schools on Technology Access and Use In Eighth-Grade Mathematics Classrooms." *Journal of Educational Technology Systems* 24(1): 83–92.

Picciano, A. 1991. "Computers, City and Suburb: A Study of New York City and Westchester County Public Schools." *The Urban Review* 23(3): 191–203.

Price, C. D. F. 1991. "Four Year Study of Colorado Entrepreneurship with Minority and Women Business Owners." In *Frontiers of Entrepreneurship Research*, edited by W. Bygrave. Wellesley, MA: Babson College.

"Parents Must Ensure That Children Have Access to Information Technologies." 1995.

Black Child Advocate (Summer): 3–7.

Putnam, R. D. 1993. *Making Democracy Work: Civic Traditions in Modern Italy*. Princeton, NJ: Princeton University Press.

Quality Education Data. 1991. Microcomputer Uses in Schools: A 1990–91 Q.E.D. Update. Denver.

Reynolds, P. 1995. "Who Starts New Firms? Linear Additive Versus Interaction Based Models." In *Frontiers of Entrepreneurship Research*, edited by W. Bygrave. Wellesley, MA: Babson College.

Rush, B., et al. 1987. "The Use of Peer Networks in the Start-Up Process." In *Frontiers of Entrepreneurship Research*, edited by N. Churchill, B. Kirchoff, W. Krasner, and K. Vespero. Wellesley, MA: Babson College.

Sandefur, G. D. M. T., ed. 1988. *Divided Opportunities: Minorities, Poverty, and Social Policy*. New York: Plenum Press.

Schumpeter, J. 1938. *The Theory of Economic Development*. Cambridge, MA: Harvard University Press.

Teach, R., F. Tarpley, and R. Schwartz. 1985. "Who Are the Microcomputer Software Entrepreneurs?" In *Frontiers of Entrepreneurship Research*, edited by B. Kirchoff. Wellesley, MA: Babson College.

Teach, R., F. Tarpley, and R. Schwartz. 1986. "Software Venture Teams." In *Frontiers of Entrepreneurship Research, 1987*. Ronstadt. Wellesley, MA: Babson College.

Teach, R., F. Tarpley, R. Schwartz, and D. Brawley. 1987. "Maturation in the Microcomputers Software Industry: Venture Teams and Their Firms." In *Frontiers of Entrepreneurship Research, 1987*, edited by N. Churchill, B. Kirchoff, W. Krasner, and K. Vesper. Wellesley, MA: Babson College.

U.S. Department of Education. 1996. "Private Companies Already Offering Computer Aid To Schools." *Department of Education Reports* 17(9): 5–8.

Wilson, W. J. 1987. *The Truly Disadvantaged*. Chicago: University of Chicago Press.

Wilson, W. J. 1996. *When Work Disappears: the World of the New Urban Poor*. New York: Random House.

10. Action Knowledge and Symbolic Knowledge: The Computer as Mediator

Jeanne Bamberger

This chapter addresses a small set of troublesome but pervasive educational issues that are illuminated as we look at the possible roles for computer technology in classrooms. I begin by stating some of these concerns in a rather abrupt fashion, in part as a response to others' views as expressed in earlier chapters. In the remaining sections I play out these initial responses, propose some alternatives, and give one extended example of how such alternatives actually look when played out in an unusual classroom.

• To assume that "knowledge" and "information" are equivalent can be destructive to learning. Information lies quietly in books, is gathered from others, or accessed via the Web. Knowledge is actively developed through experience, interpretation, constructions, questions, failures, successes, values, and so forth.

• Children can be active makers and builders of knowledge, but they are often asked to become passive consumers—the target of selected others' goods and information.

• Children are also makers and builders of *things*. In this context, *"grasping"* is not a metaphor as in grasping an idea, the truth. For children living in an unstable, unpredictable world, literally grasping, holding, holding still, holding on is a persistent need.

• For children whose worlds are spinning too fast already, and who are vulnerable to a sense of loss of place—in space, in a family, in a community—using the computer for speedy access to vast spaces and quick, efficient, packaged-up, ready-to-go information may be more confounding than helpful.

Background: The Laboratory for Making Things

The work with young children began as a project and a place that we called the Laboratory for Making Things (LMT). It took up residence in the Graham and Parks Alternative Public School in Cambridge, Massachusetts. The project was initially motivated by my interest in a well-recognized but poorly understood phenomenon: children who are virtuosos at building and fixing complicated things in the everyday world around them (bicycles, plumbing, car motors, musical instruments and music, games and gadgets, or a club house out of junk from the local construction site) are often the same children who have trouble learning in school. They are children who have the ability to design and build complex systems, who are experts at devising experiments to analyze and test problems confronted along the way, and who can learn by extracting principles from the successful workings of the objects they make. But they are also children who are frequently described as having trouble working with common symbolic expressions—numbers, graphs, simple calculations, written language. With knowledge in schools equated mostly with the ability to deal with conventional symbolic expressions, it is not surprising that attention focuses on what these children cannot do. Thus, instead of seeing these children as virtuosos, they are seen as "failing to perform."[1] Thus, my primary question was this: If we could better understand the nature of the knowledge that the children were bringing to what they do so well, could we help them use this knowledge to succeed in school, too?

Getting Started

Work at the Graham and Parks School began in the fall of 1985. Susan Jo Russell, who had been a teacher and was now completing her Ed.D. in math education, joined me in starting the project. The school, located in a working neighborhood of Cambridge, is named after Sondra Graham, a social activist and former member of the Cambridge School Committee, and Rosa Parks, well known for the role she played in the struggle for equal rights in the 1960s. The core of the student population mirrors the diverse population of Cambridge, and in addition includes most of the Haitian-Creole-speaking children in the city.

Our initial goals derived from hunches concerning the hands-on knowledge of children, together with the years of experience Susan Jo and I already had in working with children in the computer lab run by Seymour Papert at MIT—called the Logo Lab. We imagined a learning environment where children could use computer technology as a resource for inquiry and invention in a world that fit their size of space/time. It would be an environment where children would easily alternate between action and symbolic description, between sensory experience and representations of it, between the virtual world inside "the box" and the familiar world of their own powerful know-how in real time/space/motion. It would be a world in which children could catch up with their own under-standings—*slowing down* events and actions so as literally to grasp the "goings on" of things and how they relate to ideas.

We began with the teachers. All the teachers in the school (grades K–8) were sent an invitation to join the project. We described it as an opportunity to spend two hours once a week after school thinking together about children's learning through sharing puzzles and insights from the classroom. Teachers would learn how to program a computer. Eventually we would design and equip a lab, and develop activities for the children who the teachers would bring to the lab on a regular basis. We were able to offer participants $300 for the school year. Twelve teachers signed up, with a core group of eight becoming regular participants. We had expected the initial planning period to last perhaps two months, but the teachers felt ready to bring children to the lab only after we had worked together for nearly six months. As it turned out, those six months were critical in shaping the form that the lab itself took.

A month into the planning period, the Apple IIE computers arrived.[2] Unpacking and putting them together was, we believed, a neces-sary first step toward helping the teachers gain a feeling of intimacy with the machines. Learning the computer language, Logo, was a further step toward this sense of intimacy, and it had a surprising spin-off: perhaps because "the computer" was a totally new medium, the teachers shed their initial fears and became fascinated, instead, with their own and one another's confusions around their interactions with the machine. Probing their confusions came to be seen as a source of insight: what was behind the confusion and how could you find *that* out?

This new productive source for inquiry had another unexpected spin-off: the conversations about children's learning changed their shape and focus. Stories from the classroom turned now to *children's* confusions and how to understand them. Just as the teachers came to appreciate their own confusions as a step toward unveiling new or previously hidden ideas, so appreciating children's confusions could also be a source of insight into learning. Making the assumption that no matter what a child said or did, it made sense to him, the question was: How could we find the sense he or she was making at the time? As one teacher, Mary Briggs, put it, "I hear a child saying this weird thing, but if only I could look out from where that child was looking, it would make perfect sense."

During these six months, the lab, a large room in the school, was gradually "furnished" with a great variety of materials for designing and building structures that work—gears and pulleys, Lego blocks, pattern blocks and large building blocks, cuisenaire rods, batteries and buzzers for building simple circuitry, foamcore, wood and glue for model house construction, as well as drums and keyboards for making music. And the ten Apple IIE computers took their place as another medium for building structures that work and make sense—what we came to call "working systems." The children renamed the room the "design lab." The project, including the weekly meetings with the teachers, continued until funds ran out in 1992. Some three hundred children ranging in age from five to twelve participated in lab activities during those seven years.

Emerging Questions

In our work with the teachers, one of our goals was to design projects that were overtly different on the surface, but embodied similar underlying principles: projects that differed in the kinds of objects and materials used, that utilized differing sensory modalities, that held the potential for differing modes of description, but that shared conceptual underpinnings. The idea was that by juxtaposing such projects, shared principles would emerge as conceptual structures in themselves, rather than remain associated with and embedded in just one machine, one kind of material, or one kind of situation. In designing these projects, we were, in fact, drawing on the effective learning strategies that the children brought with them from outside of school: to learn by noticing and drawing out principles from the success of the objects and the actions that worked.

Children were encouraged to move back and forth between making working systems in real time/space (Lego cars, huge cardboard gears, pulleys, and rhythms [played on drums]) and working systems using the Apple computers as a platform (Logo graphics, music, quiz programs). A cluster of interrelated questions emerged, including: how do children (or any of us) learn to turn continuously moving, organized actions, such as clapping a rhythm, bouncing a ball, circling gears, into static, discrete, symbolic descriptions that represent our experience of these objects and our sensory mastery of them? How do we learn to make descriptions that hold still to be looked at?

The computer played a role as mediator in addressing these questions by helping the children make explicit the shared principles that might otherwise have remained hidden in the objects that embodied them. The computer, as the children would use it, was another medium for designing and building working systems. But unlike making objects through actions in real time/space, in making objects in the virtual world of the computer, one has to begin by describing in symbolic form what one wants to happen. Once made, the symbolic description becomes what has been described—symbol becomes object/action! Descriptions written on paper, or voiced loudly, remain static: the person receiving the description has to try to put its pieces together, to imagine what is meant. And it is often difficult to know if the meaning you have gleaned is the meaning intended. Did you get it right? You have to ask the teacher or wait to be told. The computer has a unique capability: you are not left in doubt— descriptions "sent" to the computer instantly turn into the things or actions described.

But these symbolic "instructions" must be made within the constraints of the computer's "understanding"—that is, within the symbolic constraints of some computer language. The result is that the computer as a mediator between description and action often turns into a strangely reflecting playground creating provocative surprises along the way. The children needed time to notice and to play with these surprises; rather than turning away, they made experiments to interrogate them— much as they knew how to do in fixing their bikes or the Lego cars they made in the lab. But the computer experiments had a special quality: because descriptions became actions, the relationships between symbols and actions could be tested. Indeed, chasing surprises, tracing the paths that led to them, turned out to be a very concrete way for the children to explore their own confusions. Much as it had been with the teachers, interrogating their confusions was often, for the children, a critical step toward gaining insight. Strange encounters of a special kind.

Design Worlds: Similarities and Differences

Learning in the design lab, then, depended deeply on the children's movement between building handmade working systems and using the computer as a medium for building virtual working systems. And in making
these moves, we encouraged the children to *make explicit* the differences
they found between these design worlds—for instance, the immediacy of
drumming a rhythm on real drums compared with the distancing involved
in getting the computer synthesizer to play the rhythm. Thus, rather than
joining handmade and computer-made systems to construct a *single working
system* (such as using a computer interface to control a Lego car), we urged
the children to pay attention to differences in the kinds of things that
inhabited these worlds. How did the differences between design worlds
influence what they thought about, and what were the differences in the
kinds of problems, confusions, and puzzles they encountered as they moved
from hands-on, real time/space situations to virtual computer situations?
Confronting these differences was important in helping the children move
more effectively between their "smart hands" and the symbolically oriented
school world.

But the children also noticed and helped us notice moments,
often caught on-the-wing, when these moves back and forth revealed surprising *similarities*. And, as we had hoped, these observations' similarities
("Hey, that reminds me of what we did ...") often led to the emergence
of a previously hidden shared powerful principle. As I show, capturing
these moments and the discussions they led to produced some of the most
significant learning for both the children and the teachers.

The movement back and forth between materials, sensory modalities, and modes of description resulted in certain kinds of ideas becoming
part of the lab culture, illuminating the children's designing, building, and
understanding across all the media. Three of these ideas were especially
present:

1. the notion of a "procedure," which initially developed in their
computer designing but was found useful in designing handmade systems
as well;

2. the sense that it is useful and interesting to look for "patterns"
that germinated in handmade designing but seeped into computer

designing; and

3. closely related to both, the idea of "chunking" or grouping, which grew out of a specific need in working with the continuousness of musical objects, but its usefulness crept into designing other objects, too. Issues around chunking became most concrete in the children's frequently heard, but rather unexpected question: As they examined one another's constructions, we would hear them ask, "So what is a *thing*, here?"

Working in the Lab with Children

Teachers brought their whole classes to the lab for scheduled hours during the regular school day. But on Wednesdays after school Mary Briggs and I spent the afternoon working with six nine- and ten-year-old children. Mary knew the children well because, as the special education teacher, she worked with each of them on a daily basis. She selected these six children because she believed they would particularly thrive in the design lab environment. But for me, actually working with children every week— instead of only listening to the teachers' stories about them—changed my whole understanding of what those stories were about.[3] While we had talked a lot about how to make sense of what a child says or does, it came as a revelation to realize how hard it is to really make contact with a child, to become intimate with her thinking so as to learn from it—especially a child for whom life in school has not been especially rewarding. And this was probably particularly so for a person like me—a middle-class academic trying to understand children for whom life was so different from anything I knew. Most of all I came to appreciate the work of teachers: what a huge difference there is between thinking and talking about schooling, and actually being there—living there every single day, not just once a week for an afternoon like I was. Working with Mary and the children made that one afternoon an intense learning experience—learning that has influenced almost everything I have done since then.

A Day in the Life of the Design Lab

A glimpse into the children's work during one day in the lab will help bring some of these ideas to life. The events on this day occurred after a

Figure 10.1: Children's invented notations

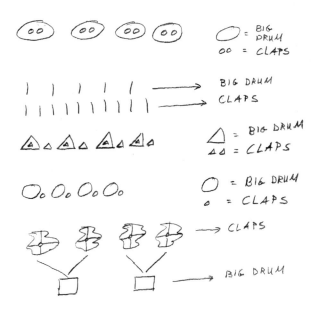

couple of sessions in which the children had been making and playing drum pieces. For instance, one child would play a steady beat on a big drum, instructing the others to clap another steady beat (a faster or slower one) that would "fit" into the first drummer's drumming. The children had also used various media (crayons and paper, cuisenaire rods, pattern blocks) to invent notations for their drumming patterns—"so someone else could play what we played."

Gears played an important role in the lab, too, especially as a means for helping children see and feel shared principles across media and sensory modalities. As Seymour Papert has pointed out: "The gear, as well as connecting with the formal knowledge of mathematics, it also connects with the 'body knowledge,' the sensorimotor schemata of a child. You can BE the gear, you can understand how it turns by projecting yourself into its place and turning with it. It is this double relationship—both abstract and sensory—that gives the gear the power to carry powerful mathematics into the mind. The gear acts, here, as a *transitional object.*"[4]

My hunch was that moving between clapping rhythms and playing with gears could be a particularly lively playground for making this "double relationship" manifest.

While working in the Logo Lab at MIT, I had designed, with the help of others, a music version of Logo called MusicLogo which was now up and running in the design lab. Thus, even within the Logo world of the computer, the children could move across media—sometimes doing graphics, sometimes doing music. The idea was the same as in other design projects: by moving across media and sensory modalities but now keeping the means of procedural designing the same, shared principles would seep out; for example, the same procedure and the principles behind it were used to make a graphic shape get smaller and smaller, to print a "countdown" (10-9-8-7 ...), and to make a synthesizer drum play faster and faster beats.

On this Wednesday afternoon we moved through several activities —from drumming, to playing with very large cardboard gears (that had been made by a group of slightly older children), to clapping, and eventually to "telling" the computer how to "play" drum patterns using Music-Logo coupled with the virtual percussion instruments of a synthesizer.

Gears and Rhythms

As we moved over to the gears, Mary asked the children, "Now how could these gears and the drumming sort of be alike?"

Ruth is standing by the gears, spinning them; her hands are actually *being* the gears as she talks. Harry is sitting at the left with Mary's arms on his shoulders, Leon is at the right. Ruth, like the other children, was having a hard time in her regular classes. But as she turns the gears, watching them go around, she spontaneously makes a proposal.

> Ruth: Well, it's a math problem: Like this one has (counting teeth on the small gear) 1, 2, 3, 4, 5, 6, 7, 8—And you bring the

Figure 10.2: Leon, Ruth, and Mary with the gears

8 around 4 times to get it (the big gear) all the way around. Now how many teeth does that one (bigger gear) have?

Rita: 24.

Ruth: No, 4 times 8, 32. And the small one goes around 4 times when that one goes around once.

Mary (changing the focus): But I wanna know which one of those wheels is going the fastest.

Harry: The smaller one.

Ruth: Both of them are going at the same speed.

Mary (to Harry): You say the smaller one?

Harry: Yah, the smaller one is going around four times and it's fastest.

Mary: But Ruth said same speed.

Ruth: Because look, you can't make this one go faster. Every time this is going ... Oh, you mean how fast it's going *around*?

Mary: Well, what do you think?

Ruth: *What kind of fastness do you mean?*

Mary: What are the choices?

Ruth: Like for one kind of fastest you could say ... like you could go ... you could say how, like (pointing to intersection of teeth) *how each teeth goes in like that*, ya know? And one kind of fastest you could say *how long it takes for this one to go around.*

Mary: Hmmm. So if you say it's the kind of fastness with the teeth, then which one wins? Which is the fastest?

Harry: The smaller one.

Ruth: No, they both go the same.

Mary: O.K. And what about if you say which goes *around* the fastest?

Ruth: The smallest one.

Clapping the Gears

At this moment, Arthur Ganson, who was also working with the children that day, sees a connection. Catching it on the fly, he turns the conversation around.[5]

Figure 10.3: Sarah claps a 4:1 rhythm

Left Hand: | | | | | Big gear

Right Hand: | | | | | | | | | | | | | | | | | | | | Small gear

Arthur: So what is the rhythm of that gear?

Mary: The rhythm of that gear? Someone want to play it?

Arthur: Yah, how about playing it?

Harry: I'll play it. (He turns the gears around making them "play.")

Jeanne: Yah, how would you play that rhythm?

Sarah: Like this ... hummm.

Sarah taps a slow beat with her left hand and a faster beat with her right. The beats have a 4:1 relationship to one another—that is, for every one tap of her left hand, her right hand makes 4 taps (see Figure 10.3).

Jeanne: Yah, do it again.

Sarah: [Taps out 4:1 rhythm again.]

Jeanne: Which is the small gear?

Sarah: The one that's going ... [taps the faster beat with her right hand].

Arthur's spur-of-the-moment question neatly brought together the seemingly disparate materials, modalities, and means of description with which the children had been working: gears were a medium for Ruth's mathematics/physics.[6] The gears for Ruth embodied, "held," principles of ratio and also "kinds of fastness": Sarah, in turn, took Ruth's description of the relationships of the two gears and expressed it in the relationship of her two hands in clapping. Two different embodiments of the same "working system." Sarah's two-leveled clapping was a kind of metaphor-in-action for the relative motions of the two meshed gears—she had *become* the gears. And yet, hiding behind that leap from one medium to the other were embodied shared principles: perhaps the most general being the fundamental idea of a "unit" and what we would call "periodicities"—what the children had been calling simply "beats."

Sarah and Ruth were demonstrating what we had suspected from the beginning: children who are having difficulties learning in school, given its symbolic emphasis, can learn in profound ways by *extracting principles* from the successful workings of their built objects and their actions on them. The question was, as it had been from the beginning, how could we help the children make functional connections between what they knew how to do already in action and the expression of their know-how in a more general, symbolic form? Ruth was clearly on the way; but what about the others? Could the computer and MusicLogo mediate between action knowledge and symbolic knowledge?

The Computer as Mediator

While Arthur's specific question and Sarah's response were unplanned events, they had been prepared by our juxtaposition of the two activities—drumming rhythms and working with the gears. The next activity was definitely planned in advance. It reflected our intention of using the computer as mediator. The question was: Could the children use the computer as a vehicle for effectively moving between their own body actions in clapping/drumming, the actions of the gears, and now, numeric-symbolic descriptions of the shared, embodied principles? In short, could they turn continuous actions into discrete, symbolic expressions?

I asked the children to gather around the old Apple IIE computers. The new task that I put to them was: "Can you get the two computer synthesizer drums to play what Sarah clapped? Except, to begin with,

Figure 10.4: I tapped a 2:1 rhythm

we'll make it a little easier. Just try playing … " And with two hands, like Sarah, I tapped out a simpler, 2:1 rhythm. The children all clapped the two-layered rhythm (see Figure 10.4).

The children were already familiar with Logo graphics and with procedural programming—what we called "teaching the computer." Now, in order to "teach" the computer to play the rhythm that I had proposed, the children would need also to find (perhaps give) meaning to numbers in this new context—to find out how numbers worked when those numbers were instructions to percussion instruments to play beats. What were the links between the actions and sounds the children made in clapping, the numbers used in doing ordinary arithmetic, numbers used in doing graphics Logo, and now numbers used as instructions to the synthesizer drums?[7]

The children were used to conversations, like the one around the gears, in which they explained to one another or to an adult how they made sense of something or how they made something work. These conversations usually arose spontaneously in response to a disagreement, to a child's surprising discovery, or when an insight led to solving a particularly intransigent problem. Descriptions of such past happenings, however, included organized, symbolic/numeric expressions; while they often pointed to an emergent similarity, descriptions were more often vague or in-action like Sarah's "clapping the gears." Compared with what the children had been used to, the relationship between actions and description would now have to be reversed. Instead of *turning back* on what had already happened, to make descriptions *after* the fact and *after* the act, in the virtual world of the computer they would need to describe what they wanted to happen *before* the act—that is, as instructions to the computer. And the *instructions must be in a symbolic form that the computer can "understand."* These were the issues as we moved to the next task and to the computers.

Leon Makes a First Discovery

To help the children get started, I typed the following instructions to MusicLogo and we listened.

> **BOOM [8 8 8 8 8 8 8]**
> **PM**

We heard a steady beat made up of seven drum sounds each with a duration of "8." At this point, however, the children (and no doubt, the reader) still had to discover what "8" meant. I gave another example, saying, "This one will go faster."

> **BOOM [6 6 6 6 6 6 6]**
> **PM**

Jeanne: Now I want to make a still faster one.
　　　Leon (who had not participated in the discussion up to now): But the lower you get the faster it gets.
　　　　　Jeanne: You answered my question before I asked it.
　　　　　Sarah: Leon's psychic.
　　　　　Stephen: Do 1 1 1 1 1 1 1.
　　　　　Jeanne: What do ya think will happen?
　　　　　Leon: If you put all ones, it'll go fast.
　　　　　Jeanne types:

BOOM [1 1 1 1 1 1 1]
PM

And it did "go fast." At this point all the children went to their computers to work on getting the synthesizer drums to play the 2:1 pattern.

For the Reader

MusicLogo and the synthesizer had the capability for making two different drum sounds, BOOM and PING. Each kind of drum could be "instructed" separately. The command "BOOM" (or "PING") "tells" MusicLogo to make a BOOM (or PING) sound. The list of numbers that follows BOOM or PING indicates the duration of each sound; the number of numbers indicates how many sounds to make in all. The numbers for durations are proportional to one another—an 8 is twice as long as a 4; a 2 is half as along as a 4. There is no sound while the user is giving instructions. The drums actually plays only when the user types the command, "PM," which stands for Play Music. Upon typing "PM," the previously typed instructions are realized in sound—symbol becomes action.

Leon Invents an Experiment

I went around to work with Leon. Leon had been an enigma to all of us: he talked very little, so we were never sure what was going on with him. Leon's teachers were often at a loss as to how to reach him. As in the conversation just reported, however, the children as well as the adults in the group knew that out of his silence came surprising, sometimes extraordinary insights. It was in the lab, too, that we discovered his most notable quality: *integrity*. If the situation, the problem to be solved, or the teacher's description or definition did not make sense to him, he, unlike more school-smart children, would just turn off rather than go through the motions to get a right answer. *Leon needed to understand for himself.* And along with this, Leon wanted to take time to think. On this occasion as on others, I learned that we adults needed to slow down to catch up with his thinking.

Leon was the quintessential example of a child for whom grasping an idea could literally be a physical experience. All of us seek ways of holding on to a new idea; but for children growing up poor and living in an unstable, unpredictable world, grasping, holding still, holding on, is a persistent need. Leon's explorations to find out how numbers could "teach" the computer to play the drums made that quite clear. And like probably so many times before, I almost missed it.

Sitting down next to Leon, I saw that he had typed into the computer, "BOOM," followed by a series of 1's.

BOOM [1 1 1 1 1 1 1 1 1 1 1]

This was, in fact, just what I had done a moment before in response to Leon's comment about the 1's going fast. I proposed a further possibility: "Leon, can you make a BOOM sound that goes exactly two times slower? What do you think? [Pointing to the screen] This is a one and you want each one to be two ones." Leon ignored me which in retrospect was perfectly sensible. My proposal made sense to me, but what could it possibly have meant to him or indeed, to most anyone: "you want each one to be two ones"? Instead, Leon, true to his integrity, continued with his own self-designed task.

Determinedly, slowly, persistently, he typed 1's and 2's. There was no sound except for his typing. With a kind of steady pulsing, repeated, rocking motion, he used two hands to type—the right hand typing numbers, alternating with left hand pressing the space bar: 1 space 1 space 1 space 1 space ... 2 space 2 space 2 space 2 space ... 1 space 1 space 1 space ... he nearly filled up the whole screen with 1's and 2's.

Despite my best intentions to find reason in what he was doing, I thought: "What can be the use of all this? Filling up the screen just to fill up time? Looks like a waste of time to me." Only later, looking back at the videotape of the whole session, did I realize how mistaken I was.[8]

After all his work, Leon finally typed "PM." The synthesizer drum dutifully played exactly what he had requested: a series of very fast drum sounds (the 1's) alternating with a series of drum sounds that went

Figure 10.5: Filling up the whole screen

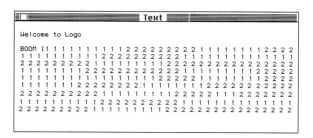

"exactly two times slower" (the 2's). As he listened, Leon followed the
numbers on the screen with his finger.

Even though I had been present while all this was happening, it
was only later that I realized the significance of what I had seen. I missed
the importance of Leon's work because I was focusing on *my task*, the task
I had set for the children—to make two levels of beats in a 2:1 relation.
Leon, with his sense of integrity, had to begin with his own questions.
What I was watching was an experiment that Leon had designed to ans-
wer questions he had silently put to himself: "What have I got here?"
What is the meaning of 1 and 2 in this context? *What do these numbers do?
And how can I find out?"*

As I studied the videotape, I learned what Leon was up to. Juxtaposing the series of 1's and 2's, the contrast between the very fast 1's and
the slower 2's was eminently audible. But listening was not enough; to
really *grasp* the meaning of the numbers, Leon needed to echo their actions
in his own actions. As the numbers on the screen played, Leon moved along
with them, keeping time. In this way he was literally coordinating symbol
with sound and action—but not quite. The 1's were too fast for his finger-

following to keep up with, but he clearly acted out the contrast between the 1's and 2's: while the fast 1's were playing, he swept his hand through the series, put his finger at the beginning of the next series of 2's, and waited. When the slower 2's started, he followed along, keeping time with each number and each steady beat as they sounded. The numbers stood still, the beat was sounding/moving, and Leon's "finger-drumming" was grasping them all. Attentively and patiently, Leon continued the process—sweeping his hand through the 1's, waiting for the 2's, keeping time with the 2's as they passed by—until the entire screen had been traversed and the whole "piece" was over.

True to his integrity and his desire to really understand for himself, Leon invented a situation to test what these numbers meant to MusicLogo, *what they did in sound and action*. Starting with what he knew already ("The lower you get, the faster it gets. ... If you put all 1's it'll go fast."), he tested that knowledge, pushed it a little further. Perhaps like a scientist working with the puzzling behavior of cells, Leon needed to differentiate between two slightly different elements and their relations. And like the scientist, he needed repetition—a critical mass of each kind of element repeated over sufficient time, and an environment where their differences could be clearly perceived. To achieve this, Leon lined up strings of elements, each string including one of the symbolic elements (1's or 2's), and each kind of string immediately juxtaposed to the other. Having repeated instances of his essential elements behaving over a sufficiently long time, the "joints" where the two kinds of elements met produced the revealing moments.

Leon was using all the available resources he had to do the work of *making meaning*. He had invented a way to use the computer and Music-Logo as a mediator between successful actions in realtime space and the world of symbols which in school are given privileged status as a measure of knowledge. In retrospect, he taught us, above all, how important it is to be able to slow down, to take time to *repeat*, to practice literally *making* correspondences; he made numbers, synthesizer drumming, and his drumming move in perfect synchrony. In this way he literally and physically *grasped* meaning.

But all of this depended on an environment that exploited the computer in a way that was unique to it: *the symbols Leon typed became what they stood for*. He was using the computer as a medium in which a symbol defines itself by becoming what it does. And he was successful! Paraphrasing Papert, for Leon the computer became a *transitional object*— a mediator between abstract and sensory experience, carrying the idea of the numbers into his mind. We needed Leon to teach us how that could really work.

A Procedure and a Performance

But there was more. After experimenting further, now trying the other drum sound, PING, and listening to what it did, Leon found he had the makings of a real piece—his own drum piece. Having worked with Logo before, he knew how to make a "procedure." Applying what he had learned in the medium of Logo graphics, Leon "taught the computer" how to play a new drum piece, never before heard. Not precomposed, perhaps not even planned, Leon followed the same process as before except for adding PINGS to his BOOMS, but still staying within the self-imposed limits of 1's and 2's. Probably as a sign of possession, of holding the procedure as his own, Leon, like so many others, gave his name to his procedure: he taught MusicLogo how *TO LEO*.

I abbreviate his procedure here.[9]

```
TO LEO
BOOM [2 2 1 1 2] PING [1 1 1 2 1 2]
BOOM [2 2 2 1 1 1] PING [1 1 1 1 1]
PING [1 1 1 1 2 2 2 2][BOOM 1 1 2 2 2 2 2 1 1]
–
–
END
```

Typing, "**END**" and pressing the carriage return," he is "told" by the computer:

LEO DEFINED

The procedure is clearly his.

The afternoon is almost over and the children are moving about:

Mary: Shhhh ... Leon's going to play his piece.

Leon (excited): "Here we go again." (He types:)

LEO (which sends the new procedure, LEO, to MusicLogo to be computed) then

PM (which sends the computed procedure to the synthesizer.)

Leon's new piece fills the lab, and the children listen attentively until the end. No one stirs. Leon looks triumphant and the children clap in appreciation.

Mary: O.K., children, we have to go now.

Later Outcomes

What can we assume that Leon actually learned through his experiment? Did he, for instance, come to understand the measured, proportional relationship between beats of duration "1" and beats of duration "2"—that "1's" go exactly twice as fast as "2's?" Events in subsequent sessions suggest that on this Wednesday afternoon, such awareness was more a glimmer than a grasp—a general idea to build on. But build on it, he did. As usual, Leon chose to move slowly, to practice, to repeat, and to find out for himself. Feeling comfortable enough with the meanings of 1's and 2's, and learning from what the other children were doing, he did try a two-layered rhythm (**BOOM** in one part, **PING** in the other), but still using the familiar 2's and 1's. To test the principle that he heard embedded in this first example, he devised a new experiment. Figure 10.5 shows how, quite on his own, he developed examples of numbers that embodied the same inner relationship—the 2:1 ratio.

Leon first wrote out each series including all the numbers, and only then typed it into MusicLogo to hear what would happen. Notice that he writes out all the numbers for each example; that is, he repeats the smaller number exactly twice as many times as the larger number. Starting with:

8 8 8 8 8

4 4 4 4 4 4 4 4 4

he gets progressively faster (6:3; 4:2) and ends up with the slowest example (10:5). However, the last of the smaller numbers is always crossed
out, making one less, because he discovered in listening that with PING
playing the smaller, faster numbers, the two instruments "never came out
together." When there were exactly twice as many faster PINGS, there
was always one extra. Was the computer making a mistake? Surely, half
as big a number meant twice as fast, and that should also mean twice as
many to "come out even." The children were intrigued with the puzzle
and worked on it for quite awhile.

Conclusions

The activities described in these stories are not intended as a recommendation for something to be literally copied—as "a curriculum" or even as
"what to do tomorrow." Nor are they intended as a recommendation for
the only way that "the computer" can be effectively used in schools. Leon
devised his experiment to explore possible answers to questions *he asked*;
for another child with different questions (even other children that day in
the design lab), his strategy could be a total bore from which they would
learn nothing.

Rather the stories are meant as a proposal for an *approach* to
learning and a whole context in which children can be helped to thrive—
especially children such as Leon who are seen as failing in school, whose
lives are rife with instability and disorganization, who often feel that
school is irrelevant and reciprocally are made to feel themselves irrelevant,
peripheral, in school settings. These are children whose personal, effective
knowledge is failing them in school largely because there is no way they
can bring it in off the street into the classroom.

For these children, most especially, we propose that a computer
can play a special role as a resource for inquiry and invention when they
can work at a *pace* and within a *conceptual space* that they can grasp and that
thus feels secure. In this environment, instead of being poor consumers
of other people's fleeting ideas and inaccessible products, children can

potentially become makers of new knowledge of which they can feel proud, with which they can give pleasure to others, and through which they can also learn how to learn what is expected of them in the school world and beyond.

The next step is to help teachers invent their own examples of resources and environments where children can make experiments and can learn how to grasp things and grasp ideas. To this end, we have recently created the MIT/Wellesley Teacher Education Program. While it is intended primarily for MIT undergraduates who wish to teach math or science in middle and high schools, the program sits in the Department of Urban Studies. The association with urban studies is exactly appropriate because we focus on issues around how children in the inner city can be helped to learn and how schools can be helped to appreciate the knowledge children bring with them from their experience outside of school. In 1996–1997, the program celebrated its third year and the education classes continue to grow. Five students have completed their certification and are teaching in local area public schools; ten more will complete their certification in June 1997. The reports back from the field suggest that life is not easy out there, but the students are gaining confidence and engendering confidence in their students as well. Meanwhile, judging from the current students' papers on their observations and tutoring, we seem to be learning how to do it better, too.

Notes

1. Of course, MIT is full of students with the reverse problem: virtuosos at pushing symbols, finding and solving equations, but often having trouble making a gadget that works—even when the gadget embodies the principles represented by the equations they know so well.

2. The ten Apple IIE computers were donated by Apple Computer.

3. Mary Briggs and I continued to work with a variety of children whom she selected over a period of five years.

4. Papert, Seymour. 1993. *Mindstorms: Children, Computers, and Powerful Ideas.* New York: Basic Books, p.viii.

5. Arthur Ganson, a kinetic sculptor, designed the materials and the tools with which children had built the big gears.

6. Ruth, quite on her own, distinguishes between one kind of fastness where "both of them [the gears] are going at the same speed ... you can't make this one go faster [because] ... each tooth goes in like that ..." This is in contrast to "how fast it's going *around* ... how long it takes for this one to go around"; that is, she is describing in terms of elements and relations of the gears that she can directly see and feel, the concrete embodiment of principles that in physics terms would be called "linear versus velocity."

7. MusicLogo, developed by Bamberger with the help of others in Papert's lab, has the computer language, Logo, as its base, adding primitives that "talk" to a music synthesizer. MusicLogo thus has all the procedural power of Logo (a dialect of LISP), making it usable for "procedural music composition."

8. All sessions in the lab were videotaped, and many were transcribed for documentation and later study.

9. To define a procedure in Logo, you begin with "TO ..." The idea is that you are going to "teach the computer TO ..." as in the infinitive form of the verb.

11. The Computer Clubhouse: Technological Fluency in the Inner City

Mitchel Resnick

Natalie Rusk

Stina Cooke

Prelude

Mike Lee never cared much for school. His true passion was drawing.
He filled up notebook after notebook with sketches of cartoon characters.
At age seventeen, Mike dropped out of high school; but he continued to
draw on his own and to help kids at a local elementary school learn
how to draw.

A year or so later, Mike's mother was participating in a
teachers' workshop at the Computer Museum in downtown Boston. She
mentioned to the staff that her son was artistically talented, but she was
worried because he was unemployed and not using his talents. They told
her about the Computer Clubhouse, a new after-school center where inner-
city youth could work on computer projects. They said the Clubhouse
needed volunteers and suggested that she encourage Mike to apply. Mike
was skeptical. "I had never touched a computer before," he remembers now.
"I didn't think of them at all." Mike's mother argued that volunteering
at the Computer Clubhouse—and learning to use computers—might lead
to a good job. Mike shrugged: "Whatever."

On Mike's first visit to the Clubhouse, staff member Noah
Southall showed him how to use a digital camera to capture one of his
comic-book drawings on the computer. Then, he learned how to use Photo-
Shop to color in the drawing. Noah asked Mike to become the first official
Clubhouse "mentor." For the next two years, Mike came to the Clubhouse
regularly. "At least four days a week," he says.

Access Is Not Enough

Ever since the personal computer was invented in the late 1970s, concerns
have been expressed about inequities in access to this new technology (e.g.,
Piller 1992). In an effort to address these inequities, some groups have
worked to acquire computers for inner-city schools. Other groups have
opened community-access centers, recognizing that schools are not the only
(or necessarily the best) place for learning to occur. At these community-
access centers, members of inner-city communities (youth and adults alike)
can use computers at little or no charge.

The Computer Clubhouse (which we organized with the support of the Computer Museum in collaboration with the MIT Media Laboratory) grows out of this tradition, but with important differences. At many other centers, the main goal is to teach youth basic computer techniques (such as keyboard and mouse skills) and basic computer applications (such as word processing). The Clubhouse views the computer with a different mind-set. The point is not to provide a few classes to teach a few skills; the goal is for participants to learn to express themselves *fluently* with new technology.

Technological fluency means much more than the ability to use technological tools; that would be equivalent to understanding a few common phrases in a language. To become truly fluent in a language (like English or French), one must be able to articulate a complex idea or tell an engaging story—that is, be able to "make things" with language. Analogously, our concept of technological fluency involves not only knowing how to use technological tools, but also knowing how to construct things of significance with those tools. A technologically fluent person should be able to go from the germ of an intuitive idea to the implementation of a technological project (Papert and Resnick 1995). Increasingly, technological fluency is becoming a prerequisite for getting jobs and participating meaningfully in our society.

The Computer Clubhouse aims to help inner-city youth gain this type of technological fluency. The Computer Clubhouse is designed to provide inner-city youth with access to new technologies. But access alone is not enough. The Clubhouse is based not only on new technology, but on new ideas about learning and community. It represents a new type of learning community—where young people and adult mentors work together on projects, using new technologies to explore and experiment in new ways.

During its first two years of operation, the Clubhouse attracted more than one thousand young people aged ten to sixteen, with 98 percent coming from underserved communities. Participants were from diverse cultural backgrounds, including African American (61 percent), Asian (13 percent), and Latino (11 percent). To attract participants, the Clubhouse initially established connections with community centers and housing projects in target communities; since then, it has relied primarily on word of mouth. Youth do not have to sign up for time at the Clubhouse; they can "drop in" whenever the Clubhouse is open.

At the Clubhouse, young people become designers and creators—not just consumers—of computer-based products. Participants use leading-edge software to create their own artwork, animations, simulations, multi-media presentations, virtual worlds, musical creations, Web sites, and robotic constructions.

The Mike Lee Style

At the Clubhouse, Mike Lee developed a new method for his artwork. First, he would draw black-and-white sketches by hand. Then, he would scan the sketches into the computer and use the computer to color them in. His work often involved comic-book images of himself and his friends (Figure 11.1).

Over time, Mike learned to use more advanced computer techniques in his artwork (Figure 11.2). Everyone in the Clubhouse was impressed with Mike's creations, and other youth began to come to him for advice; many mimicked his approach. Before long, a collection of "Mike Lee style" artwork filled the bulletin boards of the Clubhouse (Figure 11.3). "It's kind of flattering," says Mike.

Mike took his responsibility as a mentor seriously. For example, he decided to stop using guns in his artwork, feeling that it was a bad influence on the younger Clubhouse members. "My own personal artwork is more hard core, about street violence. I had a close friend who was shot and died," Mike explains. "But I don't want to bring that here. I have an extra responsibility. Kids don't understand about guns; they think it's cool. They see a fight, it's natural they want to go see it. They don't understand. They're just kids."

Clubhouse Principles

Computers, software, and networking do not, by themselves, lead to the development of technological fluency. In creating the Clubhouse, we needed to consider not only new technologies, but also new forms of social

Figure 11.1

interaction, new types of activities, new areas of knowledge, and new attitudes toward learning. In the following sections, we discuss four core principles that guided the development of the Clubhouse. These principles span multiple dimensions: social, pedagogical, technological, epistemological, and emotional. In creating new learning environments, all of these dimensions are important.

Principle 1: Support Learning through Design Experiences

Activities at the Clubhouse vary widely, from constructing and controlling LEGO robots to orchestrating virtual dancers. But these varied

Figure 11.2

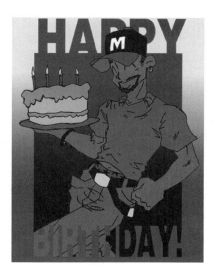

activities are based on a common framework: engaging youth in learning through design.

In recent years, a growing number of researchers and educators
have argued that design projects provide rich opportunities for learning
(e.g., Harel 1991; Papert 1993; Lehrer 1993; Soloway, Guzdial, and Hay
1994). There are many reasons for this interest in design-based learning,
among them:

• Design activities engage youth as active participants, giving
them a greater sense of control (and responsibility) over the learning
process, in contrast to traditional school activities in which teachers aim
to "transmit" new information to the students.

Figure 11.3

• Design activities encourage creative problem solving, avoiding the right/wrong dichotomy prevalent in most school math and science activities, suggesting instead that multiple strategies and solutions are possible.

• Design activities can facilitate personal connections to knowledge, because designers often develop a special sense of ownership (and caring) for the products (and ideas) that they design.

• Design activities are often interdisciplinary, bringing together concepts from the arts, math, and sciences.

• Design activities promote a sense of audience, encouraging youth to consider how other people will use and react to the products they create.

• Design activities provide a context for reflection and discussion, enabling youth to gain a deeper understanding of the ideas underlying hands-on activities.

This emphasis on design activities is part of a broader educational philosophy known as "constructionism" (Papert 1993). Constructionism is based on two types of "construction." First, it asserts that learning is an active process, in which people actively construct knowledge from their experiences in the world. People do not get ideas; they make them. (This idea is based on the constructivist theories of Jean Piaget.) To this, constructionism adds the idea that people construct new knowledge with particular effectiveness when they are engaged in constructing personally meaningful products. They might be constructing sand castles, LEGO machines, or computer programs. What is important is that they are actively engaged in creating something that is meaningful to themselves or to others around them.

At the Clubhouse, construction takes many forms. Rather than playing computer games, Clubhouse participants create their own computer games. And rather than just "surfing" on the Internet's World Wide Web, participants make waves: they create their own multimedia Web pages, such as the Clubhouse's Online Art Gallery.

To support these activities, the Clubhouse provides a variety of design tools, from introductory paint programs (such as KidPix) to high-end animation tools (such as Macromedia Director). Other software tools include digital music recording, editing, and mixing tools; desktop publishing tools; programming tools (such as Microworlds Logo); virtual-reality design tools for developing three-dimensional models on the computer screen; and construction kits for creating and controlling robotic machines (such as LEGO Control Lab). The Clubhouse also serves as a testbed for new technologies under development at research universities and companies. For example, the Clubhouse was the initial test site for the Programmable Brick, a portable computer built into a LEGO brick, developed at the MIT Media Lab (Sargent et al. 1996).

At the Clubhouse, youth learn how to use these tools. But even more, they learn how to express themselves through these tools. They learn not only the technical details but the heuristics of being a good designer: how to conceptualize a project, how to make use of the materials available,

Figure 11.4

how to persist and find alternatives when things go wrong, and how to view a project through the eyes of others. In short, they learn how to manage a complex project from start to finish.

In creating the Clubhouse, we decided to focus not just on any design activities but primarily on computer-based design activities. Why? For one thing, computers are now an important part of children's culture. As a result, computer-based activities are likely to connect with children's passions, imaginations, and interests.

Just as important, computers have the potential to engage youth in new types of mathematical and scientific thinking. It is not our approach to use computers to "teach" mathematical and scientific ideas explicitly.

Rather, we have shown that certain computer-based activities engage youth in mathematical or scientific thinking as a natural, integral part of the activity itself. For example, as Clubhouse youth use Programmable Bricks to build and program "robotic creatures," they begin to think about the similarities and differences between animals and creatures. Are their LEGO creatures like animals? Or like machines? They compare the robots' sensors to animal senses, and they discuss whether real animals have "programs" like their robots. In the process, they develop intuitions about feedback—a scientific concept traditionally taught at the university level. Programmable Bricks make the concept accessible to a much broader (and younger) audience.

Online Art Gallery

Mike Lee began working with others at the Clubhouse on collaborative projects. Together, they created the Online Art Gallery on the World Wide Web. Once a week, they met with a local artist who agreed to be a mentor for the project. After a year, their online art show was accepted as an exhibition at SIGGRAPH, the premiere computer-graphics conference.

As Mike worked with others at the Clubhouse, he began to experiment with new artistic techniques. He added more computer effects, while maintaining his distinctive style. For example, he began working on digital collages combining photographs and graphics (Figures 11.4 and 11.5).

Principle 2: Help Youth Build on Their Own Interests

In schools of education, the focus is usually on methods of teaching, not motivations for learning. Many courses emphasize how and what teachers should teach, but seldom examine why their students might want to learn. When the issue of motivation is addressed, the emphasis is often on extrinsic motivators and incentives, such as grades and prizes based on performance.

Yet if you look outside of school, you can find many examples of people learning—in fact, learning exceptionally well—without explicit "rewards." Youth who seem to have short attention spans in school often

Figure 11.5

display great concentration on projects that they are truly interested in. They might spend hours learning to play the guitar or play basketball. Clearly, youth interests are a great untapped resource. As Roger Schank wrote in 1994: "An interest is a terrible thing to waste."

When youth care about what they are working on, the dynamic of teaching changes. Rather than being "pushed" to learn, youth work on their own, seeking out ideas and advice. Youth are not only more motivated but they also develop deeper understandings and richer connections to knowledge. At first, some youth interests might seem to be trivial or shallow, but youth can build up large networks of knowledge related to their interests. Pursuing any topic in depth can lead to connections to other subjects and disciplines. The educational challenge is to find ways to help youth make these connections and develop them more fully. For example, an interest in riding a bicycle can lead to investigations of gearing, the physics of balancing, the evolution of vehicles over time, or the environmental effects of different transportation modes.

The Clubhouse is designed to support youth in developing their interests. Whereas youth from middle-class households generally have many opportunities to build on their interests (music lessons, specialty camps, and so on), the target audience of the Clubhouse has few such opportunities. For most Clubhouse participants, no other constructive after-school options are available. And many do not even have a clear sense of their interests, let alone how to build on them.

Clubhouse participants are encouraged to make their own choices. Just coming to the Clubhouse involves a choice: all of the youth at the Clubhouse have chosen to be there, and they can come and go as they please. Once inside the Clubhouse, participants continually confront choices on what to do, how to do it, and whom to work with. At the Clubhouse, youth gain experience and self-directed learning; they begin to recognize, trust, develop, and deepen their own interests and talents.

Helping youth develop their interests is not just a matter of letting them do what they want. Young people must be given the freedom to follow their fantasies but also the support to make these fantasies come to life. On the walls, shelves, and hard drives of the Clubhouse is a large collection of sample projects, designed to provide participants with a sense of the possible and with multiple entry points for getting started. In one corner of the Clubhouse is a library of books, magazines, and manuals filled with more project ideas (and a sofa to make reading more comfortable). Many youth begin by mimicking a sample project, then work on variations on the theme, and soon develop their own personal path, stemming from their personal interests.

This approach works only if the environment supports a great diversity of possible projects and paths. The computer plays a key role here. The computer is a type of "universal machine," supporting design projects in many different domains: music, art, science, math. At any time, a pair of youth might be using a computer to create a graphic animation, while at the next computer another participant might be using a similar computer to control a robotic construction.

Of course, the technology alone does not ensure diversity. In schools, more teachers are beginning to include design experiences in their classroom activities. But in many cases, these design activities are very restrictive. Students do little more than follow someone else's "recipe." In classes working with LEGO/Logo (a computer-controlled construction kit), students are often told precisely how and what to build; for example, a teacher might instruct every student to build the exact same LEGO car, using the same bricks, same gears, same wheels, and the same computer program to control it. The Clubhouse takes a very different approach; it has the feel of an invention workshop. In working with LEGO/Logo, Clubhouse youth have built, programmed, and experimented with a wide assortment of projects, from an automated hair curler to a computer-controlled LEGO city. The LEGO materials and computer technology allow this diversity—even more important, the Clubhouse community supports and encourages it.

Projects at the Clubhouse

As Mike Lee focused on his artwork, other Clubhouse youth were developing their own projects.

Emilio saw a laser-light show at a science museum and decided to design something similar at the Clubhouse. He glued small mirrors onto a few LEGO motors, wrote a short computer program to control the motion of the motors, and bounced a laser light off of the mirrors to create dynamic, dancing patterns of light. The project engaged Emilio in mathematical thinking as he modified angles and speeds to create new laser patterns.

A group of fourth-grade girls came to the Clubhouse to try out the new programmable-brick technology developed at MIT. They spent several sessions discussing what to build. They decided to create a "city of the future"; they built and programmed elevators, buses, and even a tour guide for the city. The girls, who came from a bilingual class at school, programmed the tour guide to give information in both English and Spanish. They proudly named their creation "Nine Techno Girls City."

Marcus, a ninth grader, began designing and programming computer games at school. He came to the Clubhouse to learn to develop

more sophisticated games, and received help from Paul, a student at
Wentworth Institute of Technology. Paul showed him how to program
in C, a professional programming language that Marcus had wanted
to learn. Marcus's work attracted the interest of other Clubhouse parti-
cipants —and he, in turn, helped other youth learn to design and
program their own games.

Principle 3: Cultivate "Emergent Community"

How do people become fluent in a natural language? It is now common
wisdom that people learn French much better by living in Paris than by
taking French classes in school (Papert 1980). Many American students
take several years of French class in high school, but still cannot communicate fluently in the language. The language is learned best by living in
the culture, by going to the store to buy a baguette, by joking with the
vendor who sells Le Monde, by overhearing conversations in the café, by
interacting with people who know and care about the language.

For young people to become technologically fluent, they need
a similar type of immersion. They need to live in a "digital community,"
interacting not only with technological equipment but with people
who know how to explore, experiment, and express themselves with the
technology.

To foster this type of community, the Computer Clubhouse
includes a culturally diverse team of adult mentors—professionals and
college students in art, music, science, and technology. Mentors act as
coaches, catalysts, and consultants, bringing new project ideas to the
Clubhouse. Most mentors volunteer their time. On a typical day, there
are two or three mentors at the Clubhouse. For example, engineers might
be working on robotics projects with Clubhouse participants, artists on
graphics and animation projects, programmers on interactive games. For
youth who have never interacted with an adult involved in academic or
professional careers, this opportunity is pivotal to envisioning themselves
following similar career paths.

In this way, the Clubhouse deals with the "access issue" at a
deeper level. In addition to access to new technology, inner-city youth need
access to people using technology in interesting ways. This type of access

is not possible in a classroom with thirty children and a single teacher. The Clubhouse takes advantage of an untapped local resource, providing a new way for people in the community to share their skills with local youth.

By involving mentors, the Clubhouse provides inner-city youth with a rare opportunity to see adults working on projects. Mentors do not simply provide "support" or "help"; many work on their own projects and encourage Clubhouse youth to join in. John Holt argued that children learn best from adults who are working on things that they themselves care about. As Holt wrote: "I'm not going to take up painting in the hope that, seeing me, children will get interested in painting. Let people who already like to paint, paint where children can see them" (Holt 1977).

At the Clubhouse, youth also get a chance to see adults learning. In today's rapidly changing society, perhaps the most important skill of all is the ability to learn new things. It might seem obvious that, in order to become good learners, youth should observe adults learning. But that is rarely the case in schools. Teachers often avoid situations where students will see them learning: they do not want students to see their lack of knowledge. At the Clubhouse, youth get to see adults in the act of learning. For some Clubhouse participants, it is quite a shock. Several of them were startled one day when a Clubhouse staff member, after debugging a tricky programming problem, exclaimed: "I just learned something!"

Projects at the Clubhouse are not a fixed entity; they grow and evolve over time. A mentor might start with one idea, a few youth will join for a while, then a few others will start working on a related project; for example, two graduate students from Boston University decided to start a new robotics project at the Clubhouse. For several days, they worked on their own, and none of the youth seemed particularly interested. But as the project began to take shape, a few youth took notice. One decided to build a new structure to fit on top of the robot, and another saw the project as an opportunity to learn about programming. After a month, a small team of people were working on several robots. Some youth were integrally involved, working on the project every day. Others helped out from time to time, moving in and out of the project team. The process allowed different youth to contribute to different degrees, at different times—a process that some researchers call "legitimate peripheral participation" (Lave and Wenger 1991).

This approach to collaboration is strikingly different from what occurs in most school classrooms. In recent years, interest among educators in "collaborative learning" and "communities of learners" has surged. In many schools, students work in teams to solve problems. Often, each student is assigned a distinct role in the collaborative effort. At the Clubhouse, collaboration has a different flavor. No one is assigned to work on any particular team. Rather, communities "emerge" over time. Design teams form informally, coalescing around common interests. Communities are dynamic and flexible, evolving to meet the needs of the project and the interests of the participants (Resnick 1996). A large green table in the middle of the Clubhouse acts as a type of village common, where people come together to share ideas, visions, information, and even food.

As youth become more fluent with the technologies at the Clubhouse, they too start to act as mentors. During the first year of the Clubhouse, a group of six youth emerged as "regulars," coming to the Clubhouse nearly every day (even on days when the Clubhouse was officially closed). Over time, these youth began to take on more mentoring roles, helping introduce newcomers to the equipment, projects, and ideas of the Clubhouse.

Learning about Learning

As he worked at the Clubhouse, Mike Lee clearly learned a lot about computers and about graphic design. But he also began to develop his own ideas about teaching and learning. "At the Clubhouse, I was free to do what I wanted, learn what I wanted," says Mike. "Whatever I did was just for me. If I had taken computer courses {in school}, there would have been all those assignments. Here I could be totally creative."

Mike's own learning experiences have influenced how he mentors others at the Clubhouse. "It's more important to make them comfortable rather than pushing them to do things," he explains. If they're comfortable, "then they'll do things on their own. I just try to be friends with them." When someone new comes into the Clubhouse, Mike makes sure to include them in the community. "If I'm telling someone I know there a joke, I'll include the new kids in it too. Make them aware that I know they're there."

Mike remembers—and appreciates—how the Clubhouse staff members treated him when he first started at the Clubhouse. They asked him to design the sign for the entrance to the Clubhouse, and looked to him as a resource. They never thought of him as a "high school dropout" but as an artist.

Principle 4: Create an Environment of Respect and Trust

When visitors walk into the Clubhouse, they are often amazed at its participants' artistic creations and their technical abilities. But just as often, they are struck by the way Clubhouse youth interact with one another. Indeed, the Clubhouse approach puts a high priority on developing a culture of respect and trust. These values not only make the Clubhouse an inviting place to spend time, but they are essential for allowing Clubhouse youth to try out new ideas, take risks, follow their interests, and develop fluency with new technologies.

"Respect" at the Clubhouse has many dimensions: respect for people, respect for ideas, respect for the tools and equipment. Mentors and staff set the tone by treating Clubhouse youth with respect. Right from the start, participants are given access to expensive equipment and encouraged to develop their own ideas. "You mean I can use this?" is a common question among youth when they first visit the Clubhouse and find out about the resources and options available to them.

Even with all these options, youth will not take advantage of the opportunities unless they feel safe to try out new ideas. In many settings, youth are reluctant to do so, for fear of being judged or even ridiculed. At the Clubhouse the goal is to make participants feel safe to experiment and explore. No one is criticized for mistakes or "silly" ideas.

Youth are given the time they need to play out their ideas; it is understood that ideas (and people) need time to develop. One new Clubhouse participant spent weeks manipulating a few images, over and over. But then, like a toddler who is late learning to talk but then starts speaking in full sentences, he suddenly started using these images to create spectacular graphic animations.

Clubhouse youth are given lots of freedom and choice. One participant explained why he liked the Clubhouse more than school: "There's no one breathing down your neck here." But with this freedom come high standards and high expectations. Clubhouse staff and mentors do not simply dole out praise to improve the "self-esteem" of the youth. They treat youth more like colleagues, giving them genuine feedback and pushing them to consider new possibilities. They are always asking: What could you do next? What other ideas do you have?

Many Clubhouse youth are learning not only new computer skills but new styles of interaction. Clubhouse youth are treated with respect and trust—and they are expected to treat others the same way.

The Real World

After several years of volunteer work at the Clubhouse, Mike Lee earned his high school equivalency diploma, then landed a full-time job as a graphic designer at a major high-technology company near Boston. He now designs graphics for the company's Web pages, stationery, catalogs, and brochures (Figure 11.6). "I like the job better than I thought I would," says Mike. "At first, I thought I would be stuck in a tie sitting in a box."

Mike's artwork still has the same distinctive style, but he is more fluent expressing himself with computational media. In describing his current work, Mike talks about "dither nightmares" and "anti-aliasing problems"—ideas that would have seemed alien to him a few years ago. He says his artwork is "ten times better than last year." Mike's work style has changed too. For one thing, he now relies on manuals when he gets stuck on a problem. "I never used to use manuals at the Clubhouse. I used to just hack away," explains Mike. "But I didn't have deadlines back then."

Tools for Thought

When people think about thinking, they often imagine Rodin's famous sculpture, *The Thinker*. Rodin's *Thinker* is a solitary thinker, sitting by himself, with his head resting on his hand. This image seems to say: if you just sit by yourself quietly, and concentrate hard, you will do your best thinking.

But that image provides a very restricted view of thinking—one that is becoming less and less relevant in today's digital world. In recent years, there has been a growing recognition that thinking usually happens through interactions—interactions with other people and interactions with media and technologies. New media and technologies support new representations of knowledge, which in turn provide new ways of thinking about problems.

The Clubhouse helps young people become fluent with these new "tools for thought." Two product managers from Adobe, a leading software company, spent several days at the Clubhouse, hoping to gain insights on how they might change and improve their products. Afterwards they wrote: "We were amazed at the incredible rate the kids learned complex products such as PhotoShop and Director and how they used the software almost as an extension of themselves. The kids seem to have a lot more enthusiasm and creativity in the work since they choose their own projects and determine for themselves what they want to do. I liked how the more experienced members trained the new members how to do things and how they took responsibility for the computers and their setups. Clearly the Clubhouse is their Clubhouse, not someone else's place" (Mashima 1994).

Their comments capture some of the core ideas underlying the Clubhouse approach: young people working on design projects, following their own interests, developing fluency with new technologies, sharing knowledge as a member of a community, and becoming self-confident as learners. Of course, creating this type of learning environment is not easy. At times the Clubhouse might seem chaotic. It takes trust and patience to allow youth to follow their own interests and learn from their experiences. But the Clubhouse should not be seen as an unstructured environment: although youth have great freedom in choosing their projects, there is structure embedded in the design of the materials, space, and community. Through its choice of mentors, sample projects, and software tools, the Clubhouse provides a framework in which rich learning experiences are likely to develop.

The long-term goal is to make these types of experiences available to youth in low-income neighborhoods across the country. Several more Computer Clubhouses are already under development. Youth at different Clubhouses will collaborate on joint design projects through the Internet,

Figure 11.6

and mentors and staff will share ideas across sites. Ideally, these new Club-houses will serve as models, sparking people to rethink their notions of technology, learning, and community.

Many previous technology-and-learning projects have fallen short of expectations. The Logo programming language, pioneered at MIT during the 1970s, spread to tens of thousands of schools in the 1980s. But as it spread, Logo experienced what Seymour Papert has called "epistemo-logical dilution." It was used very differently from how the designers of the language had intended, and results were disappointing in many schools.

It is now clear that technological tools themselves, no matter how well they are conceived and designed, are not enough. As new Clubhouses open, the ultimate challenge will be to disseminate not only the technology, but also the principles, philosophy, and spirit of the original Clubhouse.

Coda

Recently Mike Lee was hired as a Clubhouse manager on Saturdays (in addition to his full-time job during the week). For Mike, it's an opportunity to help others achieve what he has achieved. "I wouldn't have had the opportunities I've had without {the Clubhouse}," explains Mike. "I had no direction. I don't know what I'd be doing now. I hadn't finished school. I see kids with lots of talent. I want them to have the same chance I've had." Quietly but proudly, Mike says: "I'm on my own now." He realizes that he is a role model for others. "They see, if you work at it, you could be where I am."

Acknowledgments

The Computer Clubhouse is a group project with many contributors. Sam Christy, Noah Southall, Nancy Boland, and Brian Lee worked with the authors to turn the Clubhouse from an idea into a vibrant reality. Dozens of mentors have volunteered their time and enthusiasm. Gail Breslow, Clubhouse Director since 1995, has helped create a solid financial and organizational foundation for the Clubhouse (and also made helpful comments on a draft of this chapter). Oliver Strimpel, Marilyn Gardner, Betsy Riggs, and Ana Gregory of the Computer Museum have also provided important fund-raising and organizational support. The Clubhouse has been supported by generous financial contributions and in-kind donations from many corporations and foundations. Above all, we want to thank the young people who have made the Computer Clubhouse their Clubhouse.

The Computer Museum has been the institutional driving force behind the Computer Clubhouse project. Natalie Rusk previously served as director of education at the museum, and Mitchel Resnick serves on the museum's board of overseers and is chair of the museum's education committee. Portions of this article previously appeared in (Resnick and

Rusk 1996a, 1996b). The names of all Clubhouse members and mentors in the article (with the exception of Mike Lee) are pseudonyms. For more information about the Clubhouse, see http://www.tcm.org/clubhouse/.

References

Harel, I. 1991. *Children Designers*. Norwood, NJ: Ablex Publishing.

Holt, J. 1977. "On Alternative Schools." *Growing Without Schooling*, 17, p. 5. Cambridge, MA: Holt Associates.

Lave, J. and E. Wenger. 1991. *Situated Learning: Legitimate Peripheral Participation*. Cambridge: Cambridge University Press.

Lehrer, R. 1993. "Authors of Knowledge: Patterns of Hypermedia." In *Computers as Cognitive Tools*, edited by S. P. Lajoie and S. J. Derry. Hillsdale, NJ: Lawrence Erlbaum.

Mashima, K. 1994. Personal communication.

Papert, S. 1980. *Mindstorms*. New York: Basic Books.

Papert, S. 1993. *The Children's Machine*. New York: Basic Books.

Papert, S. and M. Resnick. 1995. "Technological Fluency and the Representation of Knowledge." Proposal to the National Science Foundation. MIT Media Laboratory. Cambridge, MA.

Piller, C. 1992. "Separate Realities." *MacWorld*, September, pp. 218–231.

Resnick, M. 1996. "Towards a Practice of 'Constructional Design.'" In *Innovations in Learning: New Environments for Education*, edited by L. Shauble and R. Glaser. Hillsdale, NJ: Lawrence Erlbaum.

Resnick, M. and N. Rusk, 1996a. "Access is Not Enough: Computer Clubhouses in the Inner City." *American Prospect* 27 (July-August): 60–68.

Resnick, M. and N. Rusk, 1996b. "The Computer Clubhouse: Preparing for Life in a Digital World." *IBM Systems Journal* 35 (3 and 4).

Sargent, R., M. Resnick, F. Martin, and B. Silverman. 1996. "Building and Learning with Programmable Bricks." In *Constructionism in Practice*, edited by Y. Kafai and M. Resnick. Hillsdale, NJ: Lawrence Erlbaum.

Schank, R. 1994. "The Design of Goal-Based Scenarios." *Journal for the Learning Science* 3 (4): 303–304.

Soloway, E., M. Guzdial, and K. Hay. 1994. "Learner-Centered Design." *Interactions* 1 (2): 36–48.

12. Computer as Community Memory: How People in Very Poor Neighborhoods Made a Computer Their Own

Bruno Tardieu

Introduction

> A bright orange electric cord dangles down from a second-floor
> apartment to a Volkswagen van parked by the sidewalk below.
> The van's open hatchback reveals an inexpensive PC computer
> to which the extension cord connects. In contrast to the bleak
> vacant lots and burnt-out buildings of the South Bronx neigh-
> borhood, the scene in the street is full of life. Children cluster
> around the van watching each other using the computer in turn.
> Others sit on blankets on the sidewalk, drawing, painting, and
> reading books. Parents watch from apartment windows; others
> are involved with the children, helping or just supervising.
> Passers-by stop, look, and occasionally offer advice. (Fanelli
> and Tardieu 1986, p. 5)

In the summer of 1985 one could find the same scene repeated in three
other neighborhoods of New York City: East New York, Coney Island,
and the Lower East Side of Manhattan, and later in the lobby of a welfare
hotel in Manhattan. The activity, called a "street library," is a pilot project
of the Fourth World Movement and its volunteer workers in conjunction
with families living in these communities.[1] Introducing computers in
these street libraries was an innovation within an innovation that I will
address here, drawing extensively from a book, *Passport to the New World
of Technology ... Computers*, in which Vincent Fanelli and I documented the
experiment. I will also describe the process of thoughts, questions, design
of action, action, and "reflection on action" (Schön 1983) that occurred
throughout this experiment in a widely uncharted field, as well as mention
new experiments that grew out of that first project.

To fully understand the approach we have taken, I will first
present some of the Fourth World Movement's founding ideas, its vision
of poverty, and its ways of operating, in particular those of the street library.
I will then explain how these ideas led us to confront the new advanced
information technology, raise new questions and concerns, then develop
new actions and learning.

Background to the Community Computer Street Library Project

Why There? Why Computers?

The South Bronx, East New York, and the other neighborhoods were not chosen by chance. The history of our action in the United States since 1964 with families constantly on the move led us there. These neighborhoods are indeed significant places. "The poorest of the poor by any standards" ... "Fear and anxiety are common. Many cannot sleep" ... "In the streets outside, the restlessness and anger that are present in all seasons frequently intensify under the stress of heat" ... "The *Times* refers to the streets around St. Ann's Church as the 'deadliest blocks' in the 'deadliest precinct' of the city. If there is a deadlier place in the United States, I don't know where it is." With these words Jonathan Kozol (1995) is describing the very same neighborhood where the street library took place, two blocks away from that church. In short, these neighborhoods are touched by the kind of extreme poverty that the Fourth World Movement has been fighting against for the last forty years throughout the world.

Yet one might wonder why children, young people, adults, trapped in idleness and coping with such extreme conditions and wordless suffering, would suddenly mobilize their energy for books, paints, and computers, create peace in the street, and dare again to express their hope, especially for the little ones. Since its beginning in France in the 1960s, and now in Europe, Asia, Africa, and the Americas, the street library program has opened the modern world to children in poverty, through reading books, telling stories, and developing art and science projects. Introducing computers in the street libraries, however, has not been easy. It took the vision of Père Joseph Wresinski, founder of the International Fourth World Movement, to convince Fourth World volunteers with backgrounds in science and computers (myself included) to start thinking about ways to do it. He was sure that poor people would get involved immediately, eager to be a part of today's world. It was us, the volunteers, who resisted.

For Wresinski the central issue of poverty is the exclusion that extends beyond economic resources—that is, to being left out of the social, cultural, educational, and political life of the nation. When computers arrived on the scene, he insisted that the poorest families be part of this modern revolution, not to be left behind once again. He was confident that the very basic humanity of the people living in extreme poverty would lead the volunteers, bringing new light to a revolution that some feared was dehumanizing relationships. After all was not that revolution precisely about knowledge, and communication between human beings, which he saw as key dimensions of the struggle against poverty?

Wresinski's Vision on Extreme Poverty: The Fourth World

When Experience Is Denied

The late Joseph Wresinski was born into poverty and exclusion.[2] He knew firsthand that misery lies beyond poverty, where people are seen as "infra human beings," experiencing a "social death." In those terms extreme poverty represents a denial of human rights (Wresinski 1994). At school the young Joseph Wresinski was told not to take the elementary school exam because teachers were sure he would fail, having come from such a family. Pushed by his mother, he took it anyway outside of school, and passed. Later he was threatened by "benefactors" of his family with being put in an orphanage to receive "better influence." Time and again the poorest of the poor are told that their children are not able to learn; and eventually they begin believing it. They also are told that the experience of their milieu is harmful, not to be transmitted to their children. It makes the poor constantly uprooted, with a denied past, doubting their own experience, knowledge, and history—the "first man on earth," as Albert Camus (1994) wrote.

Sharing Knowledge to Break the Isolation

Wresinski (1987) saw knowledge as the key, and sharing knowledge as an essential action against poverty. He launched a fight against ignorance on two sides: enable the very poor to free themselves of their "truncated culture," in which values cannot be lived, by learning from others; and help the nonpoor acknowledge and learn from the poor's suffering and struggle.[3]

(credit: Fourth World Movement)

As Mr. Dacier, a member of the Fourth World Movement who knew first-hand the extremes of poverty recently told me, "Lack of education and ignorance is a curse, but it is not the worst. The worst is that people ignore you." The learning has to be reciprocal.

Fourth World: An Identity that Allows the Poor to Contribute as Full Citizens

In 1956 in a camp for homeless families in Noisy le Grand, where he founded the Fourth World Movement, Wresinski (1983) recognized the experience of his own family and realized "that the families gathered in that camp were not just an accumulation of individual situations, of 'social cases' as the administration in these years called them. The Movement knew right away that they belonged to a same people. … Discover a people where others saw social cases, see a historic identity where others denied the social reality." These reflections led this movement to create the Institute of Research and Training for Human Relations and to forge a name, allowing the poorest of the poor to have their distinct voice heard.[4] Wresinski coined the term "Fourth World," referring to the "Cahiers du Quatrième Ordre," published during the French Revolution by Dufourny de Villiers (1789), to call attention to citizens who were so poor they could not participate in the national consultation and whose contribution had to be specially sought.[5]

These ideas, formulated in the late 1950s, have been reinvigorated with the coming of the new information society. Are not full participants of today's world those whose experience, expertise, and intelligence are sought to produce today's wealth, plan for tomorrow, and contribute to the conversations that sustain modern democracy? But what about the citizenship of the poor if their experience is not valued, sought after, or documented by the institutions that give value to knowledge, the universities (Wresinski 1996)?

That is why when advanced information technology appeared Père Joseph kept saying that short of using it with the poorest, the impossibility of communication between the poor and the others would crystallize even more into the system. Seymour Papert, working in Paris in the early 1980s, met Wresinski and the volunteers, then visited some of the poorest families in the area. "What struck me most in that first visit," Papert confided to me recently, "is that the people had no hopes to learn for themselves about computers and the modern world. But they had tremendous hopes for their children. And they felt that maybe the computer could help. The children could be the mediators for their parents." This fact that we too had observed pointed us to experimenting first with computers and children in our street libraries.

Street Library: Meeting with the Children of the Poor on Their Turf

The idea of the street library came about when, in 1968, Père Joseph met with French students occupying the Sorbonne. They were at the time rioting in Paris, and publicly stating that university knowledge was oppressive and that real knowledge was "in the streets." He challenged them to apply these ideas and share their knowledge with children in the streets of the shanty towns around Paris. Many students did and thus street libraries started in many places. In the United States, where Fourth World

Figure 12.2: Street library in Coney Island housing project, New York, 1986

(credit: Genevieve Tardieu)

Figure 12.3: Young adults, Ms. Aida Lopez and Mr. Darryl Isabel, try the computer in our Lower East Side center in New York, 1986

(credit: Vincent Fanelli)

volunteers had been introduced in 1964 by Lloyd Olin, street libraries had grown out of a joint history between the volunteers and the poor families.[6] Volunteers first lived and worked in Manhattan's Lower East Side, running a Montessori-type preschool and learning center for youth. When gentrification drove out the poorest families, the volunteers chose to pursue their links with them rather than keep their programs going. Eventually, these informal links, in which learning was always central, prompted some of these families to talk to neighbors about gathering children to learn together. These gatherings naturally found their way to the street, thus becoming street libraries.

The street is truly the center of community life in poor neighborhoods. In neighborhoods where nothing is organized for the children once school closes, the street is their only playground, and therefore the street library is a natural ground for the children. It is a resource in the hands of a community, and a public affirmation. It demonstrates that, despite all the difficulties, every child wants to learn—enjoys learning and creating—and that giving priority to children with the most difficulties is the key to peace and learning.

Preparatory Work to Introduce Computers: What Do We Know? What Should We Do?

Two Relevant Features of the Computer: Powerful Words and Associative Memory

When Père Joseph and later Vincent Fanelli told me I should use my computer skills in the street library program in New York City, I had my doubts. I had finished my Ph.D. in computer science on "learning models" only two years earlier; and I did not see how the very poor children could benefit from computers. What convinced me was realizing that Père Joseph's questions were real challenges to my own understanding about learning processes; his dialogue with Seymour Papert and intellectual links with Piaget attracted me. Yet I felt quite insecure in my ability to meet this challenge, wondering what I really knew. I kept these questions in mind while participating in these street libraries, and discussed them with Vincent Fanelli, a former science teacher who was also thinking a lot about this, as well as with others. In this context, two facts about computers became significant to me.

First, computers are machines linking language and action. Words can either be an object of word processing or an order to the computer: you can type the word "PRINT" as part of the story of Gutenberg or type it to actually make a printer print the story. In computer jargon one says that a string of bits can be either data or a command. This equivalence allows programming: words make things happen. Seeing the effect of words, making them "powerful ideas" (Papert 1980), helps us to learn. This was explained to another volunteer once by a child who renamed the computer's return key the "key that obeys." He was stunned: no such key in his difficult life would make anything "obey" his words.

Another fact that struck me about computers is that they have a "memory." "I go to school then I forget everything," Carmen told me once. And Père Joseph says that the poorest, with no memory, no history, have no future. With computers, memory technology makes a step by becoming associative. The distinction between address and content blurs. It means that unlike books or tapes, electronic memory can be searched by its content: a text can be found not only through its author or title but through the subjects it covers. Moreover, two texts can be associated according to any inquiry, not necessarily predicted by the organizers of that memory or by the authors of the texts. Could this associative memory possibly help free us from always questioning the same people who are supposed to know the answers, at the expense of never questioning others? Could it help us judge from the content rather than authority of authors, and "think together" with fewer boundaries? This has particular relevance for the poor who are cut off from this "thinking together."

First Approach, Experiments, and Survey: Computers in the Lives of the Poor

Before deciding whether or not bring computers to the street libraries, we wanted to find out what the families we knew, especially the poorest among them, thought of computers and what experience, if any, they had had with them. We did this by conducting a survey in our Tapori newsletter which reaches about five thousand children from very poor as well as middle class backgrounds throughout the United States[7]; by making a small personal computer available to families who came to the Fourth World center; and by taking another computer to people's homes to give them a chance to experiment and comment. The following observations come from the survey as well as from the Fourth World volunteers daily participant-observation reports.

Expectations Out of Reach

In the spring of 1985, among the 220 readers of the Tapori newsletter who answered the survey, almost all the children with middle-class backgrounds had used computers, while two-thirds of the children from poor neighborhoods said they had never used one. Yet families in poor neighborhoods seemed to be waiting for computers. "We will get forty-five computers for Christmas in our school," Luis told us three times with excitement. But Christmas passed and there were still no computers. Parents also told us that their children were asking for a computer for Christmas, but they could not afford to give them one. Norma spoke about a candy sale in her school to raise money for computers, but again they never appeared.

Computers Mean Success

Johnny once surprised his family and me by using common computer terminology, such as "joystick," "database," and "lightpen." He had never used a computer, nor were there any in his school. He had learned in his own way: "On Saturday afternoon I always watch TV because between the cartoons they have commercials, and most of them are about computers. Some kids have computers at home, but we can't pay all that money. ... You'd better learn about computers if you don't want to be dumb. That's why I learn on TV."

Other children told us, "If I had a computer, I could go to college. ... I would pass all grades." That message comes from television commercials, advertisements in the subway for computer-training programs, and handbills distributed in the hallways of low-income housing projects. Yet most of the families we knew had no idea of what computers can actually do, so they were easily influenced. Their expectations were not realistic. They realized computers had to do with success in today's world, but they viewed them as something beyond their control, almost magic.

Previous Contacts with Computers: Be Controlled and Play Games

When some young people tried out the small computer we had in our center, their first idea was to write their names. Fanelli would show them how their names could remain in the computer's memory. This reminded them of their experiences at public assistance offices or in the criminal justice system, where information about them is kept in computers. "They look up your name and they know more about you than you do yourself," a mother commented. After that experience they all wanted to make sure that their names were erased from the memory: "I don't want my name to stay in that thing."

We also discovered that children often used computers at the corner store—in the form of video games. The very same technology, the very same Atari computer used to play video games in the South Bronx, used the Logo language developed in MIT's Media Lab and could be found in many middle-class schools (and by us a few months later). The money was not the only factor then, but rather the expectation of a society toward its children: for some to develop their intelligence with the best tools available, for others to kill time for a quarter a minute.

One day Johnny (the same Johnny mentioned earlier), came to our center with his father to try out our computer. He was quite disappointed to find no games. His father, Mr. Pacheco, told him: "Here you can learn how to feed the computer, it's not just the computer that feeds you, like these stupid games. That's why it is harder." Johnny overcame his frustration and discovered he could do some simple math with the Basic language on our computer. He quickly got tired of watching it give the right answer. "I want to make the computer wrong," he said, and eventually succeeded in entering a number too large for it to handle. This example and many others demonstrated the basic natural need to master the computer as a tool, including exploring its limits and moving away from magic.

Designing a Project Integrating the Computer: Making Choices

Overcoming Initial Fears: A Tool among Other Tools

Some adults were afraid, when we took our small computer around the
neighborhood, that it would be broken or stolen. They were surprised at
its price—$150—the price of a TV set. Yet most remained reluctant to try
it out: "I watch it but I don't touch it. I'm afraid I hit the wrong key and
break it. Then I have to pay for it." Then Vincent Fanelli designed simple
projects in which the equipment, along with other tools, was used by
teenagers in our center—for example, to print the text of an invitation to
our next party, along with block printing for the illustration. The computer
was losing its mystique, a tool among others, being used to carry out a
specific project. Any further projects should retain this quality.

Around the same time one mother, Mrs. Gattling, a true leader
who knew her community, told me: "Well if you talk to us about this computer, and show it around, it's because you will bring it during the street
library for the children to use, right?" Others reiterated that the computer
would be broken or stolen right away in the street. But Mrs. Gattling's
calm and clear determination showed us the way. "How are they going to
get electricity for the computer?" someone asked. "Bring along an extension cord, we'll plug it in in our homes, we'll take turns," she concluded.

PC Personal Computers or CC Community Computers?

A step had yet to be taken. Being in the street would be different from
being in our center. It would mean sharing the computer with a variety
of children in a project that made sense. We had tried several software
packages. Apart from video games, most of them were traditional school
math and English drills, accompanied by flashing colors and sounds.
We quickly observed that in a group of children, some were succeeding in
giving the right answers and had no reason to let others try, while others
did not really want to try once they had failed. The computer was adding
to the exclusion of the ones with the most difficulties. Only a high moral
pressure enabled us to force the children to take their turn at the computer.
I realized how appropriate the term personal computer (PC) was. It was

not meant to be shared, and it created even more tension than usual. In the middle of the street library, with up to 100 children around, it would be terrible.

We did not have to accept the goal for which computers had been designed, but rather we had to redesign one to fit our goals. The street library project has particular constraints: it is wide open, children are totally free to walk away if they are not interested, and it has to include everyone. This means we should not impose anything, but instead bring objects that are meaningful to all children, that they can master and interact with. This forced us to rethink the use of the computer.

Tapori Encyclopedia

As stated earlier, computers can help master knowledge by storing it in its databank, and using a particular kind of "powerful idea" in which words—"keywords"—command actions of researching texts on the same subject. Could we turn the children into writers and researchers? We decided to try. We decided to make a giant encyclopedia that would include things the children knew, combining the computer's capacities mentioned above—as well as its printer—with other tools such as a paint brush to illustrate the encyclopedia, and carpentry tools to build the book itself out of wood. Children in each neighborhood would contribute what they knew from their lives or from books by entering information in the database and would be able to look up other entries by typing a keyword. This project would make the computer a common good, instead of an exclusive tool: the more skilled children would not be able to monopolize the computer because they would also need to see other children's entries. The encyclopedia project would need the computer, and the children participating in the project would need one another.

I then designed an original piece of software called Tapori Databank, making it as simple as possible. Children could enter short texts, sign them, do research by title, authors, or a keyword (any word in the text could be a keyword). For these functions not to take hours on such a small computer (Commodore 64), the software had to be written entirely in machine language, which I had to relearn for the occasion.

We used a black-and-white TV set as monitor. During the first summer it broke down, but a father immediately offered to replace it with one he had. Along the same lines, we chose to use cassette tapes rather than a disk drive to store the software and the database, because cassettes are less fragile and less expensive. More important, the children could relate to cassette tapes. "Why doesn't it talk?" a child asked. We listened to the tape on one of their boom boxes and heard the high-pitched beeps of the data, coding the texts we had entered. This multisensorial experience helped them understand the idea of coding information. Familiarity with cassettes also provided an occasion for teenagers to "fix the computer" when our tape got tangled up. They would patiently untangle the tape, rewind it with a pencil, and watch proudly as the program was successfully reloaded.

Of course a data cassette is much slower than a disk drive. But who is in a hurry when the summer feels like eternity with nothing in front of you? And who said one learns better by going faster? Speed also determined our choice between two printers, a dot matrix and a plotter. We noticed that with the dot matrix printer, things went so fast that the children could not understand what was going on. On the other hand, the plotter, which we had bought first because it was cheaper, was actually a little ink pen that drew every single letter. The children were fascinated watching it print slowly and hearing the "click-clack" it made as it printed. They were finally able to watch a computer work at their pace. Unfortunately, when we looked for another plotter, we were told it was no longer being produced—too slow. Too slow for what?

What Really Happened?

First Steps

The first week of the summer of 1985, with the help of the children, teenagers, and adults, we built and painted wooden platforms that would hold the computers in the van. The following week, however, the van broke down, so we brought the computers by subway. That week was particularly

Figure 12.4: Children show their Tapori Databank entry for the encyclopedia to their mother, Mrs. Gattling

(credit: Bruno Tardieu)

Figure 12.5: Children trying the Logo language in a street of the South Bronx and young people looking at the printouts

(credit: Bruno Tardieu)

warm, and the sight of three volunteers carrying suitcases from the subway impressed the children. They quickly organized to get tables from their parents, install the computers, help connect the wires, and get the street library started. In the van the maze of wires would be out of sight under the platforms, but now they were all open. Yet no one pulled or even touched the wires. This demonstrated to us that this was for the community a source of pride and confidence—the first condition for learning.

A Typical Session of Street Library: From One Tool to Another

After an hour of reading books, we would introduce a theme for the day's work on the encyclopedia. Often children would first play charades to suggest items to be entered in the encyclopedia on that theme. It was the first way to internalize their ideas. Then the original plan had been that the children would first read more about the entry they wanted to make, draft a text, enter it into the computer, and then paint an illustration for it or go to the carpentry workshop to make a wooden cover. At the beginning, however, the children were immediately attracted by the computer's novelty, so and when their turn came, they had not prepared what they wanted to enter. When this happened, we would send them to the painting workshop. There, the slow process of painting fixed the children's attention, helped them calm down, and gave them time to think more about what they would put in the computer and to discuss it first with others. Or perhaps they would ask for a book to learn more.

Look Up My Own Entry

At first, and for months after, the children did not use this possibility of referring to one another's entries. They did use the research function, but they did so systematically to look for their own entry. This was somewhat disappointing, given the pains it took for me to build this function. I changed the program slightly so that texts from other children using the word a child had chosen as a title would be printed together with his own text. Nevertheless, they continued to look up only their entries. We had to accept that it took time for them to internalize this new experience, and to understand that their entries were kept in the machine's memory and that their knowledge was valued. Only after six months, did they eagerly begin to look up what others had written. Conversations about a whole range of subjects took place around the computer, within the community, and from one community to another: which is the tallest skyscraper; what can you do with a pumpkin; why are firefighters heroes; can bees be bad if they are God's creatures; how pretty are our moms; who is the best wrestler; what are the police for?

Several hundred entries were written, often with four or five authors giving their views. Many entries were made by children who could not actually read or write, and feared any occasion to try. Yet for this project, because they knew their contribution was expected and no one would make fun of them, they did not count their efforts. Writing five lines, having to ask how each word is spelled and where each letter is hidden in that weird nonalphabetical keyboard, could take a long time. Observing the patience of other children waiting for their turn in the face of such efforts was always a lesson for me.

All the texts were printed and pasted in the encyclopedia and illustrated with beautiful watercolors. Pasting the other printout on a bright blue index card for the child to keep was always a very special ceremony. These cards have found their way into the children's homes. Recently, when I was visiting East New York, a mother insisted that I come up and see how she had arranged the photo of her child, who had passed away much too young: pasted on the blue card all around his picture were the four texts he had written ten years ago. "He would have been a whiz," she said.

When the Parents and the Whole Community Get Involved

Parents showed their pride and support in many ways, including the crucial one: providing electricity—our huge bright orange extension cord on occasion going up as high as the sixth floor intrigued passersby and literally hooked us up to the community. Yet by the end of the first summer many parents had come to watch their children use the computer, but none had ventured to try it themselves, and refused when invited to. It was the celebrations at the end of the summer in each neighborhood that brought the parents to the computer. It started with a parade of children carrying big cardboard mock-ups of a computer, cassette, monitor, printer, paint brushes, hammers, saw, scissors—all the tools they had used during the street libraries—and finally the completed encyclopedia itself, measuring two and a half by four feet, with the names of the neighborhoods and the title "Tapori Encyclopedia." Then, in a short play, the children explained how they constructed the encyclopedia. The adults asked a lot of questions: some asked about the computer. They seemed to want to try it. Volunteers and children quickly agreed: today the computer would be for the adults. That week hundreds of adults touched a computer for the first time, to look up what their children, little brothers, and sisters had written in the Tapori databank.

Using the Databank for Other Street Library Projects

We wrote about this project in the Tapori newsletter, inviting children from all backgrounds to send in their own entries to continue the encyclopedia. We sent them back printouts with theirs and related texts. Exchange also started with other street libraries in Louisiana and on a Sioux reservation. The following year—1987, the International Year of the Homeless, and two hundredth anniversary of the U.S. Constitution—provided new themes for conversation among children of different backgrounds. We invited children to design the ideal home, neighborhood, city, and constitution. Children from a new street library in a welfare hotel were particularly eager to share their experiences and thoughts about homes and neighborhoods. This created a whole new databank on a variety of themes, such as: why a table around which the whole family can sit is important; how a telephone can save your building from burning down; how can a street be made safer; what could the constitution for a Tapori city look like. In fact, a wooden Tapori city model built in the street libraries was exhibited at the United Nations as part of the International Year of the Homeless events.

Create Links between People

Also, in 1987, a family whose children were very active in the street library from one neighborhood suddenly disappeared. It took us months to discover that they had left in the middle of the night, out of too much chaos and violence in their building, and had ended up in one of the most terrible welfare hotels in the city. Links between two best friends, Bridget and Norma, were abruptly stopped. When I finally found Norma and her family in a small hotel room, with just one bed for the entire family, they immediately asked if I would bring them the computer. I came back with it, and Norma, quickly understanding the idea, looked up "Bridget" under "author". Her mother was surprised; she thought that Bridget and Norma would not be able to talk to each other anymore after all that had happened. When I took the computer back to the neighborhood, Bridget and her mother, looked up what Norma had written right away. Then they started to see each other again.[8]

Creating Links between Thoughts: Using the Power of Keywords

Once a mother in the welfare hotel where we had our Street Library was experiencing a very hard time. Having tried for months to raise her family in impossible conditions, two of her children had been taken away to be put in foster care, making her constantly angry. She had arguments with the social workers, other adults, everyone, including me. She refused any programs offered by various organizations (to teach her how to do her budget, how to feed her family, how to behave with her children, etc.), saying loudly that she had no time, although she obviously had nothing to do. Authorities did not appreciate her humor and interpreted her attitude as stating that she did not really care about her children or about anything else; she made no sense to them.

One day, as the mother observed the children working on the computer, she asked me: "So what do they write in there?" After a few explanations, quickly absorbed by her keen mind, she asked again: "So you can type a word and see what the children have written about it?" "Yes," I said. "Can I try?" she asked. After a moment of thought, she typed the keyword HAPPY. All the text of the children that included the word "happy" printed out. There were quite a few, and that impressed her. Then she typed the word FAMILY, and again she was moved to see that this was a topic the children often mentioned. She pasted the printouts on a blue card and then read them carefully. In her suddenly frail and delicate expression I could guess the inquiry that haunted her: "After all that we make our children suffer, what do they think of us, of their family, of life? Are they bitter? Can they still say the word 'happy'? Can they still speak about families?" She showed the printouts around (including to the social workers). I realized I would have never dared propose such themes to the children. Her research made them appear, and created sense.

Projects Grew Out of That First Experience in New York and Worldwide

Fourth World Network

At the urging of Père Joseph, Fanelli and I wrote *Passport to the New World of Technology ... Computers* in 1986. Our project and the book's publication helped convince other Fourth World groups and affiliate associations to work with computers and poor families. They also opened new avenues for experimentation. In the last page of the book, we wrote: "Our project in New York had international echoes. We are looking into how we might link up with groups in other areas, using a modem that was recently given to us which we can use with our Commodore computer." (In 1986, the Internet was not yet being used by the public at large.)

In 1988, with a grant from the European Union, Fanelli developed a computerized network that enabled all the Fourth World Universities in fifteen cities in Europe to connect and exchange summaries of their monthly discussions.[9] He then expanded this Fourth World Network to include news and internal e-mail for Fourth World teams. Soon young people and children also had their "corner" in the network. ATD Fourth World being worldwide, we extended the network to all our teams, even though telephone lines are in such poor shape in the largest (and poorest) part of the world. Despite all the difficulties, it proved quite successful, especially when we used it as a tool to support international campaigns and gatherings designed to unify the poor and their friends worldwide.

In New York, Links with the World and Street Workshop

This worldwide exchange of news and stories via new technology has had an impact back in New York, where it all started. Every month, families get together to share what has happened in their neighborhood as well as

Figure 12.6: The drawing of the marble machine and the built machine

(credit: Denis Cretinon)

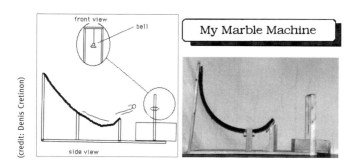

news coming from the rest of the world. People ask to answer the news or write to volunteers who have gone elsewhere. A young man, Johnny's cousin, who participated in the street library in New York and now lives in Boston, has used my computer to write to the group in New York. It has become natural for the families we know to feel in touch with other poor families from other countries as well as with people from other backgrounds who are concerned with poverty, and to use advanced information technology for that purpose.

In the street library itself the computer has also remained naturally integrated. Chris Cleary, a Fourth World volunteer working in the New York street libraries says that several parents refer to him and other volunteers as "the computer people." Most of them, he adds, however, have never heard of the Internet or rather it did not register when they heard it: "how often do we see e-mail or web-site addresses on TV or in the newspapers?" So they decided to introduce it in the street library. He writes, "When the children first got in touch with it they had a difficult time figuring out what to look for, as if thrown into a huge library and having to choose a book. We had them start with thinking about things around them, like their neighborhood of Harlem, and we found a site with a picture of a young boy and a few things he had to say about living in Harlem, a few blocks from where we had the street library. From then on the ideas came fairly quickly." Then Denis Cretinon, now in charge of the program, introduced the children to an experimental web site, allowing all the street libraries in the world to exchange information and stories— maybe the beginning of a new adventure.

Another major development in New York has been the use of computers to design science machines. Kurt Reitz, a new Fourth World volunteer, and Denis Cretinon organized small workshops building a "marble rollercoaster" with children who had the most difficulties. The idea came from seeing a large kinetic sculpture at the Port Authority where billiard balls rolled down complicated tracks, doing "tricks" and making noises and music along the way. Each child had to invent a part of the track that would do whatever "tricks" he wished. The children first designed the track and described what they wanted the ball to do. The children used the computer to enter their designs and comments about what the ball "should do" in a databank (designed by Kurt Reitz with Hypercard) with additional pages showing some basic laws of physics regarding "balls going downhill."

Then they had to actually build the track out of wood. Often the ball did not do exactly what they had planned it would. "Then they had to adjust. It was amazing to see how comfortable the children became with the tools, including power tools," wrote Denis Cretinon. "It could have been dangerous but nothing happened. It is probably due to that process of designing, recording it, making it, and reflecting back on it. They were not just playing around with tools. They had a purpose." Children would go back to the computer to write what the ball actually did, then enter new designs. Kurt wrote: "As the desire to create becomes stronger, the children naturally, gradually, develop the discipline that they lack to do the tedious work required to bring their creation to fruition."

Conclusion

Framing the issue as one of access is the ultimate success for people who have created a technology and are trying to sell it. If the poor and excluded need access, they mostly need reinvention for different aims. The fact that we saw ourselves being pushed into a somewhat unexplored area was important in freeing us to question the means, and to look for meaning behind the means. Technology by itself is meaningless, but people who design a specific application for it, give it meaning. We had to discover the meaning behind the tool, with no fear of challenging such imposing and powerful symbols of "smarter than thou." We opened choices: "printer has to be fast to gain time and money" versus "printer has to be slow for children who have plenty of time to observe and learn"; "personal computer" versus "community computers"; "computers to be fed by" versus "computers to feed"; and "technology to provide answers" versus "technology to become a researcher and frame questions."

But if freeing oneself of commonly accepted ideas is a necessary step to go beyond the status quo, it can be frightening and calls for some security. Our security came in the form of simple practice enabling us to write our travel log and draw a map of our journey along the way to learn our directions, with people as the only landmarks. By doing our participant-observation report every night I had the feeling we were more scientific than when I was at university, letting the facts sink in and challenging theories. We also had constant collective reflection on our interpretations of what we had seen and heard as well as on our own actions. We could share aloud with our coworkers our surprises and disappointments even when it hurt; and with the security of team commitment and affection for one another, we could try to decode their meaning to constantly reinvent the action. The diversity of the volunteers' backgrounds forced us to go beyond shallow consensus. These two processes—personal and collective—allowed us to face the real challenges brought by the poorest people, those who make actions and ideas fail, instead of covering them up or hardening ourselves as is often the temptation. It allowed us to remain close to the poorest people and make their humanity and quest for transformation our compass. "All came from a shared life, never from a theory," Wresinski (1983, p.152) wrote, to explain how the group started. As Denis Cretinon said recently, "In the street the children are the master, not the computer. If what's on the computer doesn't make sense to them, it is the end of it."

This opens the way to an ongoing venture in which both very poor people and people who master today's means of communication are invited to create a partnership. I have tried to show here that a genuine joint venture and reciprocal learning between them can be fruitful and promising. It is also vital. If superpowerful tools of knowledge construction and communication are mastered and put into practice by a continuously shrinking number of people, the gap between means and meaning will become forbidding, and will present a danger for our modern democracies. On the other hand, if those who design the structure of today's and tomorrow's world accept to confront their inventions, values, and visions with the poorest people in our societies, with enough patience for each other, and no fear of being attacked, they will be able to reinvent them together—broader, deeper, more humane, more meaningful. Then our advancing technology will also be an advancement for civilization, and our combined knowledge will strengthen us rather than weaken us by creating barriers of fear and violence. Père Joseph concluded the 1983 conference at the Sorbonne by inviting members from the academia to join him in the struggle against extreme poverty: "When the free and educated men and women will join the Fourth World, extreme poverty will not exist anymore" (Wresinski 1996).

Notes

Bruno Tardieu is at the Institute of Research, Action and Training for Human Relations, International Movement ATD Fourth World.

1. Fourth World Movement in the United States: 7600 Willow Hill Drive, Landover, Maryland 20785.

2. For more information about Father Joseph (1917–1988), see Vos van Steenwijk (1996).

3. This approach deepens and somewhat contradicts the idea of Oscar Lewis's "culture of poverty" (Lewis 1996).

4. The institute was created to introduce the numerous studies on the poor, some research and knowledge that would first and foremost respect the poor, and start from and be consistent with their understanding and actions.

5. The association used the term in various publications during the 1960s. Then, in 1969 published Jean Labben's "Le Quart Monde." For a definition of Fourth World (referring to the poorest as subjects, unlike in the sociological notions of underclass or lumpen proletariat), see Join-Lambert (1981).

In the colloquium leading to this book, Manuel Castells mentioned the emergence of a fourth world "from the South Bronx to Burkina Faso," with "people who are not exploited but are irrelevant."

6. Olin, a criminologist from Columbia University, inspirer of the U.S. war on poverty, and cofounder of Mobilization for Youth, learned about the Fourth World Movement in one of the first colloquia organized by its research institute in UNESCO. He then offered to have Fourth World volunteers participate in the MFY evaluation. For a history of the Fourth World Movement history in the United States, see Fanelli (1990).

7. Tapori is the children's branch of the Fourth World Movement. It was named after children Père Joseph had met in India—children living in railway stations, sharing what they had, yet despised by many. Everyone had told him not to interact with these children who would have nothing good to teach him. Tapori allows children from very poor backgrounds as well as other backgrounds to learn from one another and become friends.

8. Bridget and Norma's story has been published in *Fourth World Chronicle of Human Rights* (Paris: 1990), Fourth World Publications.

9. For a definition and history of Fourth World University, see Ferrand (1996).

References

Camus, Albert. 1994. *Le Premier Homme*. Paris: Gallimard.

Dufourny de Villiers. 1967. *Cahiers du Quatrième Ordre*, no. 1, 25 April 1789, reprint. Paris: Edition Histoire sociale.

Fanelli, Vincent and Bruno Tardieu. 1986. *Passport to the New World of Technology ... Computers*. Paris, London, and Landover, MD: Fourth World Publications.

Fanelli, Vincent. 1990. *The Human Face of Poverty: A Chronicle of Urban America*. New York: Bootstrap Press.

Ferrand, Françoise. 1996. *"Et vous, qu'en pensez-vous?"* Paris: Editions Quart Monde.

Join-Lambert, Louis. 1981. "Quart Monde." In *Encyclopedie Universalia, Thèmes et Problèmes*, pp. 341–344.

Kozol, Jonathan. 1995. *Amazing Grace*. New York: Crown.

Labbens, Jean. 1969. *Le Quart Monde*. Paris: Edition Sciences et Services.

Labbens, Jean. 1978. *Sociologie de la Pauvrete: le Tiers Monde et le Quart Monde*. Paris: Gallimard.

Lewis, Oscar. 1996. "The Culture of Poverty" in *La Vida: a Puerto Rican Family in the Culture of Poverty—San Juan and New York*. New York: Vintage Books.

Papert, Seymour. 1980. *Mind Storms: Children, Computers, Powerful Ideas*. New York: Basic Books.

Piaget, Jean. 1960. *The Psychology of Intelligence*. Totowa, NJ: Littlefield, Adams.

Rosenfeld, Jona. 1989. *Emergence from Extreme Poverty*. Paris, London and Landover, MD: Fourth World Publications.

Schön, Donald. 1983. *The Reflective Practitioner: How Professionals Think in Action*. New York: Basic Books.

Tardieu, Bruno. 1995. "Lieu de memoire." In *Revue Quart Monde,* no. 155, pp. 43–50. Paris: Editions Quart Monde.

Tardieu, Bruno. 1990. "Bridget and Norma." In *The Fourth World Chronicle of Human Rights.* Paris, London and Landover, MD: Fourth World Publications.

Vos van Steenwijk, Alwine de. 1996. *Father Joseph Wresinski—Voice of the Poorest.* Los Angeles: Queenship Publishing Company. Translated by Charles Sleeth from *Père Joseph.* Paris: Editions Quart Monde, 1989.

Wresinski, Joseph. 1983. *Les Pauvres sont l'Eglise.* Paris: Le Centurion.

Wresinski, Joseph. 1992. *Blessed Are You the Poor.* Paris, London and Landover, MD: Fourth World Publications. Translated from *Heureux vous les Pauvres.* Paris: Ed Cana, 1984.

Wresinski, Joseph. 1994. *Chronic Poverty and Lack of Basic Security: A Report of the Economic and Social Council of France.* Paris, London and Landover, MD: Fourth World Publications. Translated from *Grande Pauvrete et Précarité Economique et Sociale.* Paris: Journal Officiel de la République Française. Avis et Rapport du Conseil Economique et Social. 1987.

Wresinski, Joseph. 1995. *Father Joseph Wresinski, Founder ATD Fourth World Movement.* Excerpts from interviews. Paris, London and Landover, MD: Fourth World Publications.

Wresinski, Joseph. 1996. *Echec a la misère, conférence faite à la Sorbonne le 1er Juin, 1983.* Paris: Editions Quart Monde.

13. Social Empowerment through Community Networks

Alan Shaw

Michelle Shaw

Local Village Building

As our society has become more complex, many communities have become less cohesive. Frequently we have lost the sense of the tight-knit neighborhood, of the village, of the place where everybody knows each other's name, and where people are often working with their neighbors on projects to improve their community. Many people are yearning for that kind of world to return.

No one can know for sure what it is going to take to bring that back, and we are not always certain of exactly what the forces are that are for or against it. But whether you are rich or poor, or somewhere in the middle, it is extremely comforting to have some sense that your community is a type of extended family, where everyone is integrated in some way into one another's lives. This is the notion of the village or at least it is the ideal of the village. Recently, many people have been drawing on this ideal by quoting the African proverb that it takes a village to raise a child, or it takes a whole village to raise a child. Such a statement helps focus our attention on the idea that as social realities in our communities have become increasingly complex, we seem to have left the concept of the village behind.

Now we stand at the door of a new age of information technology. As we enter into the twenty-first century, it is becoming increasingly clear that computer networks are sure to become ever more critical in our daily lives. It is therefore important to ask if this technology can be helpful in our quest to reclaim the village. If this is at all possible, then we need to focus some of our attention on the issue of village building when we talk about computer networking. How can we use this technology to positively affect people's day-to-day life experiences? And how will this technology affect our relationships with others, especially in urban centers, and especially among our various classes and ethnic populations?

We will address these questions first by looking at certain theoretical paradigms that help clarify some of the issues involved. We will also describe the results we have gathered from using a particular networking system in a low-income community in Newark, New Jersey, which provides some concrete examples of how this technology can be an important tool for residents trying to bring the village back to an urban neighborhood.

Producers versus Consumers

Many people are wondering whether the new evolving technology is going to create information haves and have-nots. If this happens, we can expect to see already dire social problems become even worse. It is possible to imagine the day when a lot of people will not feel like they are citizens in this country because they are not connected to the technology that is at the mainstream of American life. If this is the case, we need to begin looking for alternative visions of the role that technology can play in helping combat potential societal divisions.

One alternative vision has to do with exploring ways to use the technology to help people become producers rather than consumers. Oftentimes, discussions about computer networking and the Internet have to do with a model of the end user as a consumer accessing resources. In this model the technology helps the end user get connected to something that someone else has produced. Concepts like "surfing" or "browsing" are based on the consumer model where the users of the technology are rarely the producers who are developing their own content. It is very much like the use of the television. The average television viewer watches the programs and surfs the channels. The viewer does produce programming that will be seen on another's television set. Whether it is television, movies, radio, or CD's, media technologies are rarely thought of as resources with which the average person can produce anything of real value.

Yet information technology can be a very productive medium indeed. It need not be limited to the paradigm of a commercial broadcast medium. This technology can be more like a canvas—a place where one can extend oneself and build things of value that can be shared within the same medium. A theory called "social constructionism" helps describe how this type of activity can be a force for community building and social empowerment.

Social Constructionism

Social constructionism is an extension of a theory known as "constructionism," which is itself related to the theory of "constructivism." Both constructionism and constructivism address the issue of childhood learning and development, although they also have broader social implications. Jean Piaget (1954) advanced the theory of constructivism to argue that childhood learning is more than a matter of simply pouring information into the head of a child. He claimed that learning is not just getting access to information; it is more about the active intellectual processes that a child goes through when coming into contact with new information. Learning does not happen until a child takes an active role in building knowledge with the information he has. This building process has to do with internal mental and cognitive structures that are continually evolving as new information and experiences are incorporated. Therefore, a good teacher is not someone who just supplies access to information for the child. Rather, a good teacher is a person who is more of a coach in an intellectual sense, someone who can facilitate the child's building process. The teacher is trying to find out in what stage of a building process the child is, and in each stage the teacher is helping the child with critical resources that might facilitate that process. This is an understanding of the child as an activist in her own learning process.

Constructivism focuses its attention on the internal cognitive mechanisms of learning and development. Constructionism adds to this viewpoint by addressing particular externalized aspects of developmental activity: "We understand 'constructionism' as including, but going beyond, what Piaget would call 'constructivism.' The word with the v expresses the theory that knowledge is built by the learner, not supplied by the teacher. The word with the n expresses the further idea that this happens especially felicitously when the learner is engaged in the construction of something external or at least shareable … a sand castle, a machine, a computer program, a book. This leads us to a model using a cycle of internalization of what is outside, then externalization of what is inside and so on" (Papert 1990, p. 3).

Constructionism argues that when someone investigating an idea constructs a new artifact related to that idea, then that person is able to actively engage in a developmental cycle. Rather than viewing the learner as one who just builds internal cognitive structures while learning, constructionist learning includes building external constructions that engage the environment and give the learner feedback with which to reinterpret the experience. By reinterpreting the experience in response to one's own construction, a learner is able to continue developing an internalized concept and then reexternalize it in new ways within the environment. This is a developmental cycle. When learners express themselves through external constructions, they are able to examine their constructions and rethink, relearn, and recreate. This forces the original internalized concept beyond its initial stage and allows much richer and deeper learning experiences.

Social constructionism takes these theories into the social setting outside of the classroom and focuses upon the construction of activities, projects, and relationships that help define an evolving community. Through this lens, the members of the community serve as active agents in the construction of outcomes and activities that produce a developmental cycle in the social setting. Within social constructionism, the social setting itself is an evolving construction. When the members of a social setting develop external social constructs—the shared activities, projects, and relationships in the community—they add to the setting and provide new materials and processes to the setting that can be instrumental in future shared constructions. This engagement can create a cycle of development that is critical to determining a setting's ultimate form (Shaw 1996).

Social Empowerment

Without constructivist and constructionist theories, one might not provide children with the tools and materials in a classroom that can help them become active in their own learning processes. And when children lack such tools and materials, they can be reduced to functioning primarily as consumers of information and activities that their teachers produce. This model is disempowering because the children never gain significant control over their own developmental constructions. Similarly, without the model of social constructionism, one might be satisfied with tools and materials in a social setting that relegate the members of the setting to the function of consumers of information and activities that others produce. Instead, social constructionism argues that members of a social setting need tools and materials that can help them control and develop their own social constructions. This is the key to true social empowerment. Neighbors who live in a community often are not active in shaping the social setting that they face daily. Whether the experiences in a local community are positive or negative, most neighbors are disconnected from processes that bring them together with other members of their community to develop their community to its fullest potential. In other words, living in a neighborhood can often be a very passive experience.

If every neighbor were active in social constructions, if every neighbor had a role to play in their neighborhood, then they would be engaging their social setting in a constructive developmental process. The emergence of a person in a community who pulls together a potluck once a week or once a month and invites the neighbors will make that a richer community. Someone could organize a clothing drive. Someone else could organize day care. We could have musicians adding new music to the community. We could have poets contributing poetry. We could have people actively working with young people in the community. We could have people who draw murals on walls finding ways to make the walls beautiful. We could have a community that is continually evolving and developing. Of course, this does happen in many places, but it is often rare in many more places—especially in urban social settings.

In urban centers many people are disconnected from others living in their neighborhoods. This may be because people are more busy nowadays, or because of a combination of growing fear, uncertainty, and shifting demographics. These factors present barriers to the older social tools and traditions that were used in the past to pull together activities and keep a community tight-knit. So we need new tools and a new tradition of village building in our modern communities. And in this area, information technology can certainly be of help.

Neighborhood Information Infrastructure

Networking technology has been used to make it possible for people to create new infrastructures on a national and international scale. In fact, the federal government has increasingly been addressing what it calls the National Information Infrastructure (NII). The NII is connected to the idea that business and governmental entities can enhance their activities if there is an electronic "superhighway" in place, just as the creation of the physical highway and road system made new business and government activities possible. The electronic superhighway would allow for connections to be made and for new activities to take place that would be very difficult to accomplish without this new highway system.

Yet computer networks can provide organizational infrastructure for just about any type of collaborative activity. So we need to extend the concept of the NII beyond the national scene and focus also on the local community. We must consider the possibility that this technology can help members of a community build up their neighborhood information infrastructure. Interstate highways would not be very useful if it were not for off-ramps. People need to travel on local byways and between blocks of houses, not just from city to city. In fact, people spend most of their time traveling along their local roadways. So, we will also need to address the issue of local infrastructure when considering the implications of the NII. In fact, as the following quote from Paul Resnick and Mel King indicates, many of the issues concerning social empowerment are a matter of enhancing local information infrastructure.

> There is no such thing as a poor community. Even neighborhoods without much money have substantial human resources. Often, however, the human resources are not appreciated or utilized, partly because people do not have information about one another and about what their neighborhood has to offer. For example, a family whose oil heater is broken may go cold for lack of knowledge that someone just down the block knows how to fix it. (Resnick and King 1990)

If computer networks begin to support neighborhood information infrastructure, then these networks can become tools for social constructionism. They can help members of a community rebuild a fractured social setting. Neighborhood computer networks can be used to support and augment the social infrastructure that is at the core of the cohesiveness in tight-knit communities. To demonstrate this potential, a computer networking system was developed at the MIT Media Laboratory and placed in a small neighborhood in Boston, Massachusetts and in a low-income housing development in Newark, New Jersey. The system has been very successful at illustrating the power of this approach.

Multi-User Sessions In Community

Multi-User Sessions In Community (MUSIC) is a computer system that uses text, graphics, digitized voice, and speech synthesis features to inter-act within a shared networked environment designed to support activities taking place in real communities as opposed to virtual communities. MUSIC is attempting to present a model for how local neighborhood infrastructure can be advanced by information technologies just as a national information infrastructure is also being advanced by these systems.

The nature of the MUSIC program is essentially that of a Graphical MUD, or "Multi-User Dungeon." MUDs are programs that accept network connections from multiple simultaneous users and provide access to a shared database of "rooms," "exits," and other objects. Users browse and manipulate the database from "inside" the rooms, seeing only those objects that are in the same room and moving between rooms mostly via the exits that connect them. MUDs are thus a kind of social virtual reality, an electronically represented "place" that users can visit. MUDs are extensible from within—MUD users can add new rooms and other objects to the database and give those objects unique virtual behavior, using an embedded programming language. MUDs generally have many users connected at the same time. All of these users are browsing and manipulating the same database and can encounter both the other users and their newly created objects. MUD users can also communicate with one another directly in real time, usually by typing messages that are seen by all other users in the same room.

MUDs have existed for about ten years, becoming particularly prominent on the global Internet in the past five years. Throughout the entire ten years, they have been used almost exclusively for recreational purposes. Many MUDs are specialized for playing a game like "Dungeons and Dragons," in which the players are assigned numerical measures of various physical and mental characteristics and then have fantasy adventures in a role-playing style. Nearly all other MUDs are used almost exclusively for leisure-time social activity, during which the participants spend their connected periods talking with each other and building new areas or objects for general enjoyment.

Figure 13.1: MUSIC's graphical user interface

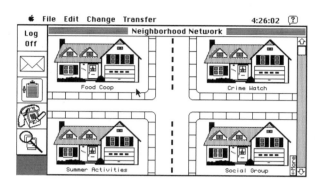

Through MUSIC, users are able to use the MUD environment to work together and provide infrastructure to their neighborhood or community organization. It is essentially an example of computer supported collaborative work (CSCW), which is a mode of productive work that has become an essential part of academic, government, and business research and development over the past two decades. In academic communities, this very important function of networking is supported mainly through electronic mail, online discussion groups, and shared database systems accessible through the Internet.

The MUSIC server for the network can be located just about anywhere; in neighborhood homes, churches, community centers, schools, and public spaces. The server turns a dedicated PC or MAC into an information resource that is connected to multiple telephone lines continually day and night. This server can give the callers access to a database developed by the local organization and neighborhood residents. The client software allows users to log in over a modem and use voice input and feedback

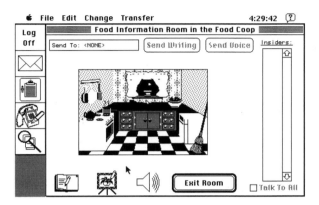

as well as normal text modes. In keeping with current user-interface trends for this type of system, the database in MUSIC has been developed around certain spatial and visual metaphors. The system is designed with a graphical user interface that has been modeled after a neighborhood with streets and buildings (Figure 13.1). The buildings represent the programs that are being organized on the system.

The data storage and retrieval mechanism is developed around the concept of "MUD"-like rooms filled with objects (Figure 13.2). When a user enters a room, her icon shows up in the "insiders" column along with anyone else's icon. Each room is organized around a topic that also serves as the name of the room. The topics identify the types of information in each room. The information in each room is contained in the objects in each room. There are text, graphic, and sound objects. Users can enter a room and list the objects; view an object; and open, create, or copy an object. When an object is open, users are able to enter and edit its text, graphics, or sounds. Although multiple users are allowed into the database at any

Figure 13.3: Icons for outgoing mail on MUSIC

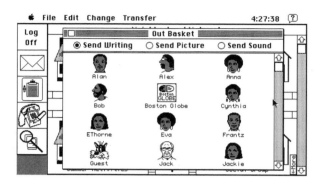

time and multiple users can enter any room, only one user may edit any
one object at a time. Multiple users may view an object that is currently
open and being edited by another user, however. MUSIC is extensible from
within—users can add new rooms and buildings to the database.

MUSIC supports bulletin board postings, discussion groups, and
real-time and voice communications among users who are logged on con-
currently. Private places are also available to support personal communications and proprietary information. Each person who has an account on the
system has his own private electronic mailbox from which he can send and
receive text and voice mail, and groups of individuals can set up spaces for
documents that only they will be able to access (Figure 13.3).

MUSIC has a mechanism for handling online voting, surveying,
and polling. Special rooms facilitate news publications. A special geocoded
graphical map database/directory room allows users to get information
about other users in the neighborhood or organization by simply clicking
on that person's street name or organizational grouping name (Figure 13.4).

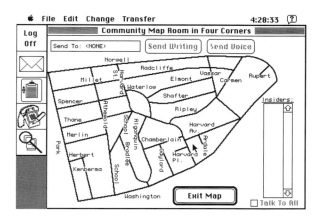

Making Healthy MUSIC

We have implemented the MUSIC networking system in a small neigh-borhood in Boston, Massachusetts, and in a low-income housing develop-ment in Newark, New Jersey. The initial implementation of the project in Boston was primarily for research purposes. This project was small in scope and lasted only one year, after which just about all of the equipment used to support the network had to be taken away, effectively ending the project. The Newark network was the first project initiated once the research work was completed and it is a good example of how technology can actually be used as a permanent tool for community building. It is at the end of its second year in existence, and it has reached many more people than the more modest Boston example. Therefore, most of our description of the results of the online activity will concern the network in Newark. Those results, as we describe them in this section, are based on an article written in 1995 by Pamela Morgan., the director of the project. The article is entitled "Making Healthy MUSIC: Technology as a Tool for Social Revitalization" (Morgan 1995).

In the spring of 1994, Pamela Morgan from the Office of Computer Education and Technology of the Newark Public Schools received a Telecommunications Information Infrastructure Assistance Program (TIIAP) grant from the National Telecommunications Information Agency (NTIA) of the U.S. Department of Commerce. The sum of $106,950 was provided for the installation of a community computer network that aimed to raise student achievement by helping improve the delivery of primary health care and the quality of life for community residents. She entitled the project, "Making Healthy MUSIC."

The project focused on the residents of a New Community Corporation housing development that surrounds the Newton Street Elementary School. The New Community Corporation provides housing, job training, and social services for the greater Newark community. New Community Corporation housing, which consists of approximately seven hundred units in low-rise buildings, now completely encompasses the Newton Street School community, and over 85 percent of the school population lives in New Community Housing.

The network is comprised of computers placed in homes, social service offices, the public library, Newton Street School, Newark Public Schools central office, an area church, and the University of Medicine and Dentistry of New Jersey (UMDNJ). The engine of the system is the MUSIC software. Hardware includes Macintosh LC 550 computers, a Quadra 950 file server, and 14,400 baud modems.

From the program's onset, a collaborative relationship was formed between the Newton Street School administration, the Office of Computer Education and Technology of the Newark Public Schools, the New Community Corporation, and the office of the dean at UMDNJ. Representatives from these institutions, as well as representatives from the office of the Provost of Rutgers University, the Newark Public Library, the *Star Ledger* newspaper, the AT & T Alliance of Black Telecommunications Employees, and other interested community members serve on an advisory board which meets quarterly to review and advise on program progress, and offer resources to support the project. Advisory committee members have helped shape the program by bringing the rich resources of their organizations to the table for the collective benefit of the Making Healthy MUSIC participants.

The selection process for families to participate in the project began in January 1995. Criteria for participation were simply that the participants (who are referred to as captains) must have a child attending Newton Street Elementary School, and must live in New Community housing. They must also agree to allow at least four people from outside their immediate families access to the computer, and they must complete a series of training sessions. The selection process included the completion of a survey (which was sent home with each student at Newton Street Elementary School), an application, and a personal interview. Fifteen individuals (who with two exceptions did not know each other) successfully completed the entire process and became the first program captains.

The training sessions started with a community-building retreat during which the captains spent two intense days analyzing community needs and developing strategies to meet those needs. By the end of the retreat the captains had developed a Making Healthy MUSIC captain's contract in which they stipulated their responsibility to the program and to the community. The preface of the contract, which was developed by the participants, reads as follows:

Once the community creates a bond,
the quality of life will improve,
and give hope to many families that life will be better.
It starts with one Victory!!
Where once we knocked on doors and they were closed,
Now, we will get them opened.

Other aspects of the contract focused on the expectations that the participants had for the program, the indicators they felt would comprise a successful program, and their identification of how the program could be a tool for empowerment for improving the quality of life in their neighborhood. Next, they ran a series of computer-focused training classes for families. A community of learners was in evidence as parents and children worked together to learn to use the Macintosh computer. Since the initial training session, they have had subsequent retreats and Macintosh computer training sessions in order to maintain the momentum of the project, and to bring new captains and their families into the Making Healthy MUSIC family.

At the date of this writing, there are about thirty captains and a total of about 180 users. Of that number, about 140 of the users are actually residents in the housing development, and the other 40 are staff and volunteers from the Newark public schools, UMDNJ, and the other affiliated organizations.

Neighborhood Activism

During the time the project has been implemented the Making Healthy MUSIC families have organized several committees that meet in person once a month, and several online discussion groups. The discussion groups online include: Circle of Sisters, Circle of Brothers, AIDS, Parenting, Recipes, Housekeeping, Allergies and Asthma, Mental Health Topics, and Men's and Women's Health Issues. Doctors have been communicating with residents online, answering real questions and setting the stage for more comfortable face-to-face meetings. A number of youths in the community view the principal of Newton Street Elementary School, Willie Thomas, as a father figure, although many of their parents were not initially familiar with him. Parental involvement in the school is greatly increasing, parents are actively involved in the school's planning process, and Thomas is now viewed as being "one of the family" by the Making Healthy MUSIC parents and their family members. Parents contact him online to get information and often just to have an open line of communication with the school principal. Thomas has included many of the participants in his school-based planning teams in order to have greater parental input into the school's operations. And, of course, one of the most important results from the Making Healthy MUSIC project has been the activism we have seen on the part of parents and students who are online. Using the network, residents have been able to organize numerous events and to come together during crises. They have organized talent shows, a recycling drive, flea markets, gardening projects, field trips, and fundraisers where food and t-shirts have been sold.

Almost all of these organizing efforts began as one person's idea that was first communicated to others on the network through the bulletin board, or e-mail, or in an online discussion. After a number of other residents respond positively, a dialogue begins that also takes place online, and that ultimately results in an activity being organized and implemented in one form or another. Projects that begin in the discussion rooms are usually projects that are related to the topic of the discussion room, or are projects that a person wants to pose to the group of people with whom they have had dialogues in that discussion room. Project ideas that begin by being posted to the bulletin board are usually ideas that a person wants to send to the widest possible audience. About five to ten messages are posted to the bulletin board on any given week, with about one hundred messages currently active on any given day. It often takes months for an idea posted on the bulletin board to be old enough to be removed.

Many items posted on the bulletin board are announcements or questions people want to pose to the entire online community. Not everything posted is a project idea. But by and large, most project ideas begin by being posted to the bulletin board, although some notable exceptions have started in the discussion rooms. In one case, a woman wrote inside a discussion room that she was recently told by her doctor that her health problems were related to her lack of exercise. She said she would have to get involved in a regular exercise routine of some sort, such as weekly walks around one of the parks nearby. However, she also mentioned that she was afraid to walk around the park alone, so if this was going to happen for her, somebody else would have to come along. Was anybody interested? Soon, at least three women responded online, saying they also needed exercise and that they would love to join her each week. She only had to pose her initiative in an open forum, and a ball started rolling that got a group of women to exercise together, each of whom would probably not have gone out to exercise alone.

In a different discussion a mother lamented that in her opinion, many of the teenage girls in the neighborhood do not behave in a very lady-like manner, and they do not seem to be willing to talk about the issue with their mothers or with any older person. She asked if anybody had any idea of what might be done about this. One person did have an idea; she suggested that because the girls are always asking to have their hair braided by these older women, and because it usually takes many hours to braid it, maybe the older women could come together and organize discussions about these issues that would happen while these young ladies were getting their hair braided. They would then have a captive audience, and with a couple of older people working together, they might be more effective than any one of them trying to get the discussion going alone. Many of the women in this discussion group loved the idea and decided that they definitely wanted to be involved in this excellent example of informal neighborhood organizing.

In another case, a mother put a message on the bulletin board that she wanted to take her children on a field trip to the airport, because she wanted to challenge her children to think about careers in fields like aviation that they never see up close. She said most of the young people in the housing development have never been to the Newark Airport—or on an airplane—and this was limiting their sense of what the possibilities were in their own futures. So she invited any other children who wanted to go to come along. Not only did ten other children and some parents write e-mail to her saying that they wanted to go, but people from Rutgers University and the Newark Board of Education wrote to her that they had contacts who could put her in touch with the person in charge of the airport. Suddenly, this parent was the organizing force behind a type of field trip that is very difficult to pull off without institutional connections. In the end, over a dozen children and a number of parents met an official at the airport and received a tour of the entire facility. They also boarded a plane, met a pilot, and visited the cockpit as a pilot described for them what they do in there and how one goes about becoming a pilot. When it was over, the tour guide told this mother that the children in her field trip were the best behaved and most well organized that had ever been on a tour with that particular guide. This was an amazing accomplishment for a mother who had never organized a field trip before. The network provided her with important organizational tools, which she put to good use.

In a different case, a father on the system used the bulletin board in a similar organizational effort. He wrote on the bulletin board that he wanted to organize a Boy Scouts chapter in his neighborhood because he could not find one anywhere nearby for his son. He added, however, that he had never organized anything like this before and so he was going to need a great deal of help. A number of people sent him messages saying they would help, and one woman wrote to the bulletin board that she was very inspired by his idea. She said that he was going to reach out to so many young people with his initiative that even if he had never organized anything like this before, he was off to a great start.

Once, in a time of tragedy when a young teenage girl was murdered in the community, people expressed their grief in poetry and tributes that they passed around on the bulletin board. Then one girl used the bulletin board to announce that she was extremely upset that a parade was going to take place on the same day that the funeral was to be held. She felt that the parade would interfere with people's ability to grieve, and she was quite angry that nobody seemed to care. The parade had been organized a year in advance by the Catholic archdiocese that owns the housing development. They sponsor the parade every year, so it would be extremely difficult to postpone it. But the day after she voiced her opinion on the bulletin, another posting on the bulletin board announced that the parade would be rescheduled. Remarkably, the grief of one girl had been heard at the highest levels of the archdiocese. She realized that she could make a difference, especially when her community has a system that attempts to let everyone's voice be heard.

After awhile, many projects that are organized on the system become ongoing projects that have special rooms or buildings of their own. The talent shows that have been organized on the system are an example of this type of project. The young people enjoyed the first one so much that they began a room to begin organizing the next one with the help of their parents. A list of young people with different talents is kept in that room, and some sound clips and drawings by these young people are also kept there. About four talent shows have been organized so far, with no end in sight. And given that each show is another opportunity for the young people to shine, the school's principal has indicated that he will always make space available at no charge for this activity.

Various organizations in the community also put buildings and rooms on the system to announce their initiatives and to generate input from the community. The elementary school, Rutgers University, the hospital nearby, a library, a mental health facility, and the security office of the housing development all have buildings online. The presence of these organizations on the system often helps their neighbors become more comfortable with the idea of increasing their involvement with them. In fact, the school and the hospital have seen a dramatic increase in the involvement of these residents in their institutions. For example, once during a period when a lot of fights were breaking out among young people at the elementary school, some of the parents went to the principal to discuss the issue with him, and they decided to volunteer time to help monitor the hallways between classes when the trouble usually occurred. This kind of discussion and that particular solution had never occurred before, and ultimately the parents' intervention has helped to successfully resolve the problem.

Conclusion

The community in Newark is a low-income community that is not in the least bit poor. It is rich in examples of real tight-knit community experiences. But bringing computers into homes of communities like this is a solution that is much too expensive for the average low-income neighborhood. However, the computer industry will soon be bringing this technology to television sets over cable channels or phone lines. Either inexpensive computers will be available in the future to engage in these networks, or a computer will not be needed at all. The forces that are driving this are the commercial forces that want people to be able to buy their products on interactive televisions or over the Internet. These forces are not thinking of using this particular technology to help develop neighborhood-led initiatives and social constructions. Productive uses of this technology, however, are real and viable, and we must struggle to bring these possibilities into every community.

To empower our communities and ourselves, we need to make sure that we think of community networks as a tool for local neighborhood development, where the neighbors themselves are the leadership, producing their own content, and the technology is just a facilitator. Networking should help people tell their own stories and develop their own programs, not simply help them consume more of the stories and programs that come from outside forces. In this way, networking can help people recapture the magic of a community where everyone is important and each has something to offer.

References

Morgan, Pamela. 1995. "Making Healthy MUSIC: Technology as a Tool for Social Revitalization." *Journal of Urban Technology* 3(1): 97–102.

Papert, Seymour. 1990. *Introduction: Constructionist Learning*, edited by Idit Harel. Cambridge, MA: MIT Media Laboratory.

Piaget, Jean. 1954. *The Construction of Reality in the Child*. New York: Ballantine Books.

Resnick, Paul, and Mel King. 1990. "The Rainbow Pages—Building Community with Voice Technology." In *Proceedings of Directions and Implications of Advanced Computing (DIAC–90) Symposium*. Boston, July 28.

Shaw, Alan. 1996. "Social Constructionism and the Inner City: Designing Environments for Social Development and Urban Renewal." In *Constructionism in Practice: Designing, Thinking, and Learning in a Digital World*, edited by Yasmin Kafai and Mitchel Resnick, pp. 175–206. Mahwah, NJ: Lawrence Erlbaum Associates.

14. Commodity and Community in Personal Computing

Sherry Turkle

The chapters by Bruno Tardieu and Alan and Michelle Shaw describe experiments with computers in disadvantaged communities that are a decade apart. During the interim computing technology developed dramatically, both in power and in nature. In the mid-1980s, Tardieu was able to put a handful of "stand-alone" machines on community street corners and invited children to use them to record their personal stories and write an encyclopedia of questions to which they wanted answers (what you can do with a pumpkin, how you can succeed in school). By the mid-1990s, the decade of the Internet, the model of connectivity was no longer about people speaking to a machine, but of people using the computer to communicate directly with one another. The Shaws put networked computers into neighborhood homes and created an online virtual community. And yet, despite the dramatic difference in the technical resources at their disposal, what these two projects have in common is even more dramatic: both use the computer as a medium for words that validate the voice of the community; both use the virtual landscape that exists within the computer to extend a community's sense of place; and both use the computer to make a community known to itself.

In Tardieu's work, the street-corner computer gave children an opportunity to externalize the good things, the hopeful things that were within them. And as the larger community engaged with the computer, the community learned about itself through the traces people left in the machine. In the Shaws' work, the idea of the externalization of human resources was concretized in network software specifically designed to create a virtual neighborhood.

The term "virtual reality" is often used to denote metaphorical spaces within the computer that people navigate by using special hardware—specially designed helmets, body suits, goggles, and gloves. The Shaws used a type of program known as Multi-User Domains or MUDs, where instead of using the computer to immerse themselves in a vivid world of sensation, users immerse themselves in a world of words. MUDs are a text-based, social virtual reality. Logged on to a MUD, one feels inside a built environment, one has a sense of place. Tardieu was able to create a sense of place within street-corner machines, which increased individuals' sense of what they owned, what belonged to them. The MUD's software multiplies this effect. Quite literally, virtual real estate can be created where one can come to feel at home. People can make the space their own through what they write on it, and they can extend its architecture. Users of the Shaws' MUD can build their own "rooms" and their own "objects." Although these rooms and objects exist only on the computer, they take on a powerful reality because they can be used to significant purposes, both emotional and practical.

Tardieu's street-corner computers became a place for stories and for history. The community could record its accomplishments and knowledge. The neighborhood MUD builds on this strength: families can build a space to support a food cooperative or a marketplace where reading lessons can be exchanged for household repairs. A group of expectant mothers can find one another and decide to petition a local hospital for a course in prenatal care. Alone, each woman might hope to be tapped by an already extant hospital outreach program. As a group, they can create a new community resource.

Tardieu used the power of words to create identity and self-esteem. Children were surprised, then thrilled that the computer remembered their words. The printouts of computer entries became cherished possessions, validations of the fact that community members had found a voice. Writing on the computer opened a path to writing for people who considered themselves incapable of self-expression. In a MUD, the sense of finding a voice is extended and enhanced. Writing becomes conversation, fluent and charged with emotion. Unconstrained and unconventional, it is a writing through which one encounters the self. Yet the presence of a transcript of this spoken writing means that what has transpired can be edited, transformed into more conventional writing. On a MUD, one discovers that one can speak writing, something like Molière's Monsieur Jourdain, who discovered that he was speaking prose all his life.

In the development of MUDS, the software has most often been used by middle-class individuals living in disparate locations. On MUDs, they have found anonymity and attendant possibilities for experimenting with self-presentation and new relationships. The MUDs have become a place for playing with identity. The Shaws' work transforms the nature of the identity effects; in the neighborhood setting, the effects are collective: virtual society can help a community discover and better utilize its human resources. It is the community—not just individuals—that finds a new voice.

In considering the power of virtual communities in the context of middle-class users, it is helpful to think of them as new variants of the bistro, the coffee shop, the bar, where people come together and share their stories, their travails and successes. The anthropologist Ray Oldenberg has spoken of these as "third places," falling between the intimacy of the family and the anonymity of the street; they are places that create sense of belonging, of being known. For the severely disadvantaged, whose families are often broken and whose streets are dangerous, the virtual community first of all creates not a third place but a safe place. Tardieu's street-corner machines quickly became a safe zone. People had a reason to be there and were supported and protected when they visited. Almost definitionally, the Shaws' neighborhood MUDs are places where people can go without fear. There are no guns, there are no drugs. But once having found each other in virtual space, the networked neighbors find it easier to meet in person, to meet with purpose and confidence. The virtual and the real are made permeable to each other.

In recent years, a "war of the worlds" mentality has grown up in discussions of cyberspace, a sense that the virtual and the physical are in competition and that we are in danger of being "sucked away" from the physical into the virtual. But in the end, people do not live in virtual reality. Above all, computer environments that can maximally leverage the power of the virtual to increase the quality of life in the "real" need to be built in disadvantaged neighborhoods.

Computers are powerful and evocative objects. They carry models for thinking about self and community, models that are not predetermined by the shape of the technology. Rather they are the product of the myths, history, and personal associations that grow up around it. So it is not surprising that even in its short history, the political meaning of personal computers has been a contested terrain. The work of Tardieu and the Shaws underscore several ways in which our best thinking about personal computers and their relation to community draws on aspirations for the computer that were put forth in the 1970s by the early personal computer movement, but were eclipsed in the years that followed.

In the early days of the personal computer movement, in the mid-1970s, people could not buy much "off the shelf"; instead they had to make their own computing environments and band together to accomplish their goals. As the computer became a commodity, the emphasis shifted to what could be purchased, what software was being "produced." The work of Tardieu and the Shaws returns the focus to local activity and making computer users into producers of culture rather than consumers of a commodity.

Computers for the People

Personal computers came on the scene in the mid-1970s. Although the political ferment of the 1960s was over, its images of empowered communities and grassroots politics remained. But they remained in a kind of limbo, without objects or events to which they could easily be associated. The personal computer became such an object. For decades the computer had been a symbol of centralized economic and political power. It had belonged exclusively to large institutions, corporations, and the government. Yet now, it took another form: it was small, inexpensive, and in the home. The first personal computer owners, many of them veterans of the student protest movement, made technology the centerpiece of a new utopian politics. They took their relationship with what they saw as a transparent, "completely understood" home computer as a metaphor for how the political world should work.

The young people who were drawn to the world of "hobbyist" or home computing were joined by an older group of engineers who had seen their jobs and their job satisfaction in the computer industry change dramatically since the 1960s. As programmers in the 1960s, they had been relatively autonomous and were given the opportunity to see projects through from beginning to end. But as models of "structured programming" began to dominate the computer industry, their work became fragmented. Although at their jobs, programmers were no longer independent craftspeople, they found that they could recreate that secure sense of autonomy with their personal computers at home.

Despite its emphasis on autonomy, the early personal computer culture was not individualistic. Hobbyists founded a network of computer clubs large and small to share ideas and hardware; they had "fairs" and potluck suppers, and they acted on their belief that personal computers had a political vocation by reaching out to their larger communities. One group, known as Community Memory, set up free-access computers that served as message centers and information about local resources in Berkeley, California. Members of Community Memory discussed their project with some wistfulness. Many of them were frustrated that their earlier political efforts in the student movement had not borne fruit and hoped that personal computers would offer them a second chance. They argued that society could be understood much as one could understand the transparent "innards" of a computer, and from there, could be improved if people felt empowered to act.

The social philosopher Ivan Illich described the process by which knowledge is professionalized and taken out of the information commons. He wrote about the necessity of putting knowledge back into the hands of the people. For Community Memory, Illich was a hero and personal computers were a way to act on his dream. Personal computers meant that these machines were no longer icons of centralized knowledge and power: they could be put at the disposal of the grass roots. They could return knowledge to the collectivity.

The Computer as Commodity

In the 1980s the personal computer became a commodity. At the same time that Tardieu was acting in the spirit of the Community Memory Project, trying to use a personal computer to foster neighborhood life in the South Bronx, improved personal machines were being marketed, "mainstreamed," and deployed into an increasingly individualistic political culture. The 1984 Superbowl commercial that introduced the Apple Macintosh underscored how complex and contradictory the social meanings of the personal computer had become. The commercial was rich in associations to George Orwell's *1984*: In a vast hall, row after row of uniformed men in gray stare expressionless at a screen on which another uniformed man is giving a speech. We follow the progress of a lone runner, a woman, as she approaches and enters the hall, makes her way past the rows of seated figures, and finally, smashes the screen. The Apple logo appears. And then, the words:

"Macintosh. The Computer for the Rest of Us." The commercial's iconography suggests that this new computer will release us from the uniformity of centralized power, represented by the IBM corporation. The early dreams of computing for the people were thus brilliantly evoked, but the "rest of us" were no longer dreaming a collective dream. The role of the new computer was not to build community but to provide an alternate commodity. People now had the choice to reject one computer and choose another. The politics of the rebel computer was about consumer choice not community memory.

At the same time that the political meanings of the personal computer were shifting, the actual machines were becoming more complex technologies. Indeed, what made the Apple Macintosh easier to use than the machines it competed against was that it effectively hid the "computer" from the user. The Macintosh kept users at a surface level of visual representation and gave no hint of inner mechanisms. This was a tremendous technical advance; yet it undermined the kind of "transparency" that had served as a political metaphor for the early hobbyists.

Before the introduction of the Macintosh, computer users who spoke of transparency were referring to the ability to "open the hood" and poke around. But when Macintosh users talked about transparency, they were talking about something very different. For them, transparency meant "seeing" one's files and application programs simulated as icons on a screen desktop. They were referring to a new ease in making things work without regard to how they worked. One might say that this was a kind of transparency enabled by the machine's opacity. Computer language has always moved easily into popular culture. By the end of the decade transparency had taken on its "Macintosh meaning" both in technical and everyday language. Today, when people say that a thing or a process is transparent, they mean that they can easily see how to make it happen. They do not usually mean that they know *why* it is happening.

In the 1970s personal computer enthusiasts imagined a technology that would instill the habit of transparent understanding and invite the marginalized to challenge political power. By the end of the 1980s this dream had been quite literally stood on its head. Now the technology suggested an acceptance of things as they were presented, and personal computers were not envisaged as part of communities. Personal computers were now marketed as an extension of self, a fashionable accessory for isolated, often elite users.

The shift in the technology's political associations did not go unnoticed by those who had grown up with personal computing. Harry, a fifth-grade teacher, had been part of the early Berkeley circle that turned to computing as political activism by other means. He built the first home computer, the "Altair," from a kit he saw advertised in a popular electronics magazine. He says that he "fell in love with the early home machines," enjoying the feeling that he could "see down from a top-level instruction to what was actually happening in the computer hardware below."

In 1992, fifteen years after he was a regular attendee at the San Francisco "Home Brew" computer club, where people shared technical information and visions of social change, Harry considered his life with computers and eventually began talking about community, politics, epistemology, and cars. To him, the early personal computers supported an empowered politics because they carried a positive message: you can understand it, you can fix it, you can ask a friend to help. Now that the computer was a slick commodity, it was part of a "toss it away" culture where no one could fix things because no one could figure out how they worked. Harry reflected on his history with computers over two decades:

> When I was a boy and my father and I used to take apart his Chevy truck, I fell in love with the idea that someday I would take complicated things apart. Chevy trucks were not my thing; that was a Nebraska thing. I went to California, got interested in politics, Marx, Ivan Illich. I worked as a teacher, but I made some money on a piece of software I wrote. That's when I began my BMW hobby. As soon as I made any money, I bought old BMWs and fixed them up. And I would always have a new one for my personal driving.
>
> I tried to teach my students what my father had taught me, or I guess it was more like what fixing up the old Chevys had taught me. Take it apart. Analyze the situation. Make it work. That's how communities should work. That's how classrooms should work. In any case, that was how I saw Illich's message and

why I liked what he had to say so much. And then, the BMW
people put [computer] boards into their new models and a bunch
of chips ran the whole damn car! If something broke down, you
replaced the chips. That was the end of the line for me. I stopped
driving BMWs. It would have been like teaching kids that when
something doesn't work in life, toss it because things are too
complicated to fix. I don't like this message.

Coming Full Circle

In computer street libraries and networked neighborhoods, Tardieu and the
Shaws have quite literally made efforts to create community memories—or
information commons—and to have computer users construct rather than
consume. They are giving active expression to powerful insights about
computing and community from the early days of the personal computer
movement. But they are avoiding something that was fragile in that earlier
technological politics. The hobbyists never thought that people could
change unresponsive political systems or intellectually deadening work
environments by building machines that were responsive, fun, and intellectually challenging. But their political optimism was based, at least in part,
on the idea that empowered relationships with a computer would translate
a demand for more empowered political relationships. But the transfer of
attitude was not so simple. The work of Tardieu and the Shaws does not
rely on the computer as a symbol or model. It is no longer the machine
that offers itself as a model of relationship or of transparent understanding.
The transparency that the early hobbyists thought was so important to find
in the computer, in the hope that it would transfer to an empowered attitude
about other things, is now sought exclusively in the machine's ability to
make the community transparent to its members. Computer-based street
libraries and networked neighborhoods do not try to use the computer's
operating system as a metaphor for an empowered relationship to politics,
but directly exploits technology to facilitate action in the world. The
computer is not simply valued as the carrier of an idea, but as a means to
increase a community's self-knowledge. It is this self-knowledge that is
the translation of the early hobbyists' optimism about transparency.

A thirteen-year-old girl in a computer classroom once commented on the computer and self-knowledge by saying: "When you work with a computer you put a little piece of your mind into the computer's mind and you come to see yourself differently." On the level of community, the computer's vocation to help in the creation of identity is even more powerful. Both Tardieu and the Shaws have gotten people to create virtual homes that became places of pride. The constructivist tradition argues that we learn by building. In disadvantaged communities the point is underscored because it carries an even greater emotional charge: build something, be someone.

With the expansion of the Internet in the early 1990s, the social meanings of the personal computer have become more complex because each personal machine is now also a communications gateway. In the search for metaphors for why this might be important, there has been much talk of a "global village," since electronic mail, newsgroups, and bulletin boards were blind to boundaries of nation or geography. Enthusiasts thrill to the new technology-mediated international conjunctures. A teenager in Naples, Florida, can find an octogenarian in Sydney, Australia, who shares her precise passion for seventeenth-century Venetian stamps. And there is much talk of a global marketplace because the Internet seems to promise a new frontier for the business of buying and selling.

In returning to the local emphasis in the politics of the early personal computer culture, Tardieu and the Shaws are again coming full circle to what was most robust in earlier dreams for personal computation. The global village is a powerful metaphor that speaks to our political, economic, environmental, and cultural interdependency. But the contribution of computing to the quality of everyday life depends on acting locally. This is true for all communities, but is nowhere more urgent than for the disadvantaged. There, communities need to discover their own strengths: their untapped human potential. All resources must be used to best advantage. There is no room for waste.

15. Approaches to Community Computing: Bringing Technology to Low-Income Groups

Anne Beamish

Could the community computing movement be in trouble? It is possible, because despite the laudable goal of bringing information and communication technology to a broader audience, there are serious problems. Project goals are too often vague, simplistic, and unrealistically utopian. Participants are frequently seen as passive consumers of information rather than active producers. Information is emphasized rather than the communication side of the technology. And perhaps worst of all, projects too often view the technology as an end in itself rather than a means to an end. The future of community computing is not completely gloomy, however. Some projects do manage to successfully navigate around these problems, and we can learn a great deal from them.

The purpose of this chapter is to help clarify what community computing is today and describe some of its problems and successes. To do this, I will examine the meaning of community computing and how it has changed over its short history, review the wide range of project types that fall under the community computing banner, and then suggest how these projects and future ones can move forward to become more relevant and useful to the communities they are meant to serve.

What Is Community Computing?

If you search for a definition of "community computing" on the Web, the two words "community" and "computing" turn up hundreds of sites. Most refer to community networks or Free-Nets which are "loosely organized, community-based, volunteer-managed electronic network servers" (Victoria Free-Net Association 1994) that provide free dial-up access to the Internet and information about the local community.[1]

After a short period of referring only to community networks, community computing gained a second common association. It became synonymous with access, and in particular with public access computing centers where hardware, software, and technical support are provided to neighborhood residents.

More recently, a third meaning has appeared. Community computing is expanding to mean providing relevant and interesting content online for specific low-income groups with the intention of motivating them to use the technology.

The word, if not the complete concept of community computing, which for so long has been the domain of community volunteers, is now also being embraced by the private sector. A number of commercial sites are appearing that claim to be a form of community computing. One example is CitySearch, which has gone into the Raleigh, North Carolina, area with the intention of becoming "the compete guide to the community" and of providing tools for interaction and buying goods in the area.

Cybercafés are also appearing on street corners, but unfortunately rarely in low-income neighborhoods. Although I applaud the appearance of these businesses and think that they can make an important contribution to the cities where they operate, I will exclude them, at least for this chapter, from the definition of community computing. I omit them because a fundamental difference exists between grassroot community computing initiatives that see their users as residents and neighbors and the commercial ventures that view their users as consumers and customers.

In summary, we have community computing referring to community networks, free online access, public access centers, and the provision of information. The expansion of the meaning of community computing is a positive step, but I still find these definitions worrisome. First, they too often focus on community computing as a thing or artifact rather than a process that can achieve an outcome. And second, although enthusiasts speculate or claim that their particular version of community computing will benefit citizens, democracy, schools, and businesses, they often cannot specify what these benefits will be.

Mario Morino of the Morino Institute offered one of the more useful definitions of community networks which I think is applicable for community computing in general.[2] Unlike the previous definitions, this one emphasizes the end result as a resolution or solution to a problem in the community. He said: "Whatever the name, we see community networking as a process to serve the local geographical community—to respond to the needs of that community and build solutions to its problems. Community networking in the social sense is not a new concept, but using electronic communications to extend and amplify it certainly is" (Morino 1994).

Types of Community Computing Projects

So far I have described community computing in terms of grassroot networks, public access centers, and information providers. These three categories are too broad, however, and hide the richness and variety of projects that shape and ultimately define community computing.

Another way of viewing community computing is to look at the dozens of types of projects that fit under this very broad umbrella. The approaches to community computing can be categorized in two ways. The first is by specifying what the project organizers consider to be the missing ingredient that they will provide. This can include: hardware, software, and training; infrastructure; online access; or relevant content.

Community computing projects most often focus on issues of access and closely follow Mitchell's access framework in chapter 6. They are most frequently involved in providing hardware and training, and information. Less often, they provide the network infrastructure or online access, and rarely are they involved in developing software, hardware, or public policy.

The second way of categorizing projects is by the target group. For example, projects usually choose to focus on: individuals; general public; schools; youth; community organizations; or specific groups such as the homeless, racial or ethic groups, or neighborhoods.

The next section very briefly reviews some of the more successful projects that illustrate each of these approaches. Table 15.1 shows how each of the projects can be categorized according to the target group and what they are providing.

Providing Hardware, Software, and Training

Of the projects that provide hardware and software, one of the first decisions they must make is whether to use old or new equipment. Many believe that the only way to provide computers at a reasonable cost to low-income households is to make older or used equipment and software available. Others, however, argue that this is an unacceptable option. They question what employable skills would be gained if users learn on obsolete and slow equipment that business is discarding.

Many reject the idea that second-rate equipment is acceptable for low-income households, but not for higher-income households. As one community activist put it, "I only want the best for my community." On the other hand, pragmatists maintain that although they would prefer to make newer and more powerful equipment available to their community, it simply is not realistic or affordable and that some equipment is better than none.

Individuals

An innovative project that took the approach of providing used equipment to individuals was undertaken by the Stockyard Association, a community development corporation in a blue-collar neighborhood in Cleveland, Ohio. In 1990 over half of the adults in the neighborhood had not graduated from high school and the median income was $22,944, with 30 percent of households having incomes of less than $10,000 (Stockyard Area Development Association 1996).

The association decided that if their community was to survive economically, they had to find a way to make computers accessible and affordable, especially to those living on low-wage jobs or public assistance (Zapinski 1996). In addition, they wanted their community to have the same rate of personal computer ownership and computer literacy as the national average, which is 35–45 percent.[3]

Their solution was the Computer Ownership for Neighbors Project, which sold "almost free" recycled computers and training to those who applied to the program. The "kits," which were donated by companies located in Cleveland, included a 286 computer with software, a 2400 baud modem, keyboard, and 9-pin printer, and sold for $50. With the system came eight hours of basic training and a follow-up session two weeks later in which participants could ask questions, receive a printer, and get additional training on using the modem and communication software.

These systems are admittedly very limited: the modems are slow and the computers cannot show graphics or run any of the newer software. But project organizers felt that at $50, it was a start that a low-income household might be able to afford.

Because the $50 systems are limited, neighborhood residents who have a job are encouraged to join a Computer Buyers' Club. Members of the club decide on the minimum specifications of the computers they want and the amount they want to pay. They then pool their funds and look for computer dealers who can provide them with their system. The most recent Buyers' Club, which had 62 participants who wanted 386 IBM-compatible machines costing no more than $350, successfully found a dealer who was able to supply them with rebuilt equipment for the price they could afford (Stockyard Area Development Association 1996).

Though the goal and implementation of this project is admirable, it will be of only limited value if it stops at this stage. An even greater contribution would be to evaluate the effect of the project on the community by following project recipients over a number of years to see how they used the equipment, if it was an influence in getting or keeping a job, or if it ultimately had an effect on the neighborhood economy.

Public

Supplying equipment directly to low-income individuals is rare, even though this approach makes access more convenient and creates a sense of ownership. However, not many low-income households can afford such an expense, few organizations are willing to give the equipment for free, and delivering timely training and technical support can be difficult. Consequently, the most common way of making computers and—more important—the human resources available to the public is through community computing centers. These centers are open long hours and almost always target lower-income residents; many are free, while others charge a nominal fee for using the facilities.

The main advantage of this approach is that expensive resources can be used by a greater number of people. High-end computers can be purchased, a greater variety of software can be made available at the center, and funding is potentially easier because donors are likely to prefer to support a public center rather than the private acquisition of technology. And probably most important, support and training are readily available when the user needs it.

This approach is not without problems, however.[4] In addition to being less convenient for individuals, outfitting a community computing center with the appropriate hardware and software can be very expensive, and it is often difficult to find and keep knowledgeable technical staff.

Schools

Providing hardware, software, and training to schools is also a priority in almost every school district. Administrators, community leaders, teachers, and parents believe that not only will the technology improve education, but that computer literacy will be a basic skill for entering higher education and advancement in the workplace in the future (Squadron and Birenbaum 1995). Although general agreement exists on the importance of bringing technology into the schools, there is little consistency in the funding. Not surprisingly, wealthier school districts with a strong tax base are much more likely to have already incorporated technology into the schools and curriculum than are inner cities or rural areas.

Although the lack of hardware and software is a major issue at most schools, it certainly is not the only issue. A report from the Office of Technology Assessment (U.S. Congress 1995b) found that one of the biggest obstacles to introducing technology into schools was the lack of teachers trained to use technology effectively in the classroom and to integrate it into the curriculum. An initiative that addresses this need is Tech Corps, a nonprofit organization that assists K–12 schools to integrate technology by sending volunteers from the high-tech community to install, repair, and upgrade equipment; advise on the design of networks; help develop Web pages; mentor students and teachers; and conduct seminars (Tech Corps 1996).

Still another problem that increases the difficulty of integrating technology into the classroom is the poor physical condition of the schools themselves. A recent survey of ten thousand schools by the General Accounting Office (U.S. Congress 1995a) found that most schools required fundamental improvements to building structure, wiring and electrical systems, air conditioning, ventilation, and security before any computer equipment could be installed.

Youth

The introduction of technology into the schools is clearly intended to
benefit the children in the educational system, but many other projects
concentrate on youth outside the school system, especially those living
in low-income households. Project organizers believe that unless these
children have access to the technology, not only will they miss out on
the basic skills needed to get a job in the future, but they could become
even more marginalized in society.

A number of projects have been started to address this issue.
California's Plugged In was one of the first. Its goal is to bring the benefits of computer technology to the East Palo Alto community, which has
not shared in the rest of Silicon Valley's high-tech boom. Although the
organization is open to residents of all ages, Plugged In's major focus is to
develop the leadership and job skills of youth. The program offers drop-
in introductory computer classes and creative projects, such as producing
digital video news features, computer programming, cartoon animations,
multimedia slide shows, interactive newsletters, and designing personal
Web pages. One of their projects, Plugged In Enterprises, is an advanced
course in hypertext markup language (HTML) programming and an
introduction to business design and management; the class operates like a
business, and students create Web pages for local and national nonprofits,
businesses, and individuals (Plugged In 1996).

Community Organizations

Still another group that frequently needs assistance are the community
organizations that serve the poor. Although they could use the technology
to more effectively serve their clients, they often lack the necessary financial, technical, and human resources to do so.

One project that is addressing this important need is the Information Technology Resource Center (ITRC) in Chicago, Illinois. Established
in 1984, this organization helps nonprofits use computer technology. Its
programs include basic information about computers and common applications, assistance in analyzing computer requirements, and hands-on

training in word processing, spreadsheet, database, desktop publishing, telecommunications, and operating systems. It also has special projects such as CompuMentor/Chicago, which matches volunteer computer professionals with organizations; the Computerized Accounting Project, which assists nonprofits in computerizing their accounting, and NPO-NET, which is a World Wide Web information service for Chicago nonprofits. ITRC is not free; it provides its services on a membership basis with annual fees ranging from $225 to $675 depending on the organization's budget. Additional funding comes from foundations and corporations (ITRC 1996).

Specific Groups

Another type of project provides hardware and software to specific groups such as the homeless, seniors, racial or ethic groups, neighborhoods, or housing developments. There are two ways to accomplish this. The first, and probably most common, is to simply include them in a public community computing center, which may or may not single them out with special programs. For example, the Public Electronic Network (PEN) in Santa Monica, California, is open to all residents of the city, and they have even established a number of terminals in the public library to enable the city's homeless to participate.

The second way is to provide hardware, software, and training for a particular group only. An example is the Information Technology Initiative (ITI) by the United Neighborhood Houses of New York, which will not only help the city's thirty-seven settlement houses become more effective, but will provide residents of the settlement's inner-city neighborhoods with greater access to the technology by creating "neighborhood-based family rooms" in participating settlement houses (Rockoff 1995).

Providing Infrastructure

One aspect that is rarely considered in community computing is the infrastructure needed to support the communication technology in neighborhoods. Few projects focus on ensuring that a community is "wired," meaning that it has access to a broadband network which allows the high-speed transmission of data, including sound and graphics. It is odd that so few projects focus on this issue, because there is a real danger that with deregulation in the telecommunication industry, electronic redlining could occur more easily.[5] It's likely that high-income neighborhoods will have new fiber-optic cable laid in their streets while low-income neighborhoods will be quietly bypassed because the industry sees them as less profitable markets. This is potentially disastrous for the neighborhoods that are left out, because without a good infrastructure, high-tech businesses would never consider locating in these areas, and new start-up businesses by local residents who rely on this technology simply would not be an option.

Projects that do focus on infrastructure aim at providing a broadband network throughout a town or neighborhood which allows households, schools, and businesses to use applications such as teleconferencing, telemedicine, distance learning, or accessing the World Wide Web at high speeds. Existing residential areas normally have a network of coaxial cable for cable television and another of copper telephone wire which can also be used to dial into an Internet Access Provider. The copper wire cannot carry high bandwidth applications, and although the cable is capable, it is still not available or feasible in most communities.[6]

Occasionally, new communities such as Celebration, Florida, built by the Disney Corporation, or Playa Vista, California, developed by Maguire Thomas Partners, Dream Works SKG, and the Howard Hughes Corporation, include high-speed fiber-optic networks as part of the infrastructure intended to attract new buyers (Howland 1996; Loar and Rainey 1996). These communities, however, are not usually intended for low-income households.

Public

Including fiber-optic cable in a new housing development is still not common, and retrofitting an existing community with a high bandwidth network is rarer still. Blacksburg, Virginia, is one of those few exceptions. The Blacksburg Electronic Village (BEV), a partnership between the town of Blacksburg, Virginia Tech, and Bell Atlantic Southwest, intends to link every household, business, and classroom to this network. It believes that a broadband network will revolutionize residential and business life and it hopes that the technology will shift the economy of the town away from natural resources and heavy manufacturing and be the driver of future economic growth. We need to remember, however, that Blacksburg is not exactly an average town: 22,000 of the 36,000 residents are students at Virginia Tech, and the town has a high technological literacy rate with a high per-capita usage rate of computers (Beamish 1995; Holusha 1994).

Schools

In addition to the few towns developing new infrastructure, schools are also witnessing some activity. Although most school districts were trying to provide adequate equipment, software, and training for their teachers and students, little attention was paid to the infrastructure needed to link the computers to the Internet. Recently, however, private high-tech companies have undertaken an initiative to "wire" the schools and link them to the Internet. The first of these projects, called NetDay 96, took place in California in March 1996.[7] Private firms volunteered labor and administrative and technical support, and worked closely with partner schools which raised funds for purchasing the materials and provided labor. The goal was to wire five classrooms and a computer lab or library in each participating school; the project managed to wire 2,000 of the 13,000 California schools. Because of the California NetDay success, many other states have decided to organize their own NetDay for the fall of 1996 and spring of 1997.

Providing Online Access

In the late 1980s and early 1990s, concern was expressed that many people would be barred from using the technology because of the high cost and the limited number of Internet service providers. This concern motivated many communities to establish community networks, which offered free or low-cost access to the Internet and community information. Residents could dial in to send and receive e-mail, browse information about the community, and link to other sites on the Internet. This approach proved to be an extremely effective way of introducing people to the technology.

Running an Internet access system was and still is an expensive proposition, however. Because community networks had no dependable revenue from the users of the service, they had to depend on volunteers, donations, and grants. The inadequate funding prevented the networks from expanding as the number of users increased, and the service in many community networks began to deteriorate; some were even forced to file for bankruptcy. At the same time, the number of commercial Internet access providers increased and prices dropped. This situation caused a crisis in many of the community networks that were founded on the premise of providing free Internet access. The decision of whether to continue offering free access or begin charging a fee was painful and divisive. Of the community networks that remained true to their original vision, some have survived while others have closed their doors. The community networks that managed to adapt and often thrive in the new environment were those that began to de-emphasize the free Internet access aspect and concentrate on being a community information server.

Providing Content

Another dimension of community computing—and perhaps one of the richest—is the provision of content. Proponents of this approach believe that even if the physical infrastructure was available, without engaging and relevant content, the public, especially low-income groups, would have little reason to use the technology. This type of project has greater long-term potential than those providing hardware and software because they often have a clearer vision of how the technology can be used to build a sense of community, encourage collaboration, or increase democracy in their group.

Ironically, although content projects have the greatest potential, they often suffer from a fatal flaw—a lack of content. Projects that start off with a vision of providing a deep and current source of information find that creating and maintaining a Web site takes a tremendous amount of work and energy that they cannot always sustain. It is unfortunately all too common for a Web site that appeared to be vibrant and interesting in its opening days to quickly become stale after three, six, or twelve months pass with nothing changing on the site.

Many community networks and city-based sites, however, do
manage to provide relevant and up-to-date community information, ranging from bus schedules to city council minutes. But of those projects that
do offer an extensive range of information to their clients, most ignore one
of the technology's most intriguing aspects—communication.

Public

A project that has embraced the technology and illustrates its potential
to enhance communication among residents and between residents and
government is the Minnesota E-Democracy Project. The project's goal is
to "increase citizen participation in elections and public discourse through
online civic forums and collections of important information" (Minnesota
E-Democracy 1996). One forum is closed and only the candidates can post
or respond to questions put to them by the organizers. The second is for citizen discussion where anyone can post questions, comments, and positions.
    This project is an example of how online sites can encourage more
in-depth public discussion. But in spite of the project's admirable qualities,
we cannot forget that until access is ubiquitous, the advantages of increased
political participation and discussion will be limited to those who do have
access—which currently excludes most low-income groups (Aikens and
Koch 1996).
    Another criticism that can be made of content-providing sites
is that they too often consider their clients to be consumers of information
rather than producers. A few projects working with youth are attempting
to reverse this tendency.

Youth

The Youth Voice Collaborative Project (YVC) at the Boston YWCA
teaches youth to think critically about media and how it is created. Their
goal is to use the media (print, radio, television, and electronic) to amplify
the voice of youth and magnify their role as contributing members of the
community. Since 1994 they have run a number of media seminars and
projects. One project that used the World Wide Web as an alternative
medium was the YVC Campaign '96 Multimedia Project. Two teams of

YVC youths went to the Republican and Democratic National Conventions as reporters in August 1996. Although they had arranged with a number of traditional news outlets to carry their stories, they also set up a Web site where they published their stories about their experiences before and during the conventions as well as an online discussion area.

Community Organizations

Community organizations often face a unique problem in that they often share the same lack of information and isolation as those they serve. A project that illustrates how these two needs can be addressed is NPO-Net.

NPO-Net is a network service that helps Chicago-area non-profits communicate, research, and manage more effectively as well as foster a sense of collaboration and community. This is done through providing information and online conferences in which issues such as fund raising, research, technology, planning, personnel, insurance, specific neighborhoods, children and youth initiatives, and the homeless are discussed.

Specific Groups

Although a wealth of sites are designed to appeal to a specific interest or demographic group, very few specifically target low-income communities. One recent effort is the Inner City Access site which is intended for the Boston communities of Roxbury, Dorchester and Mattapan. Each of these neighborhoods has a section where local businesses and individuals can place their Web page. The project also runs free Internet training classes for neighborhood residents.

Conclusion

There are many worthwhile community computing projects that have trained low-income residents, provided access, and created repositories for neighborhood information. Certainly, most of the projects described in this chapter are exemplary and worth emulating.

But there are still problems. Far too many projects, in spite of their rhetoric, have been unable to go beyond the broadcast model and still

Table 15.1: Approaches to community computing

Target Group	Providing Hardware, Software, and Training	Providing Infrastructure
Individuals	• Stockyard Computers for Neighbors Project	
Public	• Community computing centers	• Blacksburg Electronic Village • Celebration, FL • Playa Vista, CA
Schools	• TechCorp Many projects are being undertaken by individual school districts	• NetDay
Youth	• Plugged In	
Community Organizations	• Information Technology Resource Center (ITRC)	
Specific Groups • homeless • seniors • disabled • racial or ethnic groups • neighborhoods • housing developments	• Community computing centers • Information Technology Initiative (ITI)	

see their target group as consumers rather than as producers of information. Too many ignore the capacity of the technology to support communication. And even sites that emphasize information over communication are unable to maintain a high standard of updated information.

A greater problem, however, is the frequent vagueness of community computing's goals and the underlying assumption that the technology itself will automatically improve the lives of low-income residents and their neighborhoods. For example, even though access is inarguably important, we are often unclear about why low-income communities should have access. Could they use it to bring about social change? Political mobilization? Employment? Education?

Providing Online Access	Providing Relevant Content (for and/or by target group)
• Community networks	• Community networks • Minnesota E-Democracy Project
	• YVC Campaign '96
	• NPO-NET
Online access is usually supplied by the projects providing the equipment and/or content.	• Inner City Access

And once our goals are clear, we need the courage to evaluate our efforts. We may believe or predict that technology can benefit low-income communities and can lead to better education, improved job prospects, and stronger communities, but there is an alarming lack of research or evidence that any of this is taking place. Some of the most glaring examples are the hundreds of public access centers that claim to train participants for the job market, but never assess how many participants actually get jobs as a result of the project.

In spite of these caveats, many of the projects I have reviewed, including the ones described in this book suggest the potential for significant community benefit. The Computer Clubhouse, the Community Memory Project in the South Bronx, and Healthy MUSIC in Newark all point the way to a more durable and valuable future for community computing. Although they are not alike, each project has a vision of what is important to its particular group and each has been able to look beyond the machine to the people that it is meant to serve.

In summary, we need to clarify the aims of community computing and redirect its strategies of action. Instead of meaning hardware and software, or access, or a Web site, or wiring, or information, we should say that community computing is about using the technology to support and meet the goals of a community. Second, we should specify what these goals are and be prepared to evaluate our efforts. Third, we must ensure that users are producers of information as much as consumers. And fourth, we ought to keep reminding ourselves that community computing is a means to an end rather than an end in itself. If we do, community computing will have a long and valuable future.

Contact URLs

The following is a list of URLs for many of the projects mentioned in this chapter.

Blacksburg Electronic Village (BEV): http://crusher.bev.net/
CitySearch: http://www.citysearch.com/
Computer Clubhouse: http://www.tcm.org/clubhouse
Healthy MUSIC:
http://mmassey.www.media.mit.edu/people/mmassey/MUSICintro.html
Information Technology Resource Center (ITRC):
http://www.npo.net/itrc/
Inner City Access:
http://www.roxbury.com/index.html
Minnesota E-Democracy Project: http://www.e-democracy.org/
Morino Institute: http://www.morino.org/
NetDay: http://www.netday.org/
NPO-Net: http://npo.net/
Plugged-In: http://www.pluggedin.org
Public Electronic Network (PEN):

http://pen.ci.santa-monica.ca.us/

Stockyard Area Development Association:
http://little.nhlink.net/nhlink/sada/

Tech Corps: http://www.ustc.org/

Youth Voice Collaborative (YVC):
http://sap.mit.edu/projects/yvc/

YVC Campaign '96 Multimedia Project:
http://sap.mit.edu/projects/campaign96/

Notes

1. Free-Nets are community networks that belong to the National Public Telecomputing Network (NPTN). The NPTN was a nonprofit corporation established in 1989 to disseminate the software and methodology for establishing community networks. It filed for bankruptcy in the fall of 1996.

2. Morino Institute is a nonprofit organization that focuses on finding and cultivating ways in which interactive communications can be used to benefit society, empower individuals and create opportunity, particularly in the areas of economic development, governance, health, and education.

3. According to a 1995 government report, "Falling Through the Net," 8.1 percent of households with an income of less than $10,000 would have a computer, and of those, 44.1 percent would have a modem. In contrast, 63.4 percent of urban households with incomes over $75,000 would have a computer (McConnaughley 1995).

4. Some of these issues were highlighted in one of the few surveys on community computing centers (CompuMentor 1996) which interviewed twelve centers in California. The survey found that the centers' most common purpose was to improve and enhance the skills and quality of life of the residents. Interestingly, although many of the centers professed to focus on employment, there were virtually no data on job outcome. And in many of the centers, even though technology was usually fairly modest, dependable technical support and expertise were often inadequate.

5. Redlining is used to describe the illegal practice of banks or insurance companies systematically refusing to make loans or insurance policies in a specific neighborhood or community.

6. Sharon Gillett of the Center for Coordination Science, MIT Sloan School of Management, has written a paper comparing ISDN telephone service and upgraded cable TV networks. "Connecting Homes to the Internet: An Engineering Cost Model of Cable versus ISDN" is available on-line at: http://www.tns.lcs.mit.edu/publications/mitlcstr654.html.

7. The California initiative was a "virtual organization" with a presence only on the Web.

References

Aikens, Scott and Erna Koch. 1996. "Building Democracy On-line."
  CMC Magazine, April 1.

Beamish, Anne. 1995. *Communities On-line: Community-Based Computer Networks.*
  Master in City Planning, Massachusetts Institute of Technology. Available at:
  http://alberti.mit.edu/arch/4.207/anneb/thesis/toc.html.

CompuMentor. 1996. *Between a Rock and a Hard Disk: Community Computing Centers
  for Employment and Education.* CompuMentor.

Holusha, John. 1994. "Virginia's Electronic Village." *New York Times*, January 16, 9.

Howland, Libby. 1996. "Playa Vista Marries High Tech and Sustainability."
  Urban Land 55 (3): 12–13.

ITRC. 1996. *ITRC Fact Sheet.* Available at: http://www.mcs.net/~itrc/itrcfact.htm.

Loar, Russ and James Rainey. 1996. "Wiring a High-Tech Small Town." *Los Angeles
  Times*, March 5.

McConnaughley, James. 1995. *Falling Through the Net: A Survey of the "Have Nots" in
  Rural and Urban America.* The National Telecommunications and Information
  Administration (NTIA), U.S. Department of Commerce. Available at:
  http://www.ntia.doc.gov/ntiahome/fallingthru.html (October 1996).

Minnesota E-Democracy. 1996 *About Minnesota E-Democracy.* Available at:
  http://www.freenet.msp.mn.us/govt/e-democracy/about.html.

Morino, Mario. 1994. *Assessment and Evolution of Community Networking.* Paper presented
  at Ties That Bind, at Apple Computer, Cupertino CA.

Plugged In. 1996. *Plugged In Programs.* Available at:
  http://www.pluggedin.org/bropluggedin.html.

Rockoff, Maxine L. 1995. "Settlement Houses and the Urban Information Infrastructure."
  Journal of Urban Technology 3 (1): 45–66.

Squadron, William and Helen Birenbaum. 1995. "Machines, Wires, and Access:
  Information Technologies and America's Urban Schools." *Journal of Urban
  Technology* 3 (1): 81–96.

Stockyard Area Development Association. 1996. *The Stockyards Computer Ownership for
  Neighbors Project.* Available: http://bbs2.rmrc.net/sada/sadacon.htm.

Tech Corps. 1996. *What is the Tech Corps?* Available at: http://www.ustc.org/what.html.

U.S. Congress, General Accounting Office. 1995a. *School Facilities: America's Schools
  Not Designed or Equipped for 21st Century.* GAO/HEHS-95-95.

U.S. Congress, Office of Technology Assessment. 1995b. *Teachers and Technology: Making
  the Connection.* OTA-EHR-616, U.S. Government Printing Office.

Victoria Free-Net Association. 1994. *Free-Net Strategic and Marketing Plan.* Available at:
  http://freenet.carleton.ca/freeport/freenet/conference2/issues/menu.

Zapinski, Ken. 1996. "Neighborhood Learns Computer Use." *Cleveland Plain
  Dealer*, July 22.

Part III: Conclusions

16. Information Technology and Urban Poverty: The Role of Public Policy

Bish Sanyal
Donald A. Schön

There are no "technological fixes" for America's inner-city problems; social engineering has its limits; policy outcomes rarely, if ever, match policy objectives; and policies are rarely crafted neutrally by the dictum of so-called public interest. All this we knew when, at the Department of Urban Planning at MIT, we organized a colloquium on Advanced Information Technology and Low-Income Communities.

The aim of the colloquium was to provoke new analyses and generate some innovative policies. The colloquium was to serve as a conversation between academics and activists, equally engaged in understanding information technology (IT) from very different perspectives. The academic's view would offer a view from "the top," rooted in an analysis of global socio-technological-economic trends hinged on the rise of IT, and an appreciation of the likely effects of these trends on low-income urban populations and communities. In contrast, the community activists would provide a view from "the bottom" that would be rich in details about individuals and communities, the many constraints they face in their day-to-day lives, and how these constraints influence IT's impact on them. The view from the bottom was to complement the view from the top: the global, generalized, and highly abstract analysis was to be synthesized with the concrete, detailed stories of how individuals and communities were responding to the new technological possibilities. Such a synthesis, we had hoped, would generate innovative policy suggestions through a blend of the academics' theoretical and formal knowledge with the practice-based, fine-grained wisdom of the activists.

Although the colloquium spanned an entire semester and involved weekly presentations by academics and activists, it fell somewhat short of generating a real dialogue between the two groups. The mood among the academics, documented in Part I, was generally pessimistic. They saw urban poverty as worsening and argued that IT will do little to improve—and much to worsen this situation—except insofar as we can better educate and train the poor, especially in computer skills, to compete for entry-level positions in IT firms. In contrast, the activists were eager to learn about IT's intricacies, hoping to capture some of the new technological power of rapid communication for the benefit of their communities. The activist's eagerness was somewhat surprising, because in the past they had been deeply skeptical about whether technological innovations could ever lead to socially progressive outcomes. But as became evident during the colloquium, community activists are now concerned that at a time of declining government funding for inner cities, communities lacking electronic access to resource announcements will be disadvantaged in competing for scarce resources. The activists are correct to assume that as the pressure on government mounts to reduce expenditures by streamlining its operations, it is quite likely that, much like business operations, government agencies will be forced to shift to electronic communication mode to reduce costs and increase productivity.

The activists have additional reasons for their enthusiasm for IT, as we learned during the colloquium. Community activists worry that if they fail to make the transition to the new communication mode, they will be thought of as being stuck in the old mode of community organizing, creating a negative image that will hurt their capability to mobilize resources. The activists are also aware of the intense competition for government resources under the new regime of fiscal federalism. They know that quick, up-to-date information on government programs is essential to compete for declining resources. Another reason, which revealed the most about the current condition of low-income communities, is that activists cannot build a critical mass of support for their efforts by relying only on the spatial community to which they belong. Access to IT would provide the opportunity for community leaders to build a critical mass by drawing support from across the country without having to assemble everyone at the same time and place. All these reasons contributed to the activists' enthusiasm to learn about IT, even though the academics warned against the myth of technological utopianism and argued that IT is unlikely to alter the conditions of the urban poor who remain marginalized and isolated by social, political, and economic changes currently under way.

Despite the colloquium participants' difference in attitude toward IT, we did arrive at some points of agreement. These points of agreement were not explicitly articulated during the colloquium, rather, they are implicit in the discussions that followed the regular presentation of papers in the colloquium. We have grouped these areas of agreement into five parts. First, we describe two unique characteristics of the digital revolution—namely, its interactive potential and decentralizing nature, which offers the poor a new set of opportunities for social and economic integration. Second, we describe why the colloquium participants unanimously agreed that universal access to IT is essential and why the market if left to itself will not provide such access. Third, we analyze briefly current government policies regarding IT and find them inadequate for ensuring universal access. Fourth, we put forward a set of policies necessary for channeling IT's benefits toward low-income areas. Fifth, we conclude with some remarks about what kind of research is necessary to devise policies sensitive to the particular needs of the poor.

Technology and Social Progress: New Opportunities

The colloquium participants acknowledged that IT is not a discrete technological invention, but rather a broad-gauged sociotechnological system advancing in a wave over all of society, analogous to earlier systems such as those associated with industrial production, the railroad, or the automobile. We cannot forecast precisely what this new digital electronic revolution will bring for society as a whole or for its low-income communities in particular. But we believed big changes were in the offing: that IT will alter the way markets function, the mechanisms of governance, even family and social interactions. These changes will come incrementally into different aspects of our lives, but their impact will be so vast over time that, say, fifty years from now our lives will indeed be radically transformed.

We, as a society and as individuals, can choose how we shall think and act in relation to the digital revolution. But one thing is clear: to profit from the potentials opened up by IT—whatever they may be—we must participate in it. This is especially true for the poor, who are already excluded from the economic, social, and cultural mainstream. They must be helped to participate in the digital world in a variety of ways. In the economic sphere, the poor must be included in the informational economy —as employees or as entrepreneurs. They must receive better education, for which IT offers important potential in the form of educational uses of the Net, e-mail communication between teachers and students, and electronic self-paced education. In the social sphere, too, IT offers the urban poor a new set of opportunities because of two unique characteristics—namely, IT's interactive potential and decentralizing nature. Unlike television and radio, IT offers the opportunity for interaction between the computer and its user, creating the conditions necessary for learning, confidence building, and self-empowerment. As Bruno Tardieu and Jeanne Bamberger describe in Part II, computers, if used with empathy, can reduce the poor's sense of disempowerment and give them the confidence necessary for continued learning. Likewise, IT's decentralizing nature offers the poor an opportunity to be entrepreneurial. Unlike earlier waves of technological innovation, such as the industrial revolution, IT lends itself to multiple, local variations, and to the exercises of multiple forms of local control. With the World Wide Web, every user has the potential of becoming a broadcaster. Further, the new network technology opens up hitherto unrealized potentials for communication. Every individual has the potential for discovering and making connections with other individuals of like interest and mind. And, the technologies of the Internet and the computer open up essentially endless possibilities for customization. These possibilities, as Alan and Michelle Shaw point out in Part II, offer a new opportunity for grassroots communication among individuals and groups striving to re-create a strong community of place.

For Joseph Ferreira and Michael Shiffer, who contributed to Part II of this volume, IT offers even more to the urban poor. They demonstrate that the computer may function as a repository of information, accessible by grassroots neighborhood planners. The Internet can function as a digital communications network for neighborhood discussion and debate. It can also facilitate reciprocal exchange of information between local and central sources, as the poor gain the ability to enrich the central database with their local knowledge. Shiffer also describes the multimedia, multirepresentational capabilities of the computer that enable it to make planning and policy reports "come alive" for neighborhood residents, and enable those residents to present themselves, their communities, and their views on urban issues to the world outside the neighborhood.

Universal Access and Public Policy

To capture IT's potential for the benefit of the poor requires that they be connected to the digital world. Hence the key policy issue is one of access to this world. As William Mitchell argues in Part II, access is more than personal computers: it requires infrastructure, affordable hardware, user-friendly software, and the will and motivation to employ them. Not surprisingly, access to IT is unequally distributed between the well-to-do and the poor. Indeed, the world is comprised of computer haves and have-nots. The objective of public policy should be to bridge this gap.

In this regard, the current situation is somewhat gray, as we came to appreciate during the colloquium. On one hand, the costs of hardware and software are on a downward spiral. As Mitchell Kapor pointed out in one session, this technology is sensitive to the same supply and demand conditions as other goods and services—when something is available in surplus, the price goes down. Much like telephone and television, IT may eventually become part of the daily life of everyone, including the poor. This is not mere wishful thinking. As Kapor described, two distinct trends in the digital world offer this opportunity. First, there is a growing technological convergence whereby telephone, cable, and computer services can be provided together efficiently and at reasonable cost to the consumer. The set-top box, which turns the living room television into a computer monitor, is an example of this. The second trend, which complements the first, is a convergence in the industry structure, as firms that once provided telephones, cable, or computer-related services are increasingly seeking to move into one another's territories—a trend that has been facilitated by the deregulation of the telecommunications industry since 1996. Under ideal circumstances, these two trends could lead to a higher level of efficiency in the production and delivery of services, which in turn should lower the marginal cost of providing these services to low-income areas.

On the downside, a number of trends suggest that the market alone cannot provide the poor with access to the digital world, and, even if access is provided, it is unclear whether it will be enough to integrate them into the nation's mainstream economic, political, and social life. First, technological convergence is not inevitable. Without some government support, private firms may be reluctant to invest in technological innovations with property rights that cannot be controlled. Second, the convergence in industry structure may not lead to cost reduction. On the contrary, it may reduce competition and increase the price of telecommunication services. (After all, the deregulation of the telecommunications industry did not reduce the price for local cable services!) And, if the price of telecommunication services increase without a concomitant increase in real income of the poor, private firms may be reluctant to cater to poor communities. This makes the danger of "digital redlining" quite real.

There are additional reasons to be concerned about whether market mechanisms would eventually provide the poor access to the digital world. As Alice Amsden and Jon Collins Clarke note, in recent years only a few large firms have generated the major innovations—unlike in the early stages of the digital revolution when technological innovations emerged from a relatively more open system with many small innovators. One reason for this change from the "blooming of a thousand flowers" to the dominance of a few is that innovations in IT now require a large amount of finance capital as well as extensive social capital. This prohibits entrepreneurship at the bottom, and discourages innovations geared to the specific needs of the poor.

Another obstacle to universal access may be the lack of social infrastructure. Unlike electronic infrastructure, which has received some attention from policymakers, social infrastructure, or lack thereof, has received relatively little attention in policy discourse. But, as William Mitchell, Anne Beamish, Bruno Tardieu, Jeanne Bamberger, and Alan and Michelle Shaw argue in Part II, provision of adequate social infrastructure is a key prerequisite for capturing IT's benefits for the poor. By social infrastructure we mean good schools, well-equipped community centers, and, most important, educated and technology-receptive individuals, both children and adults who are capable of fully exploiting IT's interactive potential. Without such social infrastructure in place, no amount of electronic infrastructure and affordable hardware and software can ensure that the benefits of universal access will reach the poor. Tardieu elaborates on this point in Part II where he demonstrates why improved education is not simply a matter of connecting all schools to the Internet. Tardieu argues that in the absence of good teachers who can show the students how to use IT for confidence building, learning, and self-empowerment, inner-city children will become mere "consumers of technology," spending time and money on electronic video games. In contrast, children who attend good schools in upper-income communities will learn to utilize the same technology to organize their knowledge, create data banks, and search them. This will challenge their minds and build self-confidence. The point for our purposes is: Can schools in low-income areas afford to employ an adequate number of good teachers to guide their students to utilize IT in a productive way? Our colloquium participants were uniformly skeptical that under the current funding system of public schools, which relies heavily on property taxes from the area residents, schools in poor areas will ever be able to provide the kind of education necessary for tapping IT's full potential.

In a similar vein, Anne Beamish argues that to ensure the poor's access to the digital world, efforts must be made to connect public libraries, community centers, and ultimately individual households to telecommunication infrastructure. This too will require more than the provision of computers. At the household level, low-income families are unlikely to make a quick transition to the electronic communication mode even if the benefits would appear to be significant. Ironically, what would be required to make the transition is traditional, door-to-door campaigning by community activists who must patiently explain how to utilize personal computers and demonstrate how they would provide access to information vital to the well being of the poor families. Likewise, community centers and libraries too would also require assistance to switch to the new communication mode. These public facilities would need resources not only to acquire computers and user-friendly software, but also to employ an adequate number of trainers who are willing and able to help the users make the transition. And, as Anne Beamish notes, this kind of support cannot be in the form of one-time assistance only. With rapid technological advancement, old computer programs soon become obsolete; hence new programs must be installed periodically. Similarly, old computers have to be replaced with new computers with more capabilities. Without such regular improvements and maintenance of computer facilities, community centers and libraries in low-income areas are not likely to be of much use to area residents even if they are equipped with computers.

The Inadequacy of Current Government Policies

What has the government's response been to the challenges posed by the digital revolution? At the federal level, government policy has evolved gradually from Vice President Al Gore's 1993 proposal for an information superhighway[1] to President Bill Clinton's proclamation in the 1996 State of the Union Address to connect all schools to the Internet by the year 2000. This policy evolution from preoccupation with the information superhighway to attention to schools was accompanied by two congressional efforts to address IT-related issues: first, the National Information Infrastructure Advisory Council (NIIAC) was created in 1995; and second, both the Telecommunication Reform Bill and the Communications Decency Act were passed in 1996.[2]

At first glance, the NIIAC reports[3] may appear to address the concerns of poor families in inner-city areas. The Kick Start Initiative, for example, states that all schools, community centers, and other local institutions should be connected to the Internet to provide a new channel for civic participation. It does not, however, recommend any bold steps by the federal government to achieve this outcome: the initiative merely advises communities that they should make individual efforts toward this objective, given that there are success stories of such efforts at the local level. But since not all cities and towns are equipped with the same level of financial and human resources, how likely is it that, without sustained and significant support from either the state or federal government, the disadvantaged communities will achieve the goal of connecting local institutions to the Internet? And, as mentioned earlier, access to the Internet may be a necessary but definitely not a sufficient condition for educational improvement or civic participation. Schools, as well as neighborhoods, need teachers and activists who can use the technology to, in Tardieu's words, turn the students and residents from being simply consumers to producers of knowledge.

According to Mitchell Kapor, an original member of the NIIAC and a participant in our colloquium, the main purpose of the NIIAC and its reports was not to address how to wire schools and community centers. Instead, NIIAC's central objective was to respond to the concerns of the intellectual property interests in Hollywood who pushed for copyright laws to protect against loss of revenue, not to draw the nation's attention to obstacles that low-income communities must overcome to participate equally in the technological revolution.[4] Consequently, because the NIIAC did not address the key issue of how to achieve universal coverage, Kapor argued that they missed an opportunity to take advantage of the technological and industry convergence that was taking place to devise new and effective public policies.

The sponsors of the Telecommunications Reform Bill in 1996 were equally oblivious to the needs of the poor. The bill opened up competition in various sectors, such as local telephone and cable television, which may eventually lead to price reductions for all consumers; but, in the main, the bill's proponents were not motivated by a concern for the disadvantaged. As Kapor argued persuasively in the colloquium, the reform bill was primarily "a business deal" among the major players in the telecommunications industry who wanted to expand into one another's market territory. Nothing in this bill improves or guarantees the poor's access to telecommunications services. On the contrary, with deregulation universal service is likely to be even more difficult to enforce without large-scale subsidies, which are politically unpopular these days. As a result, it is quite plausible that low-income communities will be underserved or, worse, not served at all.

Policymakers have not totally ignored the possibility that the digital revolution may bypass low-income communities. So far, however, the efforts to rectify the situation have been rather limited compared to the scope of the problem. For example, at the local level, many cities participated in Net Day[5] by wiring some public schools to the Internet. Such efforts depend primarily on voluntary support, in cash and kind. To generate voluntary support, cities have relied on local universities, well-established private firms, and wealthy philanthropists. The federal and state governments have applauded this sort of effort by cities because it fits in well with the current national mood to shift fiscal and other responsibilities from the federal to the state and local levels. Not surprisingly, the impact of the locally sponsored Net Days has been spotty and somewhat regressive, because local authorities have been reluctant to take on the difficult task of technologically upgrading the most backward schools with the fewest resources.

In sum, federal government policies regarding IT have been motivated largely by business interests, with some concern that the new technology should not further accentuate the existing inequality in educational opportunities among children. The federal government has been more concerned, however, about the morality of its citizens. The enactment of the Communications Decency Act is an example of the federal government's deep concern that IT may have a serious adverse effect on the morality of teenagers who may gain access to "immoral material" via the Internet and the Web. Similar acts enforcing universal coverage of all citizens is yet to be proposed, although there are precedents of such efforts that ensured access of the poor to basic utilities in the past.

One reason why government at all levels has not actively ensured universal access is because politicians and policymakers have not yet comprehended fully IT's likely impact on relative distribution of life chances among all citizens. To date the government's approach to IT has been conditioned by the assumption that the adaptation of digital technology is crucial for business productivity; its impact on the poor has not been of particular concern because of the pervasive belief that none of the immediate problems of urban poverty can be addressed by IT. Policymakers continue to believe that the glaring symptoms of urban poverty—drug use, badly maintained public housing, welfare dependency, out-of-wedlock births, and so on—cannot be addressed by ensuring universal access to IT. The current national understanding is that these problems require better policing, more prisons, stringent laws against "deadbeat dads," and a new welfare system that would force the unemployed poor to work to earn a living. Under these circumstances, President Clinton's call to connect all schools to the Internet by the year 2000 is the only sign that the government may have finally begun to comprehend the significance of the digital revolution. Against this backdrop, we present below the policy recommendations that emerged from the colloquium.

Policy Recommendations

In thinking about policy recommendations, the colloquium participants acknowledged that, as described in Part I, the focus at the macro level is on a major economic transformation, whereas when we shift the focus to the micro or local level, as in Part II, we substitute models of education, community solidarity, and equity; as a result, economic issues at the local level do not receive much attention. As Leo Marx emphasized, policy prescriptions must take into account the changing nature of the economic base of the country, involving redefinition of work and the consequences for full-time employment.

Bill Mitchell injected another cautionary note into our policy deliberations: IT is developing so rapidly that a public policy proposed today may quickly become obsolete as technological improvements open up new possibilities and close old options. With these two caveats in mind, we propose the following set of policy recommendations for capturing the immense potential of IT for low-income areas.

IT Is No Substitute for Social Policy

The universalistic, undifferentiated language that is used to describe global trends and transformations resulting from IT lends itself to the creation of myths. These include: the myth of technological utopianism in which technological change is seen as assuring social progress, benefiting everybody, and correcting the inequities in our society; and the myth of technological leapfrogging, for example, the belief that software entrepreneurship offers unlimited opportunities for the emergence of modern-day Horatio Algers among the persistently poor.

Such myths serve the interests of politicians who are eagerly, or reluctantly, involved in cutting back the federal safety net for the poor. It is no accident that Newt Gingrich, the Speaker of the House, entertained the idea of giving a laptop computer to every homeless person! These myths, however, also satisfy a deep-seated belief in the American psyche, a profound identification of technological change with social progress. We also note that, at the other end of the spectrum, the technology pessimism is equally mythical and equally unsupported by the evidence, if it is taken to mean that digital technology offers no significant opportunities for low-income people. The correct approach, we propose, is to adopt a nuanced view, rejecting both extremes.

The Poor Must Not Be Excluded from Shared Inquiry

To devise policies that would capture IT's benefits for the poor, we need to understand that poverty is not simply lack of adequate income. As the community activists reminded us, the poor are hurt most by a sense of exclusion from the mainstream economy, society, and polity, and feel disempowered to improve their situation. This lack of a sense of effective citizenship adversely affects the poor's self-confidence and thus undermines their ability to learn from day-to-day experience. It also reinforces a sense of low self-worth, which, as Bruno Tardieu noted, causes the poor think they have no useful valid knowledge to offer. Consequently, IT reinforces for the poor the idea that machines know more than they do. Under these circumstances, the poor, even if provided access to IT, are unlikely to transform themselves from consumers to producers of knowledge.

The Government Must Ensure Universal Access

To ensure access, policymakers need to consider five elements: provision of infrastructure, affordable hardware, user-friendly software, the ability and motivation to use software, and periodic upgrading of hardware and software to keep pace with technological changes. Left to itself the market will not respond to all five needs. Furthermore, if these needs are not met, market-provided traditional services such as bank branches may be withdrawn from low-income areas.

Public policies to ensure access should be built on the premise that much of the prevailing telecommunications infrastructure has been developed by private firms, and the government needs to build off that infrastructure to provide universal coverage. To do so, the federal government should first provide incentives to private firms, but lacking results, the government should stipulate that private service providers must offer a certain minimum level of services to low-income areas. This is not a radical proposal: governments have pursued a similar approach for years to ensure the availability of adequate housing for low-income families by providing various incentives to real estate developers who otherwise would not build low-profit-yielding buildings. Similarly, many local authorities have required cable companies to provide facilities for local channels accessible to low-income consumers. The level of subsidies may vary from case to case, but the principle is the same: without government nudging, private firms are usually unwilling to provide services to low-profit areas. In the case of IT, however, the nature of government prodding must be somewhat different than, say, in the provision of low-income housing. The government cannot subsidize the construction of infrastructure for universal service because this would require a large volume of resources that the government cannot muster for financial and political reasons. Instead, the government should strategize how to achieve universal coverage incrementally, encouraging technological innovations that can facilitate the convergence of telephone, cable, and computer technologies. Such convergences are likely to reduce the cost-of-service provision, which is key to ensuring universal coverage.

One Key Objective of Universal Coverage Is to Create Better and Equal Public Education for Children and Youth in Low-Income Areas

There was a consensus among the colloquium participants on this point. We also agreed that this objective cannot be achieved by local-level, voluntary support from private firms or wealthy philanthropists, even though some localities have managed to muster resources by relying solely on their generosity and good will. A second option is to raise property taxes. But, the property tax base in low-income areas is not adequate for this purpose. Moreover, low-income families may not be able and willing to pay higher taxes. Hence the initiative will have to come from either the state or federal government and may require some form of legislation, like the Community Reinvestment Act, which requires private businesses such as banks to reinvest a fraction of their profits to revitalize economically lagging communities.

Another possibility is for state governments to encourage partnerships between private firms and low-income communities. For example, in San Francisco a community technology fund was created in 1996 by Pacific Telesis and more than one hundred community organizations. The goal was to ensure that California's neediest residents will have access to telecommunication services after Pacific Telesis's merger with SBC Communications. Policymakers everywhere can learn from this example: they need to understand business trends within the telecommunication firms located in their areas and help these firms benefit from such trends on the condition that the firms would reinvest in low-income areas. This strategy may serve the firms in more than one way: in addition to increasing their profits, it may provide them access to new markets. (Note the following comment by Phil Quigley, chairman of Pacific Telesis: "These are emerging markets of California, and we believe it makes good business sense to serve them."[6])

Financial Strengthening of Public Schools Is a Necessary but Not Sufficient Condition for Innovative Use of IT for Educational Purposes

At present, public schools in low-income areas lack basic necessities, such as classroom space and books and other educational materials. If these basic needs are not met, the quality of education is not likely to improve—even if these schools are connected to the Internet. Moreover, initial resistance to using computers is likely, particularly if the teachers are untrained and cannot perceive the benefits of IT as a new educational technology.

The best way to introduce IT into public schools is to demonstrate to the teachers and administrators how IT can help them address some of the basic problems they have been confronting for years. For example, public schools in low-income areas usually suffer from a lack of parental participation. If IT could be used creatively to enhance parents' participation, it might be adopted by these schools. Similarly, teachers and administrators might adopt IT quickly if it can be shown to enhance the students' interest in learning science and mathematics.

As an educational technology, IT is most likely to be effective where educational computers play the role of mediators—bridging between the students' hands-on, bodily knowledge and the symbolic representations of knowledge usually favored in school. As Jeanne Bamberger documents in Part II, in a mediating role, the educational computer enables descriptions to function as commands—descriptions making themselves real—so that a student can perceive what her/his description does. Often the effect is one of surprise, leading the student to question and making it possible to arrive at a new understanding of the phenomenon.

Outside the classroom, the educational computer can be modified to become a "community" rather than a "personal" computer, operating as a holding environment for the local knowledge that neighborhood children may put into it. As Bruno Tardieu describes in Part II, the associative memory of a community computer can lend itself to the retrieval of that knowledge, in an open-ended range of categories and combinations. In this context, the speed of a computer is not as important: in fact, the relative slowness of a plotter reveals more of its built-in mechanism of operations than a faster dot-matrix printer, thereby creating a better sense of transparency to those children who manipulate it.

Public Policies Should Target Prospective Entrepreneurs

Although it is not commonly acknowledged, low-income areas do not lack entrepreneurs who would like to start businesses to sell telecommunications-related goods and services. Some of these prospective entrepreneurs participated actively in our colloquium seeking information about new business opportunities. Unlike the community activists, the entrepreneurs are not principally interested in poverty alleviation, but, in the long run, they may be equally effective in reducing poverty by helping to connect their communities to the telecommunications infrastructure. But, as Alice Amsden and Jon Collins Clark noted, entrepreneurship cannot flourish by itself: it needs financing and a set of social networks. The government can provide assistance by creating quasi-public bodies that, in conjunction with banks and insurance companies, can generate capital and invest in start-up companies by local entrepreneurs. This is not a new proposition: banks that are regulated at both the state and federal level are already playing such a catalytic role in accordance with the Community Reinvestment Act. In comparison, insurance companies, which are regulated only at the state level, have not been very active in such efforts. It is time to encourage insurance companies—particularly companies providing health and car insurance—to invest in low-income areas, because residents in these areas pay relatively high premiums for these services. Similarly, governors and mayors should appeal to local colleges and universities to provide the budding entrepreneurs with opportunities to upgrade their technical knowledge. Through such opportunities, the entrepreneurs are also likely to create new social networks with individuals and institutions outside their communities of origin. The new networks will be a valuable source of social capital which, as Amsden and Clark argue, is as important as finance capital in the success of telecommunications firms.

Public Policies Must Ensure that the Computer Functions as a Repository
of Information for Interactive Use by Grass-Roots Planners

As Joseph Ferreira describes in Part II, IT has opened up new possibilities for generating, processing, and storing fine-grained data, which can
strengthen the state-society relationship by creating transparency, trust,
and accountability on both sides. For example, the 1996 welfare reforms,
which require welfare recipients to find employment, have created a new
urgency for information on job openings, availability of rental housing,
and access to public transportation. At the community level, the area
residents are anxious to know how efforts at fiscal federalism are likely to
affect resource allocation for low-income areas. On the government's side,
too, there is a new urgency to know more about low-income area residents,
so that the impact of welfare policy reforms can be monitored. Moreover,
as the burden of responsibility is shifted from the federal to state and local
levels to encourage devolution of power, there is a new need for fine-grained
data at lower levels of government regarding demographic trends, land-use
patterns, and so on.

   Who should gather and disseminate these data was not a policy
issue until very recently as IT reduced significantly the cost of data gathering, storing, and dissemination. The lower cost has created an incentive
for private firms to provide these services. As a result, a debate is ongoing
regarding the appropriate role of government in data generation and dissemination. Our position in this debate is the following: we acknowledge
that, so far, the government has been efficient in collecting meteorologi-
cal data, for example, but technological innovations in data collection or
delivery do not usually emerge from government control of the process.
We also acknowledge how certain types of information with large positive
externalities may not be provided by private firms. This suggests that the
government must be involved in gathering some basic information about
all cities. Private firms may build on that basic information (which is
expensive to collect and requires standardization that only the government
can ensure) by collecting additional, detailed, disaggregated data that may
be of interest to individuals, communities, or public institutions.

   If the Federal Geographic Data Committee (FGDC) accepts this
division of labor, what should the government do to ensure that the data

needs of low-income communities are met? To begin, someone has to identify what kind of data are important for the residents of low-income communities: for example, data on job openings; job-related training; the availability of various government programs designed specifically for urban, low-income areas; local area banks' lending practices; comparative insurance rates for cars, buildings, and health, and so on. More important than who should be collecting these data is, according to Joe Ferreira, the question of how these data are to be processed and stored, so that low-income households can access and utilize them easily for making informed judgments about jobs, investment, and spending plans—the kind of issues that are also important to suburban, middle-class families. Perhaps before the government decides to collect these data for equity reasons, it may be appropriate to inquire whether locally based entrepreneurs might want to respond to this market niche, even though the rate of return for providing this service may not be very high in the short run.

Even if local entrepreneurs respond to the communities' specialized data needs, government—particularly, local government—must gather some basic data not only about low-income communities but also about the entire city. In storing these data and making it available for use, government must make sure that the programs used are compatible with the programs used by low-income residents. Put another way: in storing information, government must not forget that even if universal coverage is achieved, the programs and computers used by upper- and lower-income residents may differ. This differential capacity to access and manipulate information between lower- and higher-income area residents is likely to continue because of the fast pace of technological innovation and the higher-income resident's greater ability to purchase new hardware and software. Hence governments must be willing to support the minimum threshold data needs of low-income communities, leaving the more advanced needs, perhaps, to private firms.

Another important issue is how low-income households should guard against the possible violation of one of their basic civil rights: privacy. As mentioned earlier, IT's rapid development has drastically reduced the cost of data collection and dissemination, thereby encouraging large-scale data gathering on virtually every aspect of the social, economic, and political lives of citizens. In some instances—such as data on medical doctors' records—the benefits of this new capability are significant. But, as George Orwell warned long ago, a line must be drawn between public and private knowledge. The separation between the two spheres, private and public, are socially produced, and like other social decisions, this too is influenced not by poor citizens but by those relatively better off. As a result, inner-city residents searching for employment could face a situation where prospective employers or service providers may know more about their lives than necessary. With national concern rising over the crime rate, "deadbeat dads," unwed mothers, "welfare queens," abortion, and so on, a lucrative new market for data provision may flourish. In some instances this may lead to the violation of civil rights of citizens, unless the government takes a strong stand against such disclosure.

On a related issue, the federal government should monitor closely the impact of fine-grained data on household income and expenditures, which can now be collected and distributed cheaply. On one hand, officials can use this kind of rich data to fine-tune public policy, but, on the other hand, market institutions may use the same data to more precisely redline certain areas. This may be particularly true for the provision of telecommunication's infrastructure, which will be needed most by families who can least afford it—that is, the unemployed engaged in job searches, the aged and disabled needing special services, and other such groups. Vulnerable and needy citizens like these must be protected against redlining. The government's record to stop redlining in mortgage provision indicates that, although it is impossible to totally stop this practice, publicity of a few demonstrative cases may discourage it.

What's Next?

In one of the concluding sessions of the colloquium, some community participants returned to the questions that had sparked the colloquium in the first place. What are the likely impacts of IT on low-income areas? And what purpose might this marvelous technology serve? The community participants proposed that these questions should be set aside for future deliberations and that instead, we continue the dialogue between academia and activists along the following lines: given an intention to achieve a certain kind of benefit for low-income people, or to help them achieve a benefit for themselves, how might a variant of the multifaceted technology serve the purpose? This shift in the intellectual focus of inquiry was welcomed by the faculty participants from the Department of Urban Studies and Planning at MIT because it fits well with the department's intellectual style of practice-based learning, in contrast to broad-brush theorizing from "the top." This is not to say that broad-brush theorizing of the kind found in Part I of this book is not useful for policymaking purposes. That is useful, we acknowledge, but only when informed by a good understanding of the complexities at the ground level which the prototype projects discussed in Part II captured well.

The prototype projects were inspiring because they suggested ways in which low-income people and communities could benefit from the fruits of the informational economy—to achieve a kind of education better suited to the needs and potentials of inner-city children; to create within low-income communities a more democratic, decentralized capability to enter into dialogue with one another and with the representatives of local government; to build a more active, close-knit community of place, fostering a sense of inclusion, rather than exclusion, from the larger social world, and at the same time enabling a more effective kind of community organization.

The few prototypes we discussed at the colloquium did not generate replicable models of how to achieve these noble objectives. They only made us more aware of the challenges and opportunities policymakers are likely to face as they try to channel IT's benefits toward low-income communities. Also, because the number of prototypes were few, it seemed that the lessons learned were still sketchy, needing answers to a host of questions that are critical for large-scale replication of the prototype projects.

How might a much larger array of design prototypes develop? And how should they be structured to answer our questions? We discussed the merits of continuing the association of the kinds of people gathered around the colloquium table: designer-architects, who like to stretch out scenarios and build prototypes, deploying particular versions of information technology, initiating public, fairly small-scale ventures; social scientists, who like to pursue empirically researchable questions; and action researchers who learn by monitoring innovations, exploring how design prototypes are used, what people make of them, and what new questions they raise.

Suggestions for new prototypes were not lacking: a storefront drop-in center for potential software entrepreneurs; a community service center that would specialize in computer-delivered social and commercial services; computer labs that would be introduced into schools and community centers in low-income neighborhoods; a computer resource center that would be placed in public space in a low-income housing project; new uses of digital networks, like the one developed by the Shaws, to facilitate community organization.

Each new prototype would have to be designed, and its design would be guided by principles that had been drawn from the discussion of existing prototypes:

• The question would appropriately be turned on its head. One would not ask "Here's the wonderful technology, what could you do with it?" but rather "What do we want to happen? How could the technology help us do that?"

• One would want to make the technology available to low-income people themselves, drawing on their local knowledge and creativity to enable them to design new prototypes of their own. At the extreme, as one participant asked, "Why not just invest in the infrastructure and see what people do?"

• But there would be a necessary addition: individuals with special knowledge of hardware, software, and applications would need to create learning communities together with low-income people. As Bruno Tardieu remarked, putting computers in the hands of poor kids (as with the community encyclopedia) led to the creation of a larger data bank shared by poor communities in different parts of the world—and one could then listen to them, learning from what they did with it.

The discussion of design prototypes gave rise to the idea of a large-scale experiment for making information technology available en masse in low-income communities. We would need design scenarios, action strategies, and action research that could influence policy and feed into longer-term planning for the use of information technology in low-income communities. In the wake of such an experiment, both the low-income community and the technology would be transformed.

And as one of the community participants then suggested, "I'd like to see a future colloquium around projects that were started as a result of this coming together."

Notes

1. In September 1993, the Clinton administration announced an initiative to promote the development of a National Information Infrastructure (NII), "a seamless web of communications networks, computers, databases, and consumer electronics that will put vast amounts of information at users' fingertips. Development of the NII can help unleash an information revolution that will change forever the way people live, work, and interact with each other." (Information Infrastructure Task Force, the National Information Infrastructure: Agenda for Action, September 15, 1993. Washington DC: Department of Commerce, National Telecommunication and Information Administration.)

2. The Community Decency Act would have prohibited the dissemination of morally offensive material over the Net. This act was turned down by the U.S. Supreme Court as unconstitutional on June 26, 1997.

3. National Information Infrastructure Advisory Council produced two reports in 1996: *Kickstart Initiative: Connecting America's Communities to the Information Superhighway* and *A Nation of Opportunity: Realizing the Promise of the Information Superhighway*.

4. Kapor resigned from the NIIAC to protest what he saw as its hidden agenda.

5. The Net Day program, an initiative to bring private resources to the schools, combines technical support, equipment donations, and volunteer labor. Participating firms select a partner school to which it donates funds, labor, and administrative and technical support; the schools contribute by raising funds to buy materials and providing volunteer labor.

6. E-mail announcement by *Business Wise*, October 15, 1996, 02.

Index

Abramson, Alan, 78
Access to technology
    advantages of, 153
    alternative means of, 153–155
    commercialization of Internet and,
        159–160
    computer and, 56
    Computer Clubhouse and, 265–267,
        277–278
    connections and, digital, 153
    education and, 11, 161
    effective, 12
    higher speed, 154
    infrastructure of, 155–156
    lack of, 7
    limits of, 133
    low-cost, 157–158
    markets and, 156–157
    motivation and, 161
    online, 360–361
    poverty and, 7–8, 12
    public policy and, 376–379
    regulators and, 156–157
    servers and, 160–161
    skills and, 161
    software for, 158–159
    Street Library Project and, 309–310
    universal policies of, 156–157,
        376–379, 384–385
Activism, community, 304–305,
    330–334, 374
Adams, T. G., 223
Adobe computer program, 282

Advanced information technologies. *See
    also* Information technology (IT);
    Technology in low-income
    communities
    center city and, 28–29, 46, 50–54,
        107
    concept of, 3–4
    death of distance and, 6, 50–54
    education and, 61–65
    information rich versus information
        poor, 54–58
    informational infrastructure and,
        48–50
    informationalization of world and,
        47–48
    poverty and, 9–10, 64–65
    public policy and, 61–65
    questions regarding impact of, 46,
        71–72
    rise of, 4, 7
    telecommuting and, 52–54
    transformation caused by, 8–9
    urban geography and, 58–61
"Advanced Information Technologies,
    Low-Income Communities, and the
    City" (1996 colloquium), 3,
    373–375
Advertising on the Internet, 159
AFDC, 73, 84, 96–99
"Age of the Machine," 143–144
Aid to Families with Dependent Children
    (AFDC), 73, 84, 96–99
Aikens, Scott, 362

Algers, Horatio, 215

Alternative means of access to technology, 153–155

Amsden, Alice, 7–8, 10–12, 19–20, 22, 231, 378, 387

Anderson, C., 55

Animation tools, 271

Apple Macintosh computer, 343–344

Aristotle, 125

Arizona Women's State Penitentiary, 53

Aronson, R. L., 218, 227

Assessor's Office (Boston), 168–169

AT&T Alliance of Black Telecommunications Employees, 328

ATMs, 114

Austin (TX), 29, 34

Automated teller machines (ATMs), 114

Automobiles, 145–146

Balkin, S., 224, 227

Baltimore, 89–90

Bamberger, Jeanne, 14–16, 18, 20, 376, 378

Banking industry, 29–30, 113–115

Barndt, M. G., 194

Bates, T., 225–227

Batty, M., 199

Beamish, Anne, 16, 19, 195, 360, 378–379

Becker, E., 217, 222

Being Digital (Negroponte), 7–8, 48, 135

Bell Atlantic Southwest, 359

Beniger, James, 47

Benner, Chris, 31–32

BEV, 359–360

BHA, 166, 181, 185

Biddle, Nicholas, 143

Bill Gates Art Gallery, 45

Black Child Advocate, 230

Blacksburg Electronic Village (BEV), 359–360

Blacksburg (VA), 359–360

Blakely, Edward J., 34, 40, 223

Boland, Nancy, 284

Bombay (India), 53

Bookstores, 117–118

Borja, Jordi, 30

Boston, 13, 77, 81, 88–90, 93, 166, 168–169, 174, 176–177, 181, 185, 199, 203–204, 363

Boston Housing Authority (BHA), 166, 181, 185

Boston Redevelopment Authority (BRA), 166, 174, 176–177, 181

Bottom-up strategy, 14, 175–176

BRA, 166, 174, 176–177, 181

Branch banks, 113–115

Breslow, Gail, 284

British Airways, 53

Broadcast services, 135–136

Browsers, 158

Brush, C., 225–227

Buck, Nick, 82

Buffalo (NY), 77, 89, 196–197

Bulletin board services, 155–156, 326

Butler, J. S., 218, 224–225

Cable modems, 154

Cable television networks, 154

CAD/CAM information, 122

California Plugged In project, 357

Capital
    growing organic composition of, 57
    human and social, 10, 221–222, 226–227

Capitalist restructuring, 28

Carnegie, Andrew, 215

Carnoy, Martin, 31–32

Cars, 145–146

Case, Anne C., 81

Castells, Manuel, 4–7, 10–11, 21, 27–32, 38, 47, 53

CBDs, 30–31
CD-ROM, 170, 202, 204
CDC, 168
Celebration (FL), 359
Cellular telephone, 154–155
Center city
    advanced information technologies
        and, 28–29, 46, 50–54, 107
    competitive advantages of, 7
    death of, prediction about, 6
    digital revolution and, 50–54
    employment patterns in, 83–96
        anxiety about, 32
        center city employment trends,
            90–95
        general trends, 83–86, 100–101
        immigrants and, 84–85
        metropolitan employment trends,
            86–90
        public policy shifts and, 95–96
        questions about, 71, 83
        sociospatial trends, 5
        welfare system and, 96–100
    evolution of, 72–82
        background information, 72–74
        data and analysis sources, 72
        immigration impacts, 80–81
        income sorting and segregation,
            78–80
        poverty in center city, 74–78
        questions about, 71
        social problems, 81–82
    poverty in, 74–78
    welfare system and, 101–102
Central Artery Project, 166–167
Central Business Districts (CBDs), 30–31
Chandler, Alfred, 143
Charitable organizations, federal funding
    for, 99–100
Chicago, 51, 65, 107, 357, 363
Chicago Loop, 107

Christy, Sam, 284
Citizen inquiry systems, conventional,
    183
City of Bits (Mitchell), 8, 50
City. See Center city; Informational city;
    specific name
CitySearch site, 352
Clark, Colin, 47
Clarke, Jon Collins, 378, 387
Cleary, Chris, 308
Clinton, Bill, 229, 379–380, 382
Collaborative learning, 279–280
Collaborative planning system (CPS), 194,
    199–202, 206–210
Commercialization of Internet, 159–160
Communications Decency Act (1996),
    380, 382
Community
    activism, 304–305, 330–334, 374
    cohesion, 125–129
    "emergent," cultivating, 277–280
    enhancement, 37–38
    enterprise, 202–203
    media based in, 37–38
    Street Library Project and, 304–305
    telecenters, 36
Community computing. See also Street
    Library Project
    aims of, clarifying, 366
    approaches to, 19
    Community Memory Project and,
        365–366
    community networks and, 351–352
    Computer Clubhouse and, 365–366
    concept of, 351–352
    creation of Street Library Project and,
        16–17
    future of, 365–366
    Making Healthy MUSIC project and,
        366
    personal computing versus, 299–300

Community computing (*continued*)
  problems, 363–365
  projects, 353–363
    categorizing, 353
    other, 363
    providing content, 361–363
    providing hardware, software, and
      training, 353–358
    providing infrastructure, 358–360
    providing online access, 360–361
  status of, 351
  URLs, contact, 366–367
Community Development Agency (St.
  Louis), 197–199
Community development corporation
  (CDC), 168
Community Memory Project, 343,
  365–366
Community networking, 205–206
Community networks. *See also* Social
  empowerment through community
  networks
  community computing and, 351–352
  community networking and, 205–206
  concept of, 352
  development of, 17–18
  as support systems for low-income
    communities, 194–199,
    205–206
Community Reinvestment Act, 385
Competitive advantages of center city, 7
Compromise of 1850, 143
CompuMentor/Chicago project, 358
Computer. *See also* Community
  computing; Personal computing
  access to technology and, 56
  Apple Macintosh, 343–344
  as commodity, 342–346
  concept of, 20
  in education, 14
    in poor urban schools, 228–229
  evolution of, 18–19

features of, common, 18
hobbyists, 342–343, 346
killer applications for, 49–50
literacy, 45, 133
LOGO language, 20, 239, 245
  as mediator, 15–16, 241, 249–251
  modem, 153–154
  success and, 297–298
Computer Buyers' Club, 355
Computer Clubhouse
  access to technology and, 265–267,
    277–278
  collaboration and, 279–280
  community computing and, 365–366
  constructionism and, 271
  creation of, 14, 266
  fluency and, technological, 266,
    281–282
  goal of, long-term, 282–284
  Internet and, 271
  mentors and, 277–278
  Online Art Gallery of, 271, 273
  participants, 266–267
  principles, 267–281
    building youths' interests,
      273–277
    creating environment of respect
      and trust, 280–281
    cultivating "emergent
      community," 277–280
    overview of, 15–16, 267–268
    supporting learning through
      design experiences, 268–273
  purpose of, 15
  software of, 20–21
  thought and, tools for, 281–284
  volunteers at, 284–285
Computer Museum, 266, 284
Computer supported collaborative work
  (CSCW), 324
Computerized Accounting Project, 358
Concord intellectuals, 143

Connections, digital, 153
Constructionism, 271, 318–320
Constructivism, 318–319
Consumers, producers versus, 318
Content, providing, 361–363
"Control revolution," 47
Cornford, J., 53–54
Corporate centers, spatial clustering of,
    5–6, 28–29, 51
Corporate-public urban partnerships, 10,
    36
Coulton, Claudia, 80
CPS, 194, 199–202, 206–210
Craig, W. J., 193–194
Cretinon, Denis, 309–310
Criminal economy, 33, 37, 62–63
CSCW, 324
Cyber-utopians, 7–8
Cybercafés, 352

Daniels, P. W., 28
Danziger, S. P. G., 223, 227
"Death of cities" prediction, 6
Death of distance, 6, 50–54
Denton, N. A., 80–81
Design activities, 268–273
Design worlds, similarities and differences
    in, 242–244
Detroit, 60–61
Devalued spaces, 31
Dial-in connections, 153–154
Dickens, Charles, 140
Digital electronics, 107
Digital revolution
    banking industry and, 113–115
    center city and, 50–54
    community cohesion and, 125–129
    economic opportunity and, 120–124
    homes and, 124–125
    human transactions and, 108–113
    low-income communities and, 8–9, 71
    nature of, 48

new economy of presence and,
    108–113
residential neighborhoods and,
    124–125
services delivery and, 115–120
shaping of, 27
technology in low-income
    communities and, 8–9
urban economies and, 5–6
Director computer program, 271, 282
Disney Corporation, 359
DreamWorks SKG, 50, 359
Dual city, 4, 6, 27–28, 34–39
Dualism, 34–39
Dubbink, D. T., 202

E-Democracy Project, 362
E-mail services, 155–156
East Palo Alto (CA), 357
Economic opportunity, 120–124
Edison, Thomas, 133–134
Education
    access to technology and, 11, 161
    advanced information technologies
        and, 61–65
    computer in, 14
        poor urban schools and, 228–229
    corporate-public urban partnerships
        and, 10, 36
    in England, 45–46
    improvement in, 11, 385–386
    income and technology and, 45–46,
        64–65
    information technology and, 36–37
    need for, 35
    Parent-Teacher Associations and, 36
    prison population and, 62–63
    public policy and, 10–11
    segregation of, 33
    services, 117–118
    skill requirement for labor force and,
        31–33, 37

Education (*continued*)
    software entrepreneurship and,
        227–231
    tele-education, 36
EIA, 167
Electricity, 133–135
Electronic delivery of services, general,
    115–120
Electronics manufacturing, 29, 107
Emerson, Ralph Waldo, 143
Employment. *See also* Labor force
    economic opportunity and, 120–124
    "hot desking" and, 53
    information technology and, 31–34
    patterns
        anxiety about, 32
        center city trends, 90–95
        general trends, 83–86, 100–101
        immigrants and, 84–85
        metropolitan trends, 86–90
        public policy shifts and, 95–96
        questions about, 71, 83
        sociospatial trends and, 5
        welfare system and, 96–100
    telecommuting and, 52–54, 121–122
Empowerment. *See also* Social
    empowerment through community
    networks
    social, 320–321
    zones, 166, 202–203
Enlightenment Project, 138–139
Enterprise communities, 202–203
Entertainment services, 116–117
Entrepreneurship. *See also* Software
    entrepreneurship
    barriers to, 12
    community information systems and,
        199
    concept of, 216
    franchises and, 224
    home enterprises and, 224
    need for spurring, 36

    self-employed and, 217–218, 225
    software industry and, 215, 217–222
    teleworking and, 36
    urban poor and, 223–226
    value, 224
Environmental impact assessment (EIA),
    167
"Epistemological dilution," 283
European Union, 307
Evans, D., 218
Exurban sprawl, 28

Fanelli, Vincent, 16, 289, 295, 307
Federal Geographic Data Committee
    (FGDC), 388–389
Ferreira, Joseph, 12–14, 21, 376,
    388–389
FGDC, 388–389
Field, A., 220
Fielding, Elaine L., 81
Fluency
    linguistic, 277
    technological, 266, 281–282
Ford, Henry, 215
40:30:30 Society, 57
Fourth World Movement, 16, 20,
    289–290, 292–293, 307
Franchises, 224
Fratoe, F., 225–226, 228
Free-Nets, 155–156, 196–197
Freeman, Richard, 62
Frey, William H., 81
Friedman, Lawrence M., 62–63
FUD (Boston), 166, 174

Galster, George C., 80
Ganson, Arthur, 247–249
Gardner, Marilyn, 284
Gary (IN), 60–61
Gates, Bill, 48, 50, 52, 215, 226, 230
Gautreaux program (WI), 65
GB Government Office for London, 52

GB Office of Science and Technology, 49
Geffen, David, 50
Geographic Information System (GIS)
     maps, 13, 199, 202
Gilder, George, 34, 39
Gillespie, Andrew, 53–54
Gingrich, Newt, 383
GIS maps, 13, 199, 202
Glade, W. P., 216
Glasgow (United Kingdom), 60
Global cities, 123
Global village metaphor, 347
Globalization, 61–62
Goddard, John, 49, 51, 53, 55
Goldsmith, W., 223
Gore, Al, 379–380
Goslin, L. N., 221–222
Goulias, K. G., 52
Government
     public policy and, inadequate,
          379–382
     revitalizing local, 38–39
     universal access to technology and,
          384–385
Graham and Parks Alternative Public
     School, 14, 237. See also Laboratory
     for Making Things (LMT)
Graham, Sondra, 238
Graham, Stephen, 28, 38–40, 52
The Great Industrial Divide (Piore and
     Sabel), 7
Gregory, Ana, 284
Guiterrez, E., 203
Gumption factor, 215–217
Guzdial, M., 269

Habitat II United Nations Conference
     (1996), 38–39
Hague, Douglas, 49
Hall, Peter, 5–7, 10, 21, 29, 60
Handy, Charles, 56
Handy, S. L., 52

Harbison, F. H., 216
Harel, I., 269
Harman, Harriet, 45
Harmon, Joe, 45–46
Harris, Britton, 165, 199
Harris, C., 220
Harry (fifth-grade teacher), 345–346
Hartford (CT), 77, 81, 89–91, 93
Haug, P., 220–222
Hay, K., 269
Herrnstein, Richard, 62
Higher speed lines, 154
Hikino, T., 231
Hiroshima, 135
Hisrich, R., 225–227
Hiss, A., 46
Historical perspective of information
     technology
     "Age of the Machine," 143
     automobiles, 145–146
     concept of technology, 137–138,
          143–147
     electricity, 133–135
     Enlightenment Project, 138–139
     impacts of information technology,
          133
     Lowell textile mills, 140–141
     mechanic arts, 142–145
     Progress and, 138–140
     railroads, 141–144
     significance of today's information
          technology, 146–147
     transformation of humanity, 135–137
     utopianism, digital, 136–137
     Webster and, 141–143
Hobbyists, computer, 342–343, 346
Hodgkinson, Virginia A., 99
Hollan, J. D., 199
Hollywood (CA), 29, 51
Holt, D., 228
Holt, J., 278
Holusha, John, 360

"Home Brew" computer club (San Francisco), 345
Home enterprises, 224
Homelessness, 145
Homes, 124–125
Horrigan, John, 34, 41
"Hot desking," 53
Housing and Urban Development (HUD), 166
Howard Hughes Corporation, 359
Howland, Libby, 359
HTML, 357
HUD, 166
Hutchins, E. L., 199
Hutton, Will, 57, 59
Hypercard, 309
Hypertext markup language (HTML), 357

IBM, 344
ICTs, 55
Identity, creation of, 347
Immigration impacts, 80–81, 84–85
Income sorting and segregation, 78–80
Income and technology. *See also* Technology in low-income communities
  computer literacy and, 45
  death of distance and, 50–54
  education and, 45–46, 64–65
  information rich versus information poor and, 54–58
  informational infrastructure and, 48–50
  informationalization of world and, 47–48
  public policy and, 61–65
  telecommuting and, 52–54
  urban geography and, 58–61
Information businesses, 49. *See also specific types*
Information and Communication Technology (ICTs), 55

Information, knowledge versus, 11, 237
Information revolution. *See* Digital revolution
Information rich versus information poor, 54–58
Information Technology Initiative (ITI), 358
Information technology (IT). *See also* Advanced information technologies; Digital revolution; Historical perspective of information technology
  community enhancement and, 37–38
  concept of, 20–22
  "control revolution" and, 47
  education and, 36–37
  employment and, 31–34
  future of, 390–393
  government and, revitalizing local, 38–39
  human transactions and, 108–113
  killer applications for, 49–50
  labor force and, 64
  land use and, 165, 170
  low-income communities and, 34
  prison population and, 37
  promise of, 4, 28
  significance of today's, 146–147
  social exclusion and, 28
  social progress and, 375–376
  social reform and, 34–39
  socioeconomic restructuring and new, 27–28
  space of flows and, 5, 28–31
Information Technology Resource Center (ITRC), 357–358
Informational city
  black holes of, 33–34
  as dual city, 4, 6, 27–28, 34–39
  informational economy and, 4–5
  processes identified as, 27
Informational economy, 4–5

Informational infrastructure, 48–50,
    107–108
Informational-digital revolution. *See*
    Digital revolution
Informationalization of world, 47–48
Infrastructure
    of access to technology, 155–156
    informational, 48–50, 107–108
    neighborhood, 321–322
    providing, 358–360
Inner City Access information system,
    199, 363
Inner city. *See* Center city
Innes, Judith E., 165
Innovation, milieux of, 5–6, 29
Institute of Research and Training for
    Human Relations, 292–293
Insurance services, 29–30
Interests, building youths', 273–277
International Fourth World Movement,
    16, 20, 289–290, 292–293, 307
International Year of the Homeless
    (1987), 305
Internet
    advertising on, 159
    browsers, 158
    commercialization of, 159–160
    community information on, 196–197
    Computer Clubhouse and, 271
    consumer model and, 318
    costs, 50, 159
    human transactions and, 109
    hyperlinks of, 126–127
    hypertext markup language and, 357
    immoral material via, 382
    NetDay 96 and, 381
    personal computing and, 347
    poverty and, 12
    public awareness of special issues and,
        204
    retailing industry and, 116–117
    self-publication and, 208–209

servers and, 160–161
statistics, international, 54–55
telepresence and, asynchronous, 112,
    118
television sets and, 157
Internet Access Provider, 359
ISDN connections, 154
IT. *See* Information technology
ITI, 358
ITRC, 357–358

JALA Associates, 52
Jargowsky, Paul A., 80
Jencks, Christopher, 52, 81
Job market trends. *See* Employment,
    patterns
Job shops, networks of flexible and
    specialized, 7
Jovanovic, B., 218

Kapor, Mitchell, 377, 380–381
Kasarda, John D., 80–81, 86, 91–92
Katz, Lawrence F., 81
Katz, Michael, 82
Katzenberg, Jeffrey, 50
Kaus, Mickey, 64
Kehoe, L., 50
Keynes, Maynard, 61
KidPix computer program, 271
Killen, Sean P., 80
Killer applications, 49–50
King, Mel, 322
Kitamura, R., 52
Klosterman, R. E., 199
Knowledge
    information versus, 11, 237
    power and, 193
    relevant, 193
    sharing, 291–292
Koch, Erna, 362
Kondratieff waves, 61
Kozol, Jonathan, 290

Krueger, Alan B., 94

Labor force. *See also* Employment
core, 33
desocialization of, 32–33
disposable, 33
general trends of, 5
information businesses and, 49
information technology and, 64
polarization of, potential, 56–57
skill requirement for, education and,
31–33, 37
sociospatial trends and, 5
spatial division of, 29
Laboratory for Making Things (LMT)
as approach to learning, 258–260
background information of, 237–238
in beginning, 238–240
children in, working with, 243
computer as mediator and, 241,
249–251
creation of, 14
day in, typical, 243–245
design worlds and, similarities and
differences in, 242–244
gears and, 245–249
goals of, 238–239
Leon and
discovery of, 251–252
experiment of, 252–256
learning of, 257–258
performance and, 256–257
procedure and, 256–257
purpose of, 14–15
questions about, 240–241
rhythms and, 245–247
Land ownership
knowledge of, 183–184
owner names and
bottom-up strategy, 175–176
categorizing, 172–174
lookup tables, 178–183

middle-out strategy, 177–178,
185–186
spelling corrections, 178–183
standardizing, 174–175
top-down strategy, 176–177
patterns of, 168–172
records of, 168–169, 172–174
Land use
information technology and, 165, 170
neighborhood planning, 170–172
new plans of, 167
patterns of, 168–172
records, 168–169
Lave, J., 278
Learning
by design experiences, 268–273
collaborative, 279–280
communities of learners and, 279–280
Laboratory for Making Things as
approach to, 258–260
Leon's, at Laboratory for Making
Things, 257–258
Lee, Brian, 284
Lee, Mike, 285
LEGO Control Lab, 271, 276
Lehrer, R., 269
Leighton, L., 218
"Leo" interface approach, 207
Levy, F., 64
Lichter, D., 223
Light, I. C. R., 22, 224–225
Lipsky, Michael, 100
Literacy, computer, 45, 133
LMT. *See* Laboratory for Making Things
Loar, Russ, 359
LOGO computer language, 20, 239, 245
London (United Kingdom), 45–46, 51,
123
London Planning Advisory Committee, 52
Long-distance telecommunications, 155
Los Angeles, 29, 34, 51
Low-cost access appliances, 157–158

Low-income communities. *See also* Center
    city; Technology in low-income
    communities
  changes in, 4
  concept of, 3
  digital revolution and, 8–9, 71
  information technology and, 34
  low-cost access appliances in, 157–158
  low-income individuals versus, 20
  support systems for
    collaborative planning system,
        194, 199–202, 206–210
    community networks, 194–199,
        205–206
    concept of, 21
    multimedia representational
        applications, 194, 202–204,
        208–210
    overview of, 193–194
    questions about, 204–210
    urban planning and development in,
        38
Low-income individuals, 20
Lowell textile mills, 140–141
Lynn, L. E., 223

Macromedia Director computer program,
    271, 282
Maguire Thomas Partners, 359
Making Healthy MUSIC project,
    327–330, 366
Manhattan, 29, 51, 77, 79–81, 87–93,
    123. *See also* Street Library Project
Markus, M. L., 205
Marris, P., 216
Marvin, Simon, 28, 39–40, 52
Marx, Leo, 6, 8, 11, 382–383
Marxism, 57
Mashima, K., 282
Massachusetts Bay Transit Authority
    (MBTA), 167
Massachusetts Housing Finance Agency

(MHFA), 166
Massachusetts Institute of Technology
    (MIT). *See also* Laboratory for
    Making Things (LMT)
  Department of Urban Studies and
      Planning, 203, 260, 373, 391
  Media Laboratory, 266, 271, 298, 322
  School of Architecture and Planning, 3
  Wellesley Teacher Education Program,
      259–260
Massachusetts Water Resource Authority
    (MWRA), 166
Massey, D. S., 80–81
Mayo Clinic complex (Rochester, MN),
    30
MBHP, 167
MBTA, 167
McGreary, M. H. H., 223
Mechanic arts, 142–145
Media, community-based, 37–38
Media Laboratory (MIT), 266, 271, 298,
    322
Medicaid services, 99
Medical services, 99, 118–119
Mercantile cities, 107
Merges, R. P., 220
Metropolitan Boston Housing Partnership
    (MBHP), 167
Meyer, Susan E., 81
MHFA, 166
Microworlds Logo computer program, 271
Middle-out strategy, 14, 177–178,
    185–186
"Milieux of innovation," 5–6, 29
Mill, John Stuart, 139
Milwaukee, 195–197
Minitel system (France), 157
"Minority majority," 75–76
Mission-Main public housing
    development (Boston), 13, 203–204
MIT. *See* Massachusetts Institute of
    Technology

Mitchell, William J., 8–9, 12, 21, 50–53, 378, 383
Modems, 153–154
Mokhtarian, Patricia L., 52–53
Mollenkopf, John, 28
Monmonier, M., 208
Monopolies, 156
MOOs, 127
Morgan, Pamela, 328
Morino Institute, 352
Morino, Mario, 352
Moss, Mitchell, 28
Multi-User Dungeons (MUDs), 17, 127, 323, 325, 339–341
Multi-User Sessions in Community (MUSIC), 17–18, 323–330
Multimedia representational applications, 194, 202–204, 208–210
Murnane, R. J., 64
Murray, Charles, 62
MUSIC, 17–18, 323–330
MusicLogo, 245, 251–252
MWRA, 166

Narrowcast services, 135–136
National Gallery, 45
National Information Infrastructure Advisory Council (NIIAC), 380
National Information Infrastructure (NII), 321–322
National Telecommunications Information Agency (NTIA), 328
NCSA Mosaic, 158
Negroponte, Nicholas, 7–8, 48, 135–137, 145
Neighborhood. See also specific name
    activism, 304–305, 330–334, 374
    information infrastructure, 321–322
    planning, 170–172
    residential, 30, 124–125
NetDay 96, 360, 381
Netscape, 158

New Community Corporation, 18, 328
New Community Corporation housing development (Newark), 18, 328–329
New Deal, 64
New economy of presence and, 108–113
New Urbanists, 125–126
New York City, 29, 51, 77, 79–81, 87–93, 123. See also Street Library Project
Newark Board of Education, 332
Newark (NJ), 18, 77, 81, 93, 328–329
Newark Public Library, 328
Newcastle (United Kingdom), 60
News services, 115–116
Newton Street Elementary School, 18, 328–329
NII, 321–322
NIIAC, 380
Nilles, J. M., 52
1984 (Orwell), 343
Nonprofits, federal funding for, 99–100
Norman, D. A., 199
NPO-NET, 358, 363
NTIA, 328
Nye, David, 134

Object linking and embedding (OLE) tools, 184
ODBC, 184
Office of Computer Education and Technology of Newark Public Schools, 328
Oldenberg, Ray, 341
OLE tools, 184
Olin, Lloyd, 295
Omaha, 60
Omnifest (Milwaukee), 195–197
Online access, 360–361
Online Art Gallery, 271, 273
Open database connection (ODBC), 184
Orfield, Gary, 82

Orwell, George, 343
Ostrander, Susan, 100
Owens, E. H. W., 229
Owner names
    bottom-up strategy, 175–176
    categorizing, 172–174
    lookup tables, 178–183
    middle-out strategy, 177–178,
        185–186
    spelling corrections, 178–183
    standardizing, 174–175
    top-down strategy, 176–177

Pacific Rim countries, 7
Pacific Telesis, 385–386
Pager system, 154–155
Paint programs, 271
Pandey, Shanta, 80
Papert, Seymour, 238, 244–245, 269,
        271, 277, 283, 295–296, 319
Parent-Teacher Associations, 36
Parental involvement, 304–305, 330
Parkes, C., 50
Parks, Rosa, 238
*Passport to the New World of Technology ...
    Computers* (Fanelli and Tardieu), 289,
        307
Patriarchal family, crisis of, 34
PEN, 358
Pendyala, R. M., 52
Personal computing
    community computing versus,
        299–300
    computer and
        as commodity, 342–346
        evolution of, 18–19
    costs, 157
    global village metaphor and, 347
    hobbyists and, 342–343, 346
    identity and, 347
    Internet and, 347
    for people, 342–343

political meanings of, 344–345
Shaws' work and, 339–341, 346–347
Tardieu's work and, 339–341,
        346–347
technological developments and, 339
transparency and, 344, 346
Peterson, P. E., 52
Philadelphia, 79, 81, 87, 91–92
PhotoShop computer program, 282
Piaget, Jean, 271, 295, 319
Picciano, A., 229
Piller, C., 265
Piore, Michael, 7
Plato, 125
Playa Vista (CA), 359
Plugged In Enterprises project, 357
Police forces, 119–120
Politics (Aristotle), 125
Pollard, Jane, 88
Porter, Michael, 7
Posey, J., 197, 202
Poverty
    access to technology and, 7–8, 12
    advanced information technologies
        and, 9–10, 64–65
    black holes of, 28
    in center city, 74–78
    concept of, 19–20
    Internet and, 12
    persistent, 20
    race and, 74–78
    rates of, 7
    transient, 20
Price, C. D. F., 227
Prison population, 37, 62–63
Producers, consumers versus, 318
Professional services, 29–30
Programming tools, 271
Progress, 138–140
Prototype projects, 391–393
Providence (RI), 81, 91, 93
Public Electronic Network (PEN), 358

Public Facilities Department (FUD)
  (Boston), 166, 174
Public policy
  access to technology and, 376–379
  advanced information technologies
    and, 61–65
  education and, 10–11
  employment patterns and shifts in,
    95–96
  inadequacy of government, 379–382
  income and technology and, 61–65
  recommendations, 382–390
  software entrepreneurship and,
    387–388
  universal access policies, 156–157

Quality Education Data, 229
Quigley, Phil, 386

Race
  "minority majority" and, 75–76
  poverty and, 74–78
  software entrepreneurship and,
    224–226
Railroads, 141–144
Rainey, James, 359
Rasmussen, J., 200
Rathgeb, Steven, 100
A Region at Risk (Yaro and Hiss), 46
Regional cities, 59–60
Regional Plan Association, 46
Registry of Deeds (Boston), 168–169
Regulators, 156–157
Reich, Robert, 34, 48, 56
Reitz, Kurt, 309
Relevant knowledge, 193
Residential neighborhoods, 30, 124–125
Resnick, Mitchel, 14–16, 20, 279,
    284–285
Resnick, Paul, 322
Respect, creating environment of,
    280–281

Retailing industry, 116–117
Reynolds, P., 217–218, 222
Richardson, R., 53–54
Riggs, Betsy, 284
Right-to-buy policies, 63
Robert Taylor Homes (Chicago), 65
Rockoff, Maxine L., 358
Rodin, 281
Roman cities, 107
Route 128, 29
Roxbury, 65
Rush, B., 227–228
Rusk, Natalie, 284–285
Russell, Susan Jo, 238
Rutgers University, 328, 332

Sabel, Charles, 7
St. Louis, 13, 197–199, 202–204
Salamon, Lester M., 99–100
Salt Lake City, 60
San Francisco, 29
Sassen, Saskia, 28, 59
Satellite, 154–155
Sawicki, D.S., 193
SBC Communications, 385–386
Schank, Roger, 274
Schön, Donald A., 165, 289
School system. See Education
Schumpeter, Joseph, 216
Schwartz, R., 215, 221–222, 227
Security services, 119–120
Self-employed, 217–218, 225
Servers, 160–161
Service providers, digital, 155
Servon, Lisa, 34, 41
Shaw, Alan, 16–18, 21, 320, 339–341,
    346–347, 378
Shaw, Michelle, 16–18, 21, 339–341,
    346–347, 378
Shiffer, Michael J., 13, 21, 199–200, 207,
    376
Silicon Alley, 51

Silicon Graphics, 50

Silicon Valley, 5–6, 29, 51, 357

Smith, 100

Social constructionism, 318–320

Social empowerment through community networks

    community networks and, 334–335

    local village building and, 317

    Making Healthy MUSIC project and, 327–330

    Multi-User Sessions In Community and, 323–330

    neighborhood activism and, 330–334

    neighborhood information infrastructure and, 321–322

    producers versus consumers and, 318

    social constructionism and, 318–320

    social empowerment and, 320–321

Social exclusion, 28

Social problems, 81–82

Social progress, 375–376

Social reform, 34–39

Social Security, 73

Social services, 30

Sociospatial trends, 5

Software,, 20–21 158–159. *See also specific computer programs*

Software entrepreneurship

    barriers to, 12

    capital and, human and social, 10, 221–222, 226–227

    education and, 227–231

    entrepreneurs in, 217–218

    gumption factor and, 215–217

    overview of, 215–217

    public policy and, 387–388

    race and, 224–226

    research on, 221–222

    revenues in industry and, 218–220

    urban poor and, 223–226, 230–231

Software industry

    entrepreneurship and, 215, 217–222

    revenues of, 218–220

Soloway, E. M., 269

South Bronx, 65

Southall, Noah, 284

Space of flows, 5, 28–31

Spatial clustering of corporate centers, 5–6, 28–29, 51

Spielberg, Steven, 50

SQL, 170, 172, 178

SSI, 73, 99

Star Ledger (newspaper), 328

Stockyard Area Development Association, 354–355

Storper, Michael, 88

Street Library Project. *See also* Community computing

    access to technology and, 309–310

    community involvement and, 304–305

    creation of, 16, 289

    entries and, looking up, 303–304

    in first week, 301–303

    Fourth World Networks and, 307

    links

        between people, 306–307

        between thoughts, 306–307

    location of, 290–291

    New York's expansion of, 307–309

    other street library projects and, 305

    parental involvement and, 304–305

    preparatory work for, 295–301

    purpose of, 16

    session of, typical, 303

    Wresinki's vision and, 291–295

Strimpel, Oliver, 284

Structured Query Language (SQL), 170, 172, 178

Supplemental Security Income (SSI), 73, 99

Support systems for low-income communities

    collaborative planning system, 194, 199–202, 206–210

Support systems for low-income
communities (*continued*)
    community networks, 194–199,
        205–206
    concept of, 21
    multimedia representational
        applications, 194, 202–204,
        208–210
    overview of, 193–194
    questions about, 204–210
Susser, Ida, 34, 41

Tapori Databank, 300–301, 305
Tapori newsletter, 305
Tardieu, Bruno, 16–18, 20–21, 289, 295,
    307, 339–341, 346–347, 376, 378,
    384, 386–387
Tarpley, F., 215, 221–222, 227
Taylor, John, 48–49, 55
Taylor, Winslow, 145
Teach, R. F., 215, 221–222, 227
Technology in low-income communities.
    See also Income and technology;
    Owner names
    colloquium on (1996), 3, 373–375
    digital revolution and, 8–9
    employment patterns in center city
        and, 83–96
        anxiety about, 32
        center city employment trends,
            90–95
        general trends, 83–86, 100–101
        immigrants and, 84–85
        metropolitan employment trends,
            86–90
        public policy shifts and, 95–96
        questions about, 71, 83
        sociospatial trends, 5
        welfare system and, 96–100
    evolution of center city and, 72–82
        background information, 72–74
        data and analysis sources, 72

        immigration impacts, 80–81
        income sorting and segregation,
            78–80
        poverty in center city, 74–78
        questions about, 71
        social problems, 81–82
    in future, 390–393
    land ownership and
        knowledge of, 183–184
        patterns of, 168–172
        records of, 168–169, 172–174
    land use and
        information technology, 165, 170
        neighborhood planning, 170–172
        new plans of, 167
        patterns of, 168–172
        records, 168–169
    promise of, 34
    questions about changes caused by,
        71–72
    summary of findings, 100–102
    urban planning and development,
        12–14
    urban revitalization and, 165–168
Telecommunications, 50–52, 107–108,
    155, 385–386
Telecommunications Act (1996), 48,
    380–381
Telecommunications Information
    Infrastructure Assistance Program
    (TIIAP), 328
Telecommuting, 52–54, 121–122
Tele-education, 36
Telephone network, 153–154, 156–157
Telepresence, asynchronous, 109–113,
    118
Telesprawl, 52
Teleworking, 36
Thatcher, Margaret, 63
The Thinker (Rodin), 281–282
"Third industrial revolution," 215
"Third place," 341

Thomas, Willie, 330
Thought
    links between, 306–307
    tools for, 281–284
TIIAP, 328
Tobin, S., 78
Top-down strategy, 14, 176–177
Transparency, 344, 346
Transportation-rich sectors, 60
Tri-State New York region, 46
The Truly Disadvantaged (Wilson), 61
Trust, creating environment of,
    280–281
Turkle, Sherry, 16, 18–19

Uffizi, 121
UMDNJ, 18, 328
Unemployment, rising, 62
United Nations, 305
United Neighborhood Houses of New
    York, 358
Universal access policies, 156–157,
    376–379, 384–385
University of Medicine and Dentistry of
    New Jersey (UMDNJ), 18, 328
UNIX workstation, 158
Urban economies, 5–6
Urban geography, 58–61
Urban planning and development
    in low-income communities, 38
    technology in low-income
        communities and, 12–14
Urban poor, 223–226, 230–231. *See also*
    Poverty
Urban revitalization, 165–168
URLs, contact, 366–367
U.S. Constitution's 200th anniversary
    (1987), 305
U.S. Department of Commerce, 328
U.S. Department of Education, 228
Usenet News Groups, 196–197
Utopianism, digital, 7–10, 136–137

Value entrepreneurs, 224
Valued spaces, 31
Vasari, Giorgio, 121
Villiers, Dufourney de, 293
Virginia Tech, 359–360
Virtual reality, 339–341
Virtual society, 21, 340–341

Wacquant, Loic, 63
Wall Street, 29
"War of the worlds" mentality, 341
Washington, D.C., 77, 81, 87, 90, 93,
    207
Webster, Daniel, 141–143
Welfare system
    center city and, 101–102
    employment patterns and, 96–100
    weakening of, 33, 96–100
Wenger, E., 278
When Work Disappears (Wilson), 64
Williams, Raymond, 138
Wilson, William Julius, 57–58, 61–62,
    64, 81, 223
Wolpert, Julian, 7, 10–11, 71–73, 99
Work. *See* Employment; Labor force
Works Program Administration (WPA),
    64
World Wide Web (WWW). *See* Internet
WPA, 64
Wresinski, Father Joseph, 16, 290–295,
    307, 310–311
WWW. *See* Internet

Yaro, R. D., 46
Youth Voice Collaborative (YVC) project,
    362–363
YVC project, 362–363

Zapinski, Ken, 354
Zeisel, Hans, 63
Zip code redlining, 62